Paul Harrington is a retired New York State corrections officer and a Desert Storm and Operation Restore Hope veteran, having served in the U.S. Air Force from 1989–1993. He has received multiple commendations for his service and is currently active in several law enforcement and fire organizations throughout the Hudson Valley region of New York. Recently, he has been advocating on behalf of multiple law enforcement officers, during their time of need. Paul is working on developing a not-for-profit to assist all lines of law enforcement within New York. It took Paul almost four years to write this memoir; working from several saved documents as well as current administrative law cases to gather all the facts needed to complete this timeline of events. He is originally from upstate New York, growing up in Malone, and now resides in the Hudson Valley with his family and two children.

To all the men and women who work inside the prisons within New York State and beyond; to those that sacrifice their safety on a daily basis so that our communities can feel secure knowing that you are walking some of those toughest beats in America. We salute them all for their service and their unrelenting determination to protect us all. Stay safe in there, watch each other's backs, and stand up for what's right when all else falls against you. Thank you, brothers and sisters.

Paul Harrington Sr

JUSTICE OR NOT

My experience as a State Correction Officer inside New York's Prisons

AUSTIN MACAULEY PUBLISHERS™

LONDON • CAMBRIDGE • NEW YORK • SHARJAH

Ordering Information
Quantity sales: Special discounts are available on quantity purchases by corporations, associations, and others. For details, contact the publisher at the address below.

Publisher's Cataloging-in-Publication data
Sr, Paul Harrington
Justice or Not

ISBN 9781649796400 (Paperback)
ISBN 9781649797018 (Hardback)
ISBN 9781649797025 (ePub e-book)

Library of Congress Control Number: 2022904579

www.austinmacauley.com/us

First Published 2022
Austin Macauley Publishers LLC
40 Wall Street, 33rd Floor, Suite 3302
New York, NY 10005
USA

mail-usa@austinmacauley.com
+1 (646) 5125767

I would like to thank many of my friends and colleagues who have supported me during this long road to retirement, especially those who were there for me when my well-being was in turmoil. A special expression of gratitude to Dr. Marc Habif, Dr. Virginia Feldman, Dr. Martin Ogulnick, Dr. Jeff Newton, Dr. Robert Lustbader, Dr. Kenny and the many other specialists who treated my injuries. I am truly in debt to the Roth Law Group in White Plains, New York, for winning all of my cases when I thought all else would fail. A special shout out to Dave G, Mike P, Wally P, JR, Al, Dean D, Joey G, and Ed V and his family for truly caring and being there in any way possible to support my endeavors. Lastly, to my family from all around who were there every step of the way, either physically, emotionally, or in prayer. Thank you for getting me to where I am today.

Cover Photo Credit: J.M. DeSousa

Chapter One
The Beginning

Not too many people grow up in their lives saying they want to go work in a prison. It just kind of happens. Either you already have family who works in corrections, or like me, you hear of the upcoming civil service exams. What seems to be an exciting new job on the horizon blinds one looking into the distance seeing where it will take them into their future. You will never know until you try. I started at Sing Sing Prison and then spent most of my corrections career, ending it at Fishkill Correctional Facility. Fishkill's prison sits not too far from the banks of the Hudson River in Beacon, New York, in Duchess County. Built and opened in 1892, as the Matteawan State Hospital for the criminally insane, it housed some of the most violent felons that New York could get their hands on. While the history of that era could go on and on, I wanted to introduce the beginning of what soon became known as Fishkill Correctional Facility. The Matteawan "colony farm" was closed in the mid-1960s, when the director decided that farming was not relevant training for a patient population, drawn principally from New York City. "Relevance" was a consideration that arose during the 1960s for many institutions. In this case, the prison system de-emphasized farming. Since then, the Department of Corrections and Community Supervision (DOCCS) has reduced its agribusiness program. On January 1, 1977, Mental Hygiene opened the Central New York Psychiatric Center (CNYPC), a special forensic mental health facility on the grounds of the Beacon complex (CNYPC was relocated to a portion of Marcy State Hospital in September of that year). With the creation of CNYPC, Matteawan closed forever. Fishkill housed approximately 1,700 inmates, currently operates as the regional medical unit for southern New York's prisons and offers a wide range of educational programs including Pre-General Second Language (ESL), bachelor of arts through the Bard Prison

Initiative, bachelor of science degree in Organizational Management through a partnership between Hudson Link for Higher Education in Prison and Nyack College, and various vocational classes with hands-on experience for the inmates. Of the 1,700 inmates at Fishkill, close to 45% of them are under care of the Office of Mental Health (OMH). With the closing of many psych centers around New York by Governor Andrew Cuomo, this pushed mental health inmates into the prison systems that were not designed to handle them. This created a systematic state-wide issue with how staffers now had to handle these mental health violent offenders. These inmates often would not go along with the program and things turned violent. It's a huge problem when administration does not have the officer's back. That is, in most cases, beyond things such as in-house disciplinary sanctions and outside charges and putting pressure on Duchess County's District Attorney to prosecute. The problem was that our hands were tied behind our back. It was like them being allowed to physically assault us, knowing that nothing would happen to them in return due to their mental health status. Imagine this happening to cops out on the street? Myself, and thousands of other officers in New York's prison system can and should hold Governor Cuomo ultimately responsible to the working officers whose family lives are disintegrated due to the varying consequences of these mental health "patients." There are varying levels of each inmate's mental health status and most of them are on medication and walk freely throughout general population in the medium-security portion of Fishkill, which also has a maximum security unit called "S-Block", where up to 200 inmates can be held in solitary confinement.

The State of New York owned a large parcel of what had been used for farmland which adjoined the former Beacon Correctional Facility for convicted females. It remained unused except for occasional farmers haying the fields until around 2000 when it had been sold to the City of Beacon. In 2001, construction began on what would soon become the new City of Beacon High School, hosting a large complex of buildings and sporting fields with a large parking area running along the eastern side of the school. In 2002, the school had officially opened, moving all students from the older school several blocks away into the new state-of-the-art modernized facility. What many do not know, especially most students attending there, is that just a couple hundred feet west of the high school and of the tennis courts, is an unmarked graveyard in which multiple former incarcerated mental patients and inmates are buried there. This area is hidden by trees and bushes. Back then and still today, when families do not claim the body, the state would have the remains placed in a pine wood box and buried side by side as close as can be to preserve space for future prisoners who were laid to rest there. Outside, work crew inmates would be used to dig the graves, marking it with a small block embedded into the grass that indicated the dates and their department identification number (For example 77A1234). The first 2 numbers were the year they were entered into the system, then the letter would indicate where he/she had been classified, and the last 4 numbers would be the order in which they were processed that year. This is still an active cemetery being used for dead inmates who are not claimed from their families for private burial. So next time you are at a tennis match at the school, keep that in mind. One could simply walk over and see for themselves. The markers are just above ground level unlike the headstones you would see in a normal cemetery.

I became a corrections officer trainee on December 27, 1994, and started my recruit training at the department's training academy in Albany, New York. The Academy was a watered-down version of the basic training I went through when I previously enlisted in the military right out of high school. I served 1989-1993 in the US Air Force during Operations Desert Shield, Desert Storm, and Operation Restore Hope in Africa. While in the Corrections Academy, there were quite a few officer trainees that quit during the numerous weeks of training, not being able to handle being away from home, various hardships, and the most evident one being the day of taking a tour inside one of the nearby state prisons to see the environment we would soon be working in. To me, the academy was already easy having that prior military experience. Most of our days were either in the classroom, doing physical fitness at the gymnasium, or out at the firing range for weapons and chemical agents training.

I recall when I was going through my entry processing in Albany, the psychologist doing my interview asked, "Why do you want to become a Corrections Officer?" My reply to the doctor was, "I feel as if I could assist in helping with the rehabilitative process for the inmates who were serving time for their crimes." Looking back on this over two decades later, boy was I ever wrong. There is some attempt to rehabilitate, but the recidivism rate is nearly 2/3 on average. The system just does not work. On the flip side of that coin, under 80% of the officer trainees that graduate from the Corrections Academy actually work and have a full and legitimate career. Most correction officers are good and honest public servants doing an enormously challenging and important job. But then there are those officers that become a part of the system themselves by becoming a criminal. Sometimes the academy was able to weed "those" out during training, but it would not be until they actually got into the system and they became comfortable and adapted to the new environment.

Soon after my graduation from the Corrections Academy, I was assigned to Sing Sing Correctional Facility in Westchester County, New York. Being a maximum-security facility, and amongst the oldest and most historical in the State, Sing Sing had its fair share of incidents – go figure – since most of the officers coming in to work there were transients, newly brought onto the job, and the prisoners knew this, using it to their advantage. You would see staff come and go there almost as fast as a few months, but my class was the last hired before the end of the year in 1994 when newly-elected Governor George Pataki took office and did a hiring freeze in NY state. They kept warning us of "layoffs or pink slips," but it never happened. This kept a lot of us there for quite some time, making for an extended stay, longer than expected commutes, you name it. In order to get moved, we would have to have a new class come in behind us to push us out onto our transfer list requested assignments. Prior to my transfer earlier that summer, there had been a major uprising in "B" Block on the top 2 tier galleries, once they opened up the cells for the evening chow meal. This gallery is like the size of a football field and about five stories high. It's enormous, and especially on your first visit there, it can be somewhat intimidating. One of my old roommates at the time was working up there. He soon became a State Trooper. I can recall him saying he put his back to the wall, unable to do anything as several inmates ran up and down the galleries with shanks and homemade weapons, cutting and stabbing each other. They shut the jail down and called for all available officers. I recall running up from the lower part of the prison in the Tappan area of Sing Sing with my baton in hand, sprinting with a group of officers all the way up the yard corridor stairs. Upon arrival, it was pure bloodshed. I first saw one of our sergeants on the ground, leaning against the wall, his white uniform shirt covered in blood. Complete chaos, with the incident still out of control. When we got there, we spread out trying to take control, not even knowing what we were dealing with at the time and where it had all started. Several injuries were sustained, mostly to the inmate gang retaliation where more than a dozen inmates had been cut, slashed, or stabbed. Many officers had been injured as well, it took a couple hours to get everything under control and the injured seen by medical and/or transported out to the hospital during that incident. That was a wakeup call for anyone who was new on the job, which at the time, many of us still were there with under a year on the job.

I also recall another incident that spring, when I was assigned on one of the posts that involved a fence patrol to an area that was newly constructed. It had rained a lot that spring, and it was already dark outside, with the ground being wet, but the rain had stopped. This fence ran within the walls of the prison which separated the inside buildings of this vast facility. In fact, many outsiders of the public do not know this, but Metro North Railroad has trains that run straight through the prison facility, with the high walls and fencing around it, the track areas were far below. I believe it is the only one like it from all around. There is a road and bridge that crosses over it, connecting the upper part to the lower part of Sing Sing's facility. On top of that bridge is a wall post called Tower 4. It was staffed back then by two officers on my shift. One was always patrolling the walk plank, watching down as the trains passed through to their next stop at the Ossining Train Station. I had some safety issues that evening, as I was walking along the interior fence post on an assignment, pulling on the fence checking to see it was secured and not previously tampered with. The newly constructed area, to include the ground soil, had become like quicksand, all due to the rain and thawing. Before I knew it, I was up to my crotch in the ground. Anyone shorter than me would have been up to their neck. One of the patrol units was called over the radio to assist. Upon their arrival, they could not get me out as they were starting to fall in as well. One of the officers from Tower 4 yelled over and said they could use the 20-foot rope they had. This had a large metal loop on it which they used to attach keys to and lower to the incoming relief officers so they could enter the tower door below. They grabbed that rope and threw it to down to the officer, then brought it to me and tried pulling but to no avail; it was not enough energy in the direction they were going. Now more staff had arrived and they were deciding on what to do at that point. The last thing they wanted to do was have the fire department come in there. One of the officers had a brilliant idea of wrapping me with the rope and pulling me out with the state van. But instead, a human chain was formed and within minutes I was pulled out of the pit. The watch commander's office was briefed about this as it was happening. Luckily, I was able to get out of the sink hole in one piece, surprisingly enough, without injury, but covered in mud. As I was on my way up to the medical unit to get checked out, one of the officers had overthrown the rope back up to the officer in the tower post but missed the top of the tower officer's grip by far and it landed on the train tracks below. I am told one of the rail maintenance men were able to get it removed sometime shortly afterward. Later on, as the news spread, quite a few of the senior officers told me that they saw that incident as a great opportunity to take some time off from work, but being new as I was and absent any injury, I stayed the course.

Then it was Christmas Eve, December 24, 1995, when an inmate had been murdered in "A" block on the bottom gallery, just adjacent the recreational area. He had been stabbed to death. It was late in the shift, after dinner time. There were a lot of rumors about the actual details of how this happened, but facts showed ultimately it had been a hit from a gang-related drug deal. The prison was on lockdown for a couple of days, holding all inmates in their cells. Meals were delivered in white foam trays to each cell. This is when even the civilian staff were put to work assisting in kitchen duties and whatever essentials had to be completed inside the prison. It had happened in his cell which the gate of it had been open at the time for that evening's activities. I remember working the corridor gates in that evening as several "suits" showed up, along with state police and other investigators. From the way things were going, I thought I was never going to get home that night. It was my first awakening to the worst type of violence that surrounded the officers who worked inside those galleries, locked inside with the inmates that often outnumbered staff approximately 110 to 2. I remained there for approximately 14 months before finally getting my transfer to Fishkill early in spring of 1996.

Since day one at both prisons, I had always been assigned to the afternoon shift, a very popular shift for single officers who liked to go out on the town after work and get to sleep in before going back into work. I am originally from the North Country Region of New York, not too far off the Canadian border. I had the chance to eventually make it back up north closer to home, being on the transfer list. I remained on the list but then thought about the area of where I was now living, how much I liked it, and having met many new friends, I decided to take myself off the list and make Fishkill Correctional Facility my permanent assignment. I settled in until this day where I have established a beautiful family, a new home, a thriving business, and a busy schedule of community service throughout the town I live in. In the early part of my career, many officers had been treated respectfully and were looked at individually for our skill sets which each of us had to offer. With other jobs besides your regular post that required additional training for officers to sign up for these duties, it was per the directives that we were paid no extra salary for the performance of these duties. It was strictly for those who cared about their job, wanted to help create a safer environment and working conditions for all. When the older administrations had moved on to retirement, transfers, etc., things would change. It got to the point where the politics of the administration would affect the morale of the entire staff at the facility, including that of our union, who could not for the life of them, get us to all become united as one. Back then with such a higher sense of an easier working environment, officers worked as a team and often continued working with injuries sustained while on duty from inmate related incidents. Much of the reason for doing such was their responsibility of working their swapped shift for other officers who traded shifts to get extra time off. Even if the officers had each other's backs, it was not uncommon to see that the newer administrations did not. Most of the time we worked injured while being treated in fear of losing our careers and way of life, and for the need to support our families. I can't tell you how many people walk into Fishkill's Prison, especially on the night shift, with limps, bum knees, bad backs, and being messed up by numerous orthopedic injuries. The employers of the department were always quick to get you back to work even against the advice of your doctors, surgeons, and lawyers, all in an effort for the prison to be able to avoid overtime. The more overtime there was, the worse it looked for the top brass. Albany's eyes would see it as mismanagement and frowned upon of those administrators. These administration officials wanted to keep their jobs and chances for promotions, but if they did not make the numbers appear in an acceptable form, then it was down the drain for them. We were just numbers to them, and still are today. Albany has given more rights to inmates such as parolee's right to vote, inmates getting free computer tablets to email home, and don't even get me started about the free college degrees from 3-4 recognized universities that came in weekly for those inmates that enrolled to get further education. In the state's eye, this looked to be a part of their rehabilitation, but in the eyes of the public, it became infuriating since they worked and created savings, took on college loans, all in an effort to get his or her kid through college. The inmates finish their sentence and on release, they have ZERO college loans. Do your law-abiding family members have college loans? I'll bet the farm on it.

As an officer, you are placed in a dangerous environment, and at times, a violent world of pain and despair. Shrouded from the good and innocent, love and happiness, calm and quiet. You are often secluded with society's worst. attempting to correct behavior of those that in most cases do not want to be corrected.

At that time period, the outside world did not care about the unseen prisoners. They pretended the brutal world of corrections did not exist. The politicians in charge turn their backs until something bad happens. At this point, questions are being asked and fingers are being pointed often at the officers and saying they are at fault. After all, they say shit rolls downhill, and when it's an incident that turns bad, normally the most senior officer is held responsible, depending on the situation. It certainly could mean the worst scenario for anyone working in the area of the incident. Officers would get injured there quite often. Many of those times, if the situation was unfounded, it was simply taken as if the incident had occurred, even with no witness accounts. But being a witness to incidents inside there could be an easy set-up if you did not go along with the program. If there was not much for injury, the other person involved had his time coming, not knowing if someone or something would be waiting in the least expected place. If the situation was that bad and it warranted immediate action, out to the parking lot it would go, many times occurring between shifts. And we are talking about officer-on-officer incidents of workplace violence. If either of those parties involved only had minor injuries, perhaps worse, they would take some time off using their sick leave credits. Those were the old days; it is now rare to see this occur right in the vicinity of the facility. But one thing was for sure, it would be of no secret and that individual officer would become isolated by their co-workers.

Slowly the officer who was victimized becomes desensitized and withdrawn to family and friends. On the outside of the walls, there is nobody to talk to. They don't understand because his/her life is shrouded and hidden from the public. You often find yourself sitting in the back of the room with your back to the wall. A loud bang and you jump fearing the worst.

Corrections takes its toll on your health and mind. Eating away at you from the inside out. The public should think about the correction officers and the job they do to protect you and your family from the unseen. Pray that they stay safe to return home to loved ones. Think about correction officers and how their lives are affected by this hidden world. Most of us hide the fact of what they had experienced and don't talk about it much so it does not appear to be an issue upon one's observation, but when you look deep inside of them, you will see a whole new dark side. Thank them for all that they give up for you and your family. Because they do it for their own.

In the early days of my new assignment at Fishkill, I had the opportunity to work many areas of the prison to gain more knowledge and experience so that I could better myself and my expectations within the facility. Many officers working in this prison had several family members also working there in some capacity. Whether it was a civilian truck driver, maintenance, nursing staff, or even a secretary, there had been plenty of those jobs to go around. It leads one to wonder, how so? Soon enough one would find out that after a job was posted, many applicants were brought into the administration building for job interviews, only to have the position filled that had been saved by a current employee who was already working there and had gotten first pick for their job-seeking family member. This is a large facility with several buildings that are connected by an underground tunnel that has not been in used for decades, as well as a paved road called the "Walkway" that has numerous security posts along it where inmates and staff alike traverse this area to get around the facility. There are many buildings divided amongst the compound of this vast facility within the perimeter fencing. You have Buildings 21, 21A, S-Block, the RMU (Regional Medical Unit), administration building, Buildings 12 and 13, gymnasium, industry work areas, And the largest of all, the main building. The "main building" in the lower section of the facility is divided into a north and south side, comprised of mainly housing units, recreation yards, a mess hall, and some industry areas that inmates work at making certain products for Corcraft, a division of Corrections Industry. You can actually Google it and see it clearly on maps now, whereas back in the day, for security reasons, it would have been blurred out. If you zoom in closely, you can see the open yard areas, the baseball fields, and the layout of the entire facility. The industry area primarily produced office furniture as well as heavy-duty items such as metal doors, gates, bed frames, basically anything for the prisons and other state agencies.

Fishkill Correctional Facility
Beacon, New York

Photo Credit: Robert Welsted

This main building also has a secured access entrance to the basement that is closed to everyday traffic nowadays. From time to time, staff can gain access to get in there for maintenance issues, and I had an opportunity to take a tour through there with the fire/safety team. There are basement areas facing the south side of the building that were used many years ago, when it was ran as the Matteawan State Hospital for the insane. There were a number of rooms side by side up a gallery hall with solid brick walls. These were very small rooms, maybe about 5 feet wide by about 7 feet long. There are no doors on them now, however there could have been back then. They are covered in cobwebs and very dirty from being deserted and not maintained. On those walls that very day I was down there, I observed rusty old chains still attached to the brick walls in those rooms. They were used to restrain and control the mental health prisoners. They called them the "scream rooms." You can just about imagine what occurred in those areas back in the day. The history in that place goes back well over a century and if those walls could speak, there would be some sad, sad stories told. So much has happened that the outside world would not know and did not want to know. Today, a paved road leading to other areas of the prison is called the walkway that connects most of all the buildings in the complex. This is also used for vehicular traffic within the facility. This is a common practice in prison facilities across New York. Vehicles pass slowly right in the vicinity of the inmates on this same walkway. Believe it or not, there are signs that say keep off sidewalk so that they walk on the pavement. I am surprised no inmates have yet commandeered a vehicle and take it straight out through the gate with force. Perhaps it is the highly mounted wall post tower at that gate that deters this effort on the south side of the facility above this walkway, where an officer is stationed around the clock with multiple weapons, chemical agents, among other things. Buildings 12 and 13 primarily house the work release program, inmates who come and go on schedules to their outside jobs in order to prepare themselves for their release back into society. This area also has the large visiting rooms, the school areas, the chapel, and the facility barber shop, as well as several offices and the libraries. Across from this is the gymnasium, and much money was spent to refurbish the roofs and windows, as well as the electrical and mechanical aspects of these buildings inside the facility over the last several years in that amounted to millions of dollars. Literally well over 23 million dollars. Just up from the gym is the newest part of the facility, the RMU, also known as the

Regional Medical Unit. Another multimillion-dollar three-story facility that houses an infirmary, a unit for the cognitively impaired, as well as dental offices, physical therapy, various medical areas, specialty clinics, a temporary morgue, in addition to a trauma area staffed by nurses and some doctors. Most of the time prisoners have to be sent out to the hospitals just for x-rays and whatever because of their inability to do these medical procedures in this medical unit. There are occasions that a large mobile MRI unit on a tractor trailer is brought in and set up behind the medical unit for inmates who are in need of the MRI tests.

Down the hill from the RMU is the S-Block, a special housing unit that is maximum security. It can hold up to 200 inmates. They are housed up to 2 inmates per cell, for up to 23 hours per day, and they are let out into a small caged area that is sort of like the size a small deck in your room off a cruise ship, minus the view and smell of course. They have changed policies in which inmates who have committed infractions of regulations or rules, are often sent for "keep lock" status pending their hearing based on those charges. Then you have what they call "up the hill" Buildings 21 and 21A. Probably one of the most troublesome areas of this prison. Another housing area with recreation yards, mess hall, a mental health unit, various inmate organizations, maintenance shops, and what we refer to as "the box," where inmates are segregated and put into solitary confinement. This is also the location of numerous vocational shops, but these days, those programs are starting to close up one by one and have not reopened. Building 21 is the most active. Between the age of the inmates, the gang activities, drug trades, and the various mental health inmates walking around in population to boot, it's all a ticking time bomb. It's not a question of if, but when. It is a prison. Fishkill is set up like dormitories for the most part. There are not enough eyes to watch every nook and cranny, every corner and blind spot in those units or the entire building that inmates have access to it. At that time, with the absence of security video cameras in 80% of the facility, the inmates start to learn the routines of the regular officers, so it is always a possibility for just about anything to occur.

The sex trade is another issue. Inmates in the past have reported to me that they had been pushed up on and pressured to have sex with other inmates. While it would virtually create a bad situation for them to officially report it, most of them just wanted to be transferred to another unit to get away from the individuals threatening them for sex. Like I said before, there are lots of areas in this giant facility which is way understaffed to have eyes watching over every spot an inmate knows he could go and do something without getting caught. It still dismays me that there have been no proactive efforts in installing a large network of mounted security cameras throughout the facility. The department has just recently come out with a program to address this issue called "PREA" (Prison Rape Elimination Act). While it does develop certain powers to control and determine the outcome of situations with investigation and enforcement, it is with certainty that this problem will surely not go away.

With such great morale and staff working at Fishkill when I first arrived in 1996, I had started to really jump into my job there by working many different posts as a resource officer. As much energy as I had, it was good to be able to have an unusual routine. The inmates would not know what to expect of me as I would be assigned in various areas. I was not afraid of getting dirty back then either. I would climb the tops of toilets onto the bathroom stalls to balance myself on the thin divider panels so I could reach up to the air ducts or fiberglass wrapped pipes. These were popular areas for shanks (sharpened metal rods), often made really well with taped-up handles and sometimes even a shoestring as a thong to wrap your hand around. They were sometimes as small as 4 inches and other times as long as 14 inches. I have found weapons and drugs on inmates' possession as well, which was considered to be an unusual incident. There would be outside charges filed, but only on a rare occasion. Things were handled within the prison most of the time. There were several times I was assigned to the Industry 3 and 4 areas where these prime spots for weapons and tattoo machines were being made. They would be stuffed into the wall inside fiberglass insulation. I found so much of that stuff at one point that other officers would joke that I was making that contraband up at home and bringing them in. Even I had to laugh at that.

Then there was this one officer, his nickname was "Blue." He was an old timer, a senior man, who pushed a cart around from time to time among various other duties with inmates' bagged property to sort through before the inmates were transferred out to another prison. He was a funny guy with a good sense of humor. After work, he would head out to the car at 10:30 p.m., pop the trunk, open the cooler, and have a nice cold drink. One day he told me that I was finding way too much contraband. "You know, they could send five officers into an empty cell to frisk it and then they all come out empty-handed saying nothing found in there, Sarge, but right away they send you in and you could come out with a sword." Blue meant for that to be a ball-buster, but everyone knew that each time we found this contraband, it was less of a danger to any of us working there.

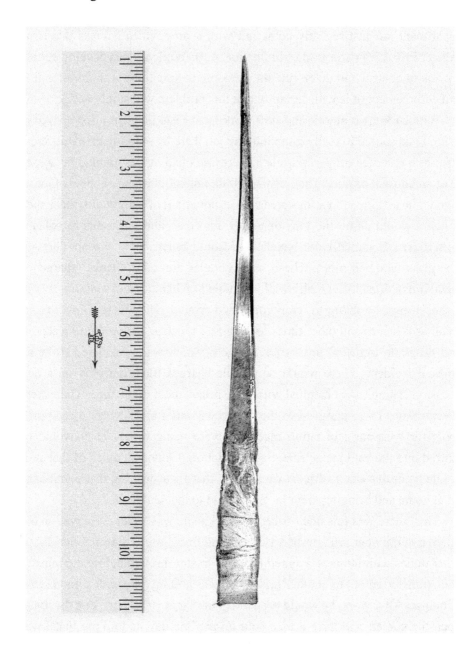

Example of homemade weapon found in common area of inmate's housing unit showers. Photo by P. Harrington

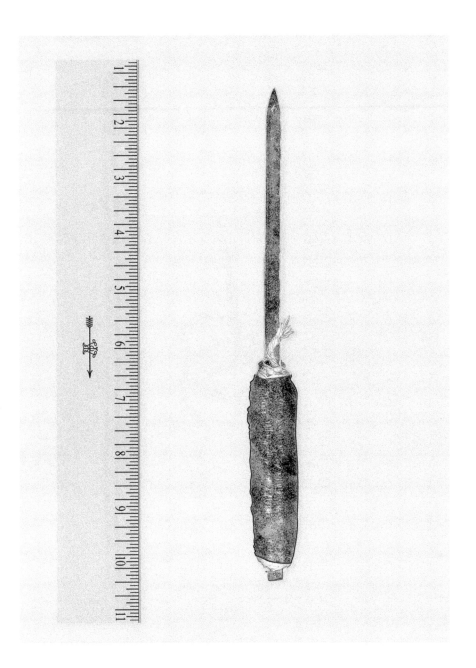

Example of homemade weapon found in common area of inmate's housing unit radiator. Photo by P. Harrington

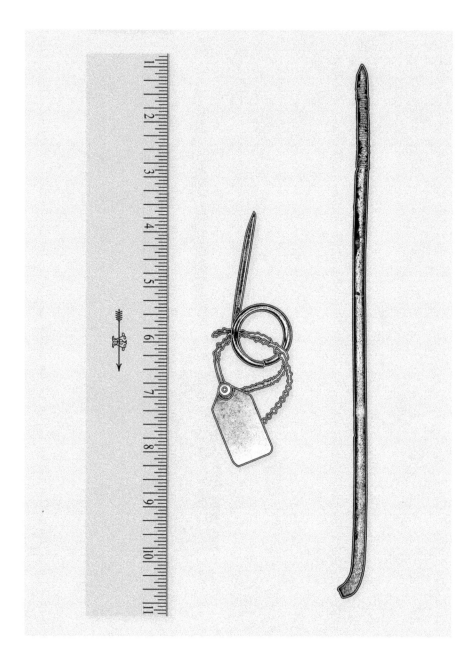

Example of homemade weapon found in common area of inmate's housing unit fire extinguisher hung on wall. Photo by P. Harrington

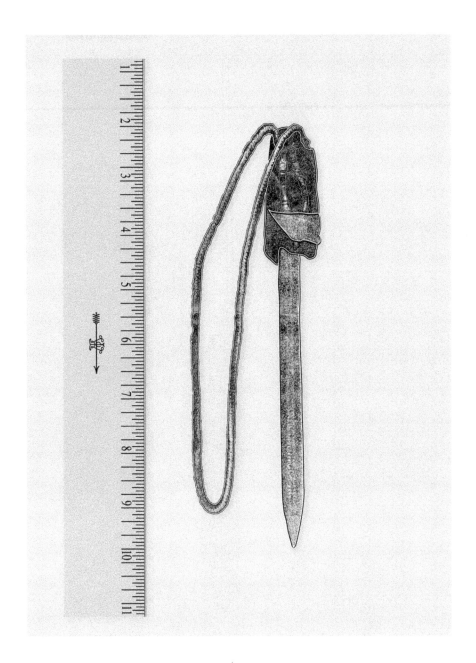

Example of homemade weapon found in common area of inmate's housing unit.
Photo by P. Harrington

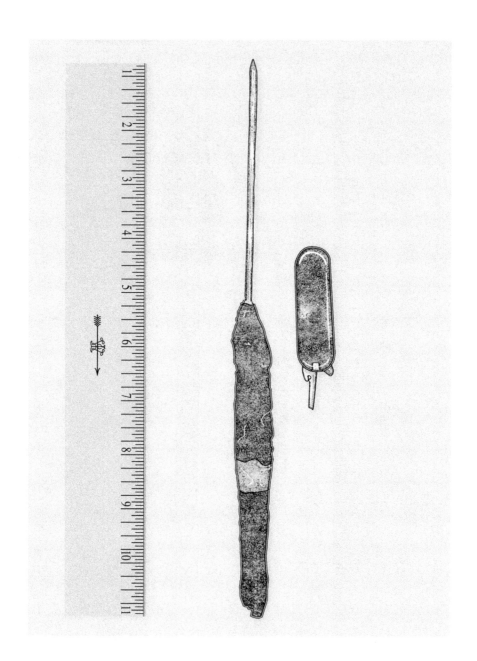

Example of homemade weapon found in common area of inmate's housing unit.
Photo by P. Harrington

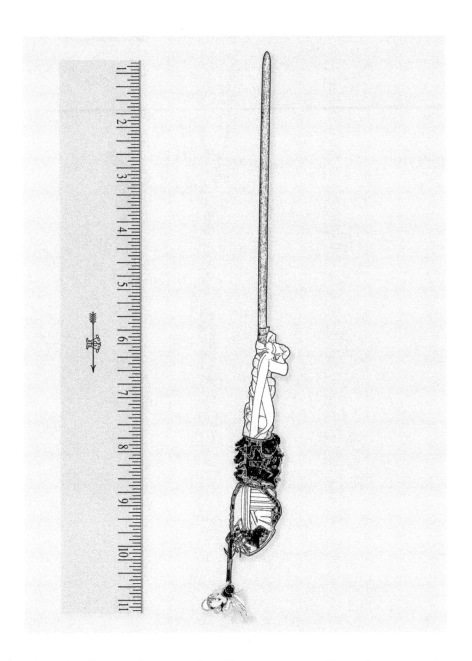

Example of homemade weapon found in common area of inmate's housing unit
showers. Photo by P. Harrington

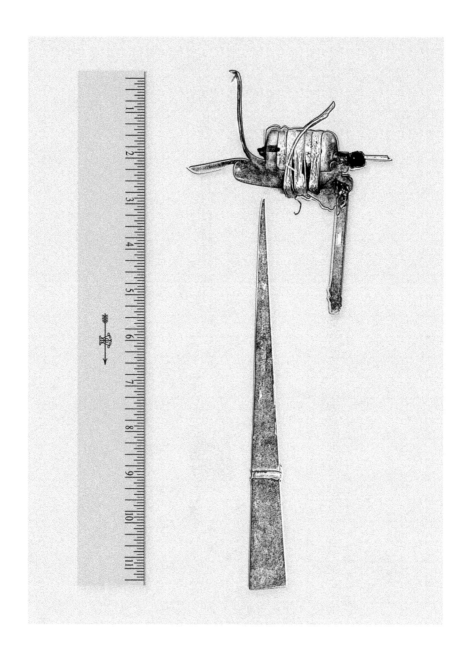

Example of homemade weapon and tattoo machine found in common area of inmate's housing unit. Photo by P. Harrington

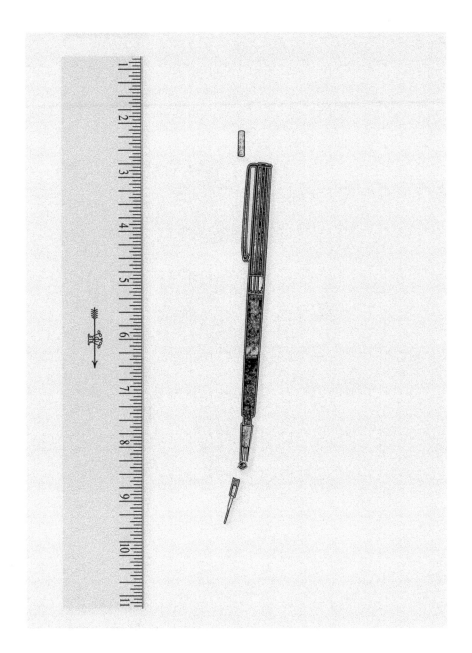

Example of homemade tattoo machine found in common area of inmate's housing unit showers. Photo by P. Harrington

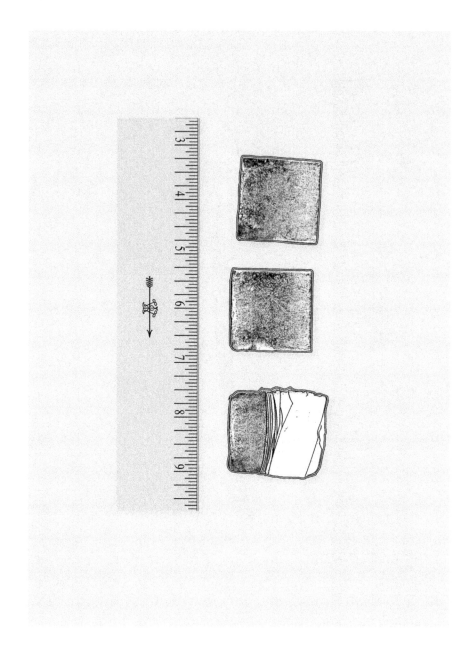

Example of homemade weapons found in common area of inmate industry work areas. Photo by P. Harrington

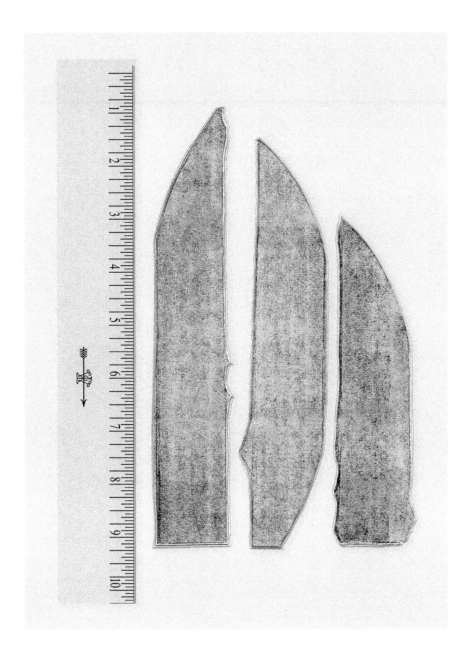

Example of homemade weapons found in common area of inmate's housing unit.
Photo by P. Harrington

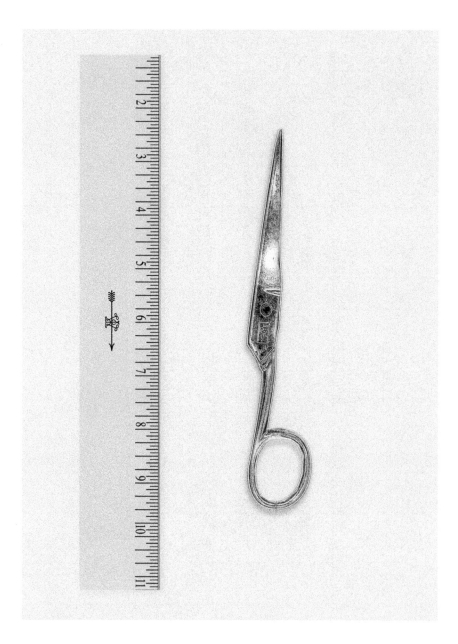

Example of homemade weapon found in common area inside cushioned seat of inmate's housing unit TV room. Photo by P. Harrington

Then in the late '90s, I can recall another officer who was very well known on the afternoon shift. His name was Teddy; he was very confident and macho, and back then things were quieter and easier to get away with. He too was a resource officer and lived on state grounds. He had a room on the 2nd floor of a three-story dormitory referred to as "Home B" which was located within a two-minute walk from the front gate of the prison. He had a special room, one that was like a small studio, complete with a living room, bedroom, and his own bathroom. There were a few studio style rooms like this in the dorm. Other single rooms in that dorm had to use public restrooms and showers. It was meant for Fishkill staff that might be staying there while temporarily assigned to the prison, and then for others who were permanent but chose to live in state housing nonetheless. There were always some sort of incidents going on, and often he was the go-to guy for transporting inmates, or doing escorts, covering posts short term, or would be just an "extra" officer who could roam an area until called upon when needed. There were ways to get out of the jail without having to go through the administration gate up front where he would be seen coming and going. Between the walkway area that is used for foot traffic by both inmates and staff, is a fenced-in trap area with a small booth but enough for one or two officers to stand in. Back then, and often times, the administration tower officer would see either a uniform at the gate or someone in civilian clothes. When the booth was not manned, the tower officer would rely on the inside admin gate officer to check the ID of the person coming through back then. Since then, there have been changes in procedures but at this time period, all one would have to do is walk through the trap after being buzzed through and walk downstairs unannounced to the empty lineup room where we had our pre-shift briefings. There was an emergency exit door in the northeast corner of the room that had an inoperable panic alarm bar on it, and the door was unable to be locked for quite some time. There had been work orders placed on it, but it had been a long time before it was repaired. You could easily walk out undetected into the parking lot. The administration lobby upstairs has a front gate manned 24 hours a day, but one could walk down the hallway after hours into an office on the first floor, or in this case, the copying machine room, and easily climb out the window and be gone. There were no bars on the windows of the administration building at all, even until this day. A lot of times anyone could go through the window or use the downstairs door and be undetected by front gate staff.

The administration building was a quiet place usually between 5:00 p.m. and 9:30 p.m. All the day shift civilian staffers had already left for the day. Very few staff remained, on average 3-4 in the watch commander's office, another 2-3 in the arsenal and then the administration gate officer. One day I was assigned to one of the outside vehicle patrols. My unit that day was called Patrol 90. There were two units out there, the other one being Patrol 91. In the vehicles, we carried an arsenal of weapons, chemical agents, you name it. We drove around the vast facility, its complex of state housing, and many other areas, similar to a campus. There was also a public road that passed through the facility. Since we only had two towers overseeing the perimeter and gate areas, these patrols were necessary; as I mentioned before, it is a large complex. From time to time, road posts would be manned to block unauthorized traffic from entering facility grounds. This use to be a 24/7 around-the-clock post, but they closed those posts. That allowed anyone to pass through along the facility fence line perimeter and could quite easily make that "drop" of contraband to be picked up by the inmate crews that came outside for the daily work details. Getting back to the matter of Teddy, the well-known officer who had more fear from his co-workers than respect. I recall the sergeant sitting at the assistant watch commander's desk dispatch me over the radio to landline his office. Once I called, he told me to go over to Home B and get Teddy, as he was needed for an assignment.

It took me only three minutes to get over to his room, and when I knocked on the door to inform him that he had to report to the sergeant for an assignment, he blew up and lost his temper, blaming me for possibly informing the bosses where he was at. They knew where he was, a lot of people did, and it was no secret. He had another officer with him in the room who I did not know well, and that individual left the department that year to go back to work for the county sheriff in the Buffalo area. It all happened so fast as Teddy, who was taller and stronger than I was, pulling me into the room and threw me onto the bed while slapping me in the face, spitting in my face, yelling curse words, yanking my uniform shirt apart and trying to choke me. I was armed with my department issued handgun at the time and luckily nothing occurred with it. It was a dangerous situation but knowing who he was, I did not take immediate action. I laid there for a second after on the hallway floor to catch my breath. I was thankfully not seriously injured, just stressed and frustrated. After the incident occurred, about two hours later, he just about chased me down out in the parking lot as I avoided him. He wanted to get in the vehicle with me to apologize and talk to me about why all of that anger came out of him in our incident. I was pretty new at the time and he was a top senior officer on our shift. Not knowing what to do about it and the lack of any serious injury allowed me more easily to forgive him, but I never would forget. I do not even understand why it all happened, we had hung out before on our days off, and I even helped him move into a new house. He got away with a lot of this stuff; he had fights with officers all the time. Sometimes he fought inside the prison, and I can recall a time on the back dock of 21-A building, he had beat up another officer known as Franklin while on duty. They had a disagreement and Franklin basically walked away battered up but ok. Word got around quicker than lightning about it. Teddy would fight other officers in night clubs and bars when off duty, only soon to make up with them days later. It was always over some stupid issue. He had asked to borrow money from me, about $30,000 to cover his gambling debts and other items, but I didn't have it. He assumed I had collected a settlement from a workers' comp case. He was pretty pissed off about that. It wasn't too long before karma would come back to haunt him. He got caught in a cocaine ring with two other officers and a sergeant. Everyone got canned for it and lost their jobs except for one officer who caught wind of the heat coming down and immediately got checked into rehab. As for himself, he fortunately suffered some low-end consequences but until my final day before I went out on injury, he still had his job working at Fishkill.

Contraband such as weapons were commonly found throughout the facility inside fiberglass pipe insulation, tucked behind radiators, taped beneath lockers, hidden in holes in the wall, just about any place an inmate might think their regular officer's routine would not expose the potential of them finding it. Some of those officers couldn't get up and climb up to the ceiling areas to get these weapons. It was one less thing we would have to worry about if we were able to get all of those confiscated and out of the areas. I still have numerous photos of these contraband items on file at home when I documented these with my paperwork. It was the first week of February in 2001, we had heavy snow that week. One of the female officers going off duty had inadvertently forgot to turn in her key ring at the arsenal window drop box on her way out of the administration gate. With all the snow falling and being in her winter uniform gear, she had grabbed her car keys from her key ring under her coat and at that moment, unbeknownst to her, key ring #287 belonging to the chapel area had 14 keys on it, and it dropped into the snowy ground as she got into her car. The snow accumulations had muffled the clinking sound of keys dropping that one would notice at any other time. I had been assigned by the watch commander to use the metal detector and search the inside perimeter walkway snow banks as well as the parking lots outside the facility. On the second day of searching, I noticed a plow pushing snow into about a 12-foot pile up near a utility pole. I put the metal detector to it, not knowing if this might had been the location, and I was picking up readings off the scale. I dug into the snow and there you have it, the entire key ring still intact but covered in ice. I brought it up front to the watch commander's office which was around dinner time. An immediate notification had been made to the higher-ups via phone and email of this finding. In more than one of my previous annual employee evaluations, I was even called "one of the best area searchers of Fishkill Correctional Facility" by the supervising sergeant who conducted my reviews at that time. I was requested to work certain buildings by many sergeants back in those days. They wanted me in those areas as ambitious as I was to get the job done. I wanted to stay as resource though, making my way around the facility so I could learn the inside workings of most areas. Then it was soon time to start working on the outer perimeter outside too. I gained some additional training to join the mounted horse patrol unit, comprised of seven horses located in a barn several hundred feet down from the rear perimeter of the facility. The old white horse barn was in clear view from Interstate 84 and still stands today. We had multiple officers with different skill levels riding these horses, and no two were ever alike. That made the horsemanship experience that much more difficult. Like humans, animals like to have routines too. But no routine was the same for these horses, as they were often donated to the state after being retired from another agency or organization. They found their new home at the facility and were taken care of in the barn by more senior officers who had experience and the occasional veterinarian visit. After only a few years that I got into the program, the facility decided to dismantle the horsemanship program due to the numerous injuries occurring, with officers getting hurt in accidents, including myself, when at about 1:30 a.m. on a cold night in October of that year, tragedy soon found my path when my horse was spooked by something in the dimly-lit grassy field. I had already made a full round of the perimeter prior to that in his mind and he was ready for trip back to the barn. Soon enough, we went into a full gallop and struck a utility pole where I was then dragged 30 yards, finally landing in the deepest part of the field. Fortunately, even though I had the wind knocked out of me, I was able to utter a few words over the two-way radio to get assistance. Soon help from the other patrol unit, the watch commander, as well as the Beacon Fire Department along with two ambulances arrived to transport me to the emergency room. There I was admitted days at St. Luke's Hospital in Newburgh for various injuries. I ended up being out from work for multiple weeks which was due to the trauma. After about two months of light duty and some time off, I was back full duty in no time at all. The Horse Patrol Unit was soon replaced with 4-wheel drive vehicles in which the officers would patrol the perimeter and large properties bordering Interstate 84.

Since I was an active volunteer firefighter in my community, I decided to join the facility's fire brigade. Fishkill has a fire station outside of the perimeter on grounds which houses an older refurbished pumper and a utility van. Inside the station were offices, records, and several self-contained breathing apparatus bottles, the kind that firefighters use when going into a burning building, as well as numerous lengths of hose, fire extinguishers, and turn-out gear, helmets, etc. Very typical of your normal working fire station, but in a prison setting. This building is normally occupied by the facility's fire and safety officer during the dayshift, which is more formally known on the radio as "Fishkill 100." This officer has a vast array of assignments and responsibilities throughout the facility. I had become the deputy fire and safety officer on my tour of duty on the evening shift. I often would be requested to respond to smaller fires within the prison, sometimes for nuisance alarms going off in the fire panels, or to conduct the required assigned fire drills for each area that inmates were housed. This would often take me from my assigned post on any given day to complete those additional duties. Many officers did not like to volunteer for extra training because that meant extra work, work that they were not additionally compensated for, or that it meant you were supporting the administration's politics, etc.

Then there were those weekly fence checks of the entire perimeter, close to a half mile long, and that could be a greatly underestimated. All year, regardless of weather, a resource officer would be picked to go out to do this assignment. A supervisor, such as the watch commander, was supposed to go with the assigned officer as the rounds were made. This would only happen when it was convenient and on a sunny day. Otherwise, you were on your own out there with a two-way radio in touch with the officer watching the video monitors. This was coordinated with the central monitoring staff as the fence line was set up in zones. Each zone had a sector alarm and camera that would alert the monitor control officer if there was activity. Sometimes a good windy storm or an animal would set these off, causing false alarms that our motorized patrols would have to respond out to investigate. Anyhow, I was often chosen for this assignment. Even if there was two feet of snow and even larger snow drifts, you would still have to go out and do it, and that could take hours. Occasionally, there would be areas with security breaches such as I have shown in my reports and photos. Those were immediately reported and a work order was put in to have the maintenance repair company come and take care of the gap in the second fence. You would think that knowing this was a scheduled security detail that the administration would have been proactive enough to plan for these weather events. It was on an extremely rare occasion that civilian staff would take a snow blower between the fence perimeters to clear a path for staff making these checks. It was the talk of the prison, who would be the next one to go out there to do this unfavorable task during winter? I can recall coming back in beat, red in the face from the cold, pants from my knees down soaked, including socks and boots from climbing through the snow. I had asked the female lieutenant that evening if I could run home and change (I lived 15 minutes away and it was only mid shift.) She did not believe me; she was hesitant and did not want to approve of this request. She told me to lift my pants and she physically felt my socks on both of my legs up to my calves to see if they were wet. I felt like I was back in catholic school trying to prove my truthfulness to my teacher. After confirming that I was right, she allowed me to go home to change and then come back. Some thanks I got for going out there and getting it done. She should have been charged by the department for even making physical contact like that with male staff while on duty. Speaking of fence patrols, there was this officer by the name of Chester, he had been assigned to go out in the knee-deep snow and complete this inspection one cold evening. He was pretty upset about it, given his seniority and all. He hesitantly started from the main trap area and made his way around 21 Building in the area of the Water Tower, and this was caught on the facility video security camera as monitor officers noticed he had fallen straight back in the snow making snow angels and started eating an apple from his pocket. Obviously, this was reported to the watch commander and staff had to go make their way out to his location to get him. This was his way of giving up and not doing the assignment. Although he was not hurt, he just mentally went off the edge and put up some resistance so someone else would have to relieve him. At Fishkill, if you screw something like a task up enough, you would get reassigned. Often times this is done on purpose when a staff member did not want to work in that position.

I heard about openings of training in the prison's drug lab. This was a course that was given by a supervisor who had been certified for years. It was done while on duty, so it got you off your post for most of the shift, and after passing your written exam, you would become certified and then along with some "on-the-job" training, you were soon off on your own. I was also a professional photographer off the job and owned a corporate photo studio in Orange County. The administration at that time would often use me for my expertise and the fact that I already had the professional equipment to do photos around the facility, either officially for incidents, or for the more relaxed occasions of special visitors to the facility, one of my favorites being that of Cardinal Timothy Dolan. But they also had me cover the Puppies Behind Bars program that is run at Fishkill for a special documentary on *The Oprah Winfrey Show*, among other events as well such as retirement parties and even photos for the Commission on Accreditation.

Now, let's get back to that drug lab. I received my certification from NIK Poly Testing System of Narcotics in August of 2010 and for the newer system NARK, in 2016. I was called upon regularly to conduct drug testing investigations which led to additional contraband charges for inmates that were found to be in possession of them. Once the contraband of suspected drugs was turned over to me on the chain of evidence forms, I would make my way to a secured drug lab area in Building 13 and begin my assignment. First thing was to get out all of the needed paperwork, the proper test kits, the digital camera, as well as the drug weight scale. Photos would be taken for identification purposes marking down all the pertinent details. Sometimes this packaging was wrapped so tight and had been secreted up the anal cavity of an inmate; wearing gloves alone with an open window were not enough to keep the stench and potential contamination away. In fact, there had to be minimal air movement in the room once the package was opened and the portion of the suspected narcotics were tested, whichever case it was; most of the time for me it was synthetic marijuana, positive for amphetamines which we referred to as K2, a drug problem all around the country that was being sold everywhere. Then many occasions it would be suboxone, cocaine, heroin, or actually marijuana. Just one outgoing direct breath would be enough to blow the product off of the weight scale. Sometimes a supervisor would enter the room and the door swinging open would cause air movement. Once I got the weight and confirmed test results, I got a hold of the field supervisor or the watch commander to inform them of the results. This would start the process of an "Unusual Incident Report" and thus creating hours of paperwork for a number of staff involved. On many occasions, I would be called to testify at an inmate's hearing as he argued the procedures or process that was used to determine the outcome of the testing done on the contraband drugs. There was, and still is, a profound drug problem in Fishkill Correctional Facility. Actually, in every New York state prison, there are severe drug problems. Albany offers the minimal tools in order for us to combat these issues. Because of this, many officers and other staff are put into harm's way each and every day they walk through those gates. I have been there and done that, seen the worst-case scenarios of how an inmate reacts to the side-effects of the drugs he ingested or consumed. Too many unnecessary injuries have occurred due to uses of force with out-of-control combative inmates who are high on drugs. Once in a while when we were on point and vigilant enough (depending on what day and shift was on duty), we were able to find these dangerous drugs and get an inmate placed in solitary confinement pending his hearing. You really have to know your stuff in there; any screw-ups in documentation could toss an entire charge. I was called upon to do the drug testing one day for a use of force when an inmate was trying to throw his drugs while being taken down to the floor by officers. One of those items was a large clove of garlic. At first, Sgt. Cameras thought it to be something used to throw off the scent of the other drugs he was carrying. While I was in the drug lab, I had finished up the testing of the other drugs, and then I peeled the garlic all apart while weighing it, taking photos, and it looked and appeared to be ordinary garlic. I had notified that I had finished up. I cleaned up the lab, signed out of the log, and began to lock up. Then I stopped. Then I thought, wait a minute. This inmate was fighting to get rid of these drugs, even throwing his garlic. Why would he bother throwing away an allowable item on his person? I opened the door back up, turned on the lights, got the test kits out, and placed my sample amount in the poly tester kits and within two seconds, I had bright purple colors indicating that it had been laced with amphetamines, what we also referred to as K2. Apparently, this garlic had been soaked with the drug, dried, and then mailed in through the package room to the inmate. Nobody had heard of this before so since it was an allowable item, he was given the garlic as part of his package. I immediately called Sgt. Cameras back and told him I had tested the garlic and it was positive for K2 amphetamines. I am glad I took the time to go back and check this out. Inmates always had ways of getting over on us, but now I uncovered one of their secrets. Since most of the drug charges were being handled in-house by the department, many times they would get off with little to no additional disciplinary measures that had to be applied to the results of their hearing. It could take as many as 5-6 staff numerous hours in paperwork, investigation, and other procedures just to have it all thrown out in the end. This became a losing factor in the morale for the staff that actually did their jobs. Every day it seemed as if there was something that pissed off staff. It was not a secret either. But all too often it was just moaned and groaned about, which kept the phones busy. But these words were never enough to take action and actually do something about it. Besides the fact that there were nearly 750 officers working at Fishkill in it, we had never been a united group that acted as one. It was the same at many prison facilities. There were always differences and excuses. The administration officials saw this, took action to divide and conquer. Our union did not get the support it needed because they became their own worst enemy on their own, the whole system just fell short of its goals.

A lot of times officers would find contraband drugs toward the end of shift and score their selves some overtime a few times a week. Not that this was a coincidence each time, but the inmates knew as the shift winded down, so did the officers' searches, security rounds, and found the opportunities that those were the best times to make their moves. I can recall several times making last-minute rounds on units and running into drug transactions or other assaults with inmates occurring. Something they did not expect seeing when I came around that corner. Another issue was that supervisors were on different shifts, so let's say our shift was 2:30-10:30 p.m., the sergeant's would be 2:00-10:00 p.m. The same applies for the dayshift and overnight tours where supervisors come in one-half prior to officers. The incoming shift sergeants do not usually head into the inmate population buildings until after the pre-shift briefings are wrapped up and shift change commences. After each shift, they would head out of the buildings up to the administration area to finish up their paperwork prior to that and pretty much for the last part of our shift there would be no supervisors in our areas at all. If there had been some sort of an incident, they would respond back to those areas which sometimes meant it was the following shift's sergeant running in to handle the event. Day by day, inmates saw the movement of each staff member, be it a civilian, correction officer, or supervisors. Most had routines, many inmates would know who was off on what days, they would hear us talking amongst each other with other staff about swapping days off, and you can bet for sure some other inmate was making notes of this so that they had this "intelligence" handy if needed to know who was going to be on duty and who would be off in order to move their contraband, conduct their drug transactions, or perhaps worse, find that hidden area to have sexual relations. One can research and find documented cases where just at Fishkill itself, there had been literally numerous cases of female officers having inappropriate relationships with inmates who under the letter of the law, being a ward of the state, cannot, and do not, have the ability to consent to such activity. That's just involving staff on inmate cases, there many more inmate on inmate, at least much more than are reported.

There continues to be huge drug problems in every prison in New York. There are a variety of ways in which they come into the facility. There are trained staff and procedures in place to prohibit the attempts to introduce contraband into a correctional facility. Visitors on the weekends, packages, mail, and even on a family reunion visit (reserved for married inmates and their family only). Who knows what they are dropping into areas of the prisons at night. While there are preventative measures taken, sometimes someone on the outside gets real clever in hiding this dangerous contraband within a food or toiletry product, or if during a visit, it is brought in while hidden in a visitor's body cavity. Fishkill had the occasional K9 Unit come to the prison on visit days to catch the contraband before it comes inside the facility. The department also deploys officers from neighboring facilities that have specialized training in the ION scanning, an additional method often used in secure entities to detect the handling of any illegal drugs. But going through all of this is only one of the many ways to combat the drug problem. Another route of entry at Fishkill is through Gate 2, the truck trap area that is the main entry for vehicle traffic such as commercial deliveries, transportation of inmates to other facilities, construction crews, etc. As many as 20+ inmates go in and out of under security officer escort to do work on the outside grounds during the weekdays. These inmates go through a background check and get top security approval before they can become eligible for this program, often referred as "outside gang crews." These inmates do everything, from mowing, picking up garbage, tree limb removal, clearing debris, as well as snow removal. This was probably the easiest way for an inmate to get drugs into the facility. Anyone, when arranged to do so, could drop off the contraband in a hidden place where the outside crews can pick it up and simply hide it in their body cavity or even their boots. You see, once their day of work is over, all they do is walk back into Gate 2, where two or three officers will line them up and give them a quick pat-down. They are then escorted back to their housing unit to be dropped off where they go back to their rooms or cubicles to prepare for the evening meal, perhaps take a shower, get ready for the count, and even possibly, if lucky enough, get that letter in the mail from a loved one. Things tend to get done quicker in security situations when there are larger than normal numbers of inmates present. These inmates know the routines and find loopholes on how to get around the rules each day as they come back inside. If not, then surely you know they would all quit and request their counselor to put them into another program. Then there lies the problem, who is going to mow the numerous acres of grass, shovel all the snow, remove the garbage, help load and unload trucks, etc. The facility weighs its options and sees fit to keep the present established procedures in place. Sometimes it has been overheard that by turning a blind eye to these issues, everyone goes home from work safe and happy without the fear of reprisals or violence.

Chapter Two
Violence on Violence

1999 was one of the worst years I had seen in the department. Besides the multiple incidents, one of the biggest ones yet was a homicide of an inmate on Housing Unit A-West, in 21-Building. To cut the details short, responding staff had to control a combative inmate and by doing so, they had to use the help that they had available. The supervisor in charge of the area that day, Sgt. Johns, had undergone quite a lengthy investigation due to the inmate's death. You see, at the time, no one in the department had yet to have been trained in what was called "positional asphyxia." This is caused when there is so much weight upon a person, it causes their chest to collapse and breathing becomes impossible. Later that evening, the state police had collected Sgt. John's uniform boots due to the investigation. It was not too long afterward that he ended up going out on stress comp and then getting disability retirement. A number of years ago, he had passed away due to an unknown illness. But going back to that time period in 1999, things became difficult for officers, we were all on edge. I happened to be working on December 30, 1999, with a partner, Officer Peter, in Building 21-A that evening, on Housing Unit "K", with about 58 inmates on the unit. I was conducting my unit search and without any fear of heights, I climbed high above the inmates' shower walls and observed the top of the exhaust fan. I noticed what appeared to be an envelope that was sealed. I opened it up to inspect its contents and found what appeared to be a coded letter with an answer key. I went back up front to advise the area supervisor of my findings and I was immediately sent up to the administration building to see the on-duty captain. It took me nearly an hour to decode the letter, and after I wrote out the two-page letter, the captain had ordered an immediate investigation which ultimately caused approximately 39 inmates to be shipped out days later, transferred away, due to their involvements of this letter, which was a combination of the homicide and Y2K. Here is what the letter from these inmates had said – this is the first time anyone, even most officers and staff at Fishkill, will be ever hearing word for word about this letter. It was kept secret for the longest time.

"Attention, all prisoners: The time for us has come for us to start up in Fishkill and stop being passive inmates we have allowed ourselves to be. Hear our pleas because we take no action when we are wronged by our paid keepers. They cheat us, we cry. They beat us, we cry. They lie to us on and on, and we cry. They treat us like dirt, we cry. Now they murder us, we cry no more, no more crying. Now we take action. Starting January 1, 2000, we start the new years the Y2K way, starting at 6:30 a.m. on the above date. No one leaves any housing unit in this entire facility point blank. No one is allowed to come into any housing unit for any reason. Until the news media is present and the past word is spread throughout to all. Any staff in the area is to be locked down and not allowed any hype or say period. All keys, radios, and equipment are to be taken from all staff members in your area. Any staff member who fights will be dealt with the same way they deal with us when problems arise. All snitches and inmates who go against us is to be dealt with in the same manner as staff. No one is to speak or stand alone, everything will be said and done as one. All heads are to meet when the jail is fully taken over in agreed area at agreed times. When all is well as already agreed, start on movement two, look out for the word and more to come on this in days to come."

ATTENTION ALL PRISONERS

THE TIME HAS COME FOR US TO START UP IN FISHKILL AND STOP
BEING THE PASSIVE INMATES WE HAVE ALO UD OURSELVES TO

OHEAR OUR PLEAS Because WE TAKE NO ACTION WHEN WERE
WRONGED BY OUR PAID KEEPERS,

THEY CHEAT US WE CRY

THEY BEAT US WE CRY
THEY LIe TO US AND ON US WE CRY
THEY TREAT US LIKE DIRT WE CRY
NOW THEY MURDER US WE CRY no no more CRYING
NOW WE TAKE ACTION

STARTING JAN 1ST WE START THE NEW YEAR THE
Y2K WAY START-ING 6:30AM On THE ABOVE DATE.
NO ONE LEAVES ANY HOUSENG UNIT IN THIS ENTIRE
FACILITY FOR NO REASON POINT BLANK

NO ONE IS ALLOWED TO COME ON ANY HOUSNG UNIT FOR
ANY REASON. UNTIL THE NEWS MEDIA IS PRESENT AND
THE PAST WORD IS SPREADED THROUGHOUT TO ALL.
ALL STAFF IN AREA IS TO BE LOCKED DOWN. AN NOT ALOUD
ANY HYPE OF SAY SO PERIOD.

ALL KEYS RADIOS AND ETC IS TO BE TAKEN FROM

ALL STAFF members IN YOUR AREA.
ANY Staff members who FIGHTS IS IS TO BE DEALT
WITH THE WAY THEY DEAL WITH US. WHEN PROBLEMS
ARAISE.

ALL SNITCHES AND INMATES who GO AGAINST US IS
TO BE DEALT WITH IN THE SAME MANNER AS STAFF

NO one IS SPEAK OR STAND ALONE everyoneING
IS TO BE SAID AND DONE AT one.

ALL HEADS IS TO meeT when the Jail IS FUllY
TAKEN over IN AGReed AReA AT AGReed times.

when All is well AS ALReADY Agreed STArT on
movement two Look out FOR next
word And moore on This in DAYS
come.

Example of takeover note after being decoded by myself on Housing Unit "K" Unit
Showers. Two days later, over 40 inmates were shipped out to other facilities around
New York State with over 200 large bags of property inventoried by staff. Copy by
P. Harrington

I was so pissed off at this when I figured out the coded letter, and the captain that evening gave a few of us an order a cease and desist of any word getting out to the troops. He wanted his staff to show up to work on New Year's Day. This alone would cause a major problem if word had gotten out to other officers working that day. Once I finished my briefing with the bosses, I went back to the housing unit to continue my searches. Knowing what I had just found, gave me instinct to dig further. I had thought that areas around the facility must have a cache of homemade weapons hidden. I went back into the inmates' bathroom, and about 10 minutes later, I ended up splitting my head open on a metal pipe valve, holding my head as it was bleeding and going back up from to the office. Many inmates saw this and headed to their rooms/cubes expecting some incoming trouble. My partner contacted the area supervisor and I was immediately transported to St. Luke's Hospital E.R. in Newburgh for stitches and treatment. I was back to work on New Year's Day without any further problem. I made it in time for the chaotic transfer all of those inmates and their bags of property.

As years have gone by, we have begun dealing with more and more drug problems, which in recent years have shown that across New York's prisons, the biggest problem has been with suboxone, K2 (synthetic marijuana), and heroin. These drugs create a vast number of incidents inside these secure facilities. If it's not gang related, you can bet it's drug related. I can't tell you how bad the violence has become with drug problems. There have been serious issues where many inmates have been transported to outside hospitals for emergency treatment. If it's an inmate acting out over the side-effects of ingesting these drugs, then you can bet on a response of officers coming in to take control of the situation. These drugs can make most of these inmates into superhuman. I have been at incidents which the smallest sized inmate would be able to outmatch 4-5 officers trying to get control of him and into cuffs – or what we term "mechanical restraints." The most serious incident at Fishkill I was involved with was on April 21, 2015, for a Code 10 emergency transmitted via two-way radios to all staff that required the immediate response of officers to an area. You have no idea what you are running into with these situations. Upon my arrival to this unit, called B-Center in Building 21, I was exhausted and completely out of breath from running all the way there and up numerous flights of stairs. Right away, I had observed a totally chaotic scene. This building was infamous for its gang activities and drug problems. There was a lot of yelling with multiple officers around trying to control a combative inmate and contain the situation from other inmates who were close by on that unit, and it took a second to size up this scene before I decided where I was needed the most. It was crazy to say the least, with so much happening there. Seeing that this inmate was still not secured while the struggle ensued on the floor, I took the handcuffs off the back of the belt of another officer and placed them on the inmate's right wrist first, and with the help of others, was able to get his left wrist over to get the other cuff on him. For the sake of all involved, I wanted to get the situation under control just as much as the next officer. With the amount of time it took for me to get up there from my post, about two minutes later, one could only imagine the struggle that these officers were having with this inmate that whole time. Being under some type of drug, which at the time was believed to be K2, one of the behavioral factors of this is that it gives one incredible strength. It is known to drive up your body temperature, wreak havoc on your cardiac system, among other things. More help was called for over the radios. Soon after, many more staff started to show up from other areas of the facility, the first I have witnessed that happened in a very long time. Finally, the inmate was stood up against the wall with assistance by staff and held in place while being interviewed by the sergeant. Just prior to this, a Code Blue medical emergency was called on the radio because another officer was on the floor holding his chest and ribs. Medical personnel from the facility's Regional Medical Unit (RMU) responded and the officer was taken by stretcher out of the unit. As they rushed this officer down the narrow staircase head first going down, his pants pocket had caught the end of hand rail and almost yanked him right off the stretcher. In the time of all this stress, it was unusual to see this happen with his pants getting caught up on the handrail. They corrected the problem and moved on out of sight. Eventually, the inmate with the use of force was sat down in a wheelchair and secured to it with white bed sheets. This was one of the older style wheelchairs, the best available we had at the time. The state was not frequently eager to go out and buy new equipment until something happened. This again was a good example of my point about the administration being reactive. This wheelchair did not even have foot pedals on it. At the time, the facility had no other way of securing an inmate to a stretcher or wheelchair other than the use of these bed sheets. This building had minimal, outdated equipment for these types of incidents, and there was no working elevator. Many of the inmate "witnesses" testified that this inmate was cuffed and was thrown down the stairs. Funny how this was claimed while not one inmate was in the immediate area, let alone any that were in the line of sight. However, across the officer's desk is a door leading to the recreation TV room/kitchen area. In this door was a plexiglass window, probably about 24" x 30". Since the inmates are the ones that clean those areas, and in order for them to get some "privacy" in those areas to shield the officer's view without having to actually go into the room itself, it's not uncommon to see many of these windows scuffed and scratched up, causing a fuzzy, hazed, and blurry view. They create this effect by using the state-issued green scrub pads when they clean. So anyone in the recreation room that night of the incident would not have clear vision of the incident, let alone the fact that the door is also inset into the wall almost a foot or more, making it that much harder to see to the sides left and right. But for the accusations that came from these inmate witnesses were probably looking for payback now that they had a platform to speak, and this could not be farther from the truth. It had become proven in the investigation that these inmates were contradictory, found to have the wrong information, and were eventually designated as not credible. There were four of us carrying the wheelchair with the inmate down flight by flight in the narrow staircase. I had injured my left finger badly as the metal frame of the wheelchair smacked against the metal handrail. I had immediately let go so someone else could take over. I thought my finger was broken at the time. So they continued to carry the wheelchair down to the first floor going through unit one-center to gain access to the wheelchair ramp and down the walkway to the RMU. Ambulances began to arrive for injured staff as well as the inmate. Upon arrival to the RMU, the inmate was put into an exam room and was found to be unresponsive and medical staff began CPR. He was brought to the nearest emergency room at St Luke's Hospital in Newburgh where he was eventually pronounced dead. The Orange County medical examiner's office quickly ruled it a homicide. This kicked off a fury of fire for all of those involved at the facility, including the command center in Albany. It was time for everyone to get their reports in order. That evening, there were several officers injured, but only two had gone to the hospital right away. One of them was me, for what turned out to be a severely sprained left finger and a contusion to my left inner forearm after being assaulted by the inmate. I also had anxiety issues. The other officer and I were both across from each other at Vassar Brothers Hospital emergency room, in our beds waiting testing and treatment. After being triaged by the nurse, I was placed in Room 29 at about 10:00 p.m. I had x-rays and a CAT-scan done. We had a few other corrections officers who were there with us. This is standard procedure. I had requested numerous times for a union representative to come to the hospital for us once we learned that the inmate had died. We found this out when we called Fishkill's watch commander's office to check in with our status update while at the emergency room. More phone calls were made to the facility, a very busy place now due to the severity of the incident, that was filled with several investigators from the state police and the Corrections Office of Special Investigations. Union representatives from Corrections and Police Benevolent Association showed up to the facility as well, but no one came out to us at the hospital. Within an hour of being at the emergency room, we were approached by two State Police Bureau of Criminal Investigation officers and a forensics investigator. Still no response from our union reps. The investigators asked me my name, where I worked, what I did for my job in the facility, etc., and as things started to get more specific, I told the investigators no more questions. Their response was vague, but with the look in their eyes, you could tell they were up to something. They walked out shutting my curtain. Moments later, the forensics investigator walked in my room with a handful of things. He told me he was there to collect my uniform. I have heard of this happening in the past in other incidents, so I thought they were doing this for everyone involved. It appeared that they only collected my uniform as well as the second officer across the hallway from me. Nobody at the prison who was involved went through this process like we had to at the E.R. When this began, I was ordered to remove my uniform piece by piece, and photos were taken. First my shirt was removed, handed to the forensics investigator who was wearing blue latex gloves, with the item being placed in a labeled brown paper bag. Digital photos were taken of all four sides of me with his department-issued camera. Next was the white undershirt, same process repeated, as I removed my pants, boots, socks, and underwear. There were approximately 35 photos taken of me. I was visually inspected naked, standing barefoot on a cold tile floor. I was provided with a one-size-fits-all hospital gown, with no undergarments and yellow disposable socks. By that time, the facility was aware of what we were going through yet not one official had responded to the hospital. We were held there by the state police for several hours until they got word that we could be released to go home. Well, I was not able to go home, because I was driven

51

back to the facility in the prison transport van, arriving back at approximately 4:45 a.m., walking across the administration building parking lot in those small yellow socks on a cold 42-degree morning. As I approached the administration gate with the American flag whipping in the wind off to my left shoulder, I entered the foyer into the gate area where all eyes were on me. It was getting close to shift change with the arrival of several transportation officers. I had been ordered back in to make out a report by Lieutenant Dryer. When I found out that nobody else had gone through the same process, I felt angry and relieved at the same time, knowing that they did not have to endure the same humiliating experience. I, however, remained anguished, disrespected, criminalized, demoralized, embarrassed, discomforted, and furthermore, discriminated against. The Deputy Superintendent of Security at that time, whom I personally knew, came out in the first-floor administration hall just outside his office and looked at me, confused, asking what happened to me while at the hospital and why was I dressed like that. I was just as confused. I figured by that time he would have heard. One of my supervisor sergeants went to get me some emergency clothing, flip flops, and a sweat suit. He was angry that BCI investigators never gave us the courtesy of getting our reports together. I was able to wear that sweat suit somewhat, but due to my tall frame, I often find it difficult to fit into the average sizes of clothing. Later in the weeks following, I did many follow-ups regarding my uniform items.

It took me several months to file my claim with the department to replace the items that were taken from me that normally are not standard issue, especially those expensive work boots. Numerous inquiries were documented in my handbook about getting my department-issued frisk gloves reissued to me just to be told some excuse as to why I would not be able to get one yet. It was well into July and even Union Steward Officer Sanka had been aware of my need and request. Other things happening in the form of retaliation toward me from the hospital incident with BCI included harassment from other staff, and more importantly, my time card kept coming up missing. My overtime from that night was not paid for months since the assistant watch commander conveniently misplaced the notation to document my overtime from the night of April 21st. Additionally, as also noted in my pocket notebook, my claim paperwork to get the items confiscated from me was misplaced, and after resubmitting, I was given the run around over it for the next several months. I also sent my written complaint, as requested, to Regional Vice President Mr.

Mallory of Corrections and Police Benevolent Association, to be forwarded up to the Union President's Office the following day. But to no avail; no action was taken had resulted in anything favorable for what I had gone through. There again was no surprise. It was in no time at all that we were soon ordered to report to Building 2 in Albany, which houses corrections commissioners and multiple other staff. There we met up with Bureau of Labor Relations and investigators from the Office of Special Investigation for our interview. This event drew attention from major media news outlets, and soon it landed into the hands of the United States District Attorney's Office. We were now on our way to speak to the feds, interviews about the roles we played during the incident. Many of us ended up in White Plains to undergo Federal Grand Jury proceedings. We were not able to speak up against the misinformation that was out there, the "witness accounts from inmates" that were incredibly wrong and off key, or to all of those civilians who had been protesting us on the streets in Poughkeepsie, Beacon, and Fishkill, amongst other regions. We had written notification and orders from the law firm representing us that we were not allowed to speak to anyone about this case, except to the lawyers or the union. That kept things bottled up for many of us involved. Stress built each day as new reports came out. It was incredibly hard, especially for those officers who had been publicly named, not to be able to defend ourselves. Many nights were sleepless, wondering what was around the corner, hearing the rumors, but really it was the unknown that had the best of me. For well over two years, we had to bottle it up. A lot of us just did what we had to do, spoke about it amongst each other to get some peer support, maybe with our immediate family, but other than that, it was a really tough situation for anyone to go through, especially for a first time. It took over two years to finally be cleared of any criminal wrongdoing by the feds in August 2017, and it is now a civil rights lawsuit from the inmate's family. After speaking for an hour on the phone with the Assistant Attorney General, it was likely that this would end up in the laps of the Office of Mental Health and the Medical Unit of Fishkill Correctional Facility.

Over the years during my career prior to this homicide investigation, I had been involved with many other incidents which occasionally involved the use of force on an inmate or inmates to gain compliance and control, which often resulted in injuries that required medical treatment and sometimes even worse, surgery. As officers walk into work each day and go to a pre-shift briefing, we would get information on any incidents occurring in the facility, general memos, assignments for the tour, as well as notifications on whom your area supervisors were going to be. Sometimes they would not even read anything, if you were lucky enough for the Lieutenant to show up to the briefing, or if someone had "forgotten" the clipboard with the memos of information to be announced. I had worked many areas of the facility, but eventually when you gain time on the job and seniority, you have better chances at bidding an open job location. Sometimes the more popular areas were hard to get...but occasionally one would get lucky. I had placed numerous "bids" for openings on occasions, and in 2004 I took an opening on my afternoon tour. My new job where I would be assigned daily is known as Vocational TC #2 (The TC stands for Traffic Checkpoint). It was located in the basement tunnel area of 21-A Building, the upper part of Fishkill Correctional Facility, adjacent to the enormous water tower. It was at this location, due to its proximity to certain locations and the duration of my time on that post, I had experienced the most injuries due to inmate related incidents. On January 2, 2005, I recall while I was at the medical unit getting my mandatory annual TB test, an inmate by the name of Flanders had lost control and became belligerent in the holding pen waiting area. He kept yelling he had HIV and wanted to get his blood on us as he began smashing his forehead on the cinderblock walls. I placed my right hand in the area he was hitting his head to prevent injuries to his head and we ended up going to the floor pretty hard with me taking the full weight of the fall, injuring my left forearm, wrist, and hand. Everyone fell on top of me. I had remained on duty wearing an ice pack and an ace bandage. I ended up getting mandatory overtime that evening but was sent home about two hours into the shift due to my injuries from earlier. There was another time I have documented from December 6, 2005 that I had to use large bolt cutters to cut a pad lock off from one of the lockers during a search of an inmate organization area. As the handle flew back, it snapped and hit me directly in my left knee. Of course, with these incidents, they were reported and I had been checked out medically. As time went on, so did the number of incidents. I am only mentioning some of the more serious ones. While many of the days were routine, I did experience all types of situations at my various assignments. On August 22, 2007, I was interviewing an inmate about some rule violations when out of the corner of the entrance from the staircase came flying a green pepper filled with a yellow liquid which was determined to likely be urine. I was hit in the face, stomach, and leg. The inmate that was nearby was also struck. I was photographed, taken to the prison's regional medical unit, and put into a shower and given an emergency change of clothes. The superintendent of the facility had declared the area a crime scene, and was going to have someone go up to photograph it, but some of the officers had already ordered some inmates to mop up the floors and wipe down the areas of the walls, desk, etc. By then it was too late to conduct the proper investigation for a Felony Aggravated Harassment case. It appears to me that someone was in a hurry to cover this up. I was then sent to Cornwall Hospital emergency room where blood had been drawn and the ER doctor had ruled it a bodily fluid exposure. Now the stress began to pile on. Not only did we not know who did it, but the person responsible was never found, even after an investigation by the Office of Special Investigation, which back then, was formally known as the Inspector General's Office. Like I said, cover-ups inside there can be done quickly. The uniform that I had been wearing was bagged and never seen again. In fact, the facility had misplaced the employee accident/injury report. I only found that out when just recently it was requested by Albany to review my disability retirement application. I kept all of my documents. Within five minutes, I located my copy of that report and it was scanned and emailed to them where they confirmed receipt. We have always been told from day one on the job to keep copies of our documents. Another thing was to write down your work location each day of duty in your yearly calendar book for quick reference. No one else could be relied to have this accurate information. It was best to keep it for yourself, or as they say in Corrections, "Cover your ass." Don't get me wrong, we had good days at work, but they were far outweighed by the bad. Many of the different areas in Fishkill had their own cliques of officers, each of them making the shift go as smoothly as possible. In the early days of my career, the administration made sure there was good morale amongst the rank and file. Then came those days when you did not know what you would be walking into when you came on duty. There had been numerous acts of violence around the prison, and here are some of those that I had been involved with.

On October 1, 2008, having just arrived at work, one of the vocational instructors in the Building Maintenance classroom was having a problem with an inmate in his classroom. I knew this instructor well, he did some electrical work for me at our home as his side job, and I too, of course, did photos for his family. He has since moved on and became a state trooper. Upon arrival to make relief of dayshift, I did not even get a chance yet to sign into the logbook that afternoon. I was called into the classroom, about 30 feet down the hallway. Before I knew it, the situation intensified with inmate Pines. I attempted to calm him down and remove him from the class in front of the other inmates. Once we got in the hallway, a passing officer stopped to assist me. He was found to have had a screwdriver in his pants pocket outside of his shop area during a pat frisk and with the assistance of that officer who was walking in coming on duty, we had called for assistance over the radio for a supervisor to respond to my post. Next thing you know, we are on the ground rolling around as I activated my radio for emergency assistance. The inmate was wearing green and was of African American descent, but somehow in the pile, another officer had my arm pinned down as if he was color blind. On the floor, a mere two-three inches from each other, that inmate and I were face to face. I was lucky not to have him spitting into my face at that moment. There had been over 23 officers that had responded. We were able to get the combative inmate into handcuffs and off to the solitary confinement box, but not without a couple of us suffering from injuries, mine being my chest, left foot, and left leg, as documented by my area supervisor. Off to medical to be assessed we all went, and to follow up with our own doctors going off duty. Another more serious incident occurred when I was doing one of those mutual swaps of shifts, working for another officer on dayshift in Building 21, on Housing unit B-Center.

On April 18, 2011, while working my post, I had to call for assistance from a fellow officer working at Checkpoint 3. I had begun to deal with an irate inmate who was in violation of facility rules. When he was placed on the wall to be pat frisked, he had turned on me and I attempted to hold him up to the wall, but he overpowered me as we fell to the floor, again, sustaining injuries from those concrete floors. It was not much later on May 31 of that same year, I had been assaulted when I was involved with a use of force on an inmate Ortega, injuring my right knee cap and my left knee, as well as the right side of my back when we fell striking the floor. This was the incident in which I had attempted to get help via my two-way radio but the battery was not working. The battery issues with our radios were ongoing problems. The administration tried to come up with the easiest remedies they could to fix the problem without having to spend additional money replacing batteries in the previous years. As always, they pointed the finger and blamed us for the issue. You can't put an entire basket of eggs in the garbage for one bad egg. Deal with the issue at hand, individually. But they never did, even with union intervention. That night I had called in for a new battery request, but it had already been 30 minutes and one still had not arrived. I even logged it in my logbook to show that on a regular occasion we would have no radio communications due to these issues. When this incident occurred with inmate Ortega, he had already given me a false ID of another inmate and was completely uncooperative and combative toward me. We had been rolling on the floor with each other in combat for what seemed like an eternity without any help. My wall-mounted telephone by the desk was a mere 20 feet away, but I had not been able to get over to it, not until he gave up and tired out. At that point, I ordered him to stay on the ground and not to move. I ran over to the phone 15 feet away and called the arsenal control stating, "Code 10 Checkpoint 2, Code 10 Checkpoint 2!" Before help got there, I ran back over to hold onto the inmate to keep him still until we were able to get him into handcuffs. I was able to get escorted with assistance over to the medical facility to get assessed. I personally would have held the facility responsible if I had been more seriously injured. It was their continued failure to remedy the radio battery situation. Ultimately, they are responsible for providing us with a safe working environment. There had been another time, as entered into my pocket notebook, while working in an area active with inmates, my radio battery went dead and became operable at 7:30 in the morning and I did not get one until after 11:00! Not only could I not hear announcements, but had there been an emergency response I was supposed to report to, or an emergency in my own area, I would not have the communication ability unless I was able to get to a phone.

As part of my duties as the afternoon shift deputy fire and safety chief, on the evening of March 5, 2013, a "Signal One" was called over the radio, indicating that there was a fire on Housing Unit 14-18. I responded from my post up the hill of the facility from 21-A Building down to the Main Building. As soon as I got outside of the 21-A Building, I saw an officer from transportation sitting with the van running. I asked her to give me a quick ride down to the main building. That saved me a few minutes, and definitely some energy and breath. I ran up the backdoor into unit 14-18 and found several officers dealing with fire hoses and extinguishers to control the fire in a single room that had filled the entire corridor with blinding smoke. This room belonged to an inmate Ball, who had not been present in the unit, but was signed out to be at the facility's gym area at the time. Once the fire was under control, I contacted the watch commander and told him I needed addition supplies, staff, cameras, as well as fans, and to declare this area a crime scene. I also told him what I would need and the officer of the day was notified, as well as the off-duty fire and safety officer. Upon inspection of the room, I observed two points of ignition in both corners of the room. Some type of odor was present to indicate that possibly an accelerant fluid had been used. As my investigation continued, and with all the inmates evacuated and being assessed by medical, some staff were sent to the hospital for smoke inhalation. I had written a four-page investigative report to the watch commander with a copy to the captain's office and the fire and safety officer as well. That evening state police investigators, members from the Office of Special Investigation, as well as the Deputy Superintendent of Security all showed up to observe the fire location. The unit was on lock down for two-three days with inmates being relocated to other units. I found myself in the captain's Office having a discussion with him about the entire incident. Despite all of my years of experience in firefighting, all of my schools and training, they wanted this one to go away. No matter how I fought in words that day to back up my report, it was shot down by the administration. It was soon after that I found out why. This whole fire was caused by the actions of the Deputy Superintendent of Security, who had made the discretionary decision to move this inmate into a one-man private room, bypassing the seniority listing on that unit for other inmates waiting to get their own room. Once this inmate went to the gym that evening, his room was lit on fire which caused heavy damage to his personal property as well as state property. If we had pushed this as an arson, it would have come back on the Deputy of Security, so again, another cover-up. They took care of it in-house, paid the affected inmate's claim for property loss, moved him to another unit, and dropped the investigation.

On July 25, 2013, I had been injured by another inmate who was coming out of the vocational shop area attempting to hide contraband in his hand, while standing in a line of about 22 inmates waiting to be walked through the metal detector. He was one of the first in line. Inmate Flores, I remember it well. He was making a scene in front of the others. When I pulled him out of line and out into the hallway to be frisked, I had noticed a female officer passing by, I asked her for assistance. He began sliding down the wall horizontally away from my grip. She said, "Pull your pin," while watching us fall to the floor, still standing at my desk. She did not move an inch. As help arrived, I made it clear, as any other officer would, that this female officer had not assisted. It is a major rule in our manual, to come to the assistance of another officer in need. I was pretty pissed off, not that it mattered at that point. Female or not, if you want to work in a jail that has male inmates, you need to handle yourself and comport your actions accordingly to your surrounding environment. For a few weeks, word got around about her actions that day, but with any incident, normally dies down in discussion when the next "incident" occurs. I ended up having to have left knee surgery for a torn meniscus that kept me out for quite a few months.

In November of 2014, somewhere about on the 9th, an escort with an inmate in cuffs had been coming by my checkpoint from down the hill in the main building, about a 10-minute walk. I had heard by phone to expect the arrival of what we termed a "keep lock" about to come through my area, on their way to the box area. My job at the time was to stop all traffic of inmates, clear the halls, and open the doors to the secure special housing unit staircase for ease of access so there was no delay in the movement of this keep-lock inmate, officers escorting him, and the supervisor, walking together as a group. As many of those that I had go by me over the years, this one was entirely different. One of my fellow officers from the other checkpoint was at my post just after we got out of our mess hall duty. We were not yet officially opened up as it was our moment of "downtime," where we would be able to grab a quick bite to eat for our dinner. JR and I were chatting away when Sgt. Cameras had come through with a couple of officers who were struggling with a combative inmate. They had stopped at our checkpoint. JR and I looked at each other. Here we go, I thought. Sgt. Cameras had us bring the inmate into the staircase as we were told to wait there and secure the inmate while he interviewed his staff at my checkpoint. We were only about 30 feet away but obscured from view by the corner and a doorway entrance to the stairs. We both held each of his arms while he was handcuffed and faced him into the corner. All of the sudden, this inmate began to bash his head into the wall while we stood there. It was time to gain control of him and the only way in that tight area was to bring him down to the floor. We yelled to the Sarge, they all ran over to us hearing the commotion and he told me to activate my radio for a

Code 10 emergency. This brought assistance from multiple officers in the areas. I could hear stomping feet coming down the stairs from above and from down the hallways. Once the situation was under control, the inmate was brought up to the box area (special housing unit) and then seen by medical staff. The rest of us had to go down to the medical unit for assessment, photos, and to begin our reports. It literally took several hours to do this; we never even made it back to our posts before our shifts ended at 10:30 p.m. I once again had injuries to my left hip, knee, and left leg. All the other officers had various injuries but we remained on duty and were told to follow up with our own doctors.

Sometime around this time period, Fishkill's administration obtained the green light to lock down the facility to hire overtime at an alarming rate, one that has not been seen in years since Y2K. The purpose of this was to go through every area of the facility to sweep it for contraband. Although this may have been the mission at first, someone up top decided to come up with the idea that now that the facility was so well staffed, they could take advantage of the manpower. I can recall working days at Gate 2 on dayshift, doing a mutual swap for another officer who normally worked that post, at the main truck trap gate area leading out of the facility. It was a busy area. They began using all of the officers for "out of title" work. They had us ordered to move heavy appliances, furniture, and other metal and wood products to a central location, one at the lower end of the facility outside of the main building, and one at the top for 21/21A Building. It was backbreaking work. Even some of the old timers had to go out on workers' compensation due to numerous orthopedic injuries. The union would kick in dozens of pizzas daily for most of the staff doing this work while the administration provided bottled water. This detail would occur on the day and afternoon shifts, wrapping up in the evening normally by 10:00 p.m. I believe this went on for almost five days or so from what I recall. So much of this furniture, appliances, and other multiple items were brought out by dump trucks located down in the motor pool area of the facility where the maintenance garage is at. This was complained about every day, something we were very good at doing, but not putting those words into action. When it came to the department's decision on their missions, there was not much to do about it.

On one particular evening shift, I could recall some unusual situations happening. Keeping in mind that during this large-scale detail, high-ranking officials were on duty well into the evening hours, which was rare for the normal day-to-day activities. A couple of officers were sent down to pick up a small dump truck to load up a lot of this scrap metal and furniture to get it out of the facility. Even civilian staff was kept on overtime into the evenings to help out with this large operation. These two officers, unbeknownst to them, had their dump truck loaded and went down to the far back of the facility where a lot of clean fill and other debris were usually dumped. Once they lifted the dump up in the air, there were issues noticed with the hydraulics and they could not get the dump back down. They drove back around the front of the facility. It was almost comical to watch. They ended up parking the truck at the motor pool with the dump up in the air to let the dayshift handle it. They decided to get the second truck to continue getting their loads to move outside of the facility perimeter to load into the dump piles. Coincidentally, following the same procedure, making their second drop off, the dump stayed in the air upright once again, not being able to get it back down. Apparently, something was wrong with the hydraulics. This was nothing new since the fleet of facility vehicles were usually pretty beat up. If it came in new, it was pretty much guaranteed that it would not be for long. So, on their way back around the front of the facility, they drove past the administration building with the dump way up in the air. Eventually they got flagged down by the captain asking what the hell they were doing, but after some quick explanation and some laughs, it was parked next to the other truck down in the lot with the fleet. The following morning was going to be quite the surprise for incoming dayshift.

Later that night, I was assigned to a housing unit search on Unit "J" in 21 A building. This was located on the first floor. I happened to be in the recreation area which had a clear view through the windows and bars of the 21-A loading dock and Gate 4 truck trap. This particular trap was unmanned and had no security tower above it as most truck traps have at prisons in the state. But since this one was rarely used, the facility did not take the extra measures other than calling one of the outside perimeter patrols to bring the keys over to unlock the gate. In all truck traps, there are two gates. One is always closed; it is a high security risk to have both gates open at once, for obvious reasons. At the time I had been looking out the windows; it was raining pretty well. I noticed a truck coming through the gate and it was a civilian employee coming through with a truck to pick up a load off the 21-A loading dock. Apparently, to save time and from getting too wet, both trap gates at

Gate 4 were left open. One of the supervisors next to me was talking on the phone. I said, "Hey, Sarge, take a look at that!" He could not believe his eyes. He ran faster than ever downstairs to the back dock area to have them lock those gates. There had been no officer assigned to Gate 4 so it was wide open, and with the movement and all the unusual activity going on, this would have been a perfect opportunity for inmates who were being used as laborers to make a run for it. So here I am thinking, this whole time, we are moving all of this furniture and metal lockers, appliances out of the facility to clean out most of the areas, but yet they leave gates open. Even if it was inadvertent, it had taken away from the idea that due to the lockdown, we were supposed to be at higher security awareness. That whole operation was put in place to simply use us to do all of that out-of-title work for the administration.

Another incident to recall was on November 18, 2015, the same year as the homicide on Housing Unit B-Center back in April. I had been sitting at my checkpoint, processing inmates that were coming into the area for the general movement into the organizational area. They had opened up the evening program for "Porter Pool," where inmates were assigned to cleaning duties. I recall dealing with this inmate, his name was Maximus. He approached me asking for access to some cleaning supplies I had stored in our backroom, such as a broom, mop, and bucket. Once I gave him this equipment, I told him he had to go down this long empty hallway to get to the "slop sink" where he could fill the bucket with water. Maximus looked back at me with great fear in his eyes. I asked him, "What's wrong? There's nobody down there, it's ok to go, that's where you get the water to fill the mop buckets." He looked at me shaking his head sideways, "No. No. No…" I asked another inmate perhaps to tell him in Spanish that this was normal procedure. That did not work. Even the other inmates knew that Maximus was a "bug," a mental health inmate, perhaps one that did not take his meds that evening. Maximus began to freak out. I stood up from my desk ordering him to go do his task. He backed away from me and appeared to be scared. At this point, I did not know if he was a Level 1 mental health inmate, someone who was on drugs, or whatever, but I knew I had to deal with it. Before I could even take control, Maximus took off into a full sprint down the hallway and as he approached the corner, he ran into another inmate that was carrying several brown bags of groceries he had just got as a package from his family. There were cans of food, vegetables and fruit, boxes and bags all over the floor. I kept running past it and got on the radio to call for assistance. The inmate was running toward Checkpoint #3 and another officer who was filling in that day at that post stood up in the inmate's path as he ran into him, and as I caught up to the him, the inmate was on the floor kicking the two of us, with another officer completely tearing open his pants in the leg, and with the inmate kicking me in my knees. With much difficulty, we were able to gain control of him as several officers arrived. I had been on the bottom of the pile and had the wind knocked out of me. Someone standing above us called a Code Blue staff medical emergency over the radios. Before long, staff from the medical unit arrived and those of us injured were brought to the get checked out. Photos were taken, the usual documentation filled out, the state police had been notified. Ultimately, since this was a mental health inmate, he suffered no consequence of either internal or external charges as a result of the incident or any of our injuries incurred by him.

On July 25, 2016, I had been assigned to move inmate property on the dayshift while working another swap shift. Normally you would be able to obtain inmates to do this work, but neither time nor availability permitted this. The Sarge wanted this property moved before the shift ended. I remember this day was over 90 degrees outside – blistering hot. The cart we used to move the property had rails on the side of it, almost as high as about three feet or so. Most of these bags weighed well over 100 lbs. With all of my back and knee injuries from the previous cases, I tried my best to get the job done but without fail, both knees made a crack and popping sound, causing severe pain, sending me to outside hospital where they took x-rays, treated me with pain meds, and referred me to my orthopedic for immediate follow-up. I had left work early that day, ultimately missing only a few days of work since I had such a busy schedule to keep with everything for my outside business as well. Sometimes you had to grin and bear the pain to keep the pace going. If the incident occurred in one of the very rare areas that there were actual working cameras, or had been videotaped by hand (pre-planned, such as a cell extraction), then we would watch the footage over and over again to match up the video to our exact actions word for word on paper. If it was not on video, I can't recall how many times we have been ordered to change our paperwork in order for it to reflect what the story of the incident was to coordinate it with the other documents of staff. For me, and for many others who complained, it was our names going on the report, our signatures, so it should have been in our own words. Not too long after the April 2015 homicide incident, there had been some policy changes made. Any time after a use of force incident, we were all supposed to be held in different rooms to do our reports to avoid any collaboration. This, along with many other changes, really did not affect us since it was business as usual. Even if they did put us in other rooms apart, which was rare, on our way to the medical unit to get checked out, was normally a good time for those involved to make discussion.

Not too long afterward, it was about September 11, 2016, there had been a commotion over the radios about an incident going on in the box, Special Housing Unit "P", which was only about two-three floors above me from my location in the basement tunnel. I had no inmates in my area so I began to make my way to the area, arriving with a few other officers. There had been an inmate by the name of Paquito; he was a small guy, not much to him, but a hell of a fighter. He was all kinds of wiry. Hard to get a handle on. This unit was a long gallery of cells, and this was almost 3/4 of the way down. This area had video cameras monitoring everything. There was already a supervisor on the scene. The officers had fallen out onto the gallery floor trying to control this combative inmate. At that point, I jumped in where I could gain control of his upper body. There were already four other larger-sized officers who were not able to successfully gain control of him. He had continued to slip from their grip. In fact, inmate Paquito fought as they tried to get cuffs on his right wrist, but as I reached over to pull it behind him, he made numerous attempts to bite my hand. Inmate Paquito grabbed the cuffs from one of the officer's hands while I was yelling for someone else to get control of his head and that's when another officer came over and was able to pin his head down, allowing me to pull his arm back and get the cuffs on his wrists. Soon, more help had arrived and off we went for medical assessment. I had once again reinjured my previous injuries from my lower back as well as my left and right knees. I could no longer take the abuse to these areas of my body. I had had it with this. All of us went to get checked out and reported our injuries, but none had gone off duty. It was close to the end of shift. I followed up with my treating doctors, both of whom did my knee and lower back surgeries. We were basically deemed as walking wounded that evening. One of the officers even had a big tear in the crotch of his uniform pants, something he was teased about the rest of the shift to follow. I had followed up with both of my back and knee surgeons after this incident. After some major diagnostic testing and numerous visits to specialists, it was decided that soon I would possibly need knee replacement and additional back fusion surgery.

Prior to 2015, when a Code 10 emergency was dispatched over the radios, you would have a minimum of 15-20 officers respond to the area. Often times, during my emergencies at my post, I had seen as many as 20 officers on average each time. I was posted in a tunnel checkpoint area which was in vicinity of both 21 and 21A buildings, and above me on the next floor were the special housing units, recreation yards, as well as the mess hall. It was good knowing you had lots of help on the way. The downside of this is that the inmates would take advantage of the absence of these other staff as they had left their areas to respond. That's when one could assume that transactions and moves were made during the incident which distracted everyone's normal routines. I know many officers would be waiting by their unit phones to get the scoop on the event's details and what had happened. News spread that quickly. Some supervisors would break down the minimum of those involved in the reports had there been an altercation. It was always easier to make out your reports with the actions of four officers rather than 10-12, or even more. But since the homicide of 2015 at Fishkill, a lot had changed. Not only in responses by the numbers, but also assignments were given to those who were designated to respond. With all of the new sanctions coming down the pipes from Albany, you would be lucky to see half as many officers show up to your call for help. One small misstep in your split-second decision to help out a fellow officer in need, could spell suspension, disciplinary documentation, perhaps loss of pay or time, and even worse, being fired. This of course would depend on the incident. But it was always important to keep those involved in the incident on the same page with what happened. As I mentioned earlier, the new directive on use of force policy dictates that everyone is placed in different rooms while they are doing their reports to refute the possibility of any type of corresponding to get the facts straight. Funny thing is, all staff involved need to report to the regional medical unit first to get checked out and if necessary, be brought to outside hospital for treatment. This gave us plenty of time to talk things over. Each and every directive in the state's prison system seemed to have gray areas and loopholes in it that would be found and taken advantage of. Those in Albany who wear the suits and never had worked in a prison environment before, always put the advantage into the inmate's hands, and frequently took away more tools to do our jobs. With the new introduction of pepper spray that was used before any force of going hands-on with a combative disruptive inmate, this became a popular tool to use which would help out in most cases, but would often expose the officers as well who would need to be decontaminated. Not being able to physically see in an altercation can and will get staff into a bad situation pretty fast. This method had its pros and cons of its effectiveness.

Chapter Three
Working the Bids

The number of incidents were mountainous compared to the injuries described above while at my checkpoint, Vocational TC # 2. The job area description included the Vocational Building Maintenance and Small Engine Shops where two civilian instructors would teach classes Monday-Friday, and often times would keep schedules current with the schools on the outside as far as holidays and summers go. This was an area that had a walk-through metal detector, used to scan inmates for illegal contraband when they exited from the classroom shops. From time to time, an inmate would be caught trying to smuggle out metal objects or tools. This checkpoint also had the duties of overseeing the inmate organizations area. This had numerous offices that included Caribbean African Unity, Community Minded Organization, Hispanics United for Progress, as well as Inmate Liaison Committee, and Nations of God and Earth. Inside these volunteer organizational offices, inmate members of these organizations would have fundraisers selling items such as greeting cards, cereal, various candy, juices, snacks, even once a week they had a night for photos called "Click-Click," where an inmate would previously purchase these items on his commissary sheet with funds being withdrawn from his account. He would come in and get a Polaroid photo taken of him in various poses. Although they were subject to visual inspection, occasionally I would find a photo or two that violated policy. No money was ever exchanged hand to hand; all of this was done on paper and kept track of in their bookkeeping and receipts. Having been on that post for nearly 14 years, I have dealt with just about every attempt to scam, smuggle, or the popular unauthorized exchange of inmates attempting to get these "goods." I was hip to the game so I was able to catch onto these acts many times, often resulting in bare minimum discipline to the inmate, but hours of paperwork for me. I had written to the Deputy

Superintendent of Program Services after conferring with my supervisors on many occasions to get suspect inmates removed from these areas, and to bring light to the issues of how inmates are handling their "fundraisers." Somehow, they were able to keep business as usual back there in those offices while inmates would come from units on a pass to pick up their purchased items. Although the administration got their required monthly "paperwork and sales reports" from each organization, these were done by inmates who knew how to work the numbers. As long as everything lined up by the book, then it was business as usual. But I can almost guarantee that sometimes the physical inventory of these products was not reflecting what was on papers submitted. They would often take care of their own, allowing other inmate members of that organization who worked the offices and fundraisers to take items before they were able to purchase them. These organizations, while each had their issues, were kept open because the money that was raised by their fundraisers would at times be apportioned for the benefit of the facility, whether it was that the organization "sponsored" an activity, or an event that was held inside the facility. I recall one time before opening of the offices prior to 6:00 p.m. one evening; I was doing a search of an inmate organization's computer, as at that time we were permitted to doing in order to ensure they were being used in compliance. None of them had access to the internet, but had used them for in-house documentation, recordkeeping, etc. These were much older styled computers, I believe Apple brand. I noticed in one of the offices where one inmate clerk frequently would come down to work, that there was a manila cardboard folder cut out in the shape of a square to cover up an opening in the front of the tower, where one might usually see a CD drive located. I pulled it open and found an external hard drive illegally wired into the computer where unauthorized files were being hidden. I notified my supervisor and they immediately responded to my area for further investigation. This brought conclusion to the use of computers for over six months within the community services organizations, amongst other disciplinary sanctions of those inmates who were involved.

My post at this checkpoint also required those working there to respond to incidents in buildings within that area, when we had no inmates present in either the organization offices or the vocational classrooms. Some days were routine but then many of them, unfortunately to say, became those busy kinds of days no one wanted to deal with. I would often need additional days off to run my photography business, so I would swap shifts with a variety of officers, most of them working dayshift. This works when you fill out the staffing forms requesting a mutual exchange of shifts with another officer. I would work a double shift to cover him or her for one day and they in return, the same would be done for me. Although most officers I swapped with did not complain about my post during the winter or fall months, it certainly was a hassle in the late spring to summer. Being that my post was in a basement tunnel, numerous large steam pipes were only about eight feet above my desk area. Between the heat of the masonry surrounding you and those steam pipes above that were active 24/7 for the mess hall kitchen on the floor above me, it sometimes made it unbearable. Some days when supervisors made their rounds, they did not stick around long; all they could say was, "This heat is horrible, I got to get out of here." They would sign the logbook and beat feet. We did have some reprieve, in the form of a small break room located adjacent to the tunnel area near the checkpoint. Inside were our lockers, a microwave, a fridge, a table, 4-5 chairs, and a 10,000-BTU air conditioner that had to constantly fight the heat. Little did those of us working this checkpoint over the years know right above our desk area was an asbestos problem. Late in 2015, we started to see asbestos abatement. Now we all know in older buildings these days, we are surrounded by asbestos, and that's ok, as long as it is not disturbed and it becomes airborne. On this notice was a listing for the abatement of floor tile, air handler unit covers, window glazing, duct insulation, cloth vibration, and asbestos removal in our areas.

I recall one day while working on a swap outside at the Gate 2 truck trap, I was checking the IDs of the inbound construction workers and among them was an OGS (Office of General Services) supervisor. While I had his attention, I briefly asked him, "Hey, I work over at Checkpoint 2 in 21-A building where the project is starting, I noticed that the pipes above my desk have red spray paint marks on them, what does that mean?"

He replied, "That area was slated for asbestos removal, but don't worry, it's harmless unless it becomes airborne, just as long as it stays intact."

I immediately became concerned and again responded, "Sir, those pipes move and the wrapping around them are ripped and exposed. They are moving because of water hammer." The OGS supervisor looked back at me surprised I knew that…but I further told him, "Those pipes move all the time due to steam pressure. They shake and rattle, causing dust and other debris to settle upon the Plexiglas portion of our desk. We have to constantly wipe our desk off each day from debris such as fiberglass, dust, dirt, and possibly asbestos."

We parted with his advice for me to go get medically checked out if I felt it was necessary. So later that day, I began to write up my complaint to our union representatives on our shift. I had a few other officers sign it who also work this post and then I gave it to one of the afternoon shift representatives, Officer Smurf. The next day word got around and nearly 15 more officers wanted to sign this, but it was already in the hands of our union rep. We never heard about it again, nothing was ever done, even after multiple requests to follow up and get copies made. Officer Smurf never took action on it, kept bringing up excuses, and he never ended up getting those copies. Once again, the union has shown they take care of their own and picked their own fights. He was often known for not acting on other officers' complaints about their work environments. We had to fight our own fight, sometimes taking it to the top on our own. In the end, if they did not look out for you as your union is supposed to do, and as they claim to do to the general public, then you, the officer, had to stand up for what was right knowing if was your health, safety and other issues that would affect you. It was your family first, job second.

The project was being done by Abatement out of New Jersey with air monitoring being done by environmental health associates out of Brewster, New York. While what appeared to be the proper measures taking place during the project of abatement, often times on our shift the construction crews would be finished up by 3:00 p.m. In our areas, I would notice during security rounds that areas they were working were not properly cordoned off. Even plastic wall barriers taped to the masonry walls would peel off by dinner time, exposing the elements of that day's work progress. They would close it off to all inmates since if they got exposed, they could sue the state, and the state does all it can to avoid lawsuits. But staff had to remain in those areas. We are not allowed to sue our employer, the state, due to an agreement and the Worker's Compensation Program and union contract. Those areas that were cordoned off still were accessible. Staff all had keys to these hallways that were shortcuts to get outside. Even with posted signs saying closed, go around, danger, many would ignore it and choose convenience over health. It took several weeks before finally upper-level administration would have the locksmith change those locks to cordon off those work zones. Funny though, those same higher-ranking officials had keys to still cut through those areas. I guess they only wanted it to be for their convenience. After all, Fishkill is a huge sprawling facility.

With the event of the escape of the two prisoners from Clinton Correctional Facility in upstate New York, about an hour from the Canadian border, the department had been forced to changes its operational guidelines. With that came numerous policy changes that affected 20,000+ officers and even thousands more civilian staff with the implementation of a clear plastic bag that was made only to hold a couple of essential items during your shift, and maybe a meal, but if you were on a double shift or overtime, it was tough to fit all of your food and beverage. By no means was this a cooler either. If you had a fridge in your area, you would be fortunate enough to keep your items cold during your shift. The actual size of it was 11"x7"x10" and had a small zippered pocket on the front which was 6"x10" in approximate size. The handles and zippers were made so inexpensively that they often broke only weeks after normal wear and tear. Complaints came in across the state from the membership and the union started action in court to try to stop the implementation by DOCCS on their new bag policy for staff and what they could bring into work. They filed charges with PERB, trying to take this to court at the time. We all know ultimately this was caused by the events at Clinton; after all, the state is reactive, not proactive. Never has been, never will be. At least not in this day and age. Many females complained about the privacy issues of inmates being able to see hygiene products, and other staff had the same stance about their medications. Now everyone would know what you had as you came into work. As until this day, the policy remains in effect and it is the sign of only worse things to come.

As time went on working this checkpoint area, I decided that maybe it was time for a change. Having only so many months left until my retirement eligibility approached, with nearly 14 years just working at Vocational Checkpoint 2 alone, it was now time to move on. In the early winter of 2016, I was out on Worker's Compensation Disability to have my second lower back surgery due to another injury from an inmate related use of force. I was out for a few months and during that time I had heard from friends that certain jobs were being posted for bidding. I pondered on what I wanted to do next, as there were several openings, but only a few favorable ones. So, I went for it and dropped a couple bid slips pretty close to the closing date. As to my surprise, and much more to the surprise of others, I won the bid of my choice. As of

March 1, 2017, I would be officially starting my new job as "Fishkill-84," otherwise known as the 21-21A Porter Pool Officer. This job was located down the hallway from my old checkpoint, in Building 21A, right near the back dock and dumpster, as well as the elevator. It had been located there and was worked by many other seasoned officers for decades. Right outside my office area was Vocational Checkpoint 1. Essentially, there were two of us working in that area and could assist each other if needed. This office had storage cabinets in there for cleaning supplies, personal lockers, a fridge, microwave, and even an old air conditioner unit, along with a desk and two chairs. My new job consisted of a variety of duties. When I first came onto shift, I would have to go to my office, ensure I had an adequate amount of supplies for the evening's tour, and then go over to the regional medical unit to escort the nurse to the Special Housing Units to administer insulin shots to inmates who were diabetic. These inmates were on these units locked up 23 hours per day for disciplinary reasons. Since the nurse was carrying around needles, it was necessary for her to be escorted. By the time this was done, I headed down to the mess hall for the evening meal at about 4:00p.m. After some assigned activities there, generally I would get a few minutes to eat my meal and by 6:00p.m., we would open up the porter pool program for assigned inmates to come down and perform their cleaning duties in different areas. After about two hours of this, we would then call for the garbage to be brought down from the units. I would then go over to Delta Checkpoint in 21 Building to meet with the nurse to escort them around for medications in the Special Watch and Special Housing Unit areas. That would take at least an hour if being used on the overnight shift; it was about time to wrap it up and end the shift. On my very first day on my new post, one of the night locks required was the emergency door leading to a brand-new wheelchair and handicapped ramp used to evacuate injured persons to the regional medical unit. There was no other ramp in that building. There were two doors, one on the outside that led into a small foyer, then another door leading onto Housing Unit One Center, right into the officers' station. This use to be the entrance for staff that worked that building many years ago. There still remains a caged gated door in the officers' station that once was used as an arsenal where staff would pick up their assigned equipment such as batons, radios, keys, handcuffs, etc. Anyhow, I had found this heavy-duty door to be inoperable, off its hinge and with its dead bolt housing being dislodged, there was no way to lock this door, let alone night lock it for extra security. I immediately reported this to the watch commander and filled out a Form 1611, Maintenance Work Order Request, with the words "Security Expedite" written by me at the top of it. It was brought to the attention of the Deputy Superintendent of Security, the "Chief" of Security at the prison, Deputy Superintendent of Security, Oblinski. Months later, and after several reminders to area supervisors, this door still remained in disrepair.

It was almost springtime and I felt great about my renewed routine. I had hired some new inmate porters, started to clean out the drawers in the office, had the tile floor stripped, buffed, and waxed. I even went to the supply storehouse and got a new clock for the office as well as a new telephone to replace the old broken one. I used inmates who volunteered to utilize the fire hose from the cabinet to spray down the back dock areas and pavement near the dumpster. I had worked this post a total of 13 days before I started to notice the start of something going on. When I came into work on March 20th, I came in to find that the door had been painted over, removing my job title and replaced with the words "Vocational TC 1 Officer, Vocational Rover," and at the bottom, the simple initials "PP," which stands for Porter Pool, which was my job. I interviewed Pete, the paint shop civilian instructor, who right away was aware that he would be expecting my inquiry as to what happened to the office door being painted over. He denied any knowledge of what took place but the look on his face could tell it all. In fact, Pete took a bold stance as I approached him and reacted as if he was being accused of a serious infraction. Coming from someone "who had no idea that something occurred," he sure had a pretty good idea of what had happened and to expect my inquiry about it. Not to mention the can of oil-based gray paint that was sitting right there in view when I walked into his shop. Well, before I got to this new post area, Pete had been having his share of problems on how to deal with inmates and rarely had any sick time to use, as he frequently used it as it was credited to him. And this came from both civilians and security staff that worked with him. He got into that job without having completed the full college requirements since his father used to be a civilian boss there, before leaving to become superintendent for a brief period at another facility about an hour from Fishkill, retiring not long afterward. I apparently saw this becoming a turf war. Here I am, the newcomer on the bid, starting to change a few things around, perhaps if at all, clean it up and give it a little shine. It has been a shared office that on the day shift, the Vocational TC1 Checkpoint Officer and Vocational Rover Officer (who usually makes rounds in the tunnel areas where inmates are attending shop classes) used to store their lunch, coats, etc. This office was only used as an official post during the afternoon shift, which had been that way for years prior to my arrival.

A few days later, on March 23rd, it started to happen again, harassment at its best. It was often that when someone came to work a new bid in their area that was not part of their "clique, crew, or group," that all too often it would be handled in this sort of fashion. Intimidate, annoy, harass as much as possible in order to get that officer to take the hint that he or she was not welcome there and to go find a new bid. From what I have seen in prior instances, most officers would just bid off the post to avoid conflicts and all the stress. It's already bad enough that you have to watch over your shoulder for the violence, drugs, gangs, and mental health issues with the prisoners, let alone any fellow staff you work with to create that extra hostile environment. With very few security cameras in most of the Fishkill Prison, a lot of creative things can be done without anyone to witness. On this day, I had found that my required documentation of a security tool inventory was removed from the Plexiglas frame posted on the wall. In fact, I had been approached by a dayshift supervisor, Sgt. Tallman, to get that corrected at once. At that point, this list had already been taken down twice. I told him I had one posted; I had always kept things organized. Whoever was doing this, and I was clear on whom it was, who had access during the dayshift, that they were trying hard to make it look like I was not doing my job.

With some days gone by, and my time off past, it was now back to work again and on April 4th, I arrived to another surprise; every single cleaning supply that was inventoried, along with the mops and spray bottled solutions, had been removed and tossed away. This caused me to have to go get replacements, only to be questioned as to why was I going through so much supplies. Days followed only to find that the officer(s) were climbing almost 10 foot up into an open ceiling area and literally braiding a large gauge power cord for the air conditioner and tying it up into the exposed pipes. This was starting to get ridiculous. Were we adults working in a serious job at a correctional facility, or were these college day frat house pranks? It was another day, on April 14th, that my personal locker had been tipped over with the word "dick" written on it in black magic marker. That same day, tools were used, most likely from the nearby 21A utility shop, to remove the screws from a wooden cabinet in order to access the contents that were necessities for my job description duties that evening. Whatever the case, that same day as well, my keys and assigned radio and handcuffs were not turned in by the dayshift officer who was working 21 Program Escort until after 3:00 p.m.

There were multiple announcements made over the radio system to look for this equipment. At one point, Lieutenant Richards had to inquire and make certain these were located. This delay had made me already behind schedule with my escort duties. The officer that brought it up was verbally counseled after he gave a very poor excuse as to why he did what he did.

Days passed and eventually quieted down, no more annoyances, and I thought, well, maybe it has passed and they have moved on. Well, think again. That air conditioner power cord went through torture being tightly braided and tied up into the pipes every day, and on May 2nd, I received a harassing note from Officer Thompson, who was the dayshift Vocational Checkpoint 1 Officer. I knew it was him all along, but this just proved it all. He left the note in his own handwriting, very distinctive handwriting which drew no alternatives other than him being the author of this derogatory harassing note. On May 4th, as I was coming on duty during shift change and walking past my old post at Vocational Checkpoint 2, I noticed Officer Potter sitting there doing his logbook, getting settled in for his tour of duty. Then I saw Officer Thompson approach and out of curiosity I simply asked what the problem was; apparently this set him on fire into a roid rage. He squared off to me and he proceeded to start assaulting me with his threats and vulgar language. I can recall him saying, "If it was up to me, you would be out of here tomorrow! You have messed up that job and you have left me nothing but trouble of having to fix your problems!"

I stood there as calm as can be with my hands at my side, while Officer Potter was sitting at his desk witnessing this. I asked Officer Thompson, "Why are you yelling, why are you so mad? You're really upset for no reason and what you're saying is not true." Apparently, this triggered him and he really set off and started pacing back and forth toward me. At that point, I was expecting for him to hit me but he did not. He just left out of there down the tunnel to go punch out on his time card. I had a few moments to calm myself while speaking to Officer Potter about what just happened. It was not long before word got out in the prison about what happened. There are secrets in jail, and then there are no secrets in jail. I had heard it was pretty much the main topic of discussion that lasted for a while. Thompson would complain that I was leaving the office a complete mess, probably doing it himself or with others when they came on duty at 6:30 a.m., the following morning after I went off duty. I have always kept my area clean, and in my short period of time on that new post location, the other staff, including the supervisors, knew I was doing the job and keeping it up to par beyond what was expected. I even had the go-ahead from the Fire and Safety Chief to use a 100-foot section of hose from the standpipe box nearby the loading dock to have an inmate come down and wash away the debris in the dock and parking lot, in the area of the dumpster. This helped tremendously, especially with the smell.

I had taken some vacation days for some family events, so I was off until May 8th, returning to duty with no repercussions, and I did not find anything out of place in my office area. I went home that evening hoping and praying this was all over with. I knew at that point I was supposed to report the incident as per the Department's Workplace Violence Directive #4960. This was intended to identify, investigate, correct, and follow up whenever a situation such as this was reported. But doing so would have made matters worse for me. I was certain of his capabilities. There were no security cameras in our areas. I knew there would be repercussions. I have seen him in action before, whether it was the multiple road rage incidents in the upper parking lot at 6:00 a.m. in the morning with a couple of African American or Latino female officers, or someone else before shift in the hallways at line-up briefing. This officer literally puts on a show knowing he is one of the untouchables. Obviously, everyone there is aware of his connections. Having this clout really allows him to walk the walk and talk the talk. I was in fear for my safety, and the safety of my job. Fishkill's administration, and this department as a whole, is responsible for providing us with a safe working environment. There are procedures, directives, rules and regulations in place for a reason.

Chapter Four
Staff-on-Staff Assault

On the morning of Tuesday, May 9th, I had a busy schedule in my photo studio doing baby photos for a family who regularly uses my photography services. I also had other customers in for a wedding consultation, and with that, a few errands, some quick lunch, and before I knew it, I was off to work getting there early, at about 1:45 p.m. Pre-shift briefing did not start until 2:15 p.m., so I decided to go check the bulletin boards and stop into payroll about my direct deposit. Next up was our pre-shift briefing; all incoming on-duty officers had to line up on the yellow painted lines in the basement of the administration building where we would hear the announcements and any other pertinent information. This is also the time when your uniform is inspected by a supervisor to ensure directive compliance and that you were fit and present for duty. It seemed like business as usual. Little did I know this was going to be one of the worst days of my career. I walked out with the group of officers into the administration trap gate area, and soon we were let out onto the walkway as I headed toward my post in 21A Building at about 2:30 p.m. I had to enter this building as everyone else does, at Walkway Delta Checkpoint. I walked in ahead of the other crowd, eager to get to my post. I immediately noticed Officer Omway there, who usually is assigned to that post, as he was unlocking a door to get his routine started for the shift. As I turned the corner to go down the long narrow hallway, one that measures about 80 feet from corner to corner, I observed Officer Thompson coming toward me by himself. At that point it was only the three of us in the hallway. As we approached, I noticed him make eye contact with me and yell, "Hey, did Sloman leave yet?" I was curious as to why he was asking me; I slightly turned to my left to see if he was talking to someone behind me and noticed it was Officer Omway at Walkway Delta. As I turned back forward, I was immediately stuck hard and fast, like a defensive lineman on a final play of the football game, into my left shoulder by Officer Thompson. I spun around hitting the wall with my back and immediately felt pain ripping through my neck and shoulder. He just kept walking at a fast pace, never stopped, never asked if I was ok, never even looked back. Officer Omway looked over to me as I was crouching over and stated, "Are you ok? That was bad…"

I said in reply, "No, I am hurt, I am going to report this. Did you see that? I will be back." I immediately left the area and proceeded to my office where I was able to put my stuff down and hang up my coat. I called over the radio for my supervisor that day who was filling in for the regular, Sgt. Oswald. He called my office and I told him there was an incident and I needed to come see him. He stated, "Ok, come up to see me now in my office." At about 2:45 p.m., I went upstairs to see Sgt. Oswald. His first words to me were, "Who was the other officer that did this?" I stated, "Officer Thompson." Sgt. Oswald looked me square in the eye and stated, "I know this officer, I have a good rapport with him. If you report him, it will not work out good for you. Even if they can stop his actions against you, his friends will still come after you. And, think about this, you might want to consider saying you got hurt running into a swinging door, or moving inmate property. Make out the injury report and I will sign off on it for you. Let me know what you want to do either way, but you have to decide."

Hearing this was not good news. This put me in a real bad spot. In other words, I either go for the actual incident report or make up a false insurance claim for my numerous injuries. I went back down to my office and started calling a lot of my coworker friends. A couple of them especially kept a good eye on me; Rob and George, they were genuinely concerned with me and they told me that the right thing needed to be done with this situation. All too often people get away with this kind of stuff in the prison environment we work in, but now it was time to take a stand and to report Officer Thompson. They were supportive of me and attempted to convince me that this needs to be handled seriously. After a few hours at work, I could no longer endure the pain, and by now word about the incident was widespread. I called my supervisor back, Sgt. Oswald, telling him that I can't take it anymore; I am going to the regional medical unit to get checked for my injuries. I was beyond stressed out and my thoughts were clouded by what was around the corner and about to happen to me again, for having reported this incident. As I arrived to the medical area, I was assessed by Nurse Alabama, who I had gotten to know by taking her on numerous medical escorts with inmate medications. She started out by taking my blood pressure, and it was sky high, nearly 180/120. She took me into a side room to fill out my injury report and I began to have an anxiety attack, falling from my chair. I was lifted out of the room and brought into the exam room where a medical emergency Code Blue was called. Numerous staff arrived and I found myself hyperventilating with a lot of people standing over me, holding me down as I struggled. An ambulance was called and I was transported by mobile life support paramedics to the emergency room at Mid-Hudson Regional Hospital in Poughkeepsie to be treated, tested, and x-rays of my shoulder/neck were taken. I was administered medications for muscle relaxers and pain killers. I twice requested the state police to both the paramedics and to hospital Staff, but no one followed up on this. One of my duty lieutenants arrived, Lt. Michael, and he checked in on me. I was there with another correction officer stationed at my door to watch over me and to handle any phone calls or other details during my treatment. Lt. Michael had said to me that he needs my report in writing as soon as possible. This had been reported as an unusual incident to Albany Command Post already and that due to the nature of my injuries, the Deputy Superintendent would need the report in order to send it into the Bureau of Labor Relations, so they could decide on what would happen from this point of the investigation. They were in a hurry to get my report for the "Workplace Violence Incident," which I was told was an unusual incident. I was brought back to the facility, still in uniform, so that I could complete my report. Might I add that I was under medications given to me from the emergency room physician, and I was already in so much pain and tired. I completed my five-page memo report in about an hour and handed it over to Lt. Michael. I was then able to punch out and I went to the assistant watch commander to have him put me out on work-related injury – workers' comp; date of injury: 5/9/17. I went home that night but did not sleep at all. Between the pain, stress, PTSD, and playing the incident over and over in my head, it made for a long night. By 9:12 a.m. the next morning, the phone already started to ring and the first to call my house was Captain Rogers. He had ordered me to return at once to the facility with my off-duty firearm where it would be surrendered and secured in the facility's arsenal. I was then brought into the conference room to be briefed that as per the superintendent, my post had officially been moved to another area in another building, thus adding to my already busy job description. This was done to separate Officer Thompson and I, but not much thought was put into it. The assault that took place happened in the tunnel hallway, just down from where they relocated my porter pool assigned post. It was certain that we would cross paths again during shift change. Any attempt to separate only appeared to be done so at the convenience to the officer that assaulted me. Normally the department immediately suspended an individual that was suspected of causing documented injuries to others such as mine, and if it involved an inmate claiming he was assaulted by staff, then that officer was suspended, even if there was no witness and it was alleged. The usual response to any outside inquiries regarding these incidents from the Department of Corrections was: "Officials with the state Department of Corrections declined to comment on the status of the investigation. The department has zero tolerance for violence within the facilities and anyone engaged in misconduct will be disciplined and referred for outside prosecution," a spokesman said. Where is the zero tolerance? Or maybe they mean like 5% tolerance.

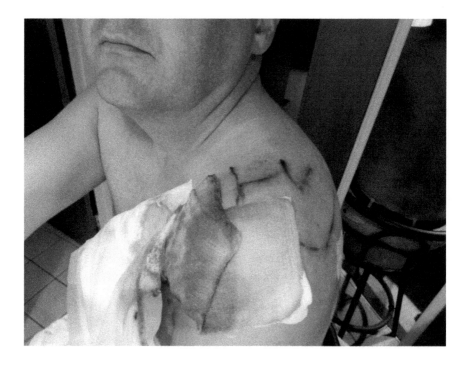

Days after my left shoulder surgery down in New York City for five
tears and to remove part of my collar bone. Painful therapy soon followed. Photo by
P. Harrington

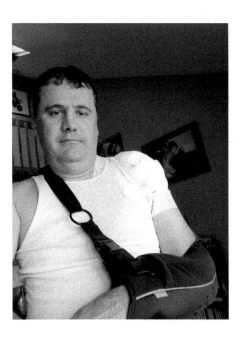

A week after the left shoulder surgery that left me helpless in even doing most common things such as getting dressed. Photo by P. Harrington

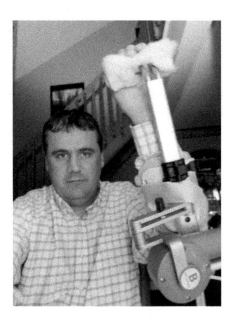

Nearly a week later, medical staff delivered my exercise chair to my house to keep my arm and shoulder moving which had to be done 30 minutes, three times a day. Photo by P. Harrington

I left the facility at approximately 10:00 a.m. and went to the Wappinger Falls Barracks of the NY State Police. There I met with a female trooper who took my report, a supporting deposition, and then had me sign off on it before she forwarded it onto a BCI investigator who handles Corrections' cases. I had dealt with him before regarding use of force incidents and investigations regarding other inmates. After about 90 minutes there, I departed and headed straight to my Workers' Comp Attorney, Dennis, someone who I have used over the last 20 years. I met with his staff to file a C3 workers' comp injury claim. I asked his paralegal at the law office about giving me referrals to other law firms that could represent me in this personal injury and assault case. I was given a referral to a Labor/Employment Lawyer Law Firm in New Paltz. I also asked them for a psychologist referral to help me deal with this situation. I was given a list and at the top was the first name I chose, Dr. Martin Ogulnick, Orange Counseling Associates located in Newburgh.

Later that day on May 10th, I had been feeling extremely stressed out, now being injured, not being able to work, having had to take leave from my position at the fire department, and having to shut down my appointments in my photo studio. They have this program for all law enforcement up in the Albany area called "Catch a Falling Star." It is run by a woman named Cindy. I was able to call her and get in touch with her that day, telling her what I had just gone through. She spoke to me briefly and sounded reassuring, only to ask me to call her back as she was on a busy schedule that day. I went to Dr. Ogulnick for a one-hour interview and evaluation. He had me come back two days later for a follow-up as I stressed to him about my loss of sleep, stress, PTSD, anxiety about this whole ordeal. I was dealing with a lot of physical pain, as well as psychological stress. I ended up going back and forth with phone calls with another law firm as they too seemed to have a full schedule. When I was finally able to get up there to meet them at their office in New Paltz, I arrived to their location to find that their law office was set up in a converted 2½-story older wood frame residence that was made into office space. Even the old wood floors still creaked and were sagging when you walked across them. It almost actually felt as if the floor beams below could not handle all of the weight of the office supplies, furniture, and equipment. I did not feel very sure about having them represent me but I rolled the dice nonetheless. I was only there to meet up with the receptionist who made several copies of my documents, I never got the chance to actually speak to one of their lawyers. I needed the attention of my union so I called two of my local representatives. On May 12th at about 10:45 a.m., I called Officer Smurf on his cell phone. He picked up and sounded welcoming on the phone. Once I told him who was calling, his tone changed immediately and he asked me what did I need. I mentioned to him that I wanted an update about my situation. He replied, "I do not know anything about this, I am about to go into a meeting, I don't have time."

I waited until about 12:37 p.m. and I called a second union rep from our local, Officer Nomore. He picked up the phone right away and I said, "Hey, it's Harrington. Is there anything you can do for me, find out details for me?"

He says in return, "I do not have any information, this is out of my hands now. No updates, it's being handled by the higher-ups. I can't help you."

As I mentioned earlier, I have had numerous surgeries for work-related injuries and one of my orthopedic doctors from Orthopedics of Duchess County, Dr. Kenny, had previously done my knee surgery. I made an appointment to go see him about treating me for my shoulder injury. He took me in and had more x-rays done, put me on some medications, and prescribed me physical therapy for 4-6 weeks for a possible sprained trapezoid muscle in my shoulder/neck.

I decided on that day, May 16th, after my doctor appointment to call into work and speak to the Deputy Superintendent for Security, Dep. Oblinksi, who I had on the phone for a good five minutes, asking him about the status of my situation…he had no updates. He said, "We will wait for your return before we can go over any details with you." I stated to him that no one from the facility has even bothered to contact me or check up on me. I wanted to know what was going on with the investigation and that I was aware of the procedures of Directive 4960 Workplace Violence. I finished the call with a simple request, "Please keep in contact with me." This directive includes many provisions and definitions. In it are some of the following details. Each employee who believes he/she has been a victim of workplace violence, is to submit a written report to his/her immediate supervisor, or the superintendent, or union representative (Please make sure a designee is appointed by the union representative). Any physical assault or acts of aggressive behavior occurring where a public employee performs any work-related duty in the course of his or her employment including, but not limited to:

An attempt or threat, whether verbal or physical, to inflict physical injury upon an employee; any intentional display of force which would give an employee reason to fear or expect bodily harm; intentional and wrongful physical contact with a person without his or her consent that entails some injury; verbal abuse that would give a person a reason to fear escalation and bodily harm; or stalking an employee with the intent of causing fear of material harm to the physical safety and health of such employee, when such stalking has arisen through and in the course of employment.

Since I now had so much time on my hands, I became more involved with the advocating on my behalf regarding the status of my case complaint. I was in the process of making notifications. After all, my family, my business, and my livelihood were now all at a loss because of this one officer. I was able to speak to a female investigator out of the Albany headquarters of the DOCCS Office of Special Investigation. She stated to me that my complaint was in the hands of a chief investigator and that they would be following up with me.

My first surprise came on the following day, May 17th. As I went into Peak Physical Therapy in Newburgh to follow up and get my appointments scheduled, I was advised by them that my workers' compensation case had been controverted. That could mean only one thing. There is a newly-promoted captain at Fishkill; his name was Captain Dryer. He had been a lieutenant, as previously mentioned, who oversaw much of the afternoon shift's watch. There were many times we did not see eye to eye on issues. He did not treat everyone equally, as an individual serving in his ranking position should do. He was a well-groomed white male, about average height with a slim frame, kind of reminded me of Woody, the character from the popular kids' movie Toy Story. His hair was always so perfectly combed. He fraternized and hung out with other officers and staff, especially when he was a lieutenant. Prior to each shift daily, we have a briefing. I recall a day in particular when he had to announce that he had a job to do. "When your supervisor calls you up and orders you to do something, you have to follow that order. There's a chain of command here and we have to follow it. I know we all go out and hang out partying, drinking together, but sometimes I have to put on the big hat and do the job. You can't call me on the phone and expect me to get you out of an assignment when a supervisor directs you to do it. You have to learn to be able to separate the job from the social life." I laughed beneath my breath. They call that fraternizing and since this was considered a "paramilitary organization," it should have been treated as such. He was talking to a line-up room full of about 70 officers, most of them pretty new to the job. If he had said that speech to dayshift senior guys, he would have been heckled out of the room. Whatever the case, he brought the misery upon himself. I soon found out that Captain Dryer, who was also very affectionate with his female subordinates, hugging them and kissing them on duty, in front of others, and even the superintendents were aware of these activities but did nothing to stop it. They probably saw it as him trying to create morale amongst the staff when in reality, it was him trying to create the morale for his own personal gain with the female staff. In fact, the New York Daily News, among other news agencies, are reporting in their publications "Fishkill correction officer sexually harassed by boss who painted her apartment pink without her permission: Lawsuit filed in Federal Court in Manhattan." More females are getting on board with that lawsuit as I was informed. Unlike the fraternizing that is strictly forbidden in the military…

Dryer was heard one day by a few staffers that I was in contact with saying as an announcement in the watch commander's office, "Harrington's case is done, he is out on his own time now." Since Fishkill had controverted my disability case claim, no one there bothered to notify me of this, not even Captain Dryer or his buddy Deputy Oblinski when I had called him the day prior. It is the state insurance fund's and the employer's responsibility to notify the injured worker that his/her claim has been controverted. Normally, reasons for this are due to inadequate physician's reports but this was far from the reason of it being as such. There was some serious digging to be done now. With that, it led me to further look into this matter as being more of a cover-up at this point. I mean come on, they flip your case by controverting your claim, denying your benefits when I clearly had physical injuries from the assault? It's bad enough dealing with the system in workers' compensation, but now you're fighting an uphill battle against the employer to boot. I immediately started touching base with my workers' comp lawyer, Dennis. His practice has grown so big now that he has offices and staff all over the region. I used to be able to talk to him on his cell phone but now if you want to speak to him, you have to go through a whole panel of individuals who will pass along your message. You actually have to make a telephone conference appointment in order to speak to your lawyer, and they told me it was over three weeks away – that was the most recent opening, three weeks! I kept calling his office, speaking to assistants and paralegals. I had never had so much difficulty getting in touch with Dennis as I was experiencing right then. There were dates for my workers' comp board hearings that needed to be requested. Without his attention, surely waiting a few more weeks was not going to help my situation anymore at that time. Here I am now, sitting at home, going between appointments five days a week, meeting with several doctors for my multiple injuries caused by Officer Thompson. I was still having lower back problems that I had two prior surgeries from due to injuries at the prison. My most recent surgery on my low back was in November of 2016 and a follow-up MRI showed that my condition had become worse with the pain in my legs. So, since I was out on my own time for the assault, I had no time benefits covering me for the inmate-related injuries.

I was used to going 90 miles per hour in life, but now I was in neutral. I was a man of many hats, working my corrections job, owning and operating my professional photography studio and wedding event business, volunteering in my community as a captain in one of the town's fire department, which does come with a pension program based on your participation, among other activities. I am active in my community helping out where I can, at the school's Backpack Program and Food Pantry, or out promoting fire prevention with over 2,000 students at four schools. I also kept busy as a photo journalist for newspapers and online websites. I often received various awards of recognition for my work in photography and for the fire department, where I was also honored to be the 2016 Orange County Fire Prevention Educator of the Year. At home, my wife and two young children and two dogs often made for some busy days.

I kept busy by immersing myself in the activities and progress of my case, even chronicling the daily updates from this case into a logbook. After all, at the time of the incident I was led to believe this was going to be investigated as a workplace violence incident. I kept that detailed logbook from the first day, along with numerous files of documents. I was told by everyone – my doctors, lawyers, physical therapy staff, and more – that I was one of the most well-documented individuals they have treated or represented. One of my doctors called me the "Library of Congress," while another one said, "You're doing an amazing, absolutely superior job documenting this case, keep up the good work." We have always been told to keep copies of our reports at work. Log books at home are another issue; this is a rarely practiced area, but it has proven to help me along many months later into my case as references had to have been made. I could tell you who I called, what we spoke about, and what day and time it was months ago.

Finally, my day came when I was called upon to meet with the Department of Corrections Office of Special Investigations. On May 22, I was able to meet up with two officers, Investigators Tonka and Thebus. They chose to meet with me at a local Dunkin' Donuts. I asked them what would I need to bring with me before I arrived. I did choose to bring a friend, Al, another Correction Officer that works at Shawangunk Correctional Facility, over in Ulster County. Al has been a friend of my family and I during this rather difficult time. He knows some of the inner workings of things and joined in on the discussion as a friend and supporter. We sat down in a booth in the rear corner of the shop, with our backs to the wall facing the door, typical of how most law enforcement officers eat out, wanting to always be aware of their surroundings. I presented documents and statements about the incidents and history with Officer Thompson. I asked them why there has been no suspensions yet and that I was in fear of my safety to return to work for having reported this incident the way that it happened, truthfully. I wanted answers as to why my workers' compensation case was denied and controverted by the prison. Without this, not only was I not working, but all of my treatments were out of pocket on my own, plus my mileage, co-pays, not to mention well over $1,000 alone just for my physical therapy that was prescribed by my orthopedic. There were so many questions they were not answering. Even my witness had not yet been required to put his version of events that he saw happen onto paper yet, Officer Potter, from the event of the verbal altercation in front of Vocational TC 2 just days before he assaulted me in the hallway at Walkway Delta Checkpoint.

Before I knew it, it was already over two and a half hours and they wanted to wrap up the interview. Investigator Tonka wanted copies of some of my paperwork, so right after we left, I made sure almost 20 copies were done and delivered to their office in Wallkill.

That evening, I went online to file a complaint with the EEOC (Federal Equal Employment Opportunity Commission) based on the retaliation and lack of disciplinary action taken since Officer Thompson was still working. The list of agencies at this point were starting to build up. Next up was the Albany office of the EAP (Employee Assistance Program); I spoke to Dave and told him the entire incident and explained to him that my stress levels were rising due to the actions from the employer. We discussed my controverted disability claim and my inability to return to work. He referred me to the New York State Division of Human Rights. I gave them a call and spoke to Investigator Tang. He apparently was having a bad day and I called at the wrong time. He was very difficult to deal with and not helpful (stereotypical for some state employees, so I am told). Having been referred to him, I called Dave back over at the EAP office in Albany, leaving him a voicemail telling him what I had just dealt with. It was on this same day that I decided to call Cindy back over at Catch a Falling Star in Albany. This program is in place to assist officers and other staff in their times of need. Unbelievably, when I spoke to her on May 23rd, I told her how bad I was feeling. She sounded upset herself and said to me, "I am just a volunteer here, I have nothing to do with your department and I can't help you." At that point I was so angry, I just hung up in disbelief. I was able to get in touch with an EAP guy that knows a lot of the same people I do. Dean, who also works at Shawangunk, was very helpful to me both on the phone and in person. We were able to work out some things and he gave me better insight on my goals and progress, saying that I was on the right track. He too also referred to my recordkeeping as very outstanding and that I was doing all the right things.

The next day I began making the phone calls again, touching base with various law firms regarding the employers' disability discrimination, lack of due process under the workplace violence policy, hindering of the investigation, the union's failure to represent, harassment, cover-up by changing the story of the witness at Walkway Delta Checkpoint that day, as well as the threat of continued issues upon my return to duty. The news that day just got worse. The State Police Investigator that had been assigned to my written complaint of the assault called me while I was at physical therapy. He stated, "I have interviewed both Officer Thompson and Officer Omway. Both denied having anything to do with this. I have a certified copy from the Mid-Hudson Regional emergency room stating that there was no injury and therefore there would be no charges and the case is being closed."

I pleaded with him stating, "I have copies from the emergency room that night, and more medical documentation from the follow-up with my orthopedic that states there are injuries. I am in physical therapy right now!"

The investigator replied back, "I am not going to use your records, I have my copies here. If you want, you can request an incident report of the investigation."

I gave a call to our own in-house Employee Assistance Program Coordinator at Fishkill Correctional Facility. His name is Mack. I left him a voicemail to have him call me back on the next day, and about 12:30 p.m., I got that call from him. "Hi Mack, thanks for calling back. Do you know anything about my situation, I mean you know, with all the news going around the jail?"

Mack was like, "Paul, I know of nothing in particular." I explained to him that despite my numerous injuries, I have not heard from anyone at work. Mack offered to get in touch with the superintendent to have him contact me shortly.

Having spoken to fellow law enforcement officers and other Corrections staff, I had heard of this big firm down in White Plains, New York. They had like seven different office locations. One of their attorneys, who is an of counsel at the firm, is Warren. I got on the phone with Warren the next day and we started talking about what his office could do for my case. He mentioned over a dozen names of clients that I personally know of, so I had them sign over my eight active injury cases from the prison and off to the races we went. I showed up to their main office in White Plains to have a meeting with the lawyers to go over my ordeals. I brought along a briefcase full of documents from each of my cases. I was assigned two lawyers, Nicholas and Jason, both covering my workers' compensation cases and my disability retirement case. Warren represents many of the police PBA agencies in my area and I have spoken to literally dozens of police officers who are all on the same page when it comes to him. Recently, the firm had done some restructuring. It wasn't long before I got a call from Dennis, my original attorney. He said he dropped the ball and apologized. He did not realize the urgency of my most recent claim that was filed but wanted to make sure that I was in good hands with my new representatives now and that if I still ever needed anything to contact him via email. He also mentioned, "Paul, you were my oldest client, having been with my firm for over two decades." I can appreciate that. Times change, people move on. That's how it works in life. I said, "Thank you, Dennis, I am in need of a larger firm that can handle all of these cases."

So in between all of this, and approximately 25 days after this incident, I still have not heard from my employer, or my union. It's not in the best interest for the prison to admit wrongdoing here as they would be open to liability. Not to mention the caseloads of paperwork it would create for the administration.

Without security cameras, anything can happen, and it does. It just appears differently in the reports when it comes down to an incident. It makes everyone's job easier when you don't actually have to explain an incident on camera. That could mean someone's career. As for our union, Corrections and Police Benevolent Association, they have always looked out for their own. I get it, family protects family. You see, Officer Thompson's brother-in-law is the Mid-Hudson Regional Vice President of this union. He has been afforded the protection, representation, and advice from this powerful union. Given this, many of the incidents that were witnessed of Officer Thompson's prior actions inside and out of the facility have gone unreported. Most know of his capabilities; even immediate supervisors turn a blind eye to these actions. After all, they too are in our same union. When you have that kind of protection, you become untouchable.

Back to my follow-ups on the phone and computer as I touched base with the State Division of Human Rights. This time I spoke with Manny. He seemed helpful and we discussed the merits of the case, and he told me to file a complaint about my disability discrimination so they can begin their investigation. After I spoke with him, I had to get out the door to my many weekly medical appointments. I was still awaiting approval to have a couple of MRIs done of my neck and shoulder. My first appointment for the day was with Dr. Ogulnick, a clinical psychologist and one hell of a man. He worked long hours and occasionally he would enjoy a bit of a tasty cigar, deservedly so. Having so much material to go over with him required multiple appointments and sessions, along with additional referrals to another psych doctor as well. He gave me a referral to a gentleman by the name of Dr. Jeff Newton, a psychiatrist in Goshen. He was a very well-written individual, understood the aspects of my job, and what I was going through. He was overseeing my progress with Dr. Ogulnick and the medications they had me on for my sleepless nights, anxiety, and mostly for all the pain I was experiencing. At one point, I was on 13 medications. They had diagnosed me with PTSD, severe stress, anxiety and depression. This was not all just from the assault on May 9th, it was a culmination of the incidents of violence I both witnessed and was involved in over the two decades in this job. It was bottled up until finally something gave in and I was finally able to let it all out. You see, on this job, it is typical for the new officer coming on the job to want to be a part of the team. With that, anything that you go through, you're supposed to "man up" and deal with it. If in fact there are situations in which if you don't do that and you take medical leave to go see a shrink, you are frowned upon and looked down as a sign of weakness. Could you be trusted in future incidents? Would something be said by you that could lead to trouble or expose any cover-up or corruption that had occurred? That was something that 9 out of 10 officers avoided. They either looked the other way or dealt with it. And if it's not in writing, it didn't happen.

Here I am back to physical therapy and then onto pain management. With so many appointments, my free time did not seem so free anymore. Most of my appointments were out of town, some of them local, but there was a lot of driving. Finding the right specialist who could treat my specific conditions, that accepted workers' compensation insurance, and had no problems dealing with the red tape, was hard to pin down. The whole system is broken. Even those who are legitimately injured go through the wringer as if they are under investigation for insurance fraud. Imagine that, originally Sergeant Oswald told me to file my injury report as if I had run into the door or got hurt moving something. But yet, I chose the right way to do it and look where it landed me. Had I done it the other way, it probably would not have been questioned. Unbelievable. How can these people wake up in the morning and look into the mirror and continue doing this? I ended up going to my primary care physician, Dr. O., to have her review my medication list and to possibly get some of them removed. I was being prescribed this and that for all that I was going through. Luckily, Dr. O. was able to take five of those off my list, so I was now down to seven medications. A far cry from those double digits. This appeared to be more manageable for me and a hell of a lot better on my stomach.

It was on June 8th that on the advice of my law firm, I started to write letters and send them certified to Fishkill Correctional Facility, addressing them to Officer Sanka. He was the union's Chief Sector Steward for our local. Since I was getting no response with the phone attempts, it was now time to start putting things in writing. The next morning, I headed out to Middletown where I had an appointment with Dr. Virginia Feldman, an ear, nose, and throat specialist with ENT and associates at Crystal Run. I went to her since Dan, my physical therapist at Peak Physical Therapy in Newburgh, had suggested that I go to my orthodontist to get the pain in my left jaw and ear checked out. She was the most down to earth, compassionate, and caring doctor for the treatment I needed. She was not one of those docs that gave you three minutes and they were out the door, she took the time to listen to you and give you some valid feedback. Dr. Lustbader, our family dentist, also in Newburgh, had diagnosed my condition as TMJ (Temporomandibular Joint Dysfunction), which is caused by sudden deceleration, relative to my assault. So, once I met up with Dr. Feldman at Crystal Run, she did a series of tests on me. Besides the Tinnitus diagnosis, there also appeared to be a balance issue and she prescribed me medicated ear drops. My left ear and jaw were in so much pain, caused from the trapezoid muscle in the left side of my neck injury. We made a follow-up appointment to come back for another visit. When I got home, a bit of good news in the form of a letter in the mail addressed to me from the State Workers' Compensation Board notified me of my pre-hearing conference to start the fight toward winning back my case that the prison had controverted. This was the start of actually something productive on my efforts toward this situation. I had been in touch with my lawyer Jason about the details on preparing for this day. It was scheduled for June 21st, which was only a couple weeks away.

The following day I was out the door again to more doctor appointments. I had a counseling session with Dr. Ogulnick. We discussed the updates of where things were at, how I had heard nothing back in response from my employer, and we even had some extra time to start talking about that 2015 homicide investigation. From there I went over to my physical therapy appointment for treatment on my left shoulder and neck. There I normally started out with electrical stimulation and a heating pad, followed by some stretching and hands-on massage. I started to get into a routine of doing my different exercises going from station to station. Each visit normally took about 45 minutes to an hour at the most. I found these sessions helpful for the day, but did not feel that I was gaining ground on getting improvement. I had not yet had my MRI approved by the State Insurance Fund. All of my medical treatments were looking at this injury as a sprain or possible tear. If they had approved the testing faster, it would be beneficial for all parties involved as the goal here was to get the injury repaired as quickly as possible so that the worker could return to duty.

I found myself home again back in front of my computer, with my desk covered in documents, my scanner busy making copies, the printer spitting out my letters, and my desktop monitor doing all of my casework. I could only do this for short periods of time due to the neck and shoulder pain. I was on the phone right away, always keeping in touch with the Office of Special

Investigations. My investigator, Officer Tonka, was rarely in the office. He told me he was handling large caseloads, literally dozens of investigations at one time. I could now understand why things took longer than normal. Did you notice I mentioned he was an officer? That's right, the department selects applicants to become investigators that look into matters like an Internal Affairs Unit of a police agency would do. These are officers investigating officers. And of course, they are going to get lied to when the questions start flying. When I went into the Wallkill office to drop off my paperwork for Investigator (Officer) Tonka, I could not believe my eyes. There were six other staff sitting at their computers in there, and I knew five of them. I had wondered where they went, maybe they transferred? Now I knew. Fishkill employs about 750 officers, as I mentioned, it's a huge facility, and there is always something going on in there. But as hard as these investigators work, there are so many times when they come to a conclusion of no findings. It's like a lieutenant at work once said, "Those guys couldn't get to the bottom of their coffee cups!" A few years back, this special investigation unit use to be called the Inspector General's Office (I.G.). But a scandal broke out on the top level, finding many to be reassigned, fired, or whatever else, and the department was forced to restructure the unit. Filling in some empty desks and changing the name hardly made anything different. It was thought by many, who was policing the police? So getting back to Tonka, whenever I did speak to him, he was very tight-lipped. So many things he could not divulge, understanding of course, but I was the victim, the complainant. I was getting nowhere anytime soon. It was a hurry-up-and-wait approach. One of the things I did need from Tonka was a copy of my supporting deposition that I gave him when I delivered those copies. I mistakenly gave him the original. It took a few weeks of reminders but finally I had received it in the mail.

Chapter Five
Stress Beyond Comparison

I needed some R and R, so I contacted my lawyers and doctors to see if it was ok for me to go upstate visiting with family. "As long as you're within your physical limitations," said one of my docs. My lawyer had texted me back saying, "Go ahead, it is ok." This was much needed. I was thankful. A few days and before we knew it, we were back on the road on our way home. Messages, emails, mail, all to catch up on. It was time to get back to my appointments as well. By now I was seeing about 12 medical doctors/specialists. Sometimes I was the youngest one in those waiting rooms, but my body pain felt as if I was the oldest. The medications would only mask the pain. What I needed was answers. I needed those MRIs to figure out what was going on; it was beyond frustrating. Since I was not working or even doing my photography business at that point, I needed to file a claim with my Aflac Disability Policy. This helped to offset the additional loss of income. Just from the summer of weddings that I had to cancel and refund alone, I lost close to $22,000+ and that was not including the studio sessions and additional bookings coming in. I estimated close to over $30k in losses so far to date. Once I got that out in the mail to Aflac, I was off to see Dr. Ogulnick again to say that I was having major problems with getting sleep at night, between the pain in my shoulder and neck, as well as the bad dreams and ruminations that kept waking me up, even with the meds that helped me to sleep. I was constantly worried about what the future held, what the fate of my family's welfare would be, among other things. I had always worked hard, just like my father did, and I wanted to be sure to provide for my family. But now I was put in this position by one individual and it has affected so many people, too many to count. Yet he remains working, held harmless of his assault on me.

I got a call from my lawyers, Jason and Nick; Nick wanted to get me the Disability Retirement application for me to fill out and to send back. This also included a decent amount of money as a retainer fee. This was another process that needed to get started, so I ensured that I took care of it as fast as I could. Jason wanted to go over details for tomorrow's workers' comp board hearing, the first of three. I was actually looking forward to this as I had needed some good news. June 21st arrived and 9:00 a.m. sharp, we proceeded into the workers' compensation board hearing room in New Windsor. Everything was just a preliminary formality, so there were no actual gains in the progress I was hoping for at that point. It was a quick 15 minutes and out the door we went, with a scheduled hearing for July 27th in which the state would call upon four witnesses to come in to testify. The judge made a note for the record that Officer Thompson, Officer Omway, Sgt. Oswald, and Deputy Oblinski would be ordered to appear on the next hearing date to give their testimony.

Looking at my calendar with the appointments looked like my schedule when I was doing dozens of family photos for Christmas cards during the busy days in my photo studio. But sadly, this was just the opposite. Literally on average I had about six-seven doctor appointments each week. Before I knew it, looking at the clock, I had to get out the door to my pain management session with Dr. W in Middletown. Somehow, he was able to get overnight approvals on most testing, treatments, or diagnostics from the State Insurance Fund. How he had that influence over many of the other established doctors is one for the record books, especially with the State Insurance Fund. I sat in his waiting room and was called in to the exam room. One of his techs came in to get things started for Dr. W. When he was finished, it would take 15-20 minutes of sitting on the exam table before the Doc would make it into your room to see you. He would take a lot of hand-written notes, talk to me about my pain levels, medications, and then stand me up for a range of motion exam. A prescription of meds and I was out the door, off to my next appointment.

Now that school was out for the summertime, my two children had to endure the dozens and dozens of appointments that I had to bring them to. Thankfully for their iPods and tablets, things kept them busy. For the most part, the kids were well-behaved and cooperative during these visits, much to my relief.

It was becoming more and more of a nightmare for me to deal with this. My family had seen the changes in me; my wife felt as if I was more of a dark person than I use to be. From someone like myself that had large social circles and always liked to bring people together, I was now completely the opposite. I had been reaching out to many friends from work, talking to them about what I was going through, keeping them posted. You find out real fast who your actual real friends are in these situations. These friends – Ed, Father K, Joey G., Tim, Dave and Tara, Al, Pat, O'C, Frank, Mike, JR, Rob W, George, Paul S., Chris C., Todd W., Bruce and Nancy, Richards, Kris, Eric, not to mention some others over at my fire station as well as the neighboring firehouses, to name a few – were always there whenever I texted them, emailed, or called. Guys from the police department, Emerald Society, and DC 10-13 that I knew, were there as well, either with a phone call or out for some socializing. These guys were always calling and checking in on me. My family, as well as my wife's, were genuinely concerned and had started to understand all that I was going through. I was getting almost daily calls or text messages from my sister Kate to check up on me, as well as from my brother John and my niece Kathleen, my other side who were all upstate as well as Grace and the rest of the family, my wife's side of the family, her mom and dad, aunts and uncles, cousins, so many to name, were all so supportive if and when I needed it, I was just to ask. Much of my family lived upstate or out of state. All of them kept me in mind when it came to their thoughts and prayers. There was this one night in particular when I had started to bottom out, I texted Joey G. and Al. I had gotten into some language that worried them as to what my current welfare was…

I got an immediate call back from Joey G. His wife was next to him on the phone, I was telling him the meds I was on. She works in the mental health field, so while she was not actually talking to me, she had been relaying information back through Joey G. Apparently at that time they got in touch with my wife asking her if everything was ok and what was going on. It got to the point where Joey G. had contacted the Orange County Mobile Mental Health Unit. They called my wife and had stated they were going to come out the next morning since I had already taken my medications and went to sleep. When I woke up the next morning, my wife went to work and nobody from the Mobile Mental Health Unit showed up. I called Joey G. back about this and he was furious that they did not do their follow-up. I felt somewhat better that morning since I had slept ok. I ended up calling Dean to speak to him about what was going on. He set up a time to meet with me so we could talk in person, rather than over the phone.

Finally, some good news. Got a call from One Call Care; they told me my MRI for my neck was approved and we went ahead and scheduled it with Hudson Valley Imaging later that week. I wanted to find out what was going on with my neck so I could finally get the right treatment. With that in hand, I decided to follow up with the EEOC, whom I filed a complaint with back on May 23rd. They responded back stating they never got my packet in the mail, even though it was mailed certified to them by USPS. I gave the New York District Office a call about this and left them a voicemail on two occasions before they finally replied back. They gave me a number to call for the intake hotline and I was on hold for 65 minutes to finally get through to a representative. I spoke to Tonya who told me she could not locate my file on the computer system. I spoke in detail about my case and she stated this appears to be a valid case for the Americans with Disabilities Act, protected from harassment and intimidation. She issued a reference number for this incident and had me fax her the documents from the intake questionnaire. Tonya then told me that this would be elevated to the next level and that a supervisor would be assigned to this. Within a short period of time, I would expect to hear back from someone.

I received a message from Dr. Kenny's office stating that my MRI request authorization for my left should injury had been denied. I called his office back and spoke to Lindsay. Dr. Kenny had been treating me all along for my shoulder injury, prescribed the physical therapy and medications, but could not get the MRI approved. How could it be that Dr. W's office can get my neck MRI approved overnight for the same case and injury date, but Dr. Kenny's office could not? I called Lindsay back, under the stress I was dealing with, and tried to explain the situation. She was quite short with me over the phone. Anything regarding the requests I had made were forwarded to Jillian who handles the legal aspects for Dr. Kenny. He sure showed patience on dealing with the State Insurance Fund; I mean, between all of their paperwork requirements, red tape, delays, and payment schedules, it would almost be better just to go under your health insurance. I have tried to see other doctors and specialists for various injuries in the past, but many of them do not accept workers' compensation, and if they do, they are not accepting new patients. Our own family physician, Dr. O., does not take workers' comp, so this makes it tough when I want to be treated by my own physician who has a history with me.

The day came and I got to meet with Dean, the EAP program coordinator from Shawangunk. I had decided to meet with him since I was getting a lack of support from my own facility. Having done what I had to do in that situation, I did not exactly win a popularity contest with some of the officers at Fishkill. Not all of them cared or even paid attention to this incident I was in. But that did not stop me from getting the support I needed from all of those who believed in me and still cared for what was going on. We eventually met over at a picnic table at their QWL building (Quality of Work Life). This is used for social functions and various events by both Shawangunk and Wallkill prisons. We sat down for a while and spoke about everything. It was a beautiful sunny day, a slight breeze, overlooking a wooded area and a grassy field. A group of an outside crew of inmates passed by on a small green bus to head out for some cleaning details, escorted by a correction officer. Dean was very supportive, of course, that's why he does what he does. I told him that later that day I was finally going in for my MRI of my neck. He mentioned to me that there was not much guidance he could give me, and that was a good thing, because I was already on track doing it. I have already been keeping records, copies, making notes, following up, going to all of my appointments, obtaining lawyers, just about everything that I was supposed to be doing. I was helping me help myself, for whatever case, who else would do all of this for me?

It was now time to go in for my MRI. I had to show up early to have them input all of my information, and they had to ensure that I was not wearing any metal at all in my clothing. If you have never had an MRI, they lay you on a table, place headphones on you, and play whatever kind of music you like. They go into another room with monitors where they observe the testing results as they appear. The whole exam takes about 20-30 minutes. You're inside this small tunnel, very cramped, and not likely to be very comfortable for the larger than average person, or anyone who may be claustrophobic. All kinds of noises are made from the magnets in the machine, sounding like a band of tools pounding away, some louder than others. Even with the headphones on, you can still hear all of this going on. If you move at all, chances are the test will have to be restarted, only making it harder on yourself. Soon enough for me, and having had MRIs in the past, I was all done. I was immediately given a CD of the test and the results would be made out into a report the next day. I wasted no time going over the next morning. I was able to get my report from Debbie; she was more than helpful to ensure it was ready for pick-up upon my arrival. The findings concluded that in my C-Spine, from C2-T1, there was mild degenerative disc changes and disc bulging, however, specifically C3-C4 there was foraminal stenosis on the left side. Even worse on C4-C5 was moderate disc bulging with slight retrolisthesis and foraminal stenosis bilaterally. This was causing the nerve pain in my shoulders down both of my arms and into my hands, most days with tingling and numbness occurring. There were no previous serious injuries to my neck involving my discs and there were no previous testing comparisons to refer to once this MRI for my neck was completed.

Now that I was back home again, I decided to contact New York's Public Employee Safety and Health (OSHA-PESH). I spoke to Joe on June 29th; he is the PESH Supervisor up in Building 12 in Albany. We spoke at length regarding my case and he seemed quite concerned and helpful for me. "The only thing we can do right now is enforce the employer to implement programs and training for workplace violence." He later sent me an email with more details, but at that point I put this on the back burner because Fishkill already has a Workplace Violence Policy, it's defined under Directive 4960. In fact, this is statewide for all correctional facilities, and according to Acting Commissioner for the Department of Corrections and Community Supervision, there is a zero-tolerance stance taken against any violations of such incidents. At this point, I figured I would follow up with the EEOC again; this time calling them had me on hold for 125 minutes, literally over two hours. I kept the phone on speaker and handled paperwork the whole time while I was waiting. I spoke to Jonathan who gave me a reference number. He told me it was assigned out to staff, but there was no charge number yet, no investigation. There was a great concern on how they were approaching this matter, especially when there was a window of time in which things had to be done with them. I did not feel so confident with them so far, even though they had massive caseloads. They are a federal agency, but I am told they are a very small one with limited budget, limited resources. They have to pick and choose their fights, focusing primarily on the most serious ones.

Now here I am looking at my calendar for July, and that too was starting to fill up with appointments, meetings, and other things. I went to Dr. Ogulnick for my usual counseling session, this one being more upsetting for me. I explained that I had an appointment with Dr. W. in Middletown. When I went in to go over the results from my neck MRI testing, I was left in the exam room for about 20 minutes with my two children. When he finally came into the room, he started questioning me as usual, but this time he did not sound the same, he almost sounded sarcastic. We went through the range of motion; I was telling him about all of my meds, the pain levels, and about all of the stress I was under dealing with this. He looked at me and said, "Look, if you are trying to get out of work and have me write notes for you, then you need to find someone else. I am here to treat you, not to do all these notes you are requesting!" I looked back at him almost in shock and said, "You know my history and current injuries, I have been treated by you for two years or so. what do you mean by that?" At that moment he turned away and walked out, literally leaving me in the room for close to 30 minutes. Maybe he was thinking I was going to give up and leave, but I sat in the room with my two children who were ever so patient, I mean the best I could expect. All of that time I was thinking, how could he do this and say that? He knows that I am required to get notes for work under workers' compensation. That was very unprofessional of him. Finally, he came back into the room, a totally different person than he was a half hour ago. In his hand he held documents faxed to him from Hudson Valley Imaging. He sat down and said, "OK, your MRI does show injuries and we will need to get you started on pain management. I will prescribe you some medications, and we will get that note for you, you are not able to work." At that point we walked out to the receptionist and made my follow-up appointment. They also requested authorization for me to get epidural injections for my neck; it's a big procedure as it is same day surgery but it involves much more than just a walk into the office.

Finally heard back from the EEOC via email. They assigned me an investigator by the name of Orfelino. He is located in the New York District Office in Manhattan. On the notice, it had numbers to call, often times directing you to different offices depending on your situation, but coincidentally, it was the same man on each voicemail at each different office. They would not allow anyone to just show up there, you would have to schedule an appointment ahead of time and go down with paperwork in hand. I had a feeling this would not be happening for me. Seemed as if I was doing more of the legwork than they were. Now it had also been some time since I last sent out the certified letter to the Chief Sector Steward at Fishkill Correctional Facility, Officer

Sanka. I mailed out another one on July 5th requesting assistance to file a grievance on the matter. I was hoping at some point I would be hearing back from someone since I was still not back to work yet. I only had a certain period of time in which to file a grievance. Something was telling me at this point there was definitely a cover-up going on. With no word from my employer as required per the workplace violence directive, no union follow-up, my case being controverted denying my medical benefits, nobody knows nothing, it was a hush-hush situation.

My family and I attend church as often as we can each week. In fact, our children just received their first communion this previous spring. Our priest, Father K., is not like any other priest I know. I was an altar boy for many years growing up, and going to church regularly I have gotten to know many priests. He is down to earth, a regular guy who you could talk to about anything. He was brutally honest, and in some instances, that was necessary. A touch of humor to top it off made for some really nice church services. Father K. has been to our home on numerous occasions, and he was quite aware of my situation. From the beginning I had spoken to him at great length and detail about what I had gone through and what I was about to face. He had always been there to talk to me about how to handle and deal with this type of stress, anxiety, and other mitigating factors. Sometimes we would sit around our fire pit with a fire roaring away. It's amazing how much people can open up and talk while watching the firewood burn away. One Sunday in the first part of July, Father K. gave a wonderful service. During it, his sermon related to my ordeal; without saying my name or other details, he spoke about stress and the fight to provide for one's family in a situation such as this. I knew right away he was referring to me as my family sat midway back in the pews. The church was packed full that morning. I could not hold back my emotions as I felt the power of his words. Afterward I recalled thinking, "I thought the only time you heard someone talking about you in church to the entire congregation was when you were up front laying in a closed casket." I was speechless, never having experienced this before, but I was able to thank him after mass as he greeted parishioners upon exiting the church to their vehicles in the parking lot.

A few days later on July 10th, I got a hold of Investigator Tonka through the Albany office. I asked him about the status of the investigation, why it was taking so long. Additionally, I inquired as to why my witness Officer Potter from Vocational TC 2 Checkpoint was not yet interviewed and allowed to give his written statement of what he saw when Officer Thompson verbally threatened me and screamed upon me in my face just days before his physical assault on me. I informed Tonka that I have been advocating this for myself and many people have been notified to look into this case. Tonka said that Superintendent Shields spoke to Labor Management and that he had to meet with them to go over details. Other than that, the conversation was short. I felt as if this was getting no worthy attention that it deserved. Too much protection was being afforded to Officer Thompson who was already on his way to be promoted to sergeant. He had taken the Civil Service Exam a couple years back and when his number came up, they sent him to sergeant school up at the Albany Training Academy. He still remained an officer at that time but soon he was promoted and remained at Fishkill. It is highly unusual for a newly-promoted sergeant to remain at the same facility. Normally they are transferred away to another prison and have to work their way back based on openings, availability, and seniority ranking.

Chapter Six

There's a New Doc in Town

My lawyer Jason had referred me to a chiropractor doctor down in Spring Valley, one who took workers' compensation insurance. I checked on a few of them up here in my area and there was no luck. Dr. Habif scheduled me for my initial consultation for my back surgery issues, something I needed to get attention for. At this point, I was hurting all over the place. This was good news for me. Dr. Habif was great to work with, he knew exactly what treatment options I needed, and he happily accepted the extra documentation I needed for my case. He also has an office in White Plains, not far from where my Law Firm is located, but as often I can, I go to the Spring Valley Office, it's much closer and a straight shot down the Thruway. Dr. Habif also helped me out with referrals for pain management regarding my shoulder injuries, as well as having more exams done for nerve testing and range of motion. Appointments were easy to come by, normally I would go the same days of each week, usually in the mornings. I could just show up and he would get me right in and onto a table. On the day of my first visit, I had to get back up the Thruway to make it in time to my next appointment in Goshen to see Dr. Newton, the other referral that came from Dr. Ogulnick. Dr. Newton listened as I spoke in detail about my stress and depression, showing him supporting documentation. He was well aware of the corruption inside the prison. He had dealt with others and seen it before. I could barely get a word out, but softly I was telling him about my lack of sleep, the nightmares, and how I was living this in my mind over and over and over. It was virtually destroying my way of life, my family lifestyle, my health, my sanity, and our economic situation. We had about an hour in session, so we wrapped up with some advice on what I should do and that he wanted to see me again in two weeks. When I got home that day, I received another email from the EEOC, this time from Investigator Orfelino.

He mentioned that my retaliation claim does not fall into any of the protected statutes. I directly replied back about the disability discrimination issues by the employer. I wanted to call him but would only be getting his voicemail as usual. I awaited his reply to follow up with me. I took off to the Price Chopper Pharmacy in Newburgh that my family uses and has done so for many years. I was getting my medications filled and when I went to check out, the computer said that per their claims' adjuster, my case for the incident on 5/9/17 was now closed. Talk about roadblock after roadblock. I found out that it was not worth the debate, so they billed it to my private health insurance and I paid numerous co-pays. I saved the receipts and mailed them to my lawyers to be submitted for reimbursement. I soon found out that this was entirely illegal for them to be doing, as I will get into more details about later in this story.

Back to Dr. Kenny's Office, I went for a follow-up. I explained the treatment I have been receiving so far and that my shoulder MRI authorization is still being denied. In order to help me along with my pain, Dr. Kenny offered me a shot into my shoulder. I think the shot itself hurt more than ever, but was expected to feel relief in the next few days. Relief that never came. Whatever was going on in my shoulder was more than what we were looking at on x-rays or in physical therapy. And since I was not improving in physical therapy, Dr. Kenny ordered me to stop my visits. I was so eager at this point to get something done for my shoulder, I ended up calling the Hospital for Special Surgery down in Manhattan that day. I spoke to one of the doctors who does the surgeries there, we went over my injuries, medications, and all of my personal information including the case document numbers for billing purposes. After this lengthy conversation, they finally decided to tell me that unless I was considering immediate surgery on a serious level, then they would not be able to accept me as a new patient, not even for conservative treatment. After that call, I got ahold of the staff over at Peak Physical Therapy in Newburgh and told them that I have to cease my visits due to orders of my orthopedic.

Investigator Orfelino from the EEOC emailed me requesting me to substantiate my allegations based on any coverage of the Americans with Disabilities Act. Now I have contacted him in writing numerous times but he has failed to call me as requested. This is a failure to communicate. I sent the descriptive reply back to him stating, "Under the ADA, you have a disability if you have at least one of the following: A physical or mental impairment that limits one or more of life's major activities." The next morning, he finally called me back. It was not the productive call I was hoping for. He was not understanding or cooperative with my concerns at all. He told me that he notified my employer that I filed a complaint even though they were not going to investigate this. "We are understaffed, low budget, and you have 100 people in line in front of you." He told me to get my lawyer to send them a letter of representation so they could discuss this further. "At this time, we are declining your charges and are closing the case." We hung the phones up and I laid down, with my stress and heart rate above normal; what the heck was I going to do about this? My lawyers were representing me for my workers' compensation case and my disability retirement case. What I needed was a labor lawyer, and I had already interviewed two of them; as expensive as they were, they too picked and chose their cases, just like these agencies.

It was now July 13th, the summer was starting to fly by fast with it being as busy as I tried to keep myself despite my physical limitations. I arrived for my appointment with Dr. W. in Middletown again. We went over my C-Spine findings, pain levels, medications, the same as usual. Since there was no luck from Dr. Kenny's office on my left shoulder MRI authorization, I had Dr. W. put in for the authorization. Believe it or not, right away it was approved. As I said about my neck MRI, how could this be? Dr. Kenny was a part of a large reputable group of doctors and specialists. What was being done so differently? So, within a few days, I spoke once again to One Call Care, they had me schedule my MRI at Hudson Valley Imaging for July 21st. I really needed this boost, at least at this point I would be able to find out what was wrong with my shoulder. So, during those next few days, more appointments followed, visits with Dr. Habif, Dr. Ogulnick, Dr. Feldman, and now with Dr. S. who specializes in General Medicine. By now with all of these appointments and billing starting to pile up, the State Insurance Fund was sending me official notices scheduling me for IME (Independent Medical Examinations) also referred to as the "State Doctor." When you go in for an IME, you fill out a questionnaire, bring your x-rays and other test results, and then go in for an exam with a doctor that you have never been seen by before, who only knows of your condition based on reading reports from the State Insurance Fund and others. How can this be an independent medical exam when you're being seen by a doctor who is hired by the State Insurance Fund? Obviously, it is in the doctor's best interest to get you back to work, even if you are not ready and

105

you need surgery or more treatments. Most of the time you are in there for ten minutes, they do a range of motion exam, ask you a few questions, observe your body parts in question, and make their determination. If they tell the state that nobody can go back to work all too often, you can bet that doctor's office is going to be dropped by them and lose a lot of business and a lot of money. So clearly this is far from independent. So many professionals in the medical field describe that this system is so one sided, hardly independent, and all too often they were denied or not paid.

So, with the medication refills or new prescriptions being given, I made my way back to the Price Chopper Pharmacy. Here we go again, the pharmacy tech telling me that my case was closed and that I need to contact my case handler. I tried to explain to them that it is not closed. I had to come out of pocket with more co-pays again. The State Insurance Fund was starting to stress me out bad and adding to my already complex issue, they were denying most of my doctor's requests and delaying everything. Now keep in mind my injury case is still controverted so this is to be expected, but then how come they are approving other things like those really expensive MRIs? Without any work right now or my secondary income from the business, we were starting to feel the crunch. Is this what the facility wanted? They think I'd give up and that this will go away? How can they sleep at night? "Delay delay, go away" seems to be their motto these days. Speaking of the MRIs, I was on my way finally to Hudson Valley Imaging to get my left shoulder done. Once again, same deal, no prior surgeries, no comparative contrast given for my shoulder. This was an injury being looked at for the first time. After about a half hour, I was given the CD and told that I could come back in the morning for the written report. I was anticipating the worst outcome from this test. When I got the report and read it, it was unbelievable. All of this time since Officer Thompson assaulted me on May 9th, I had been in pain from a series of trauma throughout my shoulder and neck. The findings were arthrosis in the AC Joint, subacromial bursitis, mild distal supraspinatus, infraspinatus, subscapularis tendinopathy without tear. There was tearing of the superior, posterior and inferior labrum, as well as moderate biceps tendinopathy, tearing/splitting of the rotator cuff, and a torn tendon. Also found was a large posterior inferior Para labral cyst, as well as a smaller one due to the trauma of the labrum. I was in need of immediate surgery but before I could get that done, the lawyers would need to win my case so I could get my treatments approved. We continued with pain management, medications, home therapy, as well other specialist appointments.

With my lower back case still being active, and seeing how I was still getting treatments for it, I went to my scheduled independent medical exam. The appointment was with Dr. Al up in New Paltz. After a very thorough questionnaire, I was called into the exam room. I was very surprised by this visit. A lot of it was surfaced on the incident from my assault on 5/9/17. This exam was supposed to be for my lower back injury from an inmate use of force on 11/18/15. Although he did a range of motion on my lower back, he kept asking me questions about my shoulder and neck, all the while feeling my neck and moving my shoulder around. In his final report, he stated I had no limitations for my lower back and could go back to full duty with no restrictions, however, he stated that he could not return me to duty due to the numerous injuries I had from the assault on 5/9/17 by Officer Thompson. It took a while to hear back any follow-up on this. I left the appointment to return home and I began to reach out to numerous personal injury lawyers. Out of about 10 different firms, nobody wanted to take a case like this against an individual officer based on a contingency. The amount of money to be spent on going to trial would not be worth it in the end. After all they said, what could you get from him as an individual with no pockets? He has a mortgage, a family? You can't touch his retirement, so really, you would be left with some sort of payment plan and a lot of liens placed on him for the rest of his life. Even if I were to pay out of pocket for the retainer and hourly rates, most of the lawyers were being fair to me when they said that honestly it would not be worth it all in the end. But I wouldn't let it end there. Consequences were yet to come.

The next day I went to Spring Valley for EMG nerve testing at Dr. Habif's office. I gave them a copy of my shoulder MRI. We then scheduled my next appointment for my range of motion exam. I had to be quick as I needed to be back up to Newburgh following this appointment to meet with Dr. Ogulnick. This session was especially important because I wanted to discuss with him the details for the second part of my workers' compensation board hearing scheduled for the next day. I was expecting to see the witnesses that were called to testify for the first time since this incident. I was also fighting bouts with my depression. It was like a roller coaster ride. Some days were up, but more often they were down. Anxiety was in the air with the hearing the following day. I was able to touch base with my lawyers to go over the plans for tomorrow. After that it was time to make some more phone calls and send out emails. I was trying to stay on top of this as best as I could. Prior to going to the hearing, I had another appointment with Dr. Kenny to review my left shoulder MRI findings. As he came in the room, he told me how surprised he was with the outcome, that it was worse than he originally diagnosed. I told him that the last shot in my shoulder that he gave to me had no effect. With that I was out the door headed over to the worker's compensation board offices in New Windsor. As I arrived early, I walked into the waiting room to check in with security. I noticed Officer Thompson already there, sitting in his Class A uniform, now with sergeant stripes on each arm. When I was told to have a seat, there were few seats left, directly next to him. Probably not a good idea, I thought, and with that in mind, I moved myself back into the hallway to wait for Jason to arrive. When he got there, we stood in the hallway and discussed paperwork, and during this time, Officer Omway, in plain clothes, walked by us making little eye contact with me as he made his way directly into the waiting room. The hearings were running behind schedule. We had to wait an additional hour to be called into Hearing Room #1. I was called in first and testified for 25 minutes or so. Upon my request, I was allowed to wait outside when Officer Thompson went in to give his testimony. He was in there for about 15 minutes.

Some things were learned during questioning. The prior incidents such as the harassing letter he had admitted to doing, since it was clear that he wrote it in his handwriting. He had faced 30 days suspension but it went to arbitration and he ended up losing three days of vacation. He also told the judge that the investigation was over and that he denied any wrongdoing or knowledge of the assault incident on 5/9/17. Following his testimony, he was allowed to depart the building, and then Officer Omway was called in to testify for only about 10 minutes. By this time, the waiting room had cleared out and I was the only one left in there, so when Omway walked out of the hearing room, I was called back in. Present were still my lawyer, the State Insurance Fund representative and the workers' compensation judge. The judge questioned the state's representative about his other witnesses, Sergeant Oswald and Deputy Oblinski. They had not appeared under order to show and give testimony. Right away in my mind, I knew that they did not come because then they would be under oath, on tape, on record, testifying what had happened on 5/9/17 and as a result of their "so-called" investigation. It was a cover-up at its best.

Additionally, the state was questioned as to why they failed to have my independent medical exams done by the deadline in time for the hearing. He ended up tossing out those exams as well as the state's request to recall and examine Sergeant Oswald and Deputy Oblinski. The judge called for the next hearing date for September 5th to hear closing arguments and to render decision on my case. The hearing was then adjourned and I walked out in the hallway with Jason. We spoke about what to expect next and some of the things that were testified about during my absence from the room. It was now time to go home and relax with family.

July 27th was here before I knew it, not an important day but a sign that another month has flown by us. I was on the phone to the Albany Office of Special Investigations. Tonka was on vacation so they put me on with his supervisor, Investigator Donners. We talked about the status of the investigation and he said when things are complete, that I would be getting a letter in writing in the mail. Further, he would be checking in with the Bureau of Labor Relations. I had driven down to Orangeburg after this call to meet with my other lawyer Nick. I needed to hand-deliver other paper documents to him that I needed to add to my case files. We sat down for a bit and talked in length about what my goals would be. Since I was so involved with what was going on, having immersed myself into the matters probably more than anyone else might have, there were certain details that needed to be decided upon. I had to chart my course of action and the union representation issue came up again. When I got back home, I telephoned the (Corrections and Police Benevolent Association) headquarters office in Albany to get in touch with President Peters. They gave me his correct email address so I sat down and immediately typed out a letter concerning my multiple attempts to get in touch with my steward and representatives at Fishkill. I was expecting an immediate response but did not get one, so I waited it out to see.

Dr. W. had referred me to his partner, Dr. Oscar, also of the same office at Crystal Run in Middletown. He treated patients for spinal injuries, including the neck. I brought in all of my documents, in a briefcase, to include my recent MRI test. I was in the exam room for about 20 minutes, the average waiting time for that office, before Dr. Oscar walked in. He came in with no charts, no notes, just a blank yellow legal pad.

He started to ask me questions and out of curiosity I asked him, "Do you have my chart or any information on me from Dr. W's referral?"

He looked up at me and said, "No, do you have anything for me?"

So, then I opened up my case and handed him over the MRI report and some other doctors notes, physical therapy reports, my medication list, among other things. Upon a quick read of those documents and an exam, it took him all of two minutes to decide that he believed that these injuries were not caused by the assault, but possibly they were already there and only made symptomatic as a result of the crushing injury from being slammed into. There's no way that over a dozen other doctors and medical specialists concur with the mechanism of injuries and yet Dr. Oscar walks in the door for five minutes and reads from his crystal ball what the future holds. He said he did not want to handle my case and referred me to other doctors to go and see. Right away I was angry; this was unfounded, unjust, and warranted my decision to cease all future visits to Dr. W's office. He even sent a report to the State Insurance Fund that depicted me in a negative way. I mean, why would a doctor do this? One who is not caring or compassionate? I looked up Dr. Oscar that evening online and found his ratings to be low; apparently, he has pissed off many other patients as well. The next day I called and canceled the epidural injection surgery as well as my follow-up appointment.

Chapter Seven
More News, More Legalities

Another morning as usual, a quick stop for gas at the local mart and then seeing some surprising news in all the papers that were on the news stand that day. On the front page: "Fishkill Prison Guards Will Not Face Charges in '15 Death of an Inmate." What a way to find out, I thought, do a media release first, don't bother contacting the officers or the facility to inform us of the Fed's decision. Either way, it was good news. News that I had hopefully expected, that we all had wanted to hear. The investigation took such a long time because of due process, something that started at the local and state level, then went onto the federal level. An autopsy classified the death of the inmate as a homicide, and the prison had long been identified by inmate advocates as a place where officers routinely abused inmates. But Joon H. Kim, the acting United States attorney in Manhattan, said that prosecutors in his office had found "insufficient evidence to meet the high burden of proof required for a federal criminal civil rights prosecution." And William V. Grady, the Duchess County District Attorney, said his office had also found insufficient evidence to support a prosecution "under any state theory of homicide."

"There is no video evidence of the altercation between the inmate involved and the corrections officers, and numerous eyewitness accounts of the incident, including those provided by inmates, are inconsistent and contradictory," Mr. Kim and Mr. Grady said in a joint statement.

Given those factors and "inconclusive medical evidence of excessive use of force," the statement said, "the Department of Justice could not prove beyond a reasonable doubt that any corrections officer willfully violated the inmate's constitutional rights." There now follows a civil lawsuit, with it being over 40 pages long. I am still dealing with complete stress and other matters relating to this incident in a separate workers' compensation case.

Since the workers' compensation board judge threw out the state's ability to use an independent medical exam to uphold their case, I received a call on August 3rd, at about 9:40 a.m., from First Choice representatives stating that both of my scheduled IMEs had been canceled. The State Insurance Fund handler for my cases, Miss Jackie, probably felt that it was agreed upon to make this move. Even though in the first hearing the judge gave them more than adequate time to get me in for exams, they failed to do so, and to provide such documentation as requested by the judge. Speaking to my attorney Jason about this, he said it was not officially canceled until it was in writing. It was only a few days until it had arrived in the mail. Those documents were added to my ever-growing mountain of paperwork from my case with Officer Thompson. As I was going through my paperwork, I decided to take a look in my logbook, to review the last couple weeks so I could catch up on things I may have forgotten. "Of course," I said, when I looked at the email to the Union President dated July 27th. Here it is, already August 7th and still no reply back. So, I compiled another email to follow up and ask him as to why I had not received any response yet, from his office, or my local union office. I was getting tired of the delays, and here I am thinking, if one were to cover up something, would you play the unknown and ignore requests to avoid the subject? Of course one would. Typical behavior. Nothing surprising about that. Besides, I thought, why would they open up the communication and create a paper trail that could come back to haunt them later?

The Empire State Plaza in New York's Capitol of Albany, where I had reported for the Public Employee Relations Board Hearing against my union and my employer. Photo by Paul Harrington.

So back and forth I go with the appointments again; this takes a lot out of someone, especially knowing that your life is on hold, you're suffering physically, financially, emotionally, your family too, not many officers would go through that much effort. It would be easier to just suck it up and go deal with it once they got back to work. Nobody wants to be inconvenienced day to day. But when you truly have multiple legitimate injuries that need the kind of treatment and attention that I was seeking, then one has to do what one's gotta do. That week was full of appointments with my chiropractor, psychologist, orthopedic spine doctor, orthopedic shoulder doctor, orthodontist (for the TMJ), ENT specialist, as well as my family physician. I started to become a regular at the pharmacy. Knowing a few of the employees in there, all of them previous photo clients of mine, now saw what I was going through, although they could not make a comment. I knew that they had wondered, and were concerned. That's where a lot of my friends came into the picture. I would get daily phone calls, text messages, and emails. Some of them were helping me by obtaining documentation that was needed to help assist me with fighting for my rights in this case. This was a rare case, something that was not seen that often, if at all. This was probably why I got the looks from all of the people I know that started to hear of my situation. Remember what I was saying before, here's a family man, working 90 mph, still finding time to give back to his community, and now all of the sudden, where did he go, many asked? I consulted with my business advisor and webmaster Joe. Joe has run my business website venture for numerous years. I needed some advice from him so I called up one day and said, "Joe, hey, it's Paul. Questions for you. You know about my situation at work right…what I had mentioned to you already? What do you think I should do with the website and social media for the business?" Since I was not working and shut down the studio for the 2017 season, I did not want it to appear as if I was permanently closed. Joe gladly mentioned, "Hey, my advice is, don't take anything down, just leave it all up, there's no reason to remove it from the internet. We just won't do any updates since you're not going to be working. This way there's still a face out there. You don't want to do any social media updates either."

"Great," I mentioned, "sounds good to me." So now that this was the plan, I could now focus my thoughts back onto the case.

The next day I contacted the United States Department of Labor regarding my case and the union's breach of Duty of Fair Representation. They had immediately assigned me a service request number. Following up with this, they had me fill out the USDOL Whistleblower Complaint and it received a reference number as well. I finished filling out the forms, printed them, and then submitted it online as well. That morning I got a call from another labor lawyer out of the New York City area who said he was not prepared to take on this type of case. He kept asking me the same questions repeatedly, ones that I gave him answers for, but maybe if he had actually let me finish my sentences, he would have heard it the first time. So there goes that one, check him off the list. I was beginning to feel buried up to my neck. Hanging up the phone, I went over to my computer station and opened up both screens to start my daily multi-tasking. I had just got another email from Ray, an investigator with the Occupational Safety and Health Administration (OSHA). In his email, he stated that on the federal level they only oversee private employers and very few public employers as well. He made a referral to the New York State Department of Labor on my behalf, so I waited for their follow-up with me. I was getting my stress levels up again, so I gave Dr. Ogulnick a call. I have been seeing him for a variety of reasons besides the injuries I received on May 9th while on duty at work. We also spoke in great detail about the inmate homicide in 2015 at Fishkill. That made national news and for a while brought out protesters for a period of time. There was so much bottled up from that incident on my shoulders and in my mind, especially about how I was treated that night after the incident and for weeks to follow. The doc did not answer, probably in session, I thought, so I left him a message. I was starting to feel like all of this was against me. I said on the message, "The Division of Human Rights, my union, the DOCCS Office of Special Investigations, Bureau of Labor Relations, the Employee Equal Opportunity Commission, State Police Bureau of Criminal Investigation, and my employer all seemed to either not want to pursue this complaint, or they just did not handle something like this at all. Please call me back and help me sort through this."

At this point I figured I would reach out to some of my political contacts in Orange County, someone I knew personally from the years of community service I have been involved with. I sent him an email explaining in brief what my situation was and what he could do to put me in touch with the right people who could advocate for me. Keeping in mind once again my lawyers were not involved in this part of my case so I was doing much of this for myself. It was advised that I seek a labor lawyer but that had already been attempted and yet I would look again. This only got harder on me. I had the support of my family and friends, colleagues from the prison, all whom kept me going, telling me I was doing the right thing, that I was on the right track. My political friend ended up putting me in touch with the State Senator's office. After getting off the phone, I got that call back from Dr. Ogulnick. He was great in being able to interpret everything I was dealing with, without having to see it in my eyes. He talked me through much of it, mostly saying it's the system, it's not me, that I was doing the right thing. We addressed those agency issues as well. That's something for another day, another time. I ended up getting a call waiting beep on the phone, so I took the call and it was the New York State Department of Labor, in regards to the USDOL whistleblower complaint. I spoke to Matt and he filled out my intake form and reassured me that an inspector would be in touch with me shortly. It was only four days later and that call came in. The Public Employee Safety and Health Supervisor called me from Albany. He wanted to start an intake form for my case by that afternoon, that it would take some time to do so over the phone. There were a number of "adverse actions" by the employer that had to be met before I would be eligible to meet the requirements of their investigations. We also spoke about the retaliation toward me for reporting this incident. Like I said before, it was very rare for an officer to report another officer, but once Officer Thompson did what he did to me in the hallway, injuring me and subsequently causing the anxiety attack in such a way that required me to be sent out by ambulance to the emergency room, the game was over. At that point, once I was on the ambulance, I had to do what I had to do. One of the lieutenants from work that evening said to me, "Paul, report all of this as it happened. Don't sugarcoat it. Think of you and your family now. It's all you need to do." Normally when there are disputes, fights, or any other unresolved issues, they take them out to the parking lot to settle the dust. Whoever was injured would just go home and get a sick note from their doctor for the next few days to cover them while that "black eye" or whatever else heals up. Of course, however, word would get all around the prison about the incident faster than the world's largest news press. In fact, even though those facility phones can be monitored, 75% of the time they are used for the gossip and stories, with the remaining time for official business. Every day you would hear the arsenal officer bark over the radio, "Clear your landlines, the Sergeant is trying to reach you!" So, getting back to my conversation with the PESH supervisor, he advised me that the intake forms were complete and that Matt would be proceeding with them to the next level. I now had to wait to hear back from them.

More surprises for me…a call from Crystal Run in Middletown came in stating that the physical therapy request for my neck was denied by the State Insurance Fund due to the case still being controverted. I knew it would be some time before I would be able to get the treatments for my neck. All of this time so far they have been keeping my pain on the level with numerous medications. I have never had, nor do I currently have, an issue with prescriptions. I have repeatedly been warned about the dangers of what I had been prescribed. I took them as directed but all too often found that it really was not addressing my pain management. I was beginning to feel it hard. This was something I would not have wished on my worst enemy. If someone would have told me the day before this incident that this was going to happen, I would have taken off on a destination vacation for as long as I could. Problem is, yesterday is today, and before you know it, today will be tomorrow. I ended up channeling my energy, what was left of it, into a five-page typed report and had it notarized by my fellow neighbor Mike, who is also a correction officer and notary public. Easier than driving five miles one way to the bank to do this. Mike was always there, very helpful. He too is a family man, married with three young children. Once the ink from his stamp was dry, into the envelope it went to be sent certified mail to the Department of Labor and to the Senator's office.

Chapter Eight
Finally, Something from the Union?

Once I got home from the post office, I saw that I had a new email; finally, about three weeks later, a response from the President of our Union in Albany. In his reply he writes, "Mr. Harrington, I have received your recent correspondence of July 27th and August 10th of 2017 wherein you state you are seeking representation following an alleged incident at Fishkill Correctional Facility that is vaguely referenced in your correspondence. Contrary to what you state, I was not made previously aware of any details regarding the incident, nor do I have any details other than what you state in the same correspondence. I also spoke with the Vice President who indicated you never contacted the regional office regarding the issue." The President goes on about filing reports with the workplace violence committee, along with references to the Department's Directive 4960 in which he also stated he attached to his email. What he attached was NOT the directive, but I believe he inadvertently attached some other correspondence between himself, the regional vice president and the union's office manager. Interestingly enough, the vice president's reply to the president was simply a one liner. "This guy will sue the union with a DFR charge." DFR stands for Duty of Fair Representation. Unbelievable, I thought, not only are they actually doing this to me, they are admitting to it and expecting something legal out of it as well. One of the reasons I never contacted the regional vice president in our area was because that he is the brother-in-law to Officer Thompson. There's an obvious concerted effort on their part as the union executives as well as the local steward to protect him and to make this all go away. I ended up sending the president an immediate reply via email stating that there were reasons why I did not make the mid-level contact due to the conflict of interest. After all, at this point I am still getting no response from my local at Fishkill Correctional

Facility. Additionally, I informed the union president that I am well aware of the directive on workplace violence. That evening I did everything I was supposed to do. Report it verbally to my immediate supervisor and after I was discharged from the hospital, make out a detailed report in writing to follow it up. This report was supposed to be investigated and an immediate determination was to be made by the Bureau of Labor Relations for them to render a decision of suspension. Apparently, it did not happen that way. Once I wrapped up my reply, it was off to more doctor appointments. I was averaging close to 25-30 of them per month at this point. I saved all of my mileage to be reported to the State Insurance Fund seeking reimbursement since May, but as of this date, still nothing from them.

It was August 24th, last week's attempts to get in touch with Investigator Tonka were fruitless. He was away on vacation they said, and his supervisor was away on training. But on this day, I was able to get him on the phone again, still trying to get answers, anything that would reassure me that this was being treated as a fair and competent investigation. We got talking about my conversation with his supervisor and I inquired about the case status. Was it closed yet? Thompson testified that the investigation was over with at the last hearing in July. Tonka was not forthcoming. He did state after the pressure continued that he was going to be closing the case and that it was up to labor relations to issue me a response from Albany. My thoughts were at odds. Was he passing the buck? Today would become a busy day for me on the phone as I made the follow-up calls. I heard from the State Department of Labor Supervisor; he called to indicate that he got the "ok" to proceed with their investigation. I was to expect a call from their representatives to set up a meeting to do the questionnaire as well as provide them with about 20 copies of my documents, not including my five-page notarized report and the 14 pages of the Department's Workplace Violence Directive.

"Thank you for calling," I told him as we hung up the phones. I then called the Governor's Office of Employee Relations and spoke to some representatives. They put me in touch with the Bureau of Labor Relations Office in Albany. Their representative who handles and oversees the Corrections Agency answered the phone when I called. He almost immediately told me to contact my union about the situation but when I explained that I am not being represented, he said he had no knowledge of this incident. He asked for both of our names, putting them into his computer system. There was no record of this incident in the system at all, showing that this was reported, as per departmental directive. He took my phone number saying he would look into the matter, to contact the Office of Investigations about the matter and that he would then follow up with me. I started to think, this is all adding up now, this is truly an entire cover-up. No reports were filed, nothing was admitted to, my independent witness had been coached on his report and flip-flopped on saying what he saw, in fear for himself and his career. At that time I decided to call the Bureau of Criminal Investigation to speak to them about getting a copy of my report. Last time we spoke back in May, he indicated I could get a copy but did not mention how. When I called him, I still had his cell phone on file so I knew that would be the fastest way to touch base with him. He answered, "Who is this?" I explained to him what I needed and right away he remembered me. His tone of voice changed rapidly. He said, "Your case was closed several months ago and we already discussed it! Why are you calling me?" I told him that I needed to obtain information from him about my supporting deposition dated May 10th. "I don't give out reports, you have to go to the state police website and request a foil or you can go to the barracks and pick up the form to fill out for the foil to get a copy. Do not use this number in the future, use the office phone." We hung up.

The next morning, I called my personnel office at work. I spoke to one of the ladies working in there about looking into my personal folder to see if my last employee evaluation was in there. She took down some pedigree information and said she would call me back. A few minutes later and the phone rang. "Officer Harrington?"

I said, "Yes, did you find out anything?"

The sound of her voice was not reassuring. "I looked through your file and the last one in there was from over a year ago."

I was in disbelief. "I just had my last employee evaluation done in late April of this year, with the Sergeant giving me an "Excellent" rating. I remember signing it and notating a comment below my name about my extra training, and he said he would get me a copy afterward."

"Well," she said, "I don't see anything in here. If you want, I can call upstairs and we can track it down."

Figuring she had done enough at this point, I did not want to send her on this trail. I started wondering, it had been about almost four months and by now it would have been in my file. Was it removed by a higher authority?

Perhaps it was in with the paperwork on my investigation? Whatever the case, the original would have been left in the folder in personnel with a copy being made for that purpose. I have never been in serious trouble in my almost 23 years of service with the department, in fact numerous evaluations of excellence are dotted inside my file, as well as about 4-5 commendations awarded by previous superintendents both at Fishkill and Sing Sing. There was one time a few years ago that I had called in sick six times within a nine-month period. With my kids being home sick from school, or something else, I had always provided the proper conforming doctor's notes to my employer. With that, they followed the book and wrote me up, placing me on "time abuse" where I stayed for about three months. Many officers are placed on time abuse for having larger numbers, more likely between 15-30 sick call-ins within a nine-month period. I had the bare minimum of six. When I walked upstairs to ask the Deputy Superintendent of Administration about this and why, his first question was, "How many sick occasions do you have?"

"Six," I responded.

He looked at me over the top of his glasses and said, "That's it? Don't worry about it, I will take care of it."

I closed out the conversation by saying that I have never in all my years had this problem. He said, "Well, you should see how many other officers in this facility we have with bigger numbers. Some of them have 36 occasions!"

"Thank you," I said, walking out of his office.

You see, this time abuse program is just a way to monitor your absences. Basically, every time you use your own earned sick time, you have to bring in a valid doctor's note. Not a big deal to most, which is why those numbers are so high for a lot of officers. They established a time directive that is more important to them than it is for handling the workplace violence inside the prisons. Many of us have always said and agreed that it is your earned time. If you wanted to use it as you see fit, then that's the end of story. But based on that, if you were accused of "abusing the use of your sick hours," then you were subjected to the consequences. The state and the union have come to agreements in bargaining sessions which makes the union enforce this with their membership. There are currently hundreds of officers statewide who have had time abuse issues. If you played golf with the time sergeant or lieutenant, camped and hung out, or knew each other on that level outside of work, that officer's issues were always overlooked. But if not, you were held to the letter of the law. As the administration superintendent mentioned earlier, "Six occasions…six? That's it?"

This goes to show you, do they go after the big guys or the ones that are not in the connection? It's discrimination, and numerous officers who have families have told me they planned to grieve and sue the department regarding the facility. In more important issues, such as weather, impassable roads, storms knocking over poles, several feet of snow, officers' vehicles that are unable to get them through the elements, driving up to barricade after barricade, putting their lives as well as others at risk due to the fact that they ordered them to report to duty, simply will end in an unfavorable result for the State of New York. As reported by COPBA's Mid-Hudson Regional Vice President Mallory, "An essential employee who reports an absence due to extreme weather conditions may be allowed to charge personal leave or annual leave if staffing levels allow for the absence. If staffing levels require the employee to report to work despite weather conditions, the employee SHOULD BE DIRECTED when reporting their unscheduled absence that they are not approved to have the day off and must report for duty as scheduled. If they do not report for duty after receiving this direction, they should be assessed an AWOL for the absence. An essential employee who reports an absence due to personal or family illness during extreme weather conditions, MUST BE DIRECTED when reporting their unscheduled absence that they must supply medical documentation for the absence. If the employee provides medical documentation, the absence will be handled in accordance with Directive 2202. If the employee fails to provide medical documentation, they should be assessed an AWOL for the absence. It is imperative that staff who are given the responsibility to take absence reports, record the specific reason the employee gave for being absent when they complete Form 1202." But in weather conditions, it's 100% with certainty that staffing levels will not allow a charge to personal accruals.

Furthermore, per Vice President Mallory, "Normal workday, tardiness, early departure, and excused absences states, 'Weather/other uncontrollable conditions.' Tardiness may be excused without charge to credits when uncontrollable conditions affect the arrival time of employees. This does not relieve employees with knowledge of adverse conditions of their responsibility to make an earlier start to assure their timely arrival at their workstation. The superintendent (for facility employees) has the authority to excuse tardiness but does not have the authority to excuse full-day absences without charge to credits. The maximum amount of tardiness which may be excused is two hours. An absence for an entire day, caused by an uncontrollable condition, cannot be excused without being entirely charged to credits. The above does not apply to tardiness of more than two hours." This is the same policy that has been in place for many years. Members are under the impression that they do not have to bring in medical documentation unless they are on "attendance control," but that is not the case. Directive 2202, Section II-B, 7 states, "In exceptional circumstances, the supervisor may exercise the right to request medical documentation for any absence charged to sick leave or family sick leave regardless of duration. A diagnosis will not be required in these circumstances." As you can see, the entire ruling looks at it from a broad perspective. For every officer, they each have their own set of circumstances during these events and should be treated as such, but this is evident that due to the mass numbers of personnel, the state has chosen to handle it with a "It's my way or the highway" matter of thinking.

Well, with that weekend being the last official one of summer before Labor Day approached, I got the chance to relax and unwind a bit with family. Everything I did though, walking, standing, whatever, I was in some sort of chronic pain. It was bearable but far from enjoyable. I caught up with some friends, many of them calling to check up on things. I was really missing out on doing my weddings, that was the bread and butter of my photography studio. Although I did not miss those hot days outdoors in the sun wearing tuxedo wear, it has always been a passion of mine, and what a better way to unleash it than on a wedding day where the happiest of all celebrations take place. Joey G and Al kept busy working weddings on the weekends, along with some other friends of mine. Sometimes though, you have to take care of yourself first. I spent 17 years prioritizing clients' needs before my own, a happy customer is a repeat customer, but there comes a time when you have to pull onto pit road to get that tune-up and new set of tires. Another friend of mine, Dave, works for Parole. He used to be a corrections officer, then moved onto corrections counselor. Then he became a state parole officer. When the state decided to merge Parole with Corrections, he soon found himself in the department again, but of course working in a different role. We were roommates when we first joined the department and were in each other's weddings. Now we are both living only miles apart, raising our families. Dave has been a big help to me in many ways, and has been very supportive. Having the days I had been having, this was a welcoming gesture for sure.

Soon enough, the 28th of August had arrived. Now my private health insurance was making inquiries about this incident. They had sent me a form asking for specific details of the incident and wanted to know my workers' compensation case information. Even though my case was still controverted, I did have assigned case numbers. They also wanted information about my doctors' visits. I am pretty sure they will be hashing all of this billing out with the State Insurance Fund. After reading and filling this information out, the phone rings; I see it's a number from the Albany area. I pick it up quick. It's the Bureau of Labor Relations' representative I had spoken to days prior. He wanted me to find him the section of the directive in Workplace Violence that requires the employer to notify the employee of their response to the investigation. I thought, wait a minute, he is supposed to know this stuff…he deals with is on a daily basis. I gave him the exact page number, section, paragraph as to where this specific wording was located. I gave him further details of the incident but he blocked all interest. He stated, "Well, good luck with your incident, the Department of Labor is investigating it now."

I told him "I will be in touch soon."

He stated, "No need to be in touch."

I countered his response, "My representatives will be in touch."

In closing, he said, "So be it."

After getting off the phone I called my lawyer leaving a message for Nick to get back to me, I needed a referral for another labor lawyer. Then my phone rang again, it was one of the investigators from the Department of Labor, his name was Jeff. We set up a meeting time and date to go over paperwork. Coincidentally, I was meeting investigators once again at a Dunkin' Donuts, this one in Saugerties, New York. It would be right after the Labor Day holiday. I started to look forward to making some progress with this.

It was time for another stress check. I went into see Dr. Ogulnick for my weekly counseling session. We had a lot of following up to do with all of these phone calls and updates. I explained that despite handling all I could with this, I was being overcome by the stress, lack of sleep, hopelessness, anxiety, and depression. I would break down just by the very thought of what was happening. I mean, here I am, broken and torn, stressed and tired, sitting still as a duck, not keeping my usual pace of my daily work schedule and activities.

It felt like many of the agencies just did not care. Even with our discussions and medications, I did not feel as if I was getting any better. I knew that in order for me to get better physically, I needed to get better mentally. Dr. Ogulnick had been so good with me, allowing me to call him almost whenever. A caring compassionate man, he too worked long hours and had to deal with so many other patients' problems.

My chiropractor, Dr. Habif, down in Spring Valley, referred me to an orthopedic surgeon, Dr. D, who has numerous office locations. My first meeting with him was in Spring Valley, where discussion ensued about the possibility of left shoulder surgery. We went into the elements of how this assault actually happened, step by step, turn by turn. We were going to await the decision about my case from the Workers' Compensation Board at my third hearing coming up. I did another follow up with Dr. D at his office in Newburgh. We went ahead and tentatively scheduled the surgery for me down in the Bronx. I had to arrange for pre-operative testing and have this done before a certain date. I was also seeing other specialists that Dr. Habif referred to me. There was a great network of physicians down in that region that accepted workers' compensation. Everyone communicated to each other, managed my treatments and handled the documentation very professionally, unlike what I have seen in other areas of the region. This network interlaced with my law firm made for a good team, someone that I needed on my side. I had appointments all around this area, from Poughkeepsie to White Plains, and from Goshen to Fishkill. Since my truck was not as good on fuel, those longer trips were made with our other vehicle which saved a lot when it all added up. There many occasions while at appointments down in Spring Valley that I often ran into other police officers from my town. We mostly went on the same days and times, even came up with the idea of possibly starting to carpool. That never panned out due to other appointments I had following those sessions. All too often I would have to run to another town in time for my next appointment. So for the meantime, we all did our own thing.

Chapter Nine
A Pound of Justice

I had arrived early on September 5th for the third and final hearing for the Workers' Compensation Board. After the routine check with security and to let the office know I was present, it was only a few minutes before my lawyer would walk in. In my hand were documents that were given to me from some other doctors, along with my multiple physical therapy receipts (each session costing an average of $60-$80), medication co-pay receipts, and my long list of mileage traveled to/from my appointments. Since there was a no-show for the case in front of us, we ended up getting called into the hearing room early at about 3:15 p.m. The judge had allowed the State Insurance Fund representative to give opening statements. I sat there on my hands, grinding my teeth, listening to these complete lies, misleading information, and contradicting material being represented by the state. They actually said that Officer Thompson was credible since how could he not be if he was just promoted to sergeant not long ago. My first thoughts hearing that were wondering if they actually did their research on this. Civil Service does not promote you to sergeant for being a good egg. If you are a good test taker, you can have zero common sense and not much education to achieve that rank. We have plenty of those around our state correctional facilities. My lawyer Jason sat close by taking notes, almost as if they were done in shorthand. I was about to burst out telling them how wrong they were. It was very difficult to sit there listening to the ten minutes of statements. The judge, sitting higher than us in the room up on his bench, spoke for a few moments before turning the floor over to our side. Jason began addressing the facts of the case, repeating previously presented materials from the other hearing, statements and reports from my doctors and testing results, and then began to tear down, piece by piece, everything that the State Insurance Fund had just stated for their case. I started to feel like we were putting points up on the board. Jason finished up with his closing statement and after a few moments, the judge had come to a conclusion and rendered his decision. It was found that the State Insurance Fund had not provided Sgt. Oswald and Deputy Oblinski for their testimony to the Board. Further, it was also found that they had not completed their state physical exams on my injuries in a timely manner. The judge went on to say, "At this time, I find in favor of Officer Harrington. His case will be established and benefits will be awarded." Officer Thompson was not found to be credible in his testimony thereby laying the groundwork we needed to further prove the serious assault and injuries inflicted upon me at Fishkill Correctional Facility on May 9, 2017. Furthermore, the testimony given by Officer Omway was not found to be credible either. At that time, Jason motioned for an adjournment date to follow up on the numbers involved regarding the reward of benefits and payments to both parties. As we departed the building, I stopped with Jason in the hallway, we spoke about what steps were next. I looked at him and shook his hand telling him, "Jason, I was worried so bad when the state opened with their statements, then you came back, showing that you did your homework on this one. Once you started speaking, a rush of relief went through me. You hit a grand slam in there! Thank you."

Off to Saugerties the next morning to meet with the two State Department of Labor investigators who I was meeting for the first time. I got there first, picked out a table in the corner and grabbed a bottle of water. Soon I saw them pull up, right away noticing the official state plates on their work vehicle. I noticed it was a woman and a man together, so I introduced myself, their names being Jeff and Penny. We exchanged some pleasantries and then got down to business. First things first. Case details. "Let's walk through this, tell us what happened, step by step, the entire incident," said Penny. She did most of the talking, Jeff was the note taker. He also had a caseload of documents with him. We had our own business meeting going on in that corner, considering a cup of coffee and a bottle of water, the use of the booth ended up being like $4.00 total. Nothing wrong with that. I ended up speaking for quite a while, stopping mid-sentence often to answer a question or two. Then came the numerous pages of a questionnaire I had to fill out, right then and there. Too many distractions and I felt rushed to get my answers down knowing they were sitting there watching me. We made for some small talk to keep things going. I also provided them with some notarized reports. The meeting itself went for

127

almost three hours. Time to get back down to the house, I thought, I had more things to do and then an appointment with Dr. O to go over my list of medications. The next day, I was actually looking forward to some relief with my pain management specialist, Dr. Kam. He ended up giving me a steroid injection into my left arm/shoulder area and gave me instructions on how to do some home exercises. We scheduled a follow-up. I felt some relief, the first in months, however temporary, at least it was something. I figured it would buy me some time before my surgery date came. Got home from that appointment and the phone rings; it's Jeff and Penny from yesterday's interview at Dunkin' Donuts. With them was their supervisor. They had me on speaker phone, and right away it sounded negative. They had gone over my case documents and said they can't do anything to help me on my complaint. I suddenly shot back saying, "We have had multiple phone interviews, I have submitted numerous supporting documents, we had the meeting yesterday and now all of the sudden you make this decision?"

"We don't handle employee matters or union issues," said their supervisor. "Since your case was awarded the other day, we are thinking there's nothing we can do for you to make you whole again as you will be seeing reimbursements soon."

They suggested that I sign a withdrawal form once they mail it to me, but I outright refused. "I want this case continued against my employer who failed to properly investigate this matter," I said in a serious voice. I have had it with these systems that are in place to help injured workers that continue to not perform their responsibilities. I explained to the three of them that the State Insurance Fund has 30 days to appeal the decision and if they do, then this case could be on hold for more than a year. We concurred that it would be a good idea to hold off until the 30 days expired, at which time I would call them back and then proceed from that point.

The calls to the State Senator's office continued on, and the person I was referred to in that office, Jim, was not very helpful. In fact, being a supervisor in that office position, he is supposed to assist their constituents especially whom are veterans during their times of serious need.

On September 11th, I finally made a trip in person to the Senator's Office in New Windsor and to my surprise, I ran into the communications director who used to be the mayor of my wife's hometown. He knew me well, as involved as I was in the region. He spoke to me along with the constituent liaison, both of them so helpful. I brought my briefcase with me giving them just about every copy they asked for. We started to get the ball rolling now and I felt as if I had some more people fighting for my side of things. I was there for about an hour, with the idea that we would follow up more by phone and email. When I got home, I decided it was now time to type up a letter, which I also had notarized, and mailed it certified return receipt to the Acting Commissioner of the Department of Corrections and Community Supervision, Mr. Anthony J. Annucci. In it were some important details from my case, and I explained to him the hardships I was facing. I further inquired as to why his own "zero tolerance" policy was not followed as the investigation initiated by Fishkill Correctional Facility. I anticipated a reply from him soon. Not hearing anything from my union local still, I drafted and typed up two letters, addressed to Fishkill's Chief Sector Steward Officer Sanka, and Regional Vice President Mallory. I mailed them both out certified return receipt on September 13th. I had hoped for at least some sort of response from Mallory. Now I had to get in touch and do some follow-ups from my prior contacts with those personal injury lawyers. We figured about what the cost of fighting this case would be versus the payout of any reward, assuming of course it would be paid, by the officer in question. It just did not seem worth it. The juice was not worth the squeeze. "Too much time, too much money," we said, my wife taking my side knowing that I would be making the best decision I could for our family. It just became so difficult, this journey in the past several months had seemed like an eternity. I got an unexpected call back from the constituent liaison at the Senator's office stating that they were making some calls and doing some follow-ups for me. All I wanted at that time was some open communication and honesty. There had to be, the situation called for it. Who the heck would go through all of this trying to fight for what happened, to make things right again, and to get what I was owed? The mail arrived. One of those green index cards with the signature of delivery came back from the Acting Commissioner's office. It was sent restricted delivery to the man himself, but obviously was signed by someone in the mail room. At least it was now at their office as I awaited a written response.

Time was growing closer for the shoulder surgery. This morning I was off to Fishkill for pre-operative testing, blood work, x-rays, you name it, the whole works, even an EKG of my heart. All of these reports needed to get back to Dr. D's office as soon as possible. With surgery now scheduled for October 4th, I waited for that date to arrive, to finally get the treatment that I needed. I had gone through the entire summer, the last five months, in pain, struggling with the neck and shoulder issues, the TMJ on my left side, as well as my already ongoing medical cases with my lower back and both knees. Dr. Habif's office had informed me that my medical equipment that was ordered had arrived. I didn't even realize it had already been ordered, but when I got there, he handed me packages, one containing a specialized back brace, and a TENS unit. If you don't know what a TENS unit is, it is a battery-powered unit that two wires plug into, and those lead to four sticky pads that you place on your skin over the areas of the injuries or symptoms. You can adjust the power for varying results and depending on my pain level at the time, the higher the frequency, the better. Keep in mind however that this is only temporary pain relief, much like taking those medications, except without the side effects. I had found myself using it a lot with a heating pad, one of the same things that they do when I go in for chiropractic care, except on a larger commercial unit.

September 20th arrived and in my mailbox I found that my other green signature card had come in finally. This one was signed by someone, but not by what appeared to be the Regional Vice President from our union. Nonetheless, I had proof that it had arrived to its intended location. Now I had to sit back and await a response. I also got another response from the State Police Acting Records Access Officer stating they received my online FOIL request and that "Due to a large volume of requests, we will not be able to send you a response until at least November 21st, or sometime before that," in regards to the investigation report on my filed supporting deposition. I figured here we go, delay delay, go away. Sitting at my computer desk, I started making some more calls, again to the Senator's office. The Communications Director and Constituent Liaison had been helping me out some, but their supervisor who I had originally contacted was always unavailable. I had heard through political affiliations it all depended on who you knew and associated with, as he did not like to deal with certain persons in those situations. I ceased my efforts with him and focused more on the others. I am not sure if there were actually any actions taken, but it sure appeared to be when I inquired. Sometimes it was by email, other times phone calls, or the occasional visit in person. I was now wondering what was going on with the OSI Investigator, Officer Tonka, with what his findings were. I thought with all that I had been finding out on my own or through other sources, something was not being played by the book with this. So I called once again to the Albany Office of Special Investigation, asking to speak to the senior investigator overseeing Tonka's progress. We spoke about the investigation, and that I knew that the case was already closed, or at least in the process of being so. What was the holdup, I thought. He said I would get a response once this is over but otherwise I would need to file a FOIL request to get that information. They were being very difficult and uncooperative to me, the one that was attacked and assaulted, in helping me get to the bottom of this. The stress levels just keep adding up…but try to keep focused, keep myself on track, I said to myself. I ended up calling a co-worker, JR, who worked with me at Fishkill for many years. Our families have joined together in the past to break bread and share some fun. I kept JR updated from time to time on what was happening. He would always reassure me that I needed to keep going on this. Even the guys I knew still working on the inside were aware of the truth and wanted to see justice done. There are always cover-ups. Where there are no cameras, there are reports made up to match, so they correspond with the supervisor before it gets passed up the line for review. If it's not on paper, it never happened. But JR told me that by now most of the talk regarding my situation had died down since so many other things were going on. Everyday things change in there throughout the multiple buildings throughout Fishkill's large complex facility. JR kept me on track saying, "Go get them, you are doing the right thing, you have won your case, all they have is denials, denials, denials." I had appreciated hearing things from that perspective. That kept me thinking positively. Like I said before, there are quite a few people I still hear from in there, but not one peep from the administration. Not even a welfare check to see how I am doing. Apparently, I have pissed them off with the pursuit of this investigation by involving outside agencies. I have personally seen this happen there in other days when there was a different administration running the show there. As state employees, sure, we have badge numbers, but it's our "line number" that counts. That's the item they hold open for your job. If that item closes, you get reassigned, or in larger cases, laid off. There is a bad mix of politics of what you see in private industry and civil service with the rights that employees have inside these institutions. We are not names, we are numbers. Sure, you might have lots of family in there, and many do. If a boss has family members looking for a decent paying job with benefits, you can bet they are already in the door there, skipping the process that the normal folks off the street have to do to apply for a civilian job. There is so many family members in there. Both on the civilian and security sides.

I finally got to get in for another appointment with Dr. Newton, the psychiatrist who was referred to me by my psychologist. He had such a full schedule, and whatever you had to say, you had better do it in 45 minutes or so. He was a great documenter just like my other treating doctors. We had spoken about recent updates as he sat in his chair facing me from the opposite side of the room. I was on a small sofa; there were no couches in there to lay on while we interviewed. Next to him was a small end table that had a phone on it with a few other notes. The tall lamp that was plugged into the wall behind it had a small lampshade. I kept looking at the lamp. It was to the far right of the table. Literally it looked as if it was going to fall off the edge, leaning slightly off balance. I remember from my previous visits that this had been the same way. No other clients had said, "Hey Doc, move your lamp over, it looks like it's going to fall off the table." Probably because like me, they had too much on their mind to be bothered by that. But for some reason, I kept looking at it. My stress was through the roof already. Dr. Newton had a very soothing calm voice as he replied back to me, all the while taking down notes, capturing my thoughts at the time. I needed prescriptions filled so I gave him my updated list. I told him that I am extremely depressed. I needed to be around people that understood my situation. My wife has even told me that I was a completely different person lately. My anxiety and blood pressure continued to be problems when I was dealing with these people who were turning a blind eye to this cover-up and refused to get out of their chair to help. I went further to explain that the Workers' Comp Board had rendered a decision in my favor, awarding me for my adjustment disorder and left shoulder, but not yet my neck. I did not know why they excluded this part, I had been treated for it that night in the emergency room, and on follow-ups with my other doctors. The MRI even showed my injuries of the neck. I continued to make my plea for assistance, I am being told no, one way or the other. Between all of the agencies involved right now, there were going to be more in the future as well I thought. This was not going to be over anytime soon. My nearly 23 years of service with this department has gone down the drain because of my inability to work due to all of the injuries I have received from inmate-related incidents, as well as the most recent one involving Thompson, who continues to work free of any inconveniences. We wrapped up the session and I headed over to the pharmacy to pick up my medication refills.

The next morning, I woke up not feeling so well, having been awake much of the night with these thoughts running through my head. But mostly it was because of the pain in my neck and shoulder. I even had to use a smaller pillow. Laying flat was ok, but then I favored to lie on my left side but continued on my right. Because I could not deal with the pain on the left side, my right side began to hurt from the continued pressure, coupled by the fact that my neck injuries were causing shoulder pain down through my arm as well. I could not escape this. It was constant. This would take a normal person and break them. It is way too much for one person's body to handle. I gave a quick call to Dr. Ogulnick, I was not feeling well, I felt as if I was going into crisis. I described all that I had been feeling and I started to have ideation. All of that came from the anxiety, feeling trapped, hopelessness, withdrawal, anger, mood changes, and recklessness. These are all warning signs, according to the National Association of Suicide Prevention. I got one of these letters attached to my payroll check back around the beginning of September in the form of a memo, with the subject line being "Prevention of Suicide by Staff." Over my tenure at Fishkill, we have seen more than our fair share of suicides at the prison, both by officers and civilian staff. More than one is too many. It is a real sad occasion for all. We always hear others say, "Never saw that coming, he/she didn't appear to look as if…or they didn't act out differently." Statistically, if and when someone cries out for help, they actually want the intervention, the help. It's when you never hear from a person and then they act, that's the real problem. It's a problem we cannot see. There are so many issues at work that we as human beings are supposed to deal with, to "man up" and handle it. That gets bottled up and stored away until the next incident, and then the vicious cycle starts all over again. Reaching out for help, when needed, usually involves someone who is trained to speak to you and to help you. It is their job to do so. A counselor is not the same as a psychologist, sometimes a person just needs a quick chat and a friendly hug, others need more in-depth therapy. Having gone what I have gone through does not make me a good candidate for just a counselor on a hotline that I can't see face to face. Sometimes it even goes beyond what a doctor can say or do for you. Medications or whatever. If you continue to be surrounded by that troubling environment, then you really are only putting a Band-aid on it all. If this entire incident was correctly handled from the start back on May 9th, I would not be in the situation I am in as badly. I of course would have had no out-of-pocket costs, I would have been treated more fairly, I would not have had to endure this pain the entire summer, you name it. We are all human. We all have a breaking point. It does not matter what your title or status is, who you are or what you do. To err is to be human. Had I walked away from this cover-up, lack of communication, zero due process, disability discrimination, and many other issues I have already described, maybe I would be better off. Or would I be? To walk away with this much injury, this much damage, a career-ending change of lifestyle is not the answer I want. What about my photo business, the fire department, my community efforts, do I just shut up and throw it all away so that this one individual can walk away from it unscathed and without penalty?

I was beginning to wonder why our union president wanted me to contact the regional vice president when in fact I had done so three weeks ago, via certified mail. I still heard no response, and he knows how to get in touch with me for sure. We know way too many people in the same social circles. So off I went to the post office and spoke to the postmaster to find out where my missing certified letter to Chief Sector Steward Sanka was at. After some quick research, she told me that it was at the post office in Beacon, so she called over there. They had sent out two notices for it to be picked up. Apparently, how this process works for the jail is that a civilian truck driver drives over to the Beacon Post Office each weekday to pick up the facility's mail. I was able to speak to him when I stopped by work that day to check in on some things. It had been picked up at Beacon's Post Office and brought to Fishkill Correctional Facility's mail room located on the second floor of the Administration Building. I popped into the mail room and spoke to the ladies working in there, right away they had both recalled my name and the series of certified letters that had come in addressed to Officer Sanka. They had not been able to get him to stop upstairs in the mail room to pick up his letter, so it went back to Beacon's Post Office. Furthermore, they said, "We told him he had to go down to the post office to sign for his certified mail," and he said to them he was not sure what he was signing for so he refused. I could not believe it when I heard that. Crazy. The facility's Chief Sector Steward and he couldn't do his job and refused to sign for his officially addressed certified mail.

I had heard from a friend who works at the Duchess County District Attorney's Office and after explaining further into what my situation was, she put me through to one of the assistant district attorneys who was the "Officer of the Day." I had called and left her a message and by the next afternoon she returned my call. It was simply a call to follow up and confirm that this was not a situation that they would handle. There would need to be criminal charges, which were lodged in the supporting deposition to State Police but never pressed. Not surprised, I thought. The same D.A. has been in that office for numerous years. He has not been an advocate for pursuing criminal charges on inmates either. Their answer, we were told at work, was that they did not have the time, budget, or staff to go after a conviction of someone who is already locked up. That's relative to inmate-related assaults on staff, and most days if it involves a mental health inmate, you can't even get inside charges brought upon the him due to his capacity. It's a struggle, it's a thankless job, and it's already bad enough in there to deal with all of these issues, including the drugs and gang violence, let alone watching out for someone wearing the same uniform as you. My wife had so much to handle now, with every portion of this case falling upon us as it did, the loss of the business income, and all of the assorted trauma. She decided to write her letter to the acting commissioner's office on October 1st. That too was sent certified.

"Dear Commissioner Annucci, my husband Paul has been involved in a very serious situation at Fishkill CF on the afternoon of May 9, 2017. I was notified my husband was brought to the emergency room via ambulance that evening where he was treated for neck and shoulder injuries, among also having an anxiety attack over this entire incident. Paul had started working his new post on March 1st while on the afternoon shift. Not long afterward he began having problems with Officer Thompson. I was under the impression during that time period prior to the physical assault my husband was being harassed and intimidated while working his newly-assigned post. He told me then there was a safety issue in reporting such incidents. My husband has mentioned, along with other employees I know, that this happens when someone does not want you working in their area. Since the evening of May 9th, my husband has not returned to work due to the numerous injuries shown from his MRI exams, physical therapy reports, and other testing. On October 4th, he goes in for major shoulder surgery and is also being seen for the neck injuries he sustained, as well as the left sided TMJ, and for the work-related stress issues at hand. He is being seen by over a dozen medical specialists and has well over 90 appointments so far and on several medications. Additionally,

135

his doctors have diagnosed him with work-related stress, anxiety, PTSD, and depression. My husband is not the only victim here, we have 8-year-old kids. My husband has always worked hard to support his family while with the state and also owning a corporate photography studio for the last 18 years. My husband has been unable to work at all. He has been a pillar of our community receiving various awards from state, county, and local officials. We are suffering from this officer's actions economically, physically, mentally, and emotionally. I have to take on the extra tasks beside working and raising our kids to fulfill the duties in which he cannot do at this time. It's hard enough to deal with the hazards of a prison environment with the inmates, let alone have to deal with a fellow officer one has to work with. My husband has endured three surgeries from inmate assaults in the past. I need you to know that I am concerned for his safety and well-being. The bad dreams about the situation are hard enough to deal with, especially at the hands of a supervisor who my husband reported this to that evening that wanted him to report the incident differently in an attempt to save harm on Officer Thompson. My husband is very well known in the area. He has spent decades of his time as a volunteer firefighter, having recently forced to take leave from his position due to these injuries. He has spoken up about suicidal thoughts in the past especially dealing with the 2015 homicide, with everything being bottled up. My husband showed me the directive you signed on workplace violence which I have read. It does not appear that Fishkill CF actually reported this as a violation of this zero-tolerance directive, in an effort to protect themselves and Thompson. The only good that has come from this so far is when the NY State Workers' Comp Board found Thompson's testimony not credible and awarded my husband his medical benefits and payments. I also know that Officer Thompson is the brother-in-law of the union's vice president. I now understand why he has been so well protected.

"My husband and I have been in contact with multiple people to report this incident. I am very upset about how this is being handled. My family, as well as Paul's, has had it with the system's lack of due process. We intend to take this as far as it has to go. We have numerous documents and logbooks since this incident has started that host the information needed to pursue this matter further. I need you to know that we are expecting a response as soon as possible. I apologize to disrupt your busy schedule but this needs to be reinvestigated."

Now to me, that letter would be convincing enough to take a further look into the matter. I can tell you from experience that if it was from an inmate's family, most likely it would be done right away, but not likely for employees.

Some news came in from the Senator's office, from the Constituent Liaison. She asked me, "Paul, did you ever contact PERB (Public Employee Relations Board) yet?"

Surprised, I replied, "NO, actually, I never thought of it. Do you have the information? I appreciate it!"

Within moments, she handed me the piece of paper with the phone number to call them. As I got home, I got on the phone and made the call to them, and they put me on the phone with an administrative law judge whose name was Bill. He explained so much to me and was helpful. He guided me through their website and told me which form I had to fill out. Once I started to do this form, I realized you needed a professor, a lawyer, and doctor to complete the form, so I called him back for some quick answers. I ended up filling out the form to file an Improper Practice Charge. With it, I attached 18 pages of supporting documentation. They wanted four additional copies made, so in all I had a large stack of 100 pages of forms, packaged up and sent certified up to the PERB office in Albany. A couple days later, I received notification that it was received. I also forward a copy of this back to the Senator's office as well. At that point, from their end, they had told me that they forwarded it onto three different agencies.

Chapter Ten

Under the Knife

Time to get some rest, I thought. Within hours I would be up and at them, getting ready for my ride at 7:00 a.m. down to New York City to have my shoulder surgery. I was told by Dr. D's office's staff that a car service would be showing up to pick me up at that time, and that I needed someone to escort me down and stay with me after I got out of surgery. So, I got ahold of my mother-in-law, Esther, a few days prior to meet me here at my house that morning early. 7:00 a.m. sharp and in pulled the "car service," a yellow Spanish cab with a driver who did not speak English, well, not so fluently. So, we climbed in as my wife chuckled, holding her coffee cup while the kids waited for their school bus. Off we tore down the road into the city of Newburgh, stopping at an apartment building to pick up another person having surgery along with her mother. Now with the four of us in the back, those van shocks seemed like they were at the end of their life span. Every bump and pothole was a wakeup call to hold on for dear life. Our driver was heading up Interstate 84 as we were on our way to the Taconic Parkway. He figured he would beat the traffic instead of going down the thruway, all the while referring to his GPS on the phone. We were passing cars like it was a NASCAR race. My poor mother-in-law sitting in front of me, those other ladies, it was the ride of our life. But not the type that one would be looking forward to. A few missed exits and here I am thinking, we won't make it on time. Every driver from Connecticut and New York on the Taconic that day was blowing their horns at us. With a bit of ease, and about 20 minutes more, we had arrived to our location in the Bronx. We could not get out of that van quick enough. Those poor ladies were saying, "Lord Jesus, help us" the whole way down. I thought, well, might as well keep those prayers going. We are about to go under the knife. I was called up to the desk to check in, and they had a stack of papers there for me to sign and initial. I noticed a few printed sheets of labels with my name and date of birth on it, as they stuck them to each sheet. I took a closer look about midway through and I stopped the receptionist in all of her productivity. I said, "Miss, did you notice the labels? They said I was born in 1917 and I am now 100 years old!" She turned red and apologized, blaming the error on someone else that must have done that. If I am at that age, you can forget the surgery, that's for sure. They soon brought me into pre-op, sitting me down after I put on my one-size-fits-all hospital gown. I had flashbacks to the last time I put one of those on, the night of the homicide in 2015 at the prison. Not such a pretty sight, I thought, but looking all around the room, all of us were wearing them, it was like a toga party except for bare butts peeking out. The anesthesiologist came to see me and to verify a few things, a very young doctor, a Korean woman, she was very pleasant to reassure me that all would be well for this routine of hers. She was off to the next patient, like an assembly line, which it was. Then I got to see Dr. D, hardly recognizing him all bloused up, wearing surgical hat and mask, and he wanted to verify where my surgery would be so he took a black magic marker and wrote on my left shoulder. They hooked me up to EKG wires and an IV giving me some meds and before I knew it, I was in the operating room. Last thing I recall is that when they sat me up, I saw a number of the staff scrambling because I did not fit on the operating table. Apparently, I was the tallest one there that day for surgery. Someone came in rolling an extension into the room to make things do for the time being, as everyone had a schedule to keep. "Didn't anyone look at my height on the chart?" I said to myself, as I went nighty night in the operating room. A couple hours and soon I was awake in recovery. Dr. D, my surgeon, had come in for 30 seconds to see how I was doing and showed me photos of everything they had done with my shoulder injuries. They had to make several holes in my shoulder to do this surgery, arthroscopic as they call it. The pain block they gave me would keep me sufficed for about 24 hours or less, and they prescribed me my medications right there to bring home. Great, I thought, more to add to my collection. Since it was same-day surgery, they got me out of there pretty fast. With my arm wrapped tightly and all stitched up, they put me into a special arm sling and off we went back into the crazy cab to head north. Same seating assignments. I managed to get our driver to stop at the McDonald's drive thru for me. "Get me a #6 medium," I quipped; boy was I starved. No one else wanted to eat. I had been fasting since early the night before so it was well-deserved. It took less time going home so we got there fast. He dropped us off first. Right inside the house to the recliner I went. The next morning, we scheduled an appointment for 10 days later to get those stitches out and to schedule physical therapy. In the meantime, a man was at my door with some furniture. I thought, did we win something? It was a chair for physical therapy, equipped with a mechanical arm that takes pre-programmed cards that exercise and move your arm around to get your shoulder loose and moving again. They wanted this done three times a day for a month. Between this unit, my back and knee braces, TENS unit, arm slings, and the ice cooler with the hose pack connection, it started to look like a nursing home around here. It was about that time now with 30 days passing that the State Insurance Fund did not appeal the board's decision, so I called the State Department of Labor back and spoke to Penny and her supervisor. I told them outright that I refused to sign a withdrawal form. They continued to interview me regarding the adverse actions for my complaint. They had to send Fishkill paperwork in which they would have to respond to in 10 days. Once they returned it for review, Penny said they will then process it and proceed if need be to the next step.

Dr. Habif set me up with an appointment to go and see Dr. Kam. I had seen him before and at this session he had planned to give me a series of four injections into the back of my neck. There were like a nerve block, where his plan was to stop the pain going up from my bulging discs that were causing me headaches every day. Before this injury, I rarely if ever had headaches. I was at wit's end. I had to try something. Too many meds every day, along with those side effects were a lot to deal with. Dr. Kam was a very strong-willed man. He always had a way to make you see it how he does. Whatever the issue was, he had a way of getting you to go with the treatment he suggested. His office staff had to keep on the ball, and when he asked for something, he wanted it five minutes ago. We proceeded on with the injections. Leaning me over the exam table while I was sitting in a chair, he proceeded with his first injection. Probably the worst pain I ever felt in my neck. He did these by hand and eye. Now that the first one was done, time for the second one. Wow, was that one worse? It had to be the same but the pain being that great, by now I was hoping that he had not hit anything important. After the third one was done, I told him, "Doc, I am done, please, no more."

He replied, "Shhhh, hold on a second, stay still, here it comes…." BAM! I was literally on fire, and soon enough the numbness set in, mostly in my neck and head area, but the headache relief was minimal, and the whole effect of his efforts would only last me a few days.

"I'm not doing that again," I thought to myself on the way home. He gave me instructions and a lecture about the medications I was prescribed by other doctors. He had made some suggestions for me to abide by, in order to protect my best interest with my health in mind. I made it home by lunchtime and got in touch with my lawyer Jason, then stopped by Dr. D's office in Newburgh to get a copy of my operative report. I was still in the arm sling at the time, so it made it difficult at times when I had to handle documents and such. I had to get this report off to AFLAC for my disability claim again; with the new surgery, it's another claim. Anything at this point would help out. No outside income from the business, and it was wedding season. When I got to the office, there was some miscommunication and apparently I had been misinformed as to when the reports would be ready. Having surgeries in the past, I had been used to getting them right away, but Dr. D's Office worked under a different policy and schedule. I had reached out to Dr. Habif about this since he had made the original referral and by the next day, everything was taken care of. This doc was a magician. He was definitely the advocating physician I needed during this difficult time.

Interesting news has come about reported by NY Fair that as you may have heard, after two decades without any meaningful rate increase, the Workers' Compensation Board ("the Board") has proposed a new medical schedule of fees that increases rates of reimbursement for most services and most providers throughout the healthcare industry. However, some of the proposals threaten to severely restrict access to healthcare for injured workers and automobile accident victims. Most troubling is a proposal to limit physical therapy to 12 visits within 180 days and eliminate the existing medical necessity standard. Proposed Ground Rule 2 provides: Physical medicine services may not exceed 12 sessions/visits per patient per accident or illness, or be rendered more than 180 days from the first session/visit. This proposed ground rule must be stopped! This rule will have dire consequences for many injured workers and all accident victims. The proposed ground rule denies patient access to care prescribed under the No-Fault statute; takes away the medical necessity standard for physical medicine, thereby restricting provider ability to practice medicine and act in the best interest of the patient; irreparably harms people who are underinsured or have a high deductible; was not formulated based on medical evidence; and directly conflicts with the enabling No-Fault statute.

There is a vote being done by the NY State Workers' Compensation Board. Although this change is to include accidents, it also involves work-related injuries as well and does not allow for the fair and equal treatment of the victims who are being once again victimized by the system. This also puts considerable hardship on the medical providers. It is not fair and just goes to prove that these state officials are putting the needs of themselves first. Most would think that this affects the average taxpayer, but it does not. Most of these costs alone come from employers' premiums and state budgets involving monies collected in fees, tolls, fines, assessments, and depending on your union, the injured worker as well, and by that I refer to the use of their personal time before the start of their compensation time.

It was now our wedding anniversary, so I had to be sure the flowers got delivered to the Mrs. while she was at work, and to make sure we were all set for dinner at Cosimo's on Union, where we had gone to eat on our first date. The room at the restaurant was buzzing as it usually does, a really popular place with some nice signature dishes. My favorite has always been the grilled chicken penne. Anyone else who has had this at Cosimo's would certainly agree. We had the kids so it was busy at the table trying to keep them occupied. We waited until we got home to enjoy an adult beverage since we were out to eat with the kids. It was a nice break to take my mind off from things; I felt as if this time I had now with my new schedule, allowed me to immerse myself as my own advocate attempting to right the wrong, fix the broken, heal the pain, and get truth from the lies.

The next morning many emails came in from the lawyers and some of the agencies. We were working on establishing my neck injuries for this case. This had not been included in the award of benefits for my case. My neck was strained the night of the assault and I had been treated for it at the emergency room, and additionally the next day, it had been listed, as required, on the C-3 form that my lawyer's office had filled out. Soon we would know a date for the scheduled hearing. Then another call came in from Jeff at the NY State Department of Labor. They asked me permission to use my name for their investigation of the facility. My reply was, "Of course, at this point, they are well aware of who had filed these notices." The State Insurance Fund started packing my mailbox with C-8.1 forms, basically a fancy name for their disputed bills, which most of them were from my neck and TMJ treatments. It was a matter of formality as I sent them off to my law firm who would bring the matters up at the next hearing and handle it from there.

I had been in touch with Father K, our priest from the church not so far from our home. He knew well of my issues, as he was updated often. Every day was full of its ups and downs. I really just wanted this to all be done with. Part of me said that, but most of the time I had been reassured by many that I needed to continue the fight to do the right thing. You did not have to hide anything from Father K. He could take anything you tossed at him. It was nice to have that. I was always telling him this favorite quote of mine from the movie, A Bronx Tale. "I don't know, Father, your guy might be bigger than my guy up there, but my guy is bigger than your guy down here!" There had to be some comedic moments with this, generally in life, you can't take that too serious either. So here we are now, it is October 13th, the mailbox is full again, mostly advertisements and political ads as Election Day began to draw close. In the mix, I found a white envelope addressed to me from the Department of Corrections up in Albany. I figured this had to be some response from my letter to the Acting Commissioner. It read, "Dear Mr. Harrington, Acting Commissioner Annucci has asked me to respond to your letter of September 12, 2017 regarding an alleged workplace violence incident at Fishkill CF. I have been advised by members of my staff that your allegations have been investigated by the Department's Office of Special Investigation. The allegations you advanced were not substantiated. Disciplinary matters are considered confidential, any action taken against other employees will not be disclosed. It has come to my attention that the NY State Police made a mental health referral for you after you repeatedly pressured them to prosecute a criminal complaint against another employee. Your assertion that you are experiencing PTSD with anxiety might give one pause and reason to seek professional services. As the Director of Public Relations previously informed you, the state may not interfere with internal union matters. Any issues you are having with union representatives are matters we cannot assist you with. The Office of Special Investigation will notify you about the completion of their investigation soon. Sincerely, Daniel F. Martuscello III, Deputy Commissioner for Administrative Services."

Reading this letter would make one think that even the Commissioner himself does not enforce his own "zero tolerance work place violence" policies and directives. This only confirms that his office, along with the other agencies mentioned in the letter, had ignored my complaint about the abuse, or were "deliberately indifferent" toward me, basically saying the allegations and charges were untrue. This letter was full of opinionated statements, false information, and misleading details. Several of the allegations were substantiated, both during the "facility investigation" of the hand-written harassing note, and of my witness, Officer Potter, who had indicated the actions of Officer Thompson that day, and furthermore, that of the NY State Workers' Compensation Board who found Thompson NOT credible in his testimony, had thereby awarded me my injury case for treatment due to his assault on me. Going into this letter further, the Deputy Commissioner additionally states that the State Police were repeatedly pressured by me to press charges and made a mental health referral on me? When and where, Mr. Martuscello? It is well-documented in my logbook and case documents that this is untrue. In final thoughts about the claims in the reply of this letter, the Director of Public Relations was not even contacted originally about the union. As I stated before, he had to input both my name and Thompson's into the computer system and we were not in there. There are a few ways that an Office of Special Investigation case against an officer who has allegedly done any wrongdoing can come out. "Substantiated" means the officer did it; "unsubstantiated" means the officer may or may not have done it, but there's insufficient proof either way, and "unfounded" which means the incident did not occur at all.

Now that it was time to get those stitches out, I had made it over to Dr. D's office on Broadway. I was seen by his assistant who not only removed the stitches, but placed sutures on my wounds and gave me follow-up instructions on physical therapy, along with other work documentation. It kind of felt good to be moving along on the progress of my shoulder surgery, but the pain was ever so great, especially laying down at night to go to sleep. The minute you roll onto this shoulder, no matter what meds you're on for the pain, it has you wide awake. After I finished up with that appointment, I figured I would make my way over to the State Senator's office to see my contacts. They sent the department's letter that I received from the Deputy Commissioner to three other agencies. By now they had also gotten the Attorney General's office involved. I also got to follow-up once again with the Public Employee Relations Board and spoke to an administrative law judge. We had spoken before, going over the charges I was about to file. I was getting to the point now that I really needed to see about that labor lawyer. The judge had told me I could do this myself, but it would be better to get legal representation since more than likely they would have it on their side. I had gotten a referral from Father K to a local law firm that has labor lawyers. He had called upon a local town judge for a name who might be able to assist me. Father K had called me with the news. "Give these guys a call," he mentioned. So with that, right after lunchtime, I had called Jacob and Gubitz, and spoke to their intake handlers. Within the hour, I had a call back from them to take some details down. We went over what the expenses would be like and after tossing some numbers around, we concurred that this would be taken to the next level. I had to email several documents and further discuss the merits of the case, whether they could take it or not (Like most law firms, they pick and choose what's going to be the grand slam for them. Obviously, who would want to be in the business of losing money, right?) I had a copy of the Union Steward's training manual and had sent that over to this form as well. With the breach of the Duty of Fair Representation, this required very specific information. That's what they needed, and that's what PERB also wanted.

Chapter Eleven
The Worst Day of My Life

The 24th of October had arrived. I awoke with the usual routine, getting myself ready, slowly but surely, with all of the joint pain in the neck, shoulder, knees, as well as my lower back. Little did I know how bad this day was about to turn out. Just about time to get the kids off to school. As soon as their bus came, I took off heading south to Spring Valley to see Dr. Habif for my chiro appointment, and to Core Care Physical Therapy for my left shoulder treatment. I had just got home from the appointments after lunch and spoke to Dean again, giving him updates and I had asked him as a reminder that our conversation details would remain confidential, with his position as an Employee Assistance Coordinator and all. I had told him about the letters that I got in the mail. I was managing, but didn't know what to expect with the bad news coming at me from the left and right. I had a few questions for an author named Ted Conover; he had written the book Newjack: Guarding Sing Sing. I sent him a message on Facebook asking him for some advice as I had begun to prepare writing my manuscript. When I had met him, I took a photo with him at that book store in New Paltz. It was back around the year 2000, and when he autographed it, had said, "Paul, be careful in there." That was advice one could take with only five years or so on the job that I had on my seniority back then, but the long haul was yet ahead for the next 20 years. I knew he would soon get back to me. I tried his website but that was not up and running. I figured for sure everyone is on social media so that made it easy to find him. So I get a call back from my lawyer at Jacob and Gubitz. She said there was nothing they could do with my case, there would be no monetary benefit at the end and the costs would not be worth going to trial. I explained to her that I needed the immediate representation for this Improper Practice Charge, but she apologized and declined, ending the conversation. I immediately called

Father K, since it was him that referred me to them so I could update him on what transpired. I then called one of my lawyers, Warren, catching him at a bad time. Apparently, he was in a meeting but he had picked up his phone so I thought he would be able to talk briefly. "What's wrong? Is this an emergency? I am busy right now and can't talk." I tried to explain to him the crisis I felt like I was about to have. Apparently, the cell service in some parts of my house breaks up, so it made for a hard time of communicating, so I hung up. Everyone has a breaking point, we are all human, but I was tired and I just couldn't take it anymore. I had tried and tried but it all fell upon deaf ears. Here I am in a really bad situation caused by this department that I gave over two decades of service to. I caved in. Everything just poured out. Between the violence that affected me at that facility, the numerous inmate assaults inflicted on me, the homicide investigation, as well as the number of surgeries I had to have or already did, it was all finally catching up to me. There was something happening that I could no longer deal in my mind with this system, its cover-up, and corruption. At that moment, I had this tunnel vision, and started making decisions without thinking of the outcome or the serious nature of the consequences. The kids were already home from school so I immediately sent them across the street to their friend's house. I did not want them to be around at that time. I did try to reach out without doing anything harmful at first. I had texted Mike next door, Father K, my wife, and Lt. Richards from work. Nobody except for Richards was immediately available to get over to my place. Richards got there in only moments, the far usual from my requests to have him over. He told me he was not sure what was going on so he came right over thinking we were just going to have a talk. Security camera footage in my house shows some of my movement at that time. I went upstairs and grabbed my fully loaded and chambered 12-gauge shotgun. I took it outside onto my back deck, as I was going through the kitchen, I had dialed 911 and hung up. I was sitting on my back deck steps in my Corrections officer uniform with the gun in the upright position leaning up against the railing within reach, but I did not have it in my hands. I was literally upset, hardly able to speak. Before I knew it, Richards came walking around the corner of the house looking surprised, not expecting the scenario unfolding in front of him. I motioned for him to keep his distance as he approached me. He started asking me questions. "What's wrong? Does this have to do with your case? Who are you dealing with?" I was able to get some answers out to him, but I needed to focus on what I was doing. I had no idea, that was the problem. I was in crisis. One does not think clearly when in such a situation. It seemed like about five minutes passed by. Richards had started making calls to his wife, my wife, and then his phone started to ring back. "Yes, I'm here, I can't talk now, bye," he mentioned quickly into the phone. I heard my dogs starting to bark inside the house. I told Richards I think the police are here now. He took several steps backward, not turning his back on me to peek around the corner of my house. "Yes, they're here," he said, "wait here for a minute, Paul, stay where you are at." As he walked off, I thought to myself, "Where am I going to go?" What seemed like an eternity of his absence was only two minutes. I later found out he had to explain to a couple of new cops in front of my house that there was a situation involving me with a gun behind the house. They had originally responded to check on the 911 hang-up call, those usually being a false alarm or kids playing with the phone. Apparently, those two town of Newburgh Police officers' eyes got really big and immediately one of them squabbled into the radio mic about the call being a gun-related incident. When Richards came back around the corner of the back to see me again, the cops were not with him. I stood up and noticed that with the sunset casting shadows, I could see the shadows of two people coming up along the wall of the house of what looked like them crouched down moving slowly. I peeked over the deck rail and looked down upon those two officers on the ground. As to both of our surprise, they had their eyes locked on mine, as big as baseballs as I stood over them. I backed off and said, "I'm done! I can't go through with this," and walked off the deck as the cops ran up onto the deck to secure the weapon. I could hear sirens coming from all directions as the entire force had been sent to the scene. Richards walked me over to our backyard fire pit and sat down with me. "Good job, Paul, you did the right thing, you made a good decision. We need to get you someone to talk to, get you checked out." More and more cops started pouring into the yard. I knew quite a few of them, and even the sergeant that eventually arrived as well. My wife had gotten home while this was going on, and Rich, my fire chief, had heard the radio communication on the scanner about the call at my residence. He came up to the scene to make sure everyone was ok. My fearful wife came outside with cops, and our two dogs headed right for me to see what I was doing with all this activity in the yard. Once I spoke to a number of people there, I went inside my house and up to my bedroom on the second floor while escorted by the officers so I could get changed out of my state uniform into some comfortable clothes. I came outside, there had to be about 7-8 police cars still there in from of my house, in my driveway, on the road. My neighbors outside in their yards had looked on with concern. I gave them a wave goodbye as we got in one of the cruisers. The sergeant had said that they were going to give me a courtesy ride over to Orange Regional Medical Center to speak to some specialists. There would be no need for an ambulance, and since there was no crime committed or any charges on me, I was able to walk freely without being handcuffed. I went voluntarily to the "access" area of the ORMC emergency room. I had my wallet, cell phone, and badge/ID with me. In my mind, I began thinking how I was walking into the hospital, not being rolled in, or even worse. I have experienced way too many officers and civilians commit suicides that worked with at Fishkill, and those that committed it had shocked everyone, nobody had any idea. Statistically, the Department of Corrections has one of the highest divorce and suicide rates amongst its rank and file. Upon arrival to ORMC, I walked into the registration area with the officers, and I got my wristband while we awaited security to come escort us into the unit. "Is he being committed?" asked the security officer.

"No!" waving both arms to clarify, "NO, he is not," said one of the town police officers I was with. "We are just giving him a courtesy ride here." Soon, I was led into a curtained closet space with a bench and changed into some provided hospital smocks and pants. Taking all of my personal property, the security staff had to inventory everything. The one thing I was allowed to keep was my wedding band. They then led me into a holding area and I went into this room, it was bare, with nothing on the walls. Inside it was a mattress and bed frame, a couple of chairs, and a night stand. Almost immediately three doctors had come in to interview me. We got about five minutes into discussion and they all had to run out for an emergency. "Two more inbound!" I heard someone yell. All of the sudden, cops and security were wrestling on the floor trying to restrain a combative man and woman. It was chaotic for about a minute, but then it was moved out of the area. Things got quiet and I was given a peanut butter and jelly sandwich. Great, I thought, I just had this for lunch. About an hour later, my wife arrived with her aunt who is a nurse at Orange Regional. They brought me some more food from the hospital cafeteria. We got about 20 minutes for a visit and the staff came back in. One of the unit's staff nurses came in to the room.

"Paul, based on the details of this situation, we are going to keep you for observation. You will be moved to a room on the second floor soon."

I was then given some meds, and as tired as I was getting, a gentleman came down to get me, bringing me up to the second floor unit. I was shown to my private room by the nurse while she went over paperwork in a folder for me to review and also spoke about the house rules. I was so tired, it was already 1:30 a.m., and I just wanted to lay down. We had to be up for breakfast by about 6:45 a.m. the next morning.

Chapter Twelve
The Stay at The Holiday Inn

When I woke up to take a shower, it was like a bad dream had become reality. All I had to wear still were those hospital clothes from the prior evening. After a quick clean-up in the shower, I was out the door down the hall to the dining room for my breakfast tray. They did a good job feeding us really well. The food was almost gourmet and plentiful, best hospital food anywhere. The room I was in had been occupied by a man who had torn things off the wall, so the walls were bare, save for the fact that there were numerous spots on the walls of unknown dried-up fluids, some of it saliva, urine colors, and who knows what. I was told by the nurse that the previous occupant had also flushed his t-shirt down the toilet which rendered my toilet useless. I had to use an alternate bathroom for my stay there whenever it acted up. The bed sheets were not full size, I had two of them and a regular white blanket. All of them were stained with gray and black marks all over them. I had asked the roaming housekeeping janitor about it and the guy told me, "Hey, this ain't the Holiday Inn!" He was in the halls chatting up with the female patients more than he was doing his job. But those were the same sheets I had to use for my entire stay. This all reminded me of the prison, we had areas very similar to this layout. About twice a day you would see security running up inside this unit for emergencies that they termed as "Code Gray." A few of these security staff in the secured entrance area were armed with what appeared to be semi-automatic side arms, but only patrolled certain areas where patients could not get access to them. They stayed mostly outside of the unit, just like in our prison setting. The other security officers came in to take physical charge of the patient until the doctors could give them a needle to settle them down.

That first morning when I walked down the hallway, trying to find my way around this new maze, a patient walked up to me staring me down and all the sudden began to scream in my face, having no idea what he was saying. He took off in a sprint and ran into an older woman around the corner, knocking her down to the floor. Every time I turned around, someone was screaming, kicking doors, breaking out in fights, one guy even wanted to sign himself out by rushing through the partially opened security doors only to be immediately tackled by staff. I continued to walk the halls looking around to orientate myself. It was always a good thing to familiarize yourself with your surroundings. Just like in the prison that I walked inside of day and day out, I could not take being there. All they did was separate you from your family. It was a fixer upper. Making sure of your safety, ensuring you took your meds and saw the doctor, that was about it for treatment. On that first day, I sat down and met with a group of five specialists there in a private room. They had asked me all about what I do in life and what happened to me. I went into numerous details and was stopped mid-sentence by one of the doctors, "How do you do so much work?"

I replied, "There's 24 hours in a day, I make good use of it." I told them that statistically, if someone calls for help, then they want it, they want the intervention. If you are going to commit suicide or hurt yourself, you're just going to do it without calling. They all nodded in agreement. We talked for about 30 minutes, and then they had a discussion to see what the plan would be for me. I was told by nurses there that normally most people stay for seven days, or 15, sometimes longer. I was already getting homesick and missing the kids, wife, and dogs.

I had inquired a few times that day about getting my required physical therapy for my shoulder from my nurses and doctors. This had been prescribed to me since I had just gotten left shoulder surgery on the multiple tears of the left shoulder from the Thompson assault. There seemed to be no problem with it, they agreed on it and said that someone would be up to see me. But nobody ever showed up to offer my physical therapy. I was lucky enough to have security bring my cell phone up to me so I could get some important phone numbers off it. I mean, who can remember a phone number these days? We were not allowed to have our cell phone, but there was a unit phone we were allowed to use at the nurse's station. I wrote down about 15 important phone numbers with my tiny wooden pencil. I was able to use the in-house phone after several other patients. There was always a line for the phone. Problem is they use to have three cordless phones on the unit. Two of them were missing and not found. That narrowed it down to one. That was all we had for a full capacity of 30 patients. Sometimes, depending on the nurse, they would let you dial out from their office phone. I had called the wife to find out what time she was arriving for visiting hours and asked her to bring me in some clothes. It was good to be in my own outfits again. Visits are only twice a day, for 90 minutes each session. My wife stayed for the allotted time and told me she would call her parents to come in and see me that evening. Her father Bob brought me that day's newspaper, something to read as boring as it got there. Sure, I attended a couple of group sessions but the TV room was always busy with someone watching their own shows so I often found myself chilling out in my own room. It was the same routine each day. Whenever I could get on the phone, I would. One time I even had to give up my dessert as well as that newspaper I had in order to get someone else's turn on the phone. I had to call my other doctors, lawyers, and family.

The next day and it was routine as usual. That's the way they wanted it on that unit. Routine. I made sure to keep talking to the supervising physician, Dr. Rojas. We spoke in great detail in his office about my situation. I mentioned that I had plans to write my first novel, a memoir. Excitedly, he told me he wanted the first copy of my book when it comes out. I had carried a great deal of responsibility on the outside, but with this turn of the events being so unexpected, there really was no plan what to do if this had ever happened. My biggest concern was how to overcome it. I explained to Dr. Rojas that it was a stigma. A stereotype. Just because a person has a position, a title, a responsibility, does not take the human factor out of the equation. We all have to be human first. Nobody is exempt from this. Dr. Rojas agreed and said that we all have a breaking point. Even psychologists have to go talk to people once in a while too. Afterward, in the hallway, one of the female resident interns on the unit kept checking in with me, her clipboard in hand, taking notes.

"What's going on, Paul? How are you feeling today? Do you want to hurt yourself or anyone else?"

"No, I answered, not at all." We went on with the usual questions and then my blood pressure was taken. They had to do that twice a day. After lunch that day, I was notified that I had another visit. I thought at first it was Father K but it was my wife's aunt and uncle. I was surprised to see them come during the busy daily schedules of their family-owned business. They came to visit, to talk to me about my problem at work, and about the incident on the deck at home. They brought me the Bible, asking me to look at certain verses inside it, and right during the discussion, Father K had arrived. He came in later so he did not get much time with me to visit. We had spoken on the phone a few times. When the visits were over, I went back to my room carrying the Bible. I sat it down on the desk in my room. I opened up the cover seeing that they wrote my name inside. There was a smaller book that accompanied it, I sat down and read it for a while. Before I knew it, dinner was served. I had a nice chicken dinner and got another visit right afterward, by my neighbor and friend Mike. He brought along some card games and a big bag of Carl's Jr. burgers, fries, and soda that we had started to eat as we played some card games of Uno. I had not played it in a while but it was nice to do something that occupied myself. Within minutes, two tables next to us were getting busy. Usually, one of the nurses watches over the visit area, which is basically a 20x30 foot room, used for dining, with numerous tables and chairs, but it was fully packed with people. I noticed one of the patients, Pat, was getting a visit from a female friend. She had brought along a dozen roses for him. They were making out, French kissing, as if it was their first date. We were only feet apart so it was not hard to notice. On the opposite side was a heavier girl, a patient who seemed laid back, her name was Beth. She had said her "ex" was coming to visit that evening. They too were at it kissing, and I noticed right away that her hand was in his open fly, moving rapidly up and down. I could not believe this was going on in front of us. I motioned for Mike to check it out, he was shocked too. Unbelievable, we thought.

"Hurry up with your fries, Mike!" I said to him. Almost as soon as the happy ending was over for the couple next to Mike and I, an announcement was made for the visits to now end as well. I am pretty sure those two had a happy ending for their visit. I was just glad to see one of my buddies come up with some grub. We said good bye and I headed right to the nurse's station phone to call Dr. Ogulnick, it was about 7:45 p.m. I knew he was on his last session for the evening. Luckily for me, he picked up the phone. I spoke to him and asked him to call the staff here in the morning to speak to them as they were in need of more "collateral information" about me. I did not feel right in this environment. Nothing was being done to really help me there, basically a Band-aid to go. To go back to your room that is. Friday morning came, up for breakfast, following my routine, still no physical therapy, even after numerous requests. Good news came as the resident intern spoke to me, she asked me some more questions and arranged for a meeting with the unit staff. On our way in there, she told me that they were discharging me that day. I thought for sure I would have to be there for the weekend. I probably would have been if it had not been for the efforts of Dr. Ogulnick making that call for me the morning of my release. It was continuing to wage hardship on my family not being home. The staff board of clinicians and myself had about a 10-minute meeting. I spoke to my social worker, an overworked individual who needed more help to handle the caseloads. I had worn one of my favorite shirts into the meeting and was complimented on it by everyone. It was the best one I had to wear, I told them. In my mind, I was so relieved that I could now be surrounded by loving family. During my in-patient status, my kids were not allowed to visit during my stay though, house rules. It was fortunate that I was going home to be with them again.

So, I was allowed to make another phone call to my wife's mother, Esther, she was always there whenever we needed something. She too used to work at Fishkill Correctional Facility as a nursing assistant but had to retire on medical disability.

"Paul," she says, "we will be out there, you tell us what time is good."

I mentioned back, "About 2:00 p.m." I had to get processed out and once she arrived, they escorted me downstairs where my wife's father, Bob, was waiting in the car at the curb. We were now on our way home. My cell phone messages had stacked up, nearly three dozen voicemails as well, just in four days. When we pulled into the driveway, my wife was still at work but the kids were home. They opened the door and immediately I was tackled by our two loving dogs, as well as my kids. It was almost a picture-perfect image. In fact, it was. It was the moment I had been waiting for. I knew what I had done was not good for my family, but I did not put myself in this environment. It was the system, everything I have mentioned so far, and yet I was home again to face it all. Only this time to be handled differently.

One of the things I learned to do was to cope with the rejection, the negative responses, the lies that they were so far into, there was no looking back. Everyone only wanted this to go away now. But yet the questions kept coming in by numerous agencies still looking into the facility's investigation, or the lack thereof. I would just have to walk away and go do something else the next time that "call or letter" came in for me…give it time to process itself and then respond back in kind when it was appropriate to do so.

The day after I was back at home, I had reached out to some neighbors and friends who were aware of the situation to let them know all was alright. I even had a nice long talk with the Police Sergeant who was on the scene that evening of my incident. I did not know what to do next to handle the stigma of all of this. There were people that knew about this that were now looking at me differently, just walking away or not knowing what to say. Perhaps they were never really a good friend to begin with? Most people were accepting of it. Things happen to all of us. In my ordeal, I had made one big bad decision in the beginning, and a bunch of smart ones following it, so I was told. I soon had a handful of friends wanting to catch up with me to go out for some burgers and beers. That helped me out a lot, to clear the air. It was sure good to be home again. I had remembered the following day to check the video cameras. We have a series of them around the house, along with an alarm and fire system at home. Turns out that some of my incident was caught on camera. I reviewed some of it and showed it to family. My lawyer Warren had said to text him if I needed anything, so I forwarded him a still photo of me in uniform with the shotgun, and a small clip of me as I went to the garage to head outside. This would be entered into my file as possible evidence down the road. Having the titles of the positions I currently held when all of this happened back in May, and with the fact that I had to put it all on hold, something in me just had to figure out where to go from here.

No matter what your title is in life, whether you are a corporate CEO, a president, a police officer, or even a congressman, this can happen to all of us. We all have to be human first. The equation always and must contain the human factors involved. One of the last things I did is write a letter to the town police chief to thank the officers for their timeliness, compassion, and care of the incident, and handling everything in a manner in which it was diffused quickly. I had forwarded this onto my fire chief, as well as the fire department president. I knew that this would have some type of effect of them as well. There were zero repercussions. Everyone was there with open arms. It was very promising. For years and years, I have always ran out the door to help others, now it was time for them to come and help me. With the holidays approaching, there was even talk about having the crews bring over the truck to get up on my roof and put up my large Christmas wreath. I was like, "Sure, they could even have a drill while they are there, but then again, my neighborhood is going to wonder what is going on now?" Funny they mentioned that, my neighbor Mike had come over and already started to do it. He wasn't someone who accepted money, just being helpful, that was all. He was very selfless, putting us before himself. He was always there at the drop of a hat. He even cleared a path between the woods of our homes, and put down pine bark on the trail and solar lights along the path.

Chapter Thirteen
To Foil or Not to Foil

With it now being November 1st, my employer got back to me about my FOIL request to obtain records regarding the investigation of my complaint. "Denied – Pursuant to Public Officer's Law ss87 (2) (A)." I forwarded this onto my lawyers since they were handling my workers' compensation case and this was related to it. So rather than fight it, I continued on with my therapy and medical appointments, trying to focus on getting myself better. I also called the Public Employee Relations Board to follow up with them about the status of my submissions. I was told by Bill, one of the administrative law judges, that it was now in the hands of the agency director and that they would be getting back to me. COPBA's Breach of Duty to Fairly Represent has clearly been evident, which is why the Improper Practice Charge was lodged against them. On May 24, 1999, COPBA was certified as the bargaining unit for our members. Since then, COPBA "continues to advocate every day on behalf of its members." All dues paying members have a share of the organization. I am still paying dues, yet I cannot get any representation from my attempts via email, phone, and certified mail. However, under State Civil Service Law, Sections 209-A, "It shall be an affirmative defense to any improper practice charge under paragraph [g] of this subdivision that the employee has the right, pursuant to statute, interest arbitration award, collectively negotiated agreement, policy or practice, to present to a hearing officer or arbitrator evidence of the employer's failure to provide representation and to obtain exclusion of the resulting evidence upon demonstration of such failure." As for the facts that I have reported the DFR complaint to outside sources, my case would clearly fall under the Whistleblower Policy. The Correctional Officers and Police Benevolent Association Inc. requires its directors, officers, and employees to observe high standards of business and personal ethics in the conduct of their duties and responsibilities. The purpose of this policy is to encourage and enable employees and members to report any action or suspected action taken within COPBA that is illegal, fraudulent, or in violation of any adopted policy of COPBA to a source within before turning to outside parties for resolution. This policy applies to any matter which is related to COPBA's business and does not relate to private acts of an individual not connected to the business of COPBA. This policy is intended to supplement but not replace any applicable state and federal laws governing whistleblowing applicable to non-profit organizations. Anyone reporting a violation, must act in good faith, without malice to any individual in COPBA, and have reasonable grounds for believing that the information shared in the report indicates that a violation has occurred.

There are many questions remaining, and this too will one day gain closure, in hopes that this does not happen to someone else. If there are policies in place within the department, then they need to be enforced regardless of the politics. As I said earlier in my story, we are all just numbers, not names. And our union should be protecting us against any violations by the employer. I had started to give it some thought about how much I was taking on with this case, with so many other officers, family, and friends all behind me to support me. Most understood how the system works and some do not. In either case, it is often mistaken that the officer who undergoes this experience is separate from the others who he or she has worked with inside the walls and fences of New York's prison system. Some people take the stress with them on their short retirements straight to their graves. Others who see a better way out find other job alternatives and set new goals. I have seen this over and over, but I do not understand why even the most senior officers or supervisors do not leave service for retirement when they are eligible to do so. These days especially, you never know what can and will happen when that gate crashes shut behind you when you show up for duty. The number one reason is it's their way of life, all they know. Others did not want to face the fact that if they needed to enter the workforce on the outside that they might be taking orders from a younger person, and many did not like the idea. Most thought that all of those seniority hash marks and stars on their uniforms were like awards of distinguished service. In most cases it was, but if you were still working there on the job, I looked at it as your failure to plan your financial future. You can't live check to check your whole career and then bounce out of there ready to go when your retirement date comes. I have also talked with far too many younger officers that have just begun their career in the last few years. Some commit havoc on their bodies on a weekly plan by the amount of alcohol and tobacco they consume. Many don't exercise, get enough sleep or watch what they eat and wonder why they feel so poorly. The worst thing I see far too often is officers that are so fixated on getting out of the system and retiring that they wish their lives away. This in law enforcement circles is called "ROD" or retired on duty. This person is a burnout that wears a uniform and doesn't do the work expected of him or her. He or she is held captive to this dysfunctional state by one or more of the factors mentioned. Not surprisingly, the ugly stats at the beginning are all about those types. To top matters off, working with RODs makes everybody else's job harder and more dangerous because you must take up their slack, often times at the expense of having nobody watching your own back. The department includes suicide prevention in its mandatory annual training that is given for up to eight hours. Using that number loosely, one attending would be able to say it was more likely to be closer to five or six hours. The focus was more on the suicide prevention of inmates, which ultimately are the responsibility of all staff assigned to those areas, and the supervisors overseeing such.

Suicide prevention training is important to help the agency pursue its goal of suicide prevention, which means achieving an annual suicide rate of 0%. All staff have responsibility for preventing suicides by effectively monitoring inmates, understanding potential suicide indicators, and knowing the appropriate responses when it is determined that an inmate may be at risk for self-harm or suicidal behavior. We all need to take precautions to ensure the safety of all inmates and help avoid the devastating impact that suicide has on the family, staff, and other inmates involved. But where does it lay on the employer when it comes to staff?

According to a department memorandum regarding suicide prevention issued by the Acting Commissioner's office, Mr. Anthony Annucci, and the Assistant Commissioner for Health, Mr. Bryan Hilton, back in September of 2017, suicide is a preventable cause of death. Most suicidal individuals want to live, but they feel overwhelmed in the moment and are unable to see alternatives to their problems. Therefore, it is crucial that all of us look out for one another and continue working diligently to prevent and address all suicide risk factors. This persistent effort "requires the cooperation of all of us."

Executive level staff, as well as direct care staff, share the responsibility to identify and address such factors in a timely manner. Suicide knows no boundaries. It affects the young and the old as well as people of all cultures, races, professions, religions, and economic status. Each person's death by suicide intimately affects surviving family members, co-workers, peers, colleagues, and friends. By working together, through awareness, prevention, education, and intervention, we can fight back and reduce the incidents of suicides and their attempts. The letter closes with some contact numbers for a local crisis hotline, as well as the names of a couple of contacts within the department who can offer more information regarding resources.

In my situation, and as you read earlier, the written response that I received from the acting commissioner's office, which was delegated to a lower assistant commissioner, Mr. Daniel Martuscello, had suggested to me that my plea for assistance in my original letter to the acting commissioner basically asserted that I was experiencing post-traumatic stress disorder and severe anxiety. He stated further, "Might give one pause and reason to seek professional services." Instead of coming off with such an unprofessional response, and seeing the signs and risk factors I had written about, his conclusion was to brush this off with a simple one-lined advisement without actually getting me the assistance that I had originally sought. This was stated in the letter from the Commissioner's Office about suicide prevention. Team effort, everyone from the executive on down to the bottom. Again with the deliberate indifference, I thought, and now I have it in writing. That letter was dated October 6th, mere weeks before my crisis. Instead of taking a stance on the issue, taking action to address my individual problem that had been created by this department, one that I had given well over two decades to, he took the easy road out, the lazy way. What would have happened on October 24th with my situation if this went the wrong way? I had kept a logbook since the incident on May 9th. A lot of people would have some serious explaining to do. But they don't care, they just don't. Just point that finger and close the office door. This is not a one-man game, it's a total widespread department issue as a whole. Everyone is afraid to do their jobs up in Albany, running away from the paperwork. Avoid lawsuits at all costs. Delay and delay all they can, hoping that the problem dissipates and goes away. The only assistance I got from the employer afterward was a third-party delivery of a one-page printed form that had local hotline numbers on it for suicide prevention from Fishkill's EAP office. There were no calls from the facility, no offers of assistance from the union or the administration. Not a care in the world. But at this point, I would imagine that they would be pretty upset with me for the way I was fighting this investigation. Funny thing though, as diversified as it is at Fishkill with officers and staff these days, if this same situation had happened to a female or even a civilian, all hell would have broken loose. Lightning speed action would have been taken. It would have been handled immediately if it had involved a female or another race. A lot of us knew this, we spoke about it often at work when incidents happened but noticed that white males were the least protected class in discrimination complaint cases. There's a difference here, but let's not play that "card" as obvious as it would seem.

Traumatic reaction can come as a single awful event, like a stabbing, a hanging, a rape, an assault, threat, or having your family threatened, hearing of your fellow officers being hurt daily, weekly, monthly over a long period of time. The first type of sudden extreme event is clear-cut, dangerous, and threatening to life, and a brutal assault on your safety or the safety of others. It is easy to understand such an event's upsetting effect. The second type of chronic slow traumatizing is more subtle. It is referred to as Complex Post Traumatic Stress, not always directly threatening but keeping you aware that danger is always present. Officers become constantly vigilant and learn that even in the safest environment, life-threatening things happen. This chronic awareness of potential violence creates an attitude of vigilance for unexpected danger. Constant exposure to risk leaves officers hardened, hypervigilant, anxious, and depressed at home and on the job. They are often removed from feelings and memories even though those feelings and memories drive behavior. The result of both single events and the chronic exposure can change the officer in many unhealthy ways.

Sometime in the course of a corrections career, there is high probability of experiencing trauma and a risk of developing symptoms of PTSD. Fortunately, not everyone will experience full-blown PTSD. Trauma is an event that is "a deeply disturbing or distressing event" according to the Oxford English Dictionary. In a prison, there are many possible such potential occurrences. Some of the possible events that may be encountered in a corrections career are:

1) Suicides, hanging or bleeding out bodies leaving a lifetime of visual memories.
2) Fights and stabbings that have the potential of spreading and of hurting officers.
3) Direct threats and assaults on officers, being pelted with bodily fluids, attacked with weapons, being sucker punched without warning or provocation, being stuck with possibly contaminated needles introducing the dangers of HIV or Hepatitis.
4) Sudden deaths of inmates while being transported or restrained.
5) Sexual harassment or violence can be traumatic for the victim. More so, if there is humiliation or retaliation associated with it. Bullying by colleagues or by fellow officers, that is associated with threats of danger, can create feelings of insecurity and danger. Isolation and feelings of being abandoned in dangerous situations such as jamming radios when officers call for help.
6) Threats to the officer and families from gang members.

This is a brief list of possible dangers that can lead to post-traumatic stress in a prison. Risk of danger rises with the level of security classification and with the level of violence among the inmate population. There has been some refinement of the diagnosis of PTSD in the longer classified as an anxiety disorder although symptoms of anxiety may be a result. More emphasis is now placed on the seriousness of the event. It needs to be life-threatening.

According to the DSM-5, "trauma is defined as exposure to actual or threatened death, serious injury or sexual violence in one of four ways: a) directly experiencing the event; b) witnessing in person the event occurring to others; c) learning that such an event happened to a close family member or friend; d) experiencing repeated or extreme exposure to aversive details of such events...actual or threatened death must have occurred in a violent or accidental manner and experiencing cannot include experiencing through electronic media ...unless it is work related." Initial experience of trauma and its impact on the victim is classified as acute stress. If the emotional and physical disruption continues beyond a month, it is re-classified as post-traumatic stress. The disabling or unsettling emotions and behaviors that result from exposure to traumatic events affect the health and safety of officers.

Reactions can range from mild to severe and disabling. Officers and others can get help for this. Good treatment will prevent more severe effects.

In 2013, Danhof and Spinaris of Desert Waters released a study of 3,599 corrections personnel and reported findings that addressed PTSD. They concluded there is a 34% PTSD rate among corrections personnel. They also noted a 31 % depression rate among corrections staff. Significantly, they found a connection between PTSD and depression with 67% of those who had a primary diagnosis of depression also having PTSD, and 65% of those with PTSD as a primary diagnosis also having depression. Tull (2016) reports that 27% of people with PTSD attempt suicide. These recent studies place better definitions and refine our understandings. PTSD and morbid conditions such as depression are significant factors and need to be addressed for the health and well-being of the officers and their families, and frankly for the well-being of the institutions. Treatments will not only provide relief from psychic pain but also will reduce addiction, domestic disturbance, suicide. and many health-related problems.

The brain has many centers and systems that perform the many tasks that our bodies and minds use to function. Simply there are centers and systems that detect events and judge them for safety or danger. Other parts of the brain react and move us to survival mode for fight or flight or sometimes freeze. The systems work at lightning speed and make judgments to insure survival. In most situations, we have perceptions of events, have emotions about them and take actions consistent with survival. Trauma by its nature is devastating and catastrophic. Survival is threatened, emotions are overridden, and action is attempted to save ourselves and those around us. The shock of the event blunts us. Often we act without recall. For the most part in trauma, it is the emotional systems that take over. For the PTSD victim, the smooth connectedness of the systems is disrupted. Some see danger when it isn't there based on a tiny piece of information, a sound, a sight, a smell or touch that recalls the trauma and misinterprets this tiny recall as the danger once encountered. Such a reminder can be crippling and overwhelming. Others stay in mental overdrive watching for and seeing danger at every turn so that the traumatic event will never happen again. They may check doors and locks at home at all hours or be overly protective of children among other negative behaviors.

Still others are hurt so badly, they avoid and often do not even recall the event but their bodies continue to react and go on alert when any reminder occurs. They tense or get defensive without being sure why. Others zone out become depersonalized and walk through danger with no concern for safety because mentally they have shut down. They sometime get the task done but do it without emotion. There is often depression, anxiety, suicidal thinking, rage, and shame for survivors of trauma. Whether an individual shuts down or overreacts, if one could take blood pressure or do an MRI, we would find the brain is very alert and the body is very responsive, the heart is beating rapidly, adrenaline is pumping. But instead of acting in concert, one system or other prevails and is out of tune with the others.

In the world of prison work as in all other places, the untreated PTSD victim is at risk. The avoider will not be available in a fight and may have high use of sick time, the hypervigilant may misjudge and either overreact or avoid when they mistake actions for danger that isn't there. Many with PTSD are high risk for substance abuse that either overly stimulates or blunts emotion. Many find other ways to blunt emotions or to stimulate dead feelings. High-risk behaviors, gambling, sexual compulsions, isolation from others, caffeine and energy drink stimulants can become coping styles.

There is no single proven treatment for PTSD. Medications, at best, only treat symptoms and often do that poorly. Treatment needs to be more intensely focused on reconnecting the brain systems that have become incongruent with one another.

In treatment Bessel van der Kolk of the trauma center in Brookline, Ma. has noted, and I agree, that the "challenge is not just dealing with the past, but to learn to enhance the quality of day-to-day experience." For the trauma victim, it is difficult to feel alive right now, they are still in the past. Treatment then is a combination of learning to be in touch with bodily feelings and sensations that occur now. It is learning coping strategies to manage the intrusions of the past memories until they can be put in a safe place that does not intrude in the present. Treatment also requires learning that an incident today is not going to be a repeat of the past trauma. It is a journey to live in the moment.

Traumatized officers need support and understanding. There is an unfortunate belief system among many that PTSD is a sign of weakness and that it can just be handled by "sucking it up." If any New York prisons cannot provide a safe environment, the fears for safety associated with the trauma will be perpetuated. It is doubtful that without a positive institutional and collegial response, an officer will have a safe recovery. The likelihood of returning to the same work environment is greatly diminished. Colleagues and local administration as well as Albany need to avoid shaming or humiliating suggestions that an officer just suck it up or be tough. PTSD is a real disabling response to trauma. They can put out all the "memos" they want and read them at line-up pre-shift briefings, but are they really enforced? And if so, for only a short brief period before it is quickly passed on and forgotten? Further, New York State's prison administrations and its superiors need to make reasonable accommodations and stick to them.

Placing an officer on another post can be helpful but only if he/she will not be required in an emergency to return to the old post. Often too, such accommodations become forgotten and an officer is forced back to a bad situation, setting them up for re-traumatization. If the prisons, in this case, Fishkill Correctional Facility, do not support an officer by accommodation and by respecting that this is an illness, if it shames and humiliates, there is a higher risk that an officer will not recover. If fellow officers, unions and administration continue to make an officer feel unsafe while they heal, it is highly likely they will not return to work. These officials have always focused on the prisoners first, and because of that many staff of the officers, and some civilians working there alike, have becomes victims and have committed suicide while working at Fishkill and other facilities around New York, some of them even doing such on duty over the last several decades.

A few days had passed. I went down to my computer station. I had made several phone calls. One of those calls were to PESH in Albany. I wanted to know what was going on with my paperwork and if my employer had replied back yet. The supervisor that took the call seemed as if he was having a bad day, either that or he was taking me the wrong way. I had mentioned that it was ironic that the very day I called, they had just received the employer's response. He stated to me, "You want us to send you the date stamp on the envelope to prove to you when we got it?"

I quickly said, "What?"

He went on saying "Well, you are insinuating that we are lying about this when you said how ironic that it had arrived the very day I called."

"Hold on, take a step back," I said, "I did not insinuate anything. Your office is there to assist employees with these types of situations. The last thing I am doing is insinuating."

His other investigator, Jeff, had been reviewing the responses and would go into investigative conference, if it was deemed necessary. They would eventually be calling me back to do another follow-up. This was an ongoing process that with any governmental agency, there would be red tape. Corrections officers suffer from post-traumatic stress disorder at more than double the rate of military veterans in the US, according to Caterina Spinaris, the leading professional in corrections-specific clinical research and founder of Desert Waters Correctional Outreach, a nonprofit based in Colorado. This in turn inevitably affects prisoners. While there is no hard data on officer-on-inmate assaults, interviews with current and former corrections officers revealed that COs occasionally take out the stress of the job on inmates. The suicide rate among corrections officers is twice as high as that of both police officers and the general public, according to a New Jersey police taskforce. An earlier national study found that corrections officers' suicide risk was 39% higher than all other professions combined. Corrections wisdom dictates that you deal with trauma by not dealing with it at all. They teach us to leave it at the gate; "eight and out the gate" is the unofficial motto. Correction officers are responsible for overseeing individuals who have been sentenced to serve time in a jail or prison. Working in a correctional facility can be stressful and dangerous. Correctional officers and jailers have one of the highest rates of injuries and illnesses, often resulting from confrontations with inmates. And on a rare occasion, from another fellow officer. Because prison security must be provided 24 hours a day, officers work all hours of the day and night, weekends, and holidays. While it is understandable that these stressors can take a toll on someone, it is vital that it does not affect the quality or integrity of their performance at work.

One study suggests correction officers have rates of post-traumatic stress disorder (PTSD) comparable to military combat veterans. Another found the risk of suicide to be 39% higher for correction officers than in all other professions combined, and a 2009 study by the New Jersey Police Suicide Task Force and by others around the U.S., found that correction officers had double the suicide rate of police officers. Other studies have found reduced life expectancy linked to stress-related conditions such as high blood pressure, heart attacks, and ulcers. The cost of this problem is tremendous. Individuals with depression or PTSD averaged approximately 30% more missed work days than individuals who were disorder-free. Those with both depression and

PTSD symptoms took off more than double the time. The human cost is equally as bad. According to a Radford University study, correction officers have a higher divorce rate than the general population. It is detrimental to the well-being of society and the general public when a correction officer is psychologically deficient. They pose a risk to themselves, the inmates, and anyone who may be impacted should a prisoner escape. As America's prison population skyrockets, it is important to maintain public trust and confidence in all aspects of the criminal justice system. While more and more offenders are being placed behind bars, the responsibility of the correction officer is increasing in both difficulty and consequence. The report examined inmate assaults on officers between 2007 and 2016, and found that they had risen from a low of 524 in 2012 to a high of 896 in 2015.

Chapter Fourteen
When Does the Talk Become Action?

"Correction officers in New York hold one of the hardest jobs imaginable. As indicated by the report we're releasing today, their jobs have only gotten more difficult. It is unacceptable to see this rise in assaults on those who are protecting us. We must ensure that dangerous drugs and other contraband are kept out of prisons so that correction officers can feel safe when they go to work every day," **said NY Senator Jeff Klein.**

"Correction officers are truly unsung heroes of our criminal justice system and go too often without recognition of the work they do as they are faced with new challenges that make their work environment extremely dangerous. Additional protections proposed today will build on my legislation that requires new correction officers and staff who regularly work with inmates with mental health issues to receive at least eight hours of mental health training related to treatment of inmates with mental disabilities. Protecting corrections officers in the face of new, more dangerous challenges is a priority for all of us," **said NY Senator David Carlucci.**

"Many of our correction officers suffer from PTSD and other mental health issues after being assaulted on the job. It's traumatic to be attacked at the workplace and we want to make sure that our officers are able to get the treatment they need through workers' compensation, which is why I'm introducing a bill to address this serious issue," **said NY Senator Marisol Alcantara.**

Senator Alcantara's legislation, S.5954, takes aim at the result of inmates intentionally throwing bodily fluids at correction officers, which may result in post-traumatic stress disorder. Her bill will allow officers facing impairment resulting from such an event be eligible for coverage in workers' compensation claims.

"Correction officers do a tremendously difficult job and face increasing on-the-job danger every day. Our facilities are understaffed and flooded with contraband including K2, which can lead to dangerous behavior. We want to support our hardworking correction officers who put their lives on the line by passing legislation that enhances their safety and helps them receive mental health treatment if they need it," **said NY Senator David Valesky.**

"Across New York, correction officers walk the toughest beat in America. The shocking numbers in this report are likely not a surprise to any of them who face the threat of assault on a daily basis. The IDC will continue to work toward finding solutions that protect these hard-working men and women," **said NY Senator Diane Savino.**

In addition to assaults on staff, the report also found an increase in inmate-on-inmate assaults, peaking in 2016 at 1,134 assaults from a low of 603 in 2009. These assaults included fights between two inmates and large-scale assaults involving over 100 inmates.

During the same period in which assaults increased, an increase in contraband seized by correctional workers was also found. These seizures include a significant rise in the amount of the synthetic drug K2 found in prisons, which is known to cause uncontrollable inmate behavior when used. The IDC report found that since 2012, K2 confiscations jumped from just three confiscations to 1,247 in 2015. Previous reports from Senator Klein and the IDC found that the products were easily available on the internet and in neighborhood stores.

Senator Klein urged the passage of his legislation to create a state analog act to criminalize substances that are substantially similar to illegal drugs to stem the tide of their entrance into the prison system. The injuries received from such assaults often result in workers' compensation claims that cost state millions of dollars. In its report, the IDC found that the increase in workers compensation claims coincided with the increase in assaults.

From a fiscal standpoint, the amount of workers compensation claims has increased from $16.6 million in 2011-2012 to $19.1 million in 2015-2016, with taxpayers footing the bill. Corrections officers play a vital role in the reentry success of the people they supervise. Effective interactions between corrections officers and people in prison or jail can reduce recidivism and improve overall long-term outcomes related to a successful transition back to the community. But the role of our officers can be hindered by the job-related stresses and challenges they often experience, including traumatic stress as a result of secondary exposure to violence, injury, and death. These high-risk job factors can lead to a negative impact on the quality of life of us corrections officers. Research shows that corrections officers have higher rates of post-traumatic stress disorder, work-related injuries, and suicide in comparison to other professions.

I look back at my history with the department, all that I have done for the good of it. When the morale was down, so was the facility's productivity. There would be times when an officer would have a down-and-out kind of day and just would not care. The inmates did not care, and the administration did not care, nobody cared. It was a pencil-whipped paperwork shift, pass the time with whatever you were able to do. The general layout at Fishkill as a medium level of security comprised of dormitories, with both rooms and cubicles. It has a maximum security level area as well. As old as the prison itself is, it is not designed as a cookie cutter. Obviously, these days when newer facilities are built, line of sight, layout and ease of access, cameras overseeing areas are all considered factors. Those provide the safest type of work environment for prison staff and corrections officers. After all, it is the responsibility of the employer to provide a safe working environment for all staff. Yes, it is a dangerous job, but there must be protections in place in order to minimize incidents would could hinder the safe working operations of that facility. When it comes to documentation required by the department on a regularly scheduled basis, the administration would assign it to someone who would venture throughout the jail to each post area. This particular paperwork is called the Monthly Environmental Inspection Report, which covers all issues such as maintenance, quality of work conditions, hazards, as well as workplace violence indicators such as dimly-lit areas, corners of areas not easily observed where one could hide, etc. During my career, I have seen these "inspections" occur many times, and they would always have the paperwork already filled out before they came to your area and all of the boxes checked off. It was maybe a three-minute visit, a quick signature in the logbook, and a carbon copy left at your post. These inspections were never "walked through." Most of the staff doing these were not familiar with those areas anyhow. Funny how the upstairs of the administration building can pencil whip the paperwork but when a subordinate does so and gets caught, then down comes the gavel on their disciplinary sanctions. Facility maintenance work orders were another issue. Several copies of them would be filled out for problem areas and were constantly misplaced or lost in the shuffle. Only until something major happened as part of that work order, or if someone got injured, would they then get the repairs completed forthwith. From the smallest items to the most major of incidents, there is some form of cover-up. Such an easy thing to do when there are no security cameras. These are issues that were brought to the attention of our union representatives on our shift. Copies of this paperwork would be given to them but sometimes nothing would ever get taken care of.

Custodial environments in Fishkill seesaw between lengthy periods of boredom and isolation, as well as physical danger. There are security posts that are busier than others. To cope with these extremes, correctional officers will sometimes disassociate themselves emotionally from their surroundings. However, this mindset also leaves officers vulnerable to job burnout. Officers focus on getting through shifts without incident, but in worst case scenarios, no longer care about what they're doing. Eventually, the officer loses the ability to empathize with those around him, a phenomenon that's commonly labeled as "compassion fatigue." There are areas at Fishkill where you will have a working partner, or close by to an area where other officers are working. About 2/3rd of the facility, you work alone, depending on the shift. As a group, correctional officers are more likely to suffer significant psychological stress. The emotional control needed to handle assaults, inmate confrontations, and other institutional realities also means no psychological reprieve for the officer who works in such environments, according to "Corrections One" magazine. Officers can suffer lasting mental trauma that makes it difficult or impossible to separate home and work life.

While working as a corrections officer may appear to be a safe occupation at first glance, it is not. Just because a prisoner's movement is restricted, does not mean that he cannot assault an officer. We face indignities such as having urine and feces thrown in our faces from a cell or being spat on. We are required to protect the lives of inmates, which means that we must often break up fights, putting ourselves at risk for serious physical injury. You might begin to see my point about what we deal with on a daily basis. It's nearly the impossible over the span of one's career to not become somehow affected. In my case, it was both the inmates and an officer that I had been injured by, requiring surgeries which reduced my physical abilities. I am told that in the near future, there is a greater chance of exacerbation, or even worse, arthritis setting in. Dr. Kenny once told me, "With surgery, we can get you as close to 100% as possible, but you will never again be the same. With time and age, the condition will only get worse. Surgery only buys you time to help you feel the best you can as you did prior to the onset of the injury."

Speaking of time, things have been coming along slowly but surely for my left shoulder recovery. My arm is now out of the specialized sling, the physical therapy chair that was delivered to my house last month was picked up just recently by the medical company, and I am in now in physical therapy with Core Care, located also in Spring Valley. They say about a few months for total recuperation of my shoulder, but recently I was told by Dr. D's staff that according to the reports, some of the tears that I suffered were only cleaned up, not actually repaired with sutures. Dr. D's assistant mentioned, "Apparently it was not done that way, son," he quipped. All that I wanted was to be back to where I was before, to be made whole again, and then some. We had another Workers' Comp board hearing scheduled two days from now. My lawyers and I had to go through the formalities of getting my neck injuries established for this case as well. For some reason when I was awarded the benefits back in September, they only did it for the left shoulder and adjustment disorder. My neck was among my other injuries sustained the afternoon of May 9th by Officer Thompson. Once this gets done officially, we can start on getting more invasive treatment to alleviate my pain without surgery. Last case scenario is always the surgical route. With a C-Spine case, they would have to enter through the front of my throat to get to the herniated discs compressing any nerves. It would be too dangerous to go into the back of the neck and involve the spinal cord.

Chapter Fifteen
Business Not as Usual

I have had a lot of family calling me to check in on my well-being this week. My niece Kathleen, my sister Kate, my mother Ann, my step mother Grace, and others as well. After going through what I went through, being apart from family that are halfway across the country is such a hard thing to deal with. One of my biggest distractions has been this book. As I sit here pondering what my next sentence will be, different ideas pop into my mind. This is way better than dealing with the details of this case as I was doing prior to my crisis on October 24th. The time clock ticks away pretty fast when your face is buried in research, both online and at the book stores. All kinds of tips and pointers go this way, go that way. It can be overwhelming all at once, but there is nothing but time to get this done. I have been lucky that I heeded the advice of a friend who told me to be sure that I kept a logbook once my incident took place. It made those details crystal clear as I looked back month by month. In between I am taking breaks from it, allowing for a physical and mental break so that I am able to keep my ideas and the facts fresh. The holidays are approaching, with Thanksgiving next week and all, I am already starting to get the emails and phone calls from my regular customers about this year's Christmas card sessions. Unfortunately, I need to continue turning away those requests for appointments. To many of them I have replied, "Thank you for your inquiry regarding your 2017 Christmas family portrait session. I am sure you have been looking forward to this with the holiday season approaching. I apologize for any inconvenience this may have caused to your family. I am in great need of this medical treatment and need to look out for my well-being as well as my own family to continue supporting them. Thank you again for understanding. Merry Christmas, Happy Holidays, and Happy New Year 2018 from our family to yours." It really hurts me to do this, something I have spent the last two decades building upon, frame by frame, photo by photo, image by image. They say nothing good lasts forever. All of my clients and customers have been more than understanding of my situation, and have shown me compassion and caring in their responses. For that, I am truly thankful.

My secondary follow-up with Dr. D's office was mostly spent in the waiting room at his office in Newburgh. I looked around and I was the only one waiting that spoke English. I had brought along my case of documents so I started to thumb through some of my materials. My appointment was already 30 minutes past the scheduled time, but I was not in any hurry since it was my last appointment that day anyhow. When I did get called in, I spoke to one of Dr. D's assistants. He read off from a report just to recap what was done during the surgery. I asked some more questions, some that concerned Dr. D, and knowing he was in the building, I had asked to speak to him. I knew that he would be able to better explain things to me as to the surgery. He did note that my recovery was not coming along as quick as he thought it would. That concern turned back to my neck injury, with that still being an issue, the pain radiating down into my shoulders and arms caused a delay in the process in healing for my left shoulder. I had to become more aggressive with physical therapy. I knew it was only for the good of me. I have heard of some other patients having similar surgery and not regaining full range of motion. Eventually they would have to go through the whole procedure of having another surgery again. I just wanted to get through it all. Work requires documentation from the doctor while you are out on workers' compensation leave. Rules state that the note has to be faxed from the doctor's office and then the original note has to be mailed in within seven days. With the office staff being as busy as they are, I am almost hesitant to once again request this. In my previous experiences with work notes, this only tends to inconvenience the office personnel and the last thing one wants to do is lose that cooperation. I already had that problem over work notes from Dr. W's office in Middletown. I did not want to play that hand of cards again.

The next day I had been scheduled for another worker's compensation board hearing in New Windsor. This was a requested hearing by my law firm in order to establish my neck injuries to this case from the assault that occurred back in May while at work. I had been called the day prior by one of my lawyers, Nick. My usual lawyer, Jason, was at another hearing and unavailable so therefore he would not be able to attend. I arrived just about on time and

Nick was already waiting for me in the building. Once I checked in, we sat down to go over some paperwork. It was not long before I was called into Hearing Room #1. Some formalities and small discussion ensued.

"Good afternoon, Mr. Harrington. How are you today?" the judge asked me.

"I am ok as can be," I replied anxiously. I wanted to get this started and over with. But nothing in the workers' compensation system or the State Insurance Fund gets started and is over with that fast. Everything is red tape, everything is an act of congress. Everything is on a time schedule. In the meantime, the injured worker, such as myself, who holds several documents, numerous test and exam results, a multitude of doctors' reports, and a law firm to back me up, sits in the waiting zone, taking weeks, months, if not longer. The pain, the stress, the physical and mental anguish, the process and systematic denials as they put you through the gauntlet to weed out those who are fraudulent and those who are legitimate. There is nothing for the pain and suffering. Sure, they put you on meds and have you talk to specialists, like everything, to only buy them time. The people who work for these agencies are human beings just like the rest of us. These "professionals" who have the experience, the trained eye, need to be able to recognize the right from the wrong and take care of those who really need the help. In my case, how much more can one reach out for this help? Having exhausted almost every avenue I can take to remediate this has led me into a vicious cycle where these public officials are self-serving, not doing their jobs or taking responsibility for what is right. And you can bet the farm that this is not just happening in the State of New York. This is all over the country. During my workers' compensation board hearing, there appeared to be some issues with the vocabulary in the doctor's report from both Dr's Habif and S. A simple administrative fix would be in order but it was not accepted and as my lawyer Nick noted to the judge his exception to the decision, we basically had to have the reports redone and request another hearing. This takes time. And with time comes more pain and suffering.

The issues with my neck are already slowing down my recovery of the left shoulder surgery, now I have to wait longer to get authorized treatment for my neck. We departed from the hearing room with one last request to have the judge order the State Insurance Fund audit and pay my reimbursement requests within the next 45 days. I have not received a dime in repayment for any of my

176

out-of-pocket expenses or mileage. I am literally owed nearly $ 2,500+ dollars as of this day by the State Insurance Fund for reimbursement of out-of-pocket expenses. As of Thanksgiving week, my mileage to appointments alone stands at 3,890 since the incident on May 9th. So far, I have been to over 132 medical appointments for my injuries of my left shoulder, neck and TMJ, as well as for the adjustment disorder. Without my outside business income coming in as usual, every little bit of payment helps my family out. I had previously submitted documentation and receipts months ago but there had been no follow-up since then. With the court's order to produce payment, I am now confident in seeing that I will begin to be made "whole" again in that aspect.

I got a call from a colleague of mine, we call him H. We have known each other for at least 20 years or more, since I first started working at Fishkill. He and I had some serious catching-up to do since it had been a while since we last spoke. I had not seen him in a while since at this point, I have not worked in over six months. H had all of his own family issues to deal with as most people do today. A change in shift at work, some other changes in routines, you name it. Things can get busy for a man and his big family.

"How's it going, kid? You alright? How's the family? Kids ok?" he asked.

"Sure, we are as good as can be for someone who has been through our situation."

"I hear ya, Paul, it ain't been easy here either. You know all that I have been going through as well."

"Oh yeah," I said, "that too. How are things at work?" H went into a lengthy discussion about some of the past few months and how he has been looking to get more of that overtime. He has the seniority to get out and retire, but sometimes one has to wait for that right moment to prepare.

"You gotta get out of there. Every day it is getting worse and you never know what can happen, it's not worth it," I told H.

"On another note, Paul, listen to this," He said, "I worked some overtime and I was at your post the other day. The dayshift officer who used to be there quit his post to be reassigned elsewhere. The boss was messing with him and changing his routine. The new officer that took the post bid on dayshift where you work has it now. I saw your locker there. Must have been they moved it from the old office you used to be at. They probably thought since you had not yet returned to work, that maybe it would be better to move your stuff into the new assigned office area. The only thing is that your locker is in the storage area of the staff bathroom. You know everyone has a key to that door. Someone noticed one day that it had been altered and messed with on the front door of it."

I could not believe it. But after some thought, it had occurred to me that this kind of stuff is to be expected. You would think in our profession we would all be adults working there, but there are so many officers who act like teens in junior high school. It's a shame. They play these games and then wonder why we can't get our raises when it comes to getting a good contract. I mean, it's way beyond that reason, but that's just the tip of the iceberg. At this point the way my locker is being handled, I would have to object to anything that may come back against me since there are a group of officers there that are out for revenge. Each staff employee inside the facility is responsible for the contents of his or her personal locker, work areas, and office desks, etc. Most of our personal lockers are about seven foot tall. It has gaps on the edges and fins on the swinging door to allow for air circulation. It could be very easy to "set someone up" by slipping contraband into one's locker. Upon inspection, it could wind up looking very bad for me, or whoever this could be done to; inevitably, retaliation is the name of the game in there. You have to walk a thin line inside those prisons and to always be careful who you associate with, and know what you are dealing with in situations.

With Thanksgiving approaching this week, my appointments will start to go into a holiday schedule. I look forward to the time off from all of these visits, more time for the family, and even a road trip was in the works. This would give me time to clear my mind and focus again on family. The important stuff. I even had a chance to catch up with some out-of-town friends, and one of them, Rob, had made his way back into town as well to visit the area, and we went out for breakfast to a local diner, which was his treat. We had to catch up on the latest news. Always something happening at Fishkill.

"Who's turn was it now?" I mentioned. Another scandal in the news about a supervisor sergeant and a female officer sexual harassment incident. Sometimes it would be an inmate involved situation, some others would be civilian staff/officers, and then a few would be inmates and civilian staff/officers. The latter part happens all across the state. It just doesn't make the news as much. There had been more incidents of officers being seriously injured by inmates during physical uses of force. It's almost as if whatever happens this week would be "old news" come the following week with the amount of activity inside of Fishkill's vast complicated facility. There was also some more talk about the next helicopter trip over New York City to do our second set of aerial photos of the skyline areas. It would be quite some time before I could do this again though, I still had a long road ahead of me dealing with my shoulder recovery and my neck treatments, not to mention my treatments from other injuries from my inmate assaults that I had previous surgeries on.

During my trip home for the holiday visit, I got a call from the State Department of Labor doing their follow-up in regards to their investigation. It had been some time since we had been in contact. The supervisor and investigator, Jeff and Penny, had me on conference call to go over my employer's response to the investigative questionnaire that was sent to the prison's administration. They had a certain time period to respond back with the paperwork. We went over each item, one by one, to discuss their answers to my complaints. As usual, the facility's administration had answered them in a very vague, generalized way. Although their words were spaced normally, the gaps between them left so much space that it was left open for interpretation. So many facts were not mentioned in their replies. I had a chance to respond back and explain the reasoning. As notes were being taken over the phone by them, they became more aware of how I was being discriminated against by the employer, all from the get go. Jeff and Penny had also asked me about the facility's response about Lieutenant Michael's statement in regards to the emergency room the evening of May 9th. As with protocol, another officer or staff member always follows the ambulance to the hospital to act as a liaison when the injured officer is being treated and is confined to his or her bed. That evening in question, Officer Henry, whom I have known for almost 20 years, had been the one with me, standing in my doorway with a hospital security officer when I arrived to the emergency room that evening. Henry is probably the most laid back, relaxed, and understanding man that I know at Fishkill. He is at retirement age so he has seen his fair share of the action. I didn't know he had come with me because at the time of the transport, I had just overcome an anxiety attack and was already in the back of the ambulance. Jeff's concern was with Lieutenant Michael's response stating that I was not rushed to do my report that evening.

"I thought you read it in my report?" I said to Jeff. "I was brought back to the facility, ordered by the Lieutenant who was directed over the phone by

Deputy Oblinski to obtain my report from the incident. Although part of my treatment consisted of pain killers and muscle relaxers, they still had me go back to the facility to sit there for 90 minutes to do a five-page report." That evening I had been told numerous times that it was essential for them to get my report as soon as possible. They would need it in order to produce it by the morning for the investigation. Additionally, the Bureau of Labor Relations would need to know the details in order to make a decision on disciplinary matters. So yes, you could say it was a rush. Anyone else most likely would have had to opportunity to go home, rest and follow up the next morning with their documentation. We finished up the call that lasted about an hour long with the knowledge that this would now be sent upward to their law department for counsel to review and make a decision at that point. I would be expecting to hear something soon I was told.

Now that the workers' comp case hearing had to be rescheduled due to the paperwork snafu, what was the rush at this point. Just sit back and let this take its course. Something I never thought about the entire time between the incident on May 9th and my crisis on October 24th. Like I said before, we all have breaking points. Even someone like me who has been in this long, is looked upon by a fellow officer differently. If it does not affect them, why would it affect me? This is one of the reasons it is very hard to discuss this stuff with co-workers. It is often played down. Probably not the right person for a long-term fix, but certainly someone who would give you that momentary boost you needed, and often times it ended up at the bar having a few drinks. That only made it worse. With alcohol being a depressant, you were "buying" time, but you would only be waking up to those same issues the next day. It felt good to be able to release all of those built-up thoughts and energies to these professionals I had been seeing. No one you work with can look at you and tell what is going on between your ears just by looking at you. This is why we have always been caught by surprise whenever another officer had committed suicide. The difference was that they had just did it, but I had called for help, seeking that alternative, someone to provide that deflection, to give me a reminder of why I am needed here. Take it from me, when you are in an actual crisis, not only do you get tunnel vision, but you do not think clearly and certainly there is no consideration for the consequences of your actions. I was looking for a way out of this situation. It was a problem, and today, I am not the only one from my job with it. The first step is to admit there is one and then seek help.

At this point as I type, my neck pain is killing me. It radiates up into my head, giving me daily headaches, and down into my shoulders and into my arms, ultimately stopping at my hands where the numbness occurs, from the nerves being pinched by the bulging discs as a result of the assault on that day of May 9th. My shoulder orthopedic surgeon Dr. D's office tells me that my recovery will be slower due to the continuing issues in my neck. Here I am only in my 40s and I feel as if I am much, much older. All in all, the injuries also sustained from the multiple inmate assaults that included both knees, my lower to mid back, my hand, arm, now my shoulder and neck really tend to stop one in his tracks. I certainly can tell you that doing the same activities that I once engaged in are no longer enjoyable. That takes quality of life out of it all. These medications, the surgeries, the therapy, various medical procedures, pain injections, etc., they all just buy you time. As you get older, the chances of exacerbation increase, old man arthritis sets in, and it only can get worse. When does this end, when does this end?

Chapter Sixteen
The Pain with the Agencies

It is hard to find doctors who will cooperate with the unending paperwork requests that follow in a workers' compensation case. There's always some issue. Even when the State Insurance Fund denies treatments and requests for testing on the injured body parts relative to your case, it creates a backlog, and you begin going back and forth, all the while waiting for what you need. Before you know it, you're getting that order to return to duty, whether it's a light duty program or not. In our department, the light duty segment is limited to only 30-60 days depending on the various circumstances. Nobody wins in these cases. There needs to be reform all across the entire system. First things first, keep the politics out of it. That has nothing to do with injured workers. Everyone complains of skyrocketing costs of health insurance these days. Employers especially, who hold it over your head when it comes to contract negotiations, and threaten to change up the benefits. Is it an abused system? You betcha.' Definitely. It happens all the time. I see it over and over again. And sometimes the state creates that when they close jails down and force those officers to be transferred to other facilities much farther away from home. The obvious easy way out of that scenario for many of those affected is to go out on workers' compensation disability leave. It almost happened to me the first day of this incident when Sergeant Oswald wanted me to report my injuries differently, altogether avoiding any paperwork or an investigation on his part, and at the same time to protect his friend, "who he has a good rapport with." There are ways to weed those fraudulent workers out of the system. But instead, they just rake everyone over the hot coals. Those who are legitimately injured, even proven to be so with the administered advanced testing. One of my doctors was just called today, I had previously spoke to her assistant and office staff. I was in need of a letter stating causation and diagnosis in regards to my TMJ treatments from my injuries incurred on May 9th. Something as simple as that so I could scan and forward it onto my lawyers for us to submit at the next workers' compensation board hearing. After all, the doctor's office does want to get paid, right? Well, according to that office, they were not able to make arrangements to draw this document up to send to me. I had been there numerous times for treatment. How could they not? I was being seen under my workers' compensation case for 5/9/17. At that point, I left it as such and notified my law firm to let them handle it. I recognized that I did not need to get into the stress of this situation as I had before and luckily this time around, I was able to realize it before it happened.

Although New York has a workplace violence program that is in place, it varies from agency to agency. In the Department of Corrections and Community Supervision (which is also part of Parole), they have a program directive that is much more stringent due to the type of work environments, clientele, and other areas. While the acting commissioner of the department claims it to be a zero-tolerance policy, my incident obviously was not inclusive. After doing some additional research, I have found a lot more data pertaining to the issues with this growing problem. Like with many crime victims, they all have their reasons for not coming forward. In our field of work, like I have mentioned earlier, it would be considered crossing the "thin blue line" to do so. But that blue line is supposed to be family, right? The answer is a big fat no. You put any group together regardless of its size and you're guaranteed one thing: Politics. And where there is politics, there will be cover-up and corruption. Agency policies and protocols should be developed to provide guidance on appropriate responses to staff victimization, critical incidents, and workplace violence. Policies and protocols should reflect and augment the agency's mission, goals, and objectives for post-trauma response. They should also provide specific guidance on how the agency and its staff will respond to these types of incidents. Aspects include how incidents should be reported, how confidentiality of victims will be protected, and how investigations will be conducted. Policies and protocols should also identify available services for victims of violence that occurs within the workplace. Additional topics may also be addressed. After Corrections agencies develop new policies and protocols on responding to violent incidents within the community corrections environment, staff training is imperative. Agency staff need to receive training on both the specific policies and procedures that are in place and the resources that are available to victims following an incident. Ideally, training should also address strategies for providing support to those victimized by violence in the workplace, both in the short- and long-term. More intensive training should be offered to members of an agency's post-trauma response team to ensure they are adequately prepared to respond should an incident occur. Most of the training given these days at Fishkill like other prisons around the state are done on an annual basis, usually for an eight-hour day, broken down into segments, and between lunch and breaks, you might actually see about six hours of course time. The PowerPoint presentation normally consists of the identification of the program, its implementation, enforcement, and other areas to be addressed. A nurse working the second floor in the Regional Medical Unit recently informed me when I saw her at a friend's gathering that workplace violence is occurring on a daily basis at Fishkill's prison.

Overcoming the traumatic experience of violent victimization can take an extended period of time. In my case, it was the physical injuries as well as the psychological that took so much time. Some of it due to the fact that the prison's administration had controverted my disability claim of job-related injuries due to the assault. The State Insurance Fund works at a snail's pace, but the need to recognize a serious situation such as mine would warrant a more immediate, thorough investigation. Research indicates that the reaction of others to an individual's victimization and the degree of social support that the victim receives can have significant implications for his or her ultimate recovery. When this happens to another officer in the line of duty, especially when it is blue on blue, you as the victim are immediately labeled, and whatever reputation you had prior was now ousted. It is imperative that corrections, probation and parole agencies allow ample time for victimized staff to reconstruct their lives in the aftermath of a crime, particularly when it occurs on the job. Often there is a tendency to get back to "business as usual" as quickly as possible; however, this approach can exacerbate the trauma experienced by a victimized correction officer. Both the agency, as a whole, and fellow colleagues, individually, should respond to the victim in a supportive, non-judgmental manner. Really, you would only find that through your true friends. Those who spoke to you before that you thought may had been a friend are now going with the flow, following the other officers "nay-sayers" group's opinion and statements against me, not only for speaking out, but for doing the right thing in this type of situation that happens on a daily basis at Fishkill Correctional Facility. The rights of victimized staff should be acknowledged, including the right to be consulted in decisions related to the investigation and prosecution of the case, the right to be informed about the status of the case, and the right to workers' and victims' compensation. But I had tried numerous times to get informed, either through the prison, the Office of Special Investigation, the Bureau of Labor Relations, and even the State Police BCI, with whom I made a criminal complaint the following morning. All of them withheld information, including denying my FOIL requests, and absolutely without any doubt in my mind, treated me again with absolute deliberate indifference.

State corrections provides employees who become victims of workplace violence with information about available services, such as victim services provided within the agency, community-based services, and Employee Assistance Programs (EAPs). Depending on which prison you work at, they will not always "fully" guide you during your time in need. It would be up to you to make those telephone calls. Agencies also should be prepared to make appropriate referrals for mental health treatment. When possible, referrals should be made for treatment providers who have specialized training in treating correctional professionals. But again, this is something that should be done, but rarely has been as a past practice. I am seeing news that soon corrections staff will be required to undergo more regular annual psychological examinations unlike the required one time that they did when they first applied for the job. This has all come about as a part of the knee-jerk reaction to the escape of two inmates from Clinton Correctional Facility in Dannemora, New York. The state spent over one million dollars a day in this manhunt that took nearly three weeks to complete. This escape should have never happened, but yet again, it was due largely in part to the broken prison system and Albany's policies. Several years prior to the escape at Clinton, there had been another one, similar in some aspects, that happened at Elmira Correctional Facility in Southern New York, not far from the Pennsylvania border. This escape did not nearly involve as much as Clinton's, but the department should have learned and taken action across the state at that point. DOCCS has always been reactive, never ever proactive. Never. These days it appears the general public, the political arenas, and all of the media are now interested on what happens behind those walls and fences. Years ago, this was not the case. Basically, after a criminal was convicted and sentenced, he or she was sent off to prison and the "key was thrown away."

Agencies also should protect the confidentiality and privacy rights of staff who have been victimized while on duty. But this is not the case. Once word hits the Watch Commander's office or the Time and Attendance Control Unit, word will get out amongst the friends of those who work in those areas. Everyone likes to talk about everyone else's business. We are all guilty of it at some point, but when it comes to these types of situations, privacy is mandatory as it should be. That's why we have laws to protect us. The Health Insurance Portability and Accountability Act of 1996 (HIPAA), Public Law 104-191, was enacted on August 21, 1996. Sections 261 through 264 of HIPAA require the Secretary of HHS to publicize standards for the electronic exchange, privacy, and security of health information. Staff should be able to access victim services and treatment in the aftermath of a workplace violence incident without fear of others finding out – including colleagues and clients/supervisees. Any limitations or exceptions to the protection of confidentiality for victims following an incident of workplace violence should be explained in agency policy and discussed in resources for staff such as brochures, handbooks, and training programs.

New York State corrections agencies should coordinate with law enforcement agencies and prosecutors' offices to ensure that criminal investigations into incidents of workplace violence are conducted effectively and efficiently, and referrals for prosecution are made as appropriate. Victimized employees should be fully consulted on how the department will proceed with the case as it relates to administrative and criminal investigations, criminal charges, and sanctions. In both administrative and criminal proceedings, victimized staff should be provided all of the rights accorded by state law to "civilian" crime victims. This applies whether the violence is from an inmate, the general public, or another employee, such as a fellow officer. But this is almost laughable. There is no way this agency would even admit to this type of environment if it were involving another officer. Like in my case, especially with the association with the union executive's family member, it would be like them admitting fault and claiming liability, thus making the department culpable. The last thing this department wants is another string of lawsuits. They get enough of those from inmates and their families as it is now. And with all my years at Fishkill Correctional Facility, the District Attorney is an independently-elected public official who prosecutes or otherwise disposes of all crimes committed in the County of Duchess, including state institutions and correctional facilities, on behalf of the people of the State of New York.

"My staff and I are committed to ensuring that offenders are held accountable for their criminal conduct. We are also committed to assuring that the voices of victims are heard and that their experiences with the criminal justice system are as safe and convenient as possible," said William Grady, Duchess County D.A.

Not a fact according to many of the officers and staff who have been victims of assaults. It has long been known that the administration's response to our grief and stress of the local justice system's lack of due process was coming from the D.A.'s office. We were often told that they did not have the time, budget, or staff to pursue convictions against inmates who were already locked up and serving time for prior crimes. Unless, of course, it was a major situation at the prison. Whatever the case, regardless, the department's workplace violence prevention program directive covers all aspects of the risk factors whether it was from staff or an inmate.

It was now Monday morning, with everyone back to their normal routines following the holiday schedules. Phone calls and emails to follow up were being made. I had called one local law firm who I had been in touch with and was potentially going to be able to get me representation regarding the improper practice charges that had been previously filed with the state's Public Employee Relations Board. Their director in Albany was awaiting my follow-up since I had requested an extension in order to get representation. I finally heard back from the state's Attorney General's Office. They had left a voicemail regarding their decision on the forms that were filed and sent in by the Senator's office. It appeared to be a conflict of interest since they normally represent the state as well so it would be a conflict of interest. It is really beginning to feel as if one is at the dentist getting their teeth pulled. One after another, after another. But like the workings of most governmental agencies, these things take time. And with time, all things work themselves out, one way or the other. I have been well supported by fellow colleagues who are well aware of the way things happen in this department. They have been behind me the whole time, helping me out with research, suggestions, phone calls, documentation, and reaching out to others who would be able to get answers. When it seemed as if it was a winnable situation from the beginning, time grew and so did the outlook of what appeared to be a failure to produce the key players of this cover-up. It was plain and simple to the naked eye. State agencies did not want any part of investigating other state agencies. It was not just the politics. It was the failure to do one's job, to take responsibility and stand up for those who are rightfully deserving of the protections afforded to them during these types of situations. It has always been said that it is more difficult to deal with the people we work with than the inmates inside those fences and walls. There were ways to handle inmates that were troublesome or not wanted in a certain unit or area. But then there were also ways of dealing with fellow officers that were not part of a group or a clique in a particular area. It was similar to a gang's territory. If you were in an area that had "regular officers who worked their everyday," boy, life was sure going to be made miserable for you that day, or for whatever period of time you were assigned there. If they couldn't get a supervisor to move you from that assignment, then things would begin to happen. So now you had to deal with the inmates, your responsibilities of overseeing them, and following the procedures of the tasks for that shift. And then you had to worry about your lunch, personal belongings, and your back for any type of harassment coming your way from other officers who did not want you working there. So, looking back on it all, as much as it has been observed happening to other officers besides myself, without the presence of video cameras, it is very difficult to prove these situations in many circumstances. Most times the officer affected by this type of situation would give up the assignment and place a bid for a new area or building, allowing the other officers that were "bullying" him or her to get over on them and the system which is supposed to be there to protect them. Not even the supervisors normally want to hear these types of incidents when they are reported. They have enough to do already without having to deal with officers' incidents. That's why there are ways of sweeping up messes and covering up an incident or two. Or three.

My law firm down in White Plains, Jason, Warren and Nick, have all assured me that their work is in progress dealing with this case along with my seven other workers' compensation injury cases. They wanted me to just relax and focus on getting better physically. One cannot get better that way until they are better mentally. Funny how the mind can control your physical well-being. But stress in itself is a killer. I have already dealt with that and still do as I write this. But from my crisis last month, I have learned a lot on how to deal with the situations, how to handle them and not get overwhelmed by the negativity. Having so much time on my hands these days, I need to keep distracted by staying focused on my present-day treatments as I continue my goals at Core Care Physical Therapy, attempting to regain full use of my left shoulder and arm once again. Once I get approved for my neck as part of my injury case, we can then proceed for the much-needed additional treatments on that. The neck pain is daily and overcoming, which causes my shoulder recovery to be slower in progression than normal. I look forward to the day that I can finally say that I am no longer going through all of this hell. As large as this department is, and many of those officers around the state that can relate to my story will tell you, we are all just a number. We all have the same goal, to go home the same way we arrive to work. But we all have different jobs and sometimes we forget we are all on the same team. No one is treated like an individual when it comes to our central office in Albany. Therefore, you become tangled up in this system, only to be chewed up and spat out. The amount of pain, injuries, and stress inflicted upon me over my years on the job was horrendous. Even when I mentioned the number of surgeries alone from my injuries on the job, each and every officer took a step back in disbelief. Shocked as they were, the fact is that violence has spiked and will continue to do so until the system is fixed. But I kept going back to work after each injury. I thought I could keep doing it. I worried about what others at the prison thought way too much. But no more. It is now time to think about me and my family. Nobody else will do that for me and ultimately, I am responsible for them. I tried to take a stand on this whole matter, exhausting all avenues with my efforts and look where it got me in October. Almost dead. Another statistic for the record books. Looking back afterward, having a different prospective has changed things. Believe me, the last thing myself, or anyone else I know, is that I do not want to become a statistic.

Chapter Seventeen
'Tis the Season

Now that the Christmas season is upon us, it is the favorite time of the year for my kids and family. We have some longstanding traditions and thanks to my neighbor Mike, he took the time to come over and get up on my roof to hang the large wreath and to place some lights up around the front of the house since I was not physically able to do so. It was a busy time of the year. My wife did some holiday shopping at the store, having me tag along one day to get me out of the house. But all of that walking I found out was not working out well for me. Every bench I could find, I would be quick to grab a seat. Most days at home, the doorbell would ring with the packages being delivered. Sometimes I had no idea that she even put any orders in online. While our holiday spending was definitely going to be trimmed down this year, we were still able to find some deals on the kid's wish lists. Once again, the calls started to come in again. It was also that time for my annual family Christmas portraits in the studio. Each year in the past, I would set up a different themed set, complete with a background, fireplace or trees, presents, wreaths, and various decorations. This made for some great income during the holiday season when weddings were about wrapped up for that time of the year. It was depressing each time I had to respond back to them though, turning away the business, the clients, most of all my regulars who always used my services, all due to the fact that I was on disability due to my injuries as a result of this workplace violence.

I mentioned earlier that there are quite a few employed at Fishkill Correctional Facility that have family who work there alongside of them. I too have lots of family who have both held civilian and officer staff positions. Two of them on my wife's side worked at Fishkill and one of them at Wallkill, and on my side, I have a number of extended family who are currently officers in the upstate region. I have been fortunate to share this experience with them and to find out more about what their observations have been in their own assigned prison facilities. Even though Fishkill was not my "original home" jail as they say, it became such upon my settlement into this area when I met and married my wife, whom I have been with since the year 2000. I hope that when this is over, that myself and my family can move onto bigger and better things. I know for certain that there will be open doors. I am a person who has the ability to seek out the type of living my family would need and so much deserves. My talent and experience of being a professional photographer and photojournalist holds so much value for me. I know there will be opportunities. I just hope that physically I will be able to continue in that capacity as we move into the future. There is a stereotype for corrections officers who in the past have brought about a reputation of being involved in domestic disputes at home and then bringing their problems to work. This is another reason we have such a high divorce and suicide rate in our career. However, a statistic I am. I will never forget the time once I graduated after the academy that I met a woman who found out I was a correction officer. We had a pleasant conversation at first but without provocation, it soon turned sour. Without even a reason, I was immediately judged with her comment, "My ex-husband was a C.O., he was the worst, you're all alike!" as she turned and walked away. I should have seen the big picture at that time. But looking back at it now, I think I understand what she meant. Not that we were all the same, but there were many bad apples and not a lot of men or women who were previously married to C.O.s have many nice things to say about them. These men and women who chose this career path and made some bad decisions during its course, continue to behave in the manner that is acceptable to some, or should I say, "tolerated" by those co-workers within the area and the supervision of which they are gainfully employed. There are several officers that I know who have other professions and work outside of the prison. They usually want to do their shift and get out of there so they can get to their other jobs. Then there are those that just do the least they can possibly get away with doing at work, spreading their disgruntled attitudes amongst their peers. Bitch, moan, and cry is all you would hear them doing in person and on the phones. You could never get them to take action about an issue. It would just be easier to go to the bar after work, get drunk and drown in their sorrows. This would temporarily blind their problems, but eventually compound them when it became a financial issue, perhaps overuse of their sick hours, and then even worse, leading them to trouble with outside law enforcement agencies. I could never understand why any of them would want to do that, but then again, maybe I never really understood their underlying problems because I too have had difficulties in my relationship at home.

By now I have made a follow-up with the Public Employee Relations Board in regards to the Improper Practice Charge complaint that I filed last month. This is part of the Taylor Law (Public Employees Fair Employment Act) under Article 14 of the State Civil Service Law. I had to file an amendment in order to provide a more detailed description of the violations that had occurred over the last several months. With the help of my logbooks, documentation, printed emails, and phone records, I was able to chronologically recall specific instances. This falls into subsection 209-a, improper employee organization practices which is known as the NYS Civil Service Law, that our union has to abide by. It shall be an improper practice for an employee organization or its agents deliberately (a) to interfere with, restrain, or coerce public employees in the exercise of the rights granted in section 202, or to cause, or attempt to cause, a public employer to do so; (b) to refuse to negotiate collectively in good faith with a public employer, provided it is the duly recognized or certified representative of the employees of such employer; or (c) to breach its duty of fair representation to public employees under this article. My case was focused on part (c). Now my employer, Fishkill Correctional Facility, becomes a party to this matter. The public employer shall be made a party to any charge filed under subdivision two of this section which alleges that the duly recognized or certified employee organization breached its duty of fair representation in the processing of or failure to process a claim that the public employer has breached its agreement with such employee organization.

There is a lot of legwork do be done yet, and my amendment which was notarized and sent certified return receipt requested just today, still needs to be reviewed by the board. We will take a wait-and-see approach, but the next step would be, if the board determines that I had made sufficient showing both that there is reasonable cause to believe an improper practice has occurred and it appears that immediate and irreparable injury, loss, or damage will result, thereby rendering a resulting judgment on the merits ineffectual, necessitating maintenance of, or return to the status quo to provide meaningful relief, the board shall petition the Supreme Court in Albany County. Keeping in mind that I have all the documented evidence, I would be extremely surprised and somehow disheartened all at the same time that yet again there is more failure in our system to seek justice. The email attachment that was presumably inadvertently attached on the Union President's email reply to me back in August was damning evidence in itself. There had been a correspondence email between the Union President and the Regional Vice President Mallory. Mallory had indicated in a short summarized sentence to the President that "This guy will sue the union on a DFR charge." This is a significant implication on the union's part that they were well aware of their duties and responsibilities, as well as their breach in the duty of fair representation in the matter of the incident on May 9, 2017.

Chapter Eighteen
Get Out and Stay Out

I just got off the phone with George, a long-time fellow correction officer. He worked a different shift than I did but we would often see each other in our work station areas when we did double shifts. George was always a good source to get caught up on whenever something had happened while you were away either on vacation, or like in my case, out on disability. There were some things I needed for him to confirm for me and to reassure that certain things were being taken care of. We went into the conversation on how all of the regular seasoned veterans were getting sick and tired of all the changes taking place, and how each day stepping into the prison with the gate slamming behind you was a reminder that once you were in, you were in. One could only hope when your shift ended that you went back out that same gate, the same way you came in. Many of the officers that had been there for well over 20 years and had prior military experience, were now taking advantage of the state's "buyback program," where you could purchase up to three years of credit from your military service in exchange toward your retirement. Instead of doing 25 years, you would only have to work 22. There were many pros and cons to this, for example, it might cost you up to $3,000 or more for each year, and that money could be transferred right from your deferred compensation fund account without a dime coming from your wallet. However, you were buying the time credits to get out and would be retiring at your current rate of pay as per the contract. You would retire at your current rate of pay for 22 years, plus your overtime if you had any. If you stayed past 25 years, most likely you would have a higher pay rate which would reflect the difference in your retirement pay. Either way, you would be out of that environment. As I mentioned before, for those that were eligible to retire and had over 25 years on the job that stayed and continued to work, I would often refer to them as those that failed to plan for their financial future. Sure, some cases were unique, divorces, child support, alimony, etc., would force someone to stay on the job. But I will put it to you like this. It's like being a homeowner and your house is on fire. You keep running back inside and grabbing all of your important valuables, sentimental or not, hoping to escape the smoke and flames and getting outside as the fire trucks arrive. But if you stay in too long, the devil himself might just get you, the smoke and flames will eat your heart, soul, and body as you are consumed up in the aftermath of the tragedy. The ideas I always taught as a Fire Prevention Officer were to get out and stay out. Not one person's life is worth anything that can be replaced. The same goes for working in a dangerous prison environment. Whether you are dealing with the perils of an unknown situation regarding a well-planned or staged event by the inmates in order to set you up, or dealing with the constant gang retaliations on each other involving deadly weapons, or even the daily drug trades that can happen right under one's nose without even realizing it. The job is dangerous enough to deal with the activities inside the walls and fences of prisons, in which the employer is charged with providing a safe working environment for its staff. Sure, we took the oath and signed on the dotted line for the job, but that did not mean that we gave up our rights of protection, our rights of safety, and our rights to justice. Let a convicted felon or even another correction officer assault a cop on the street, seriously enough to disable him or her and force them to have surgery, and surely you will see them catching another jail sentence. But when it's inside the prisons, it's a whole different world. Rarely, if ever, will you see that happen on the side of justice. When it's time to go, it's time to go. Get the hell out.

A recent editorial in the *New York Times* on December 6th headlined "Holding Prison Guards Accountable," spoke in some detail about the outcome of what occurs inside the prisons as I mentioned earlier. Might I add, first of all, a guard might be someone working at a mall, or on a beach watching swimmers, or even with the national guard, but surely it is not a state correction officer. Depending on the story, good or bad, that dictates what the writer will describe the person's title as. The *Times'* story talks about officers that often escape punishment for acts of brutality because district attorneys in communities where prisons provide jobs, and are thus essential to the community's economic health, are hesitant to charge them. This should certainly apply in my case as well. Yes, there are bad eggs in every basket.

You must equate the human factor into each and every career path any person has ever taken, regardless if you are the U.S. president or just a state employee. Another factor is that the union contract with the state shields prison workers from prosecution even in many egregious cases. That contract is now being renegotiated. The *Times* reports that Gov. Andrew Cuomo needs to hold out for a new one that strengthens state control over the prison system by holding guards more closely accountable for wrongdoing. No pun intended here, but there are two sides to that fence. First of all, just getting the Governor to take action which would benefit the officers with better protections would result in less injuries. Equipping the facilities with literally an entire network of digital cameras would also prevent much more violence. But if it did not do that, then it certainly would tell the incident's details more accurately and hold those accountable for their actions. Without cameras, it's easy to say, "Ok, here's how it went down."

The union contract makes it difficult to fire an officer. I believe it's civil service in itself that makes it difficult to fire one from his or her job. The union provides protection, but unfortunately, only when its hand is forced to do so in order to protect a much larger group as a whole. When it comes down to one or two individuals, often times, like in my case once again, it goes on ignored in the hopes that it will dissipate and go away. The *Times* further reports that one particular provision gives guards the right to refuse to answer questions put to them by the police, which undermines the investigation from the start. The contract also requires a convoluted disciplinary process presided over by arbitrators who need union approval to keep their jobs, and who thus tend to lean toward suspension rather than dismissal. In my situation on the evening of April 21, 2015, the night of the use of force with the inmate at Fishkill, I laid in bed #29 inside the emergency room at Vassar Brothers Hospital awaiting a series of tests, but I had been hooked up to several wires which prevented me from getting out of bed to walk down the hall to use the phone to call the prison and request union representatives to the hospital. Ultimately, nobody arrived even after numerous calls by the escorting officers who were there with us. But the BCI still kept coming at us with the easy questions. Sure, we had the right to refuse answering questions. After all, we still had not done our official reports. As I described earlier in my book, the investigators did speak to me after they were done with the other officer laying in the next room across from me. After a few minutes of telling them how long I have been on the job, where I worked, what was my shift, etc., it got to the point where I stopped and requested a phone call. At that point, that's when most of the discrimination and mistreatment against me began, as reported to COPBA the following day at the union president's request.

Chapter Nineteen
My Family Pays the Consequences

Stress on the job in law enforcement takes its toll on not just the individual in his or her own capacity, but those that surround them at home as well. In my case, having gone through the numerous documented uses of force, assaults inflicted upon me, the environmental violence and stressful effects it has on one another, I kept going back to work thinking I had to make this work somehow, to keep my career going, to keep my business going, all in order to support my family that included two very young children. Beyond the stress and PTSD that gets bottled up from these incidents, there are officers behind those walls that seem to be able to handle it better than others. For some reason, I had been able to do so for such a long time. I had my goals, and like most of us inside those walls and fences, we just wanted to do our time and get out of there. Surely you had the responsibility to watch each other's backs but these days, with the changes being made in the department, it's everyone for themselves. The inmates know this and take advantage of this change. The physical limitations that have overcome my body at this point has rendered me unable to fully defend myself without the higher chance of exacerbation of any of my multiple work-related documented injuries. I wanted to have quality of life still, with my kids growing up and all, what good would I be if I was not capable of even taking them out to a ball game. As it was for my crisis back in October, I almost lost all of that. But now I am on the mend, trying to maintain course in a manner in which I can become the happy-go-lucky kind of guy everyone knew me as.

I wake up each morning dealing with the constant pain in my shoulder still, the surgery limiting my movement, let alone the strength I once had in my left arm. Physical therapy is picking up that ball for me, slowly but surely. I am keeping my eye on the prize, but I am only in so much control of that destiny.

The neck injuries, combined with the left sided TMJ, and left shoulder recovery, leaves me rendered disabled in such a way that I'm not physically able to function as I once did prior to this assault at Fishkill back last May. Coupled with the numerous back and knee injuries to boot, it was more of an uphill battle for me than ever. With my wife working full time, she has to do more now than before. Sometimes I call upon my neighbors Mike or Eric, even guys down at the firehouse, or other family members, to help come do things at my home for me. My kids are starting to become a big help around the house as well, like moving firewood, shoveling snow, cleaning, and much more. I hate to rely on others, sometimes I feel as if I am a burden, especially to my wife. I have become more and more dependent on their help than I ever had or wanted to. It was always me going out to help others in the past, something that I enjoyed doing, but now I find myself on the opposite side of the spectrum.

The pain and suffering, along with the psychological trauma, has done nothing but put my family through hell. All of this caused by one person. Maybe I had it coming, with all of this stress being bottled up, but this was certainly an incident which triggered my ideations, and the diagnosis of the stress, PTSD, anxiety and depression. The hardships alone make it even more complicated. Not having that extra business income during this time of the year is something I never even imagined having to experience. My wife has been actively involved with my health and well-being; in fact, she is now considering filing a lawsuit against those parties who were involved. When I signed on the dotted line to take this job, we all knew there would be some type of hazards to this type of environment. But nobody should ever have to endure the workplace violence involving another officer causing such injuries as to potentially end your career, who is protected by higher-level union executives. And who has done this before to other officers. Maybe Thompson thinks he is untouchable, maybe he feels invincible knowing a larger group like our union has his back. But when their duty to fairly represent another member of the same union who is in the same good standing occurs, then they have another thing coming. I come from a large family too, a very big one. I know people too. Sometimes that one wrongdoer does not realize that they knocked on the wrong door, picked on the wrong person, or for that matter, assaulted the wrong guy. Those involved with the cover-up to include the employer may have thought that there was no way I had the ability or aspirations to take this as far as I had, farther than any other officers would have, but this is not over until it's over. This is something that they will not hear the end of for a very long time. Not if I can help it, not if my family can help it.

My family has taken a nosedive during this ordeal in such a way that they too have been psychologically harmed for their lifetime. To have experienced what I went through back in October during my crisis, was something that they will always remember, dealing with in their thoughts, dreams, and minds from here on out and into the future. Sometimes since this has happened, I feel at fault for putting them through such on ordeal. I did not plan for this to happen, it just did. Hearing their voices on the phone while I was in the hospital, or seeing the faces of those that came to visit me really engraved in my mind just how bad this situation had become. It was brick after brick being knocked down of such a large strong wall that we as a family had built together. This is something that stays on one's permanent record as well. As my brother told me, this could be something that follows me into my future forever. He was not happy about this at all, he had a hard time understanding why all of this occurred, and what the hell was going on that it ended up in a most certain tragic situation for us. In my mind, I feel like I have to mend myself as well as those that I may have hurt during that situation. Putting others at risk who responded to the scene like off-duty Lt. Richards, who was the first to arrive before the calvary came to the scene. I am the last person on earth to ever hurt another person intentionally and without just cause, but to deal with all of this at once is not going to happen overnight. I just hope that we can get past this one day in the near future and move on to bigger and better things. I am not so sure about being physically 100 % better, there will always be issues, so I am told, but I will have to learn to live with the pain. As for Thompson, maybe someday he will be judged by the big man above, or by karma. Or by the judicial system, whether it be the state or federal level, either way, with my family standing behind me.

Chapter Twenty
The Department's Investigation Response

Just arrived home from meeting with a labor lawyer at a well-known law firm in the region and things looked pretty good in the case. They were going to represent me and my family in our case against Thompson and possibly the department as well. When I walked in the door at the firm with my briefcase, one of the lawyers looked at me and said, "Is that all of your paperwork?" as his eyes gazed at me, not being the usual sight of an arriving new client. "You're well documented and very prepared, let's sit down and show me some documents, I will need to make some copies to get us started."

Within the hour, we had wrapped up and made a follow-up appointment. These days with the holidays creeping up on us, the mail is arriving later and later each day at home. The dogs started barking this afternoon for some reason, I wasn't expecting anyone at that moment, but when I got to the door, I noticed it was my regular mail delivery woman, Kathy. She had a bundle in her arms and needed me to sign a green signature card. I was very familiar with those, having sent out so many of them over the last several months. Took a look at the manila envelope and saw it was from the State Department of Labor, Division of Public Employee Safety and Health in Albany.

"This is what I have been waiting for," I told Kathy, as she darted back to her truck for her busy route. The files had to be over two inches thick, containing records from the Department of Corrections' response to the investigation, written responses from supervisors and officers involved, as well as the Office of Special Investigation's final report, and an additional copy of my personnel file. I immediately started to go through the pages one by one, reading into reports that had not yet been made available to me. Some investigation, I thought, the Department of Corrections and its Special Investigations Unit left some details that were deficient and contradicting between the interviews and actual written reports. They were even signed off as completed by supervisors overseeing the entirety of this incident. Someone was in a hurry to shrug this off, to cover it up and turn out the lights. But when this happens, you can almost guarantee almost anywhere, sooner or later, those slip-ups will be found and exposed.

The Public Employee Safety and Health, Department of Labor investigators and I had an over-the-phone interview in regards to the response from the Department of Corrections weeks ago, however, there were numerous details that we had not caught onto until I was able to physically see the paperwork. So, I wrote back on my response in an email to the DOL investigators to inform them that I had received the packet and thanked them for their timely response. At this point, I was dealing with Jeff, who is one of the discrimination investigators that oversaw the handling of my case. On the memorandum from Sergeant Oswald to Lieutenant Michaels dated 5/9/17, he stated that I had requested to come to his office to report this incident at 3:25 p.m., yet, during his interview with investigators on 7/28/17, Sergeant Oswald told Inv. Tonka that I had reported to his office at 3:45 p.m. This assault took place at approximately 2:30 p.m., and I reported this to Sergeant Oswald at 2:45 p.m. There are obvious contradictions in his facts in both his reports and interviews. Even the copy of the unusual incident logbook from the watch commander's office stated that I had reported this at 2:45 p.m. on May 9th. His memorandum was of "complete falsehood," as I am using the same terminology as he did of my report of his actions against me.

On 10/24/17, Lt. Michael's memorandum to the investigation stated in response that I had been under no constraints to complete my statements or was under any pressure to finish it. While I was at the hospital emergency room that evening, Lieutenant Michaels had been on the phone with the Deputy Superintendent Oblinski to report to him what updates there were of my condition. They wanted my report right away as I had mentioned prior during my interview and statements. Their urgency to get it was so that they could begin to get the investigation going and have it ready for the Bureau of Labor Relations to make their decision the following morning. Even though I had been medicated with muscle relaxers and pain killers at the emergency room and was driven back to the facility from the hospital upon discharge, I only agreed to return to complete the paperwork because I had been requested to do so by Lieutenant Michaels.

Although the Department's Office of Special Investigations' final investigation report found the "allegations" to be unsubstantiated, they were far from being unfounded. Furthermore, Investigator Tonka's report only stated he spoke to certain people, like for instance, to the Deputy Superintendent of Administration whose simple response was how the system of work repair orders are processed. The maintenance staff civilians were the ones to talk to, and I told them that. They covered my work area when I had dropped work orders with to get repairs done to my office area and they had difficulties completing them as they worked on the same shift as Thompson. He would ask them to either hold off on the repairs or not to do them altogether. The civilians did not want to get in between the middle of any territorial disputes, as they mentioned to me. If you wanted things done, one hand would have to wash the other, that's how it has always worked in Corrections. Thompson complained to the superintendent even before this incident, and to other supervisors in the area about me, in an attempt to reflect discredit upon me and to shed a negative light ever since I first started taking over my new post. He claimed I was leaving the area in a total disarray after my shift, hardly a fact, as anyone that ever worked directly with me knew how I kept my areas clean on a regular basis. I always took pride in my areas of responsibility, that's what I was taught to do growing up and in the military. This was a direct attempt for Thompson to get me removed from that post so he would not be working in the same area with me.

Looking further into these reports, Thompson's claim during the investigation interview with Inv. Tonka claimed that he was the victim during the incident on May 4th. Many people knew Thompson to have a short temper. All I wanted to know is why he had left me that derogatory harassing note, and this question alone caused him to go into a rage. I just stood there with my hands at my side, as witnessed by Officer Potter, expecting him to haul off on me and hit me while he was screaming in my face. The details in the investigation report regarding this incident were kept simple and short. Although Thompson admitted to that as well, he was not counseled for improper communication with staff, or even written up due to the serious nature of it, having a witness involved to boot.

Also, on 7/28/17, Officer Omway, the Delta checkpoint officer who originally told me that he saw what happened and asked me if I was ok, was now being interviewed by Investigator Tonka. Omway stated he does not remember if Thompson asked him about Sloman in the hallway on the day of the assault and further stated he does not know Thompson. But when Thompson was interviewed that same day, he told Tonka that he did speak to the Delta Checkpoint Officer Omway, asking him if he saw Sloman leave yet. So there was communication between the two of them as I stated in my original report, but how could one of them remember so vividly and not the other? Officer Omway stated he was preparing for his shift, yet he only has ONE hallway to observe from his desk, the ONE that Thompson and I were passing each other in, alone with no others, at the time of the assault. If Thompson was talking to Omway about Sloman as he was coming down the hallway, then surely this supports my initial report statement that he was looking in our direction and observed the incident, and then acknowledged me to see if I was ok after Thompson left the area. It does not take much for an educated person to see clearly into this cover-up, and it's sad that this is another unfortunate miscarriage of justice within our prison system, one that has affected literally hundreds of people within my community, all at the hands of a single individual. Time will tell as we await word back from the Public Employee Safety and Health (Department of Labor) with the response to the contradicting and vague submittal from the Department of Corrections. Also on hand, the Public Employee Relations Board is still currently at task with the amendments of the deficiency notice from the previously filed improper practice charges against the officers' union. I am expecting nothing productive until at least after the first of the year once the holidays pass. Then at that time I will at least be following up with my fourth attorney, the labor lawyer we are seeking representation with against the damages from this case, outside of what workers' compensation would normally cover.

Chapter Twenty-One
The Opioid Epidemic with Workers' Compensation

According to the National Institute on Drug Abuse, every day, more than 90 Americans die after overdosing on opioids. Opioids are a class of drugs that include the illegal drug heroin, synthetic opioids such as fentanyl, and pain relievers available legally by prescription, such as oxycodone (OxyContin), hydrocodone (Vicodin), codeine, morphine, and many others. Any long-term use can put someone at risk of addiction, even if the substance is used as prescribed. Many people who use opioids will develop a tolerance to them – a phenomenon that can trigger the cycle of addiction. This means that the same amount of the drug no longer has the same effect as it once did. When this occurs, people routinely take more and more of the substance to elicit the desired response. This ever-increasing dosing places one at great risk for overdose. New York's Duchess, Orange, Ulster Counties and surrounding areas are being affected by the opioid/heroin epidemic. Opioid addiction can be very frightening – not only for the individual with the addiction but for their family and friends as well. Breaking free of opioid, heroin, or prescription drug abuse takes effort, and it's difficult to do safely alone. Support groups can help and at the same time, they can provide support to family members. The pharmacy industry in the United States is a 500-billion-dollar business, and it has not changed in over 100 years, according to sources at *CBS News Network*.

Centers for Disease Control and Prevention released troubling statistics on the growing epidemic of drug and opioid overdose deaths in the United States. The origins of this epidemic have been linked to prescription opioids. While it is unknown how many drug and opioid overdose deaths are associated with workplace injuries and illnesses, it is clear that this national epidemic is impacting workers and employers. A May-2014 NIOSH blog noted that injured workers are frequently treated with powerful prescription drugs. The blog reported on studies demonstrating that narcotics account for 25% of prescription costs in workers' compensation systems and that those costs are rising. An important avenue for combating prescription drug abuse are guidelines that health care providers can use to offer safer and more effective pain treatment. NIOSH's sister agency at the Centers for Disease Control and Prevention, the National Center for Injury Prevention and Control (NCIPC), has released draft opioid prescribing guidelines and has invited public comment through January 13, 2016. NIOSH invites interested stakeholders to provide input on the draft CDC opioid prescribing guidelines.

In addition to work injuries and illnesses being the reason opioids are prescribed in the first place, there are others ways in which this epidemic is undoubtedly impacting workers and employers. The use of prescription opioids may impact the ability of a person to return to work, and ultimately can negatively affect their livelihood. If workers are under the influence of opioids while they are at work, they are likely to be at increased risk for injury. For workers in safety sensitive jobs, such as transportation and operators of heavy equipment, there will be increased risks for catastrophic events that impact many besides the worker.

NIOSH remains committed to primary prevention of occupational injuries and illnesses as our primary focus. We recognize the impact of the current opioid overdose epidemic on the workplace, and have compiled resources that may be useful for workers, employers, health care providers, and other stakeholders on a new topic page. We also believe that the NIOSH Center for Workers' Compensation Studies provides a venue for research that can help inform interventions through workers' compensation systems. The California Workers' Compensation Institute (CWCI) has identified that a small percentage of physicians account for the majority of the opioid prescriptions in workers' comp. It's clear we can identify who is overprescribing these drugs, but where is the action on the part of regulators to stop this abuse? Why aren't the state medical boards looking into this? Opioids are controlled substances, but what is the Drug Enforcement Agency (DEA) doing to stop the widespread diversion of these drugs?

Oversight of opioids in workers' comp also needs to include a system to monitor the injured worker. The CWCI found that the patients receiving the most opioids received them from an average of 3.3 different physicians –

creating an even greater risk for abuse and misuse of these drugs. In my case, it had been from as many as 5-6. So, what do we do to address opioids in workers' comp? Partnering with a good **Pharmacy Benefit Manager (PBM)** is a start. Your PBM should focus on appropriate utilization of pharmacy, not just the price paid per prescription fill. It is critical that utilization – not the cost per fill – becomes the cost driver. Claim handlers also must consider the psycho-social factors that could lead to prescription misuse. Does the injured worker have a history of addictive behavior, such as smoking or alcohol abuse? Such individuals are at greater risk for developing an addiction to opioids. Additional regulatory support is also needed. The states of Washington and others, including New York, are making great strides in trying to control opioid misuse. The strict controls instituted by some states have resulted in significantly reduced opioid utilization – and more importantly, a significant reduction in deaths from opioid overdose. The time for action on this issue is now.

The system is taking on this problem as an entire issue. Rather than looking at it individually, with such a high number of workers' compensation cases, it would be too costly and highly productive to monitor this on a case-by-case basis. Because of this, it is those of us injured workers who are not abusing the system, it is its failure of putting one back on course to getting results for their health, who are becoming victims that are stuck in the middle of this red tape. The stress of being denied medications you need to help you along until you can finally get the approvals required to have procedures and even surgery done to remove the injury, pain and suffering, is what our primary goal is. To keep harming the worker in this matter is bringing about a psychological effect that will in turn become detrimental to us as a society down the road. I can understand tackling the problem head on, but let's look at each person's case individually; after all, we are all assigned our own case numbers. Case in point: On December 17th, I had been notified as usual via text message that my prescription had been filled and was ready for pick up at the Price Chopper Pharmacy in Newburgh. I have been going to this pharmacy for 23 years. Once you go out on a work-related injury and get assigned a case number, you are mailed a prescription card from CVS Caremark that has your case information on it. There really never had been issues before getting meds, simply sign and go. Now, ever since May, it has been a hallowing affair. Each time was some different answer from the staff. I was being informed per their pharmacy computer system that my case was closed. My medications were not being covered under the workers' comp case. But remember this, I had at one point been prescribed up to 13 medications for all of my injuries.

The week prior I had contacted my case handler at the State Insurance Fund. I was asking her what my status was and how come I was having so many issues getting my medications. According to her reply email, she replied, "We have checked our pharmacy record and there is nothing to indicate that your case is closed. Our records appear as they should for your prescriptions to be processed." So, after seeing that, I took my CVS Caremark card off to the pharmacy after they texted me saying that my order was ready. I arrived there about 1:10 p.m., and being second in line, I was almost immediately served, this time by a woman I did not recognize, but she had on a lab coat and her name tag said she was the pharmacy manager. I showed her my card when she rang up my order, puzzled, she looked at it saying, "I will be back, I need to call this in for approval." Here we go again, I thought. So I took a seat for another five minutes, noticing another employee closing the security gates across the front of the entire pharmacy, with the exception of the first window register. I heard him say that they were getting ready to close for lunch. I saw the employee have customers force their way under the security screen to get to the second window for service. A few minutes later, the manager called me back up to the first window telling me I was being denied, it was not approved, and I could not get my medications. Next thing you know, they turned off the lights and closed the screens. Of all the meds I had been picking up for my injuries during the summer, they kept putting the billing under my private health insurance, the Empire Plan. A couple months ago, I had received a note in the mail from the Empire Plan, wanting information and details about my work-related injuries from the case of May 9th, 2017. I was informed that I was not supposed to be putting work-related injury medical billing on my private health insurance, something I already knew, but this was something the pharmacy had been doing. That way, they would get paid quicker and get their co-pays at the time of pick-up. With workers' comp, things took much longer to process and payments were often not the same. Currently, I have several receipts of co-pays that I submitted to the State Insurance Fund to have reimbursed back to me due to the pharmacy's billing issues. Complaints had been forward to CVS, Price Chopper, the State Insurance Fund as well as my law firm.

I left there very stressed out. Thinking I was going to get some help, I called the number on the CVS Caremark card and spoke to Aubrey who was not having a good day herself. Apparently, 'tis not the season. I attempted to explain to her the issue but somehow now with this epidemic going on, there has been a new system put in place to govern and oversee a much tighter restraint on medications not only being prescribed in lower doses and smaller quantities, but also going through an approval process to get covered under the workers' compensation case. It's just another delay waiting for your necessary prescribed medications. I had called Dr. Newton and Dr. Ogulnick up on this day leaving them messages, and with it being a Sunday, I knew they would not be in their offices, but I wanted to be sure they got my messages first thing Monday morning. Wouldn't you know it, within an hour, they both called me back to follow up. I was relieved in some sense that at least someone still cared. But they too had explained to me how this epidemic and the system was causing this with many other patients, how it was affecting thousands all around the area. I wasn't alone on this one, that's for sure. I just wanted to get what I was entitled to. The cold weather snap we were having was particularly hard on my joints, both of my shoulder and neck injuries, as well as my prior work-related knee injuries which I had just gotten knee injections from by Dr. Kenny. So while I will await replies from upper-level management from these companies regarding the medication billing issues, I will be shopping for a new pharmacy. That's a shame. It's too bad for a place that I had been going to for so many years, they don't even have the same staff in the pharmacy anymore, they too have moved on. I blame the system, I blame the laziness of those responsible for creating this epidemic, and I blame those who refuse to be responsible and do their jobs. It's easy to point the fingers, that's what everyone does, that's what I have been witnessing the last several months with numerous state agencies.

The following day, I get my reply back from my email to the case handler I am assigned, Miss Jackie, at the State Insurance Fund. She states that "There have been recent changes with the protocol required with the dispensing of some medications. If the medications are not in our formulary, then prior approval must be obtained by CVS Caremark. This cannot be avoided. In addition, due to the fact that there are still body parts/conditions that are not established on this case, every medication request must be reviewed in order to determine if it is causally related to this case." I immediately replied back to her in another email and sent copies of it off to my law firm in White Plains. I reached out to Miss Jackie stressing, "I understand the system has changed for several reasons. However, you mentioned in your prior email that 'Our records appear as they should for your prescriptions to be processed.' If there was a requirement for meds to be approved, why would I be notified via text message yesterday that they were filled and ready for pick up if they were not approved? Furthermore, this particular prescription was for a causally related and approved condition. Aubrey from CVS Caremark told me on the phone yesterday, 12/17/17, that the approval had to come from the SIF, not from CVS, as you stated. They are acting as the courier in obtaining the approval from you. As I said in my last email, they kept bringing your name into this. I am just trying to simplify this matter and get it straightened out. Everyone involved here is pointing the finger at each other and I am here without my necessary prescription."

Time and persistence will eventually prevail anyone through their situation, depending on the merits of the case. Since I had not heard back from the store manager at this point, I gave the corporate offices a call. Spoke to a customer service representative who actually took the time to hear the whole story and did not once interrupt me like I had experienced with other agencies looking to pass the buck. Within an hour, I got a call back from Steve from the corporate pharmacy offices. Steve was extremely helpful and was even willing to give me his personal cell phone for any further issues. He had my whole file in front of him and was reviewing it. All said and done, there had been "26 occasions" in which the Price Chopper Pharmacy in Newburgh had billed my private health insurance for my work-related injury prescriptions. Like my lawyers wrote to me once, many pharmacies practice this method as a way to short cut the process of having to deal with the workers' compensation system. It was a way for them to be paid faster, and to even get a co-pay from the injured worker who needed his or her prescriptions. Those of us in the system were stuck between a rock and a hard place. I have spoken to literally dozens of patients who have been on workers' comp, numerous lawyers, doctors, you name it. All of them said the same thing. The state's workers' compensation system is broken and is a nightmare for everyone. It's an old tire that keeps getting patched, slowly leaking air, wasting away funds unnecessarily, with no deep tread to get any traction and gain some ground to get ahead and deal with this process. It only took about an hour and Steve had informed me that the entire list of medications that had been billed the wrong way were reversed and that anytime I was available I could head over to the pharmacy and pick up my refund of all those co-pays. I was very thankful and when I arrived, they called me right up to the window with no issues at all and away I went with my newly earned refund. Maybe they should learn from another major pharmacy who just finished up a large class action lawsuit regarding billing issues with prescriptions as well. Who knows, they could be next. This seems to be the practice all across the state. It's a huge waste of taxpayer dollars when the system does not comply with how it is supposed operate in the first place. But another typical case of someone not doing their job.

Chapter Twenty-Two
Minorities and Discrimination
in the Workplace

Back in late fall, when I had first met up with Investigators Jeff and Penny from the State Department of Labor, Public Employee Safety and Health, they had me fill out a questionnaire several pages long. Many details that took some time to retract from my documents I had carried along in my briefcase. I came prepared, but there was this one question that I did not have the answer to; it was #25 toward the rear of the packet. The question asked, "Who else has been disciplined for the same or similar offense for which you were disciplined?" Well, part of this pertained to me and part of it did not. The fact being that I was not under any notice of discipline at this time, I did not have an answer to this question. But then below were broken-down parts to the question: who, when and where were the offenses, and what was the disciplinary action? Have you or the other committed similar acts previously? If so, how many times, and what was the disciplinary action? Well, now that some time has passed, there has been a similar incident to mine which occurred in November of 2017 in Building 21 on first-floor housing unit during the 6:30 a.m. morning shift change. It had come to my attention through several officers working there at the time that Officer Coffee, who is of Jamaican descent, had worked the overnight shift and decided to do some housekeeping in the office area. Sure, it gets a bit dull at night after you have caught up on your regular duties. Upon arrival at morning shift change of the regular bid officer who works the post on a routine basis, Officer McLight, who is a female officer, took note of his activities during the overnight shift. Thinking he was helping her out in his mind, it turned out to be quite the charade, typical of a bid officer to get after someone else who works their area and does something they deem not acceptable, whether it was worthy or not. As they say, no good deed goes unpunished. Officer McLight's husband also works the same shift and building, and was apparently present when this happened. Of course, he too shared in her anger. Officer Coffee not liking how he was being treated, decided to take off and leave the building to go home off duty.

The following night on November 28th, Officer Coffee was assigned to work the same unit again, and he had found the mess he had attempted to alleviate was still there. After correcting the deficiency in the back office/break room, soon shift change once again had arrived, right on time as usual, at 6:30 a.m. Officer McLight had arrived and more words were exchanged, with Officer Coffee stating that he did not appreciate how he was treated the night before. More dialogue followed; any inmate within 30 feet of the desk area would have heard the commotion. As soon as Officer Coffee left, a supervisor was notified about the situation. Upon immediate investigation, Officer McLight had went out on workers' comp for her injury. By the time Coffee had got up to the administration building to leave, he was stopped and taken into another room to be questioned by supervisors. He was soon suspended without pay and issued a notice of discipline. Her comp case was not controverted or questioned for her claimed injury, and her husband was not ridiculed, called names, harassed, or otherwise looked down upon for writing up another officer.

This situation has merits similar to mine, however, each scenario has its own details. My problem is that Fishkill Correctional Facility has always been quick to act on a situation when it involves a female and anyone of race (Hispanic, African American, etc.) My incident, unprovoked from my side of it, involved myself, a white male, and another white male. Typical of DOCCS to ignore those types of situations and make them go away. Although white males can be considered in a racial discrimination category, it is at least not in this case. Especially when the other white male is being represented and protected by a family member who is a higher-up authoritative figure in the Correction Officer's Union. So I contacted the Department of Labor who at this time is investigating Fishkill Correctional Facility. My situation definitely shows that I was treated much differently, unfairly, in a discriminatory way that has caused physical and mental harm not only to myself but has affected literally hundreds of other people of who I had been involved with throughout my community, by studio business, my political affiliations, as well as any other of the social-economic factors. It's not too often you hear of a white male claiming racial discrimination but when you look at the facts of these two cases, it's all there in black and white – no pun intended. I am sure their case will be an ongoing enduring and seemingly never-ending situation. These things take time. Officer Coffee has already made his contacts to report this to several agencies, and guess what…he even has plenty of union representation guiding him through the entire process and even offered him application papers for our "Rainy Day Fund" in which he can apply for monetary assistance from the union while he is on suspension. All of this started with someone simply trying to help out on a unit, perhaps to the surprise of the arriving regular officers on the following shift, but in this case that did not occur. So many officers get territorial in their areas, which is exactly what happened in my case that started this whole ordeal as well. Too many of these seasoned officers who have been there for so long keep forgetting one thing. It is state property; you're responsible for maintaining it during your tour of duty. But too many of them treat it as their own property, thus creating problems. Don't we all have enough to worry about with the gangs, drugs, and sex trades, among other things such as the violence inside those walls and fences? As of this date, Officer Coffee has informed me that he has begun the process of filing complaints with many state agencies and obtaining lawyers. He is working on a deal in order to get back to work. Either way, this incident will surely follow him back inside those fences.

Chapter Twenty-Three
Miles Upon Miles

Besides keeping good records, copies of your documents, following up on your emails and documenting your phone calls, like I have been doing in my two logbooks so far at this point, one other more important thing is to keep track of your appointments and mileage to/from your appointments. Having been to well over 160 appointments since the incident in May, I was already well over 3,000 miles. This adds up at the current comptroller's rate per mile. I had submitted my first packet as I usually had done in past cases, but since my case was controverted for numerous months, it would take additional time to get the approvals done. I had been in contact with Miss Jackie over at the State Insurance Fund, who was ordered to have the six pages of documents I submitted through my lawyers audited and paid out no later than December 29, 2017. My totals were only for appointments up until November 14th. I received a note from the SIF office stating numerous variables of instances which were not eligible for reimbursement such as trips to workers' comp hearings, pharmacies, lawyers, anything to do with your case. That's unfortunate that they play these rules, these are necessary routes to travel regarding the case. Had it not been for the injuries in the first place, you would not have to take the time or expense in getting to those locations. So now they only reimburse expenses to medical appointments. The State Insurance Fund has become a typical insurance company that delays and denies, all in an effort to save money. They are only hurting the claimants more, causing conflict between medical offices that have to deal with your case. It's no wonder so many doctors do not want to deal with workers' compensation. It's a complete nightmare. I am really surprised that something worse has not happened by an injured worker who wanted to seek justice under his or her own terms. It's enough to drive anyone up the wall. Once we get this under control and figured out, I will then proceed with my third submission with reimbursements.

So just after Christmas day, but before the deadline date, I received back-to-back notices of denials along with two small checks, both totaling close to $400. This was way under the amount I expected, according to my records. I sent replies to the Workers' Compensation Board, the State Insurance Fund, and to my law firm in an effort to get another audit done. Even with the removal of those dates of service not payable, my mileage still added up and far exceeded what they had paid out. I had talked to other officers before, one in particular, Tim, from up north, who told me his horror stories of dealing with the Workers' Comp Board and State Insurance Fund, who denied much of his mileage.

Tim told me, "Fight for it, go get it, every penny, screw them and their methods." He was actually right. This was a game. These are the cards we have been dealt. What's right is right, and I will not back down, regardless of how many people get pissed off, how many "friends" I may lose, because in the end, my family is what matters. I did not ask for this and certainly did not deserve it. The time will come for those responsible for when payment will be due.

So as I await the board to get back to me, one of my lawyers responded to me via email: "They always do, they are a big insurance company. They will use tactics like these as well as recalculating routes that use less miles. They are allowed to do so under the current state of the law on this issue." I personally made my own responses to both the Workers' Comp Board Advocacy Unit and the State Insurance Fund. Turns out that a third check for around $230 arrived in the mail on Jan 5th, after additional audits were completed of my vast listing of mileage and appointments. Speaking of seeking reimbursement for mileage, I am trying to obtain benefits for my family due to the loss of my second business income, the loss of one year's credit of retirement in the Fire Department, as well as one year's loss of my Deferred Compensation Plan's automatic withdrawals from my payroll. I have smaller benefits that come in on occasion from my AFLAC Policy, however that was something that I have paid for out of pocket as a supplement to my household, god forbid something happened. I contacted the Correctional Peace Officers Foundation the other day. Looking on their site, you can see how many brother and sister officers have been given assistance for just about any type of injury, however, according to the coordinator for the New York area, he told me that due to the circumstances of how I was injured by another staff member, I would not be eligible for any type of benefit that would be approved by the board. I am withholding the individual's name due to conflict of interest and the fact that the board governs these policies. Rather than letting the board make the determination, he became the weatherman and predicted what the outcome might be. So, in order to avoid submitting an application with paperwork, he simply said it was not likely this assistance would be available under my set of circumstances. Coincidentally enough, he too is friends with our union's vice president, Mallory. Enough said about that.

Now that the new year is upon us, I have had clients contacting me about their upcoming events in the spring and early summer, wanting to get started on their planning and coordination. I had hoped by now that maybe I would have been back in business, but it does not look hopeful. Last summer I had to cancel and refund way too many weddings, more than I could afford or wanted to do, but as things were, it was necessary. I am now at the point of writing the cancellation letters and issuing refunds for all of my 2018 weddings coming up for the next six months, sections at a time to see where this all takes me. I could end up on disability retirement soon. It's already been nine months since I have been able to work. Just trying to keep my fingers crossed. Everyone that's aware of my situation has been very understanding and supportive. As much as I hate what I am going through, it has been a blessing to have this support. I am at this point where some hard decisions need to be made. I have been in the business for about 19 years. Not a bad run. Photography will always be a hobby of mine, regardless if I retire and sell the business. Family comes first. After all, the studio area would make for a nice recreational room.

Word just came in by official memorandum by Superintendent Shields that there were more changes in policy regarding personal property storage while on duty within the correctional facility. While one may be able to see it from both sides, this is a way of the department to combat the contraband that may be introduced into these secure areas. But this is no super solitary facility, items these days can be dropped in by drones, thrown over the fences, dropped on the property where outside clearance inmates work. You can walk into a club and have your driver's license ID scanned into a computer, wanded with a handheld metal detector, empty out your pockets and pass through a metal detector, but when we go into work, that's not the case at all. Visitors of course have to go through this method, however, as I mentioned earlier, every basket has some bad eggs in it and this is why things have to be done the way they are. It's a complete inconvenience to those that go to work, do their jobs, and go home without any problems. But Fishkill is not a "home jail" anymore. With the closing of many prisons in the New York City areas, this has forced many officers to transfer up to Fishkill. With that came their habits, their ways of conducting their duties, and certainly created an immense spike in female staff numbers that we had not seen there before. But with the new policy changes, and against the opinion of many senior staffers who have been there for so long, most are forced to have to share a locker, and are being limited to its size as well. This could be an issue. With each person being responsible for his or her area and locker (which primarily is used for storage of coats, hats, lunch bags, paperwork, office supplies, soap, paper towels), it has been found on occasion that other items considered contraband had been located. So if this is the case and you have two-three officers sharing one locker, what's going to happen when no one wants to take responsibility? They will all certainly be locked out from duty, suspended, perhaps without pay, allowed to use their time accruals of vacation time until it's all dried up. Done so because this "due" process is done at their leisure. Nothing happens overnight, it could take weeks, months. Then you have the other officers who are guilty until proven innocent only to be found not at fault, ordered back to duty, and awarded back pay and accruals. Meanwhile, the families of those involved must somehow maintain their home and support of their children, putting food on the table, etc. These officials sitting up in Albany at DOCCS are running these prisons, when in fact some of them have never worked in one. They come through the door with a degree, perhaps politically get on the inside, or otherwise pass the civil service test and are chosen for the job. There are more and more assistant commissioners up there sitting in these offices typing memos and making new policies, doing studies of statistics around the country of how other states are handling their prisons. But yet they cut back on staffing. The deputy superintendent of each correctional facility brings charts up to Albany and sits down to see which posts can be closed down to save money, cut back on costs. At any given time, in most areas, you could have as many as 60 inmates to one officer at a maximum security prison, and in some other facilities, half of that, given the fact that it may be only a medium. The rise in risks to security measures in place, the higher number of assaults on staff, and the more unusual incidents will continue to occur until the right thing is done by Albany. They put inmates and their families first, feeding them on their needs, all in a way in which avoids potential events from occurring, but also lawsuits, and other violence. As for the officers speaking up, which by the way, we are seriously outnumbered, it falls upon deaf ears. These changes are not being accepted by the senior officers who are buying their military time back to retire early, or are taking the initiative to move onto other jobs in other states. It's falling apart in there, folks, and with all the new inexperienced officers inside these settings, it will create the final ingredient in the recipe needed for the dangerous environment to grow even worse. On the flip side of that coin, the state, if they ever woke up and smelled the coffee, would say, Mmm, let's offer a 20-year retirement like the State Police have and allow those to retire sooner. This would save money and allow for the hiring of additional officers and staff. If you bring in a new officer at 1/3 of what the senior officer is making after he retires, you do the math. Not to mention, cutting the shifts down from 3 (8-hour shifts) daily to 2, making them (12-hour shifts), would certainly provide more officers around the facility, thus creating a safer working environment, saving the state money, and allowing them to take more money from the budget to purchase additional safety and security equipment to make the officers' jobs easier to detect contraband. There would be more time off for those needing it during the week, there would still be overtime, and officers could still do mutual swaps so there would really be no loss on anyone's part.

Chapter Twenty-Four
More News from the State

After months of going back and forth with the Thompson case from the assault that occurred on 5/9/17, more information came back after my additional information that was sent to Jeff, one of my discrimination investigators, on December 11th. Even with the multiple conflicting dates and details from the incident reports and investigation that he sent to me in that large packet of files, showing me memos from many of the staff and supervisors involved, including the Office of Special Investigation's findings by Investigator Tonka, it had been clearly pointed out and immediately documented and forwarded back to PESH investigators. It took a week with no reply on the email I sent, so I contacted Jeff and that day he got back to me finally and said, yes, it was received and placed in my files.

On January 10th, sent by USPS certified mail, I signed the green signature card. Everything that they stated in my complaint that I had "alleged" was unsubstantiated. They stated, "We have determined that your case must be dismissed as the Department of Labor did not find that you had suffered any adverse action from employment or disparate treatment under Section 27-A of the Labor Law. Nothing revealed during our investigation had risen to the level which constituted an adverse employment action, and the alleged adverse actions have not been shown to have been the result of retaliation by your employer. Accordingly, the New York State Department of Labor will not take any further action concerning this matter. You have the right to appeal this matter and determination within 60 days to the New York State Industrial Board of Appeals."

After reading this, I refused to allow the emotions to cloud my judgement. This was clearly one man doing the shoveling while 10 other employees stood around "supervising and observing." Immediate and swift action was taken to contact the Industrial Board of Appeals and I had the chance to speak to the managing attorney, Anne, while I was on the phone with her. I had never heard of this agency before, and some of my colleagues said the same. But she was so sincere and helpful to me, taking time from her busy schedule to send me the pdf file "Petition for review of an order of the Commissioner of Labor." I was able to download it, filled it out making four copies as requested, and sent in four copies of the DOL's determination report and my discrepancy report of December 11th. With that in place, I had them notarized and off to the post office I went, all within one hour, sending it out to them certified mail return receipt requested and with the green signature card. I have so many of those green cards already, I had to make a special file for them.

I had no plans on backing down on this one, but even though I had 60 days to respond with an appeal, I hope that I will be hearing something back sooner or later. You would think much of this work should be done by a law firm but with my paralegal experience, I have decided to undertake much of this labor activity. The only thing I am finding is that unless you are an actual law firm, it appears that you are not taken as serious when dealing with these agencies. There is just no way this can be overlooked. There is too much going on here that is on paper and is contradicting. Someone needs to start doing their jobs, and they need to start doing it fast.

A self portrait of me getting ready to start day one of my pre-trial conference at the Public Employee Relations Board at the Empire State Plaza in Albany. Photo provided.

A layout of my documents getting ready for trial against the Correction Officers' Union for failure of their duty to represent as well as discrimination. Photo by P. Harrington.

This past week I had been on the phone with a personal injury law firm down in Yonkers and with labor lawyers up in Saratoga Springs. I had also been making trips down to the city of Newburgh's court house to obtain the paperwork and documentation for commercial/small claims as my corporation was planning on going after Thompson as well for the assault and the loss of work as a result. There's a difference between personal injury and assault. One can be intentional, the other can be accidental. Also, my corporation would be a separate case in itself without conflicting with my consideration of a personal injury case. I recall back to the night of this incident when we left the hospital and Lt. Michaels said to me, "Paul, you have to look out for your family at this point, think of them, do not sugar coat this." I took that as meaning I had to do what I had to do. It has been so tough, like a full-time job. I had ten doctor appointments last week, with 31 scheduled for this month of January. This is definitely keeping me on a busy schedule. Even my pain management doctors told me I needed to take a vacation, to get away from it all. That will come, someday, sometime soon, but first things first. I had a great opportunity to talk to some personal friends who are lawyers in another field, and some great advice was given. In the matters of the civil suits, these can take a course of 3-4 years, maybe longer. The costs associated with the retainer and other legal expenses certainly did not feel like it was worth the gamble. After all, numerous injury lawyers had said you can't get much out of a C.O.'s pocket. Unless of course he had other stuff on the side. But what comes around goes around. I am awaiting determination on my medical retirement that was already applied for by my law firm, and to finally get my eight workers' comp cases closed up and settled while at the same time keeping my medical coverage in place. It was time to move on. After talking to my other lawyer friends, it seemed more of the right thing to do for the family. Rather than drag this out for so long, the juice was not going to be worth the squeeze. No one could say what the outcome would be on any money recovered the victory of a case. But money is only money. It comes and goes. Family does not. And that's where things need to be focused on. It's still a consideration to proceed with the suits as time permits, but decisions are being considered. I am still awaiting the outcome of the Public Employee Relations Board Improper Practice Charges that were lodged against COPBA. Speaking to my firm that I paid a consultation fee to for labor law representation over the matter, there was not much that could outcome from this other than the courts ordering the union to represent me, to file the documents that would have needed to be filed, but all of that is past tense now and why would I pay a firm thousands of dollars to represent me in court when I am already paying my dues that warrant me the kind of indiscriminate representation any active good standing union member would be entitled to. This is all really about rolling the dice. We will have to see what happens with that.

The doctor appointments continue. It is literally becoming a full-time job. It is draining on me as an individual with dealing on all these issues, the denials, the struggles to get approvals, having all of the issues with the system. I am due this week to have two more MRIs on both of my knees from prior inmate assaults, which both have had prior surgery on as well. I was last told that I had bilateral osteoarthritis in my knees. It is pretty hard for me to do a lot of activity involving the use of these knees without the pain elevating. I have been getting my shots in the knees from Dr. Kenny, but it was just buying me time. I know ultimately surgery will have to be the answer again. Some more physical therapy, chiropractor, and psychologist care this week will bring me into next week when I am scheduled with my law firm to go in for a Workers' Compensation Board Hearing, to get my neck and left ear TMJ listed as part of the injury to this assault from 5/9/17. I had to make some extra trips today to see Dr. Feldman for the documents regarding the injuries and tomorrow I have to go to see Dr. Lustbader to pick up his notes for the TMJ relation to the injury. Although we won our case back in September after the board found Officer Thompson's testimony not credible, there had been some injuries omitted from the award of benefits. We have to get our paperwork all in order and are prepared to go in for this hearing on January 24th. It took some extra running around but I quickly found out especially in the upstate areas of New York that many medical facilities that take workers' compensation do all they can to minimize the paperwork that is required of them. The minute you put extra stuff in front of them that is needed for your upcoming Workers' Comp Board Hearing, Aflac Claim Submission, or work-related documentation, you start to get very little cooperation and many of them will work harder at not doing it then actually taking the time to do so. In fact, there is one orthopedics firm over in Duchess County that farms out the paperwork. An outside company will review your records and notes, and fill out the documents for the doctors. This takes sometimes up to two weeks to have completed and they charge $20 per page. This is seriously getting out of control.

I was able to locally appear in person at a couple of my doctor's offices, Dr. Lustbader and Dr. Feldman, to pick up the required documents my attorneys needed in time for Wednesday's Workers' Compensation Board Hearing. I had made copies and notated this in my logbooks, scanning the pages into my computer to be sent down to my law firm in White Plains. I need to get the approvals for these other injuries from 5/9/17 in order for the board and judge to review and render a decision on this. I have gone on too long with this pain and albeit I have received treatment, it has been minimal due to non-approvals. It's time to be more aggressive and get a handle on this.

Chapter Twenty-Five
Watchdog Oversights and Baby Step Progress

The state agency, Commission of Corrections, charged with overseeing and inspecting state and local correctional facilities and jails is not tracking issues that could show problematic trends at those facilities and help officials head off more serious problems, according to an audit released by the State Comptroller's Office.

The state Commission of Correction receives daily data such as complaints and reports of unusual incidents at the 54 state prisons operated by the Department of Corrections and Community Supervision, but "it does not analyze and track such information to identify any trends or patterns that may warrant monitoring or review," auditors wrote in their report, which covered the period between Jan 1, 2017 and July 19. "As a result, the Commission may not identify patterns or trends, such as a significant increase in complaints at a specific facility or system-wide, in a timely manner." The data contain reports on incidents such as inmate-on-inmate assaults and other types of security and safety incidents. Analysis of the data, including "high or increasing number of incidents occurring at a certain facility or facilities; (t)he timing of the incidents and other events at the facilities; (t)he location where the incident occurred and type of incident; (f)acilities where force was used in the incident; and (f)acilities where staff and/or inmate injury occurred as a result of an incident would help the commission determine if there are significant patterns or trends authorities should be aware of and plan for," the audit report stated.

A new information management system was being put in place at the time of the audit to provide an increased ability to analyze the data, but it still would not include all the data commission needs, the auditors wrote. The new management information system also lacks the ability to produce reports on how complaints and inmate grievances are resolved, and how long they have been in process, the auditors noted. The commission improved the timeliness of its responses to complaints and grievances during the audit period, despite significant increases in both, but more needs to be done to address the issue, the auditors wrote.

"The State Commission of Correction is not adequately monitoring what's happening in our prisons," Comptroller Thomas P. DiNapoli said in a release announcing the audit findings. "The commission needs to improve its tracking of data and to identify patterns or trends that merit attention to protect the rights and safety of inmates and correctional staff. The new data system it is building falls far short of helping them identify problems and needs to be addressed. Commission officials say they plan to improve their agency's performance, and they must be given the Executive's proposal to improve the safety of New York's correctional facilities." When cover-up of an incident happens, it overall affects the statistics of these types of incidents. In a workplace violence situation, it's a tough call to substantiate even when one of the parties has serious injury without having a credible witness or security video of an incident. In my case, due to the circumstances of the relationship status involving a high-ranking union official with the other officer involved, this was going to be the fight of all fights to prove. But when you have someone determined to buck the system like this, somewhere down the line they will mess up, and that has happened twice already, and to our benefit thus far. As noted (in a written response to the audit), we worked internally – and with other state agencies – to implement a system that compiles and analyzes complaint data to identify those facilities needing further oversight. We are also developing a system to more effectively monitor data generated through complaints and grievances filed by individuals who are incarcerated. "The Commission will continue to explore new ways that will help to improve conditions at all correctional facilities and ensure they operate effectively and in compliance with all applicable laws and regulations."

With the extreme difficulties of finding a personal injury law firm that would spend 50k on pursuing a personal injury case against an individual, not one of them really seemed interested. Most of the lawyers stated they had no deep pockets, you would take forever to get paid under judgement, if ever at all. Not worth the case. Sure, workers' compensation would cover most of your medical benefits, and because of this officers were prohibited from suing their employers from injuries arising from work-related incidents. I had done some research, spoke to some legal advocates, a couple of court officers, and decided that since I have a great loss in my secondary income with my limited liability company, I decided that I would get what I could in small claims which would only cover a small portion of my losses. I obtained the documentation and proceeded down to the City of Newburgh Courthouse on two occasions. At first, I was misled and was going to file a commercial claim, but then soon realized that it needed to be a small claim, in the amount of $5,000. The court clerk took my payment and stamped my documentation, made copies and stated that Officer Thompson would be served his subpoena to appear and sent notice via US Mail certified return receipt requested. She gave us a court date of February 21st. I already had all of my paperwork, medical documents, contracts, photos, and other supporting evidence ready to go. If the court rules in my favor, there are a few ways to enforce judgement in order to get payment. I would need to obtain the services of an enforcement officer and one way could be taking payments from each check from his employer, or even worse, the enforcement officer can take his vehicle and sell it to pay the judgement. His New York State driver's license can also be suspended. The state's system has a way of getting the judgement paid off fairly. As long as this incident investigation, medical treatment, and other considerable factors have been going on, I finally get to get a foot forward to my day in court.

Today, on January 24th, was a pretty busy day. I already had 31 medical appointments scheduled just for this month alone. This is a ridiculous schedule. I am getting to know many of the local seniors in the area. I am the youngest one in the waiting room but I joke with them saying that I bet my x-rays and MRIs show that I am older than they are, as they all laugh with a chuckle or two.

My lawyer Jason and I were on our way into the scheduled Workers' Compensation Board Hearing in New Windsor for a continuation of the workplace violence injury case. We had presented a bulk of documents from three of my doctors, all of whom the board determined to be valid, but with the State Insurance Fund's noted exception, it was granted that they could appeal and set up independent medical exams for by neck, ear, and jaw, which were also injured. We cleared those hurdles and made it to the next step. Part of the judge's decision based on our presented evidence was that he found prima facie medical evidence for the neck injuries caused by Officer Thompson per Dr. Habif's report as well as for Dr. Feldman's report on bilateral hearing loss, left

TMJ, left ear, bilateral tinnitus as well as dizziness and giddiness (balance issues). The judge gave a ruling to the State Insurance Fund to have the IMEs done within a certain time and to report back for another hearing to decide on inclusion of his findings. It was not a win, but it was not a loss either. It's a process, and it takes a lot of time to deal with this stuff. I just wished that I could get some results sooner; my neck injuries are affecting my left shoulder surgery recovery and delaying my adequate treatments even more.

About 30 minutes later, we adjourned and took off into the hallway for a quick briefing. I had to head home to get some faxes out. When I arrived, I noticed the mail had just arrived. I saw an envelope in there from the New York State Public Employer Relations Board, with whom I filed improper charges with months ago against our union for their lack of duty of fair representation.

I got inside and the first thing I did was open that envelope. Inside it was the news I had finally been waiting for. Someone doing their job! The PERB board had moved forward with the charges against the State Correction Officer's Union. Notice had been sent out to the Union President Peters, as well as to the Governor's Office of Employee Relations, and the union itself. We were ordered to appear before Administrative Law Judge, Mr. Rikers, in Albany on March 7th, 2018. With all of my documents in order and already scanned and sent ahead on file, it was only a matter of time now. On this notice from PERB was that the union, otherwise hereby known as the respondent, had 10 days to file four copies and an original of an answer to the charge or motion for particularization of the charge, with proof of service of copy upon all the other parties. Furthermore, they were advised, "Failure to file in a timely responsive pleading may constitute an admission of the material facts alleged in the charge and a waiver of the hearing."

Chapter Twenty-Six
New York's Government #1 in Corruption

Lawmakers led away in handcuffs seem like clear signs of a corruption problem in New York State. But the worst in the nation? Elaine Phillips says that's the case. The Republican is running for a vacant State Senate seat in Long Island, and she has made public corruption in Albany the centerpiece of her campaign. She outlined her plan for state ethics reform in a Facebook post, in which she claimed New York State leads the nation in lawmakers in trouble with the law.

"Over the past decade in Albany, more than 30 current and former state officeholders have been convicted, sanctioned, or accused of wrongdoing – more than any other state," Phillips said in the post. She referenced the number from an article in the *New York Times*. Phillips took that claim a step further by saying New York led the pack in corruption among other states. In Albany, running afoul of the law is bipartisan, and not just for backbenchers. Two of the state's legislative leaders were convicted of corruption charges, former Assembly Speaker Sheldon Silver, a Manhattan Democrat, and former Senate Majority Leader Dean Skelos, a Long Island Republican.

Phillips, Mayor of the Nassau County village of Flower Hill, faces Adam Haber, a Democrat who most recently served with the Nassau Interim Finance Authority Board, which monitors the county's finances. So, is Phillips right? Can New York State be the worst in a nation that includes politicians from Illinois – think Rod Blagojevich – and Louisiana, where a recent headline read "New Orleans FBI chief calls political corruption in Louisiana 'robust'"? *The New York Times, The Buffalo News*, and other publications have chronicled more than 30 corruption cases in the past decade. Look what happened with former Governor Spitzer, former Comptroller Hevesi, and many other congressmen, to name a few. It all streams from the top down to the bottom.

Dr. Jeffrey Milyo and Scott Delhommer from the University of Missouri have compiled a database that focuses specifically on public corruption at the state level across the country. Their research focuses on state legislators, high-ranking executive branch officials, and supreme court justices. They tracked bribery, influence peddling and theft of public funds among other charges. Other studies have looked solely at federal convictions or public officials at all levels of government. The Missouri researchers are the only ones who looked at corruption through a state lens, the kind of cases Phillips talks about. From 2006–2015, the researchers identified 28 corruption cases dealing with state officials in New York. Including 2005, and that number rises to 30. That puts New York first for the number of public corruption cases, followed by Pennsylvania, where 24 cases have been filed over the past decade. New Jersey ranks third with 12 corruption cases.

Look further back, and New York State has topped the list since at least 1986, Milyo said. "Historically, New York has struggled with corruption and continues to do so," said Jennifer Rodgers, executive director of the Center for the Advancement of Public Integrity. "While measuring corruption is a challenge, I think it's fair to say that New York remains one of the most corrupt states if not the most corrupt state. Each agency in itself has had to deal with this or still currently does, including the State's vast prison system. The corruption in New York State is likely rooted in culture," Rodgers says.

"Much of corruption is cultural, and in New York that means that you have to think about the way the New York political system has developed over more than 200 years," Rodgers said. "So you start with these corrupt political machines like Tammany Hall, and over time the problem replicates itself as the next generation figures out how things work and how much corruption will be tolerated, and so on down the line. We've made some progress, of course, but not enough."

Much of this corruption has leaked through the cracks in the walls and the spaces between the fencing of New York's prison system. The lack of oversight, supervision, the lack of responsibility, and the inactive actions of putting video cameras all throughout the state's facilities is a major problem. New York would rather spend over 10 million dollars producing and erecting illegal road signs on New York's roadways promoting tourism (which by the way is against federal law) among other things. If the state could only follow in the footsteps of what the federal authorities have done, such as establish, develop, and implement a new agency that oversees all agencies within the state for fraud, waste and abuse, then perhaps we would be a step ahead of this issue. After all, even the police have to be policed.

A former top aide to Gov. Andrew Cuomo was convicted on federal bribery and fraud charges in a trial that further exposed the state capital's culture of backroom deal-making. Joseph Percoco, who was once likened to a brother by the Democrat Cuomo, faces up to 20 years in prison for his conviction on two counts of conspiracy to commit honest services wire fraud and one count of soliciting bribes. Jurors who deliberated off and on for three weeks acquitted Percoco of two extortion counts and one of the bribery charges he had faced. While Cuomo himself was not accused of wrongdoing, testimony also painted an unflattering picture of the inner workings of his office.

There was testimony about administration officials using private email addresses to conduct state business in secret, and about how Percoco continued to work out of a state office even after he was supposed to have left government to lead Cuomo's 2014 re-election campaign. Cuomo has repeatedly declined to weigh in on the trial, saying he wanted to let the legal process play out. Within minutes of the verdict, good-government groups called on Cuomo and lawmakers to take action this year to strengthen oversight of government contracting and boost ethics enforcement.

"Albany stays on trial," said Blair Horner, executive director of the New York Public Interest Research Group. He called the verdict "a wake-up call to Albany to do something to clean up its ethics act." Now there are headlines about State Attorney General Eric Schneiderman who is under fire for having been accused of abuse of his authority and position, and was forced to resign. He was outspoken figure in the #MeToo movement against sexual harassment. It is one thing after another and how coincidental is it that Governor Cuomo's dealing with Federal investigators and New York Gov. Andrew Cuomo's political foes reportedly want to get to the bottom of how and why the governor's office interfered with the work of a short-lived corruption commission – a commission that Cuomo himself created. Cuomo called it a conflict of interest. It was more like a cover-up. And we all know when you paint from the top, it will drip downward, and seep into the lower areas of the great wall being painted. In other words, Albany's continued corruption does not stop at Exits 23 and 24 on the State's Thruway, it goes all the way around up and to the state's border and sometimes beyond.

Speaking of cleaning up, just having cameras mounted on the walls throughout the entire prison (rather than just in the newly constructed areas or the perimeter areas), would be just as important if not more. County jails do this, federal institutions do this. Where is New York State at? They have always been reactive and just now they are trying out body cameras at a few of the prisons. This comes only after several other incidents within the prison's system. For years and years, there has always been a problem with keeping our two-way radios operative with good solid working batteries, but yet now they think an officer, especially one who is against wearing this body camera device, will wear and operate it willfully? Put the cameras up on the walls, mount them and secure them from foul play, and hardwire them. It's a whole lot easier to tell the story as shown on the camera, rather than try to get everyone on the same page that was there for their reports. I can't tell you how many times myself and several other officers over the years were ordered to change our statements in order for everything to come together solidly, with certainty, at least with what the watch commander's reports reflected. If it's on camera, then everyone will be held to a higher standard. It works both ways. We would sit there and have debates over our finished reports, all because the bosses had finished theirs and it had better reflect it or else. The inmates will have to be held accountable for their actions just like anyone else. It will no longer be a he said-she said. Not to mention like I said before, that we can't have our eyes in every spot and corner of Fishkill's prison at any given moment.

When it comes down to one person's word over another, it almost always becomes politics. Who is the one with the most connections, who has the most ties, who is the one that needs to be protected, thereby, protecting the supervisors and administration? If there had been a camera in the hallway May 9th of the physical assault that Thompson did to me, or the day he verbally attacked me on May 4th, or on the other dates that I noted of the numerous amounts of harassment all in an attempt to get me to vacate my newly assigned post he did not want me at, we would all be sitting in different spots right now. Video cameras do not lie. I am only talking about one situation, but Fishkill in itself is one of the largest most complex facilities around the region. Fishkill even had an unofficial, anonymously printed newsletter that officers print up and it made its way around the facility, complaining about the administration and its cover-ups, pointing out the recent situations that have happened and asking questions that certainly will never get answered.

Each and every day there is some form of violence, crime, drug activity, workplace violence, sex trade, and multiple rule infractions that are committed. Most of the officers in there do their jobs, some do not, and most have proven that. We can't catch everyone and each shift works independently of each other. So do the "cliques" of the officers inside that security perimeter fence. It's almost on a daily basis that I am either running into a recently retired officer on the outside at a doctor's office or hearing from some of them on the phone. "It's time to get out of there, it's a new administration, the old ways are dissipating and it's a fight just to survive in there. You don't know who to trust anymore, with the inmates, officers or supervisors. It's each one for themselves." I was astonished to hear that over and over from them, since I had not been to work due to my injuries in over nine months. Most of these men and women do not want to fight the wrongs that have been done to them, no one wants to take the time and energy. The state sees this. Conquer and divide. Strength to fight is in the numbers, but once you lose, it's time to hang up your hats. So out the door, off to their new retired life, looking forward to being free of this stressful environment. Everyone who has worked there for any period of time has said, "I've had it, I am either going to retire early, or buy back my military time and get out of here." That's if you make it to retirement qualification.

More word came in from the Governor's Office of Employee Relations; I had called one of the attorneys representing the office in response to her letter. Turns out, now that they are involved, the union will also have an attorney there for the hearing as well. All summer they dodged requests for representation, intentionally delayed as well as numerous other violations of the contract and constitution. Now they want the convenience and extra time to get their case together? The mailbox was full of letters from the State Insurance Fund, Workers' Comp Board, City of Newburgh Court, as well as other law firms representing the union.

With things moving along in my case with PERB's investigation into my charge against the union for improper practice, I began to receive letters that certain law firms representing both the union and the Governor's Office of Employee Relations. I had read one of the notifications that the union was requesting more time to respond to the charge (10 days was not enough time for them to gather their stories), so PERB and GOER both agreed, along with my acknowledgement, that they would be given until February 15th, 2018 to submit their documents, in quadruple copies.

I immediately faxed the PERB's office Administrative Law Judge Rikers, who was hearing this case, that I was objecting the union's request to also delay the date for the hearing of March 7th. My reasons were that according to the union's representatives, they had a disciplinary administrative hearing that day. I urged Judge Rikers that our union could handle more than one event per day. Secondly, I furthermore objected to their request to reschedule the date because since the workplace violence incident on May 9th, 2017, my union has done all they could to delay, deny, and dodge my efforts to obtain representation as I have evidence of by phone, email, and certified US mail. Judge Rikers understood my request but overruled it calling their request to reschedule "not unreasonable," and therefore would delay it by an additional week. I began shuffling my documents together and writing up the facts of the case for my opening statement. Even though I had previously contacted a labor law firm up north of Albany, I decided it would not be worth the costs for the remedies I was seeking. For these types of PERB hearings, we, the charging party, are not required by law to be represented. Although if this goes to Supreme Court, PERB can only order the judgement of some attorney's fees and refunds of union dues, etc. There are no punitive damages in these types of cases. The rules and regulations state that the hearing must treat the unrepresented party fairly and not less equal due to the lack of legal representation. This is what they call a "pro se" case and it would be my first one, albeit the small claims hearing coming up in a couple weeks for my personal injury/loss of secondary income wages against Thompson. I have to thank quite a few friends who are officers out there for helping me out with the research assistance, obtaining documents, and helping me out at all costs. Despite the setbacks this has cost our family, there are still quite a number of people from work and other areas who stand behind us knowing we are doing what's right for the system, and what's right for me and my family. Those of you know who you are, especially Dave, Ed, Fr. K, Mike, Al, Tim, Joey G, Todd, and JR, among others, many not named.

Chapter Twenty-Seven
State-Ordered Independent Medical Examinations

We were into the time frame when most, if not all, of any officers or staff that go out under workers' compensation leave have to be seen by a state doctor, whether medically or psychologically. In my case, it was going to be for both. What I had mentioned earlier was that they deemed these exams as "independent." How does it make it independent when the insurance company sends you to a doctor of their choosing and pays him/her to conduct such exam and report back to the insurance company with the results of said examination? In order to make this equally just and fair, I feel the system needs to change whereas workers' compensation and the insurance company, in my case, the State Insurance Fund, should each split the expenses of the exam in order to conduct an unbiased medical determination. It's bad enough of what trauma that the injured worker had suffered but now has to deal with this broken system. In most cases, we have been seeing medical specialists for our injuries for months, including tests, surgeries, therapy, but yet you go to these exams and sit there for ten minutes and the state insurance doctor makes his decision. If he or she sees in favor of the patient once, twice, maybe three times too much, it is guaranteed that the doctor will be bypassed and lose out on any future exams to be hired for by the insurance companies. If they want to keep getting paid, the doctor better work in the favor of who is writing his check. It's a game of jumbling the medical paperwork.

On February 8th, 2018, at approximately 1:15 p.m., myself, accompanied by my Registered Nurse Consultant, Nurse Jody, arrived early for my psychological IME as ordered on 1/23/2018 by the NYSIF Case Handler Miss Jackie. Notice of exam was received by First Choice Evaluations. We arrived early and well before schedule. The appointment was set for 2:00 p.m. on that day I had expected to fill out paperwork but there was no one at Dr. Claus' office. At about 2:05 p.m., Dr. Claus came rushing through the door and right into the waiting room apologizing for his lateness. He left the waiting room for a moment and came back with a clipboard full of documents for me to fill out. Now this was going to delay our schedule even more since we previously arrived early to do this paperwork. Upon completion, we entered his office and immediately Dr. Claus looked at RN Jody and had a mixed reaction of why she was with me in the room. He asked her why she was there and she introduced herself. Dr. Claus took exception and asked her if she would mind leaving the room as he normally does this without other people in the interview exam. I spoke up at that time and explained to Dr. Claus that per the IME Notice, and Section 137 of the Workers' Compensation Law, Part 7, the claimant has a right to be accompanied during the examination by an individual or individuals of his/her choosing. Once this was made clear, he permitted RN Jody to remain with us and asked her several questions about her title, qualifications, etc.

We began the exam with a basic medical history review, even way back when I was young and had my tonsils out, and when I had braces, which I believed at the time had nothing to do with the psych exam but he continued to focus on the medical. As he asked more questions, I told him I could not remember most incidents, but that had I known this was going to be medical related, I would have brought my accident/injury reports with me to help recollect those details. He faulted me for not being able to recall the body parts that were injured even if I didn't know the dates. I had over 20 different injury reports in my two decades of service but only about eight of them were actual workers' compensation cases on file. I was able to refer to most of my surgeries that I had from my work-related injuries. We then spoke about the incident of 5/9/17, and he typed out from the start of my work day up until the end of when I had left in an ambulance to go to the hospital that evening of 5/9/17. He asked me a lot of questions of my injuries, what body parts were injured prior to my incident. We discussed other types of work that I might be able to do. He stated he had to determine if I was going to be psychologically disabled for life. I told him I did not know, I was not sure what tomorrow would bring, what the future holds. None there had any certainty of what would happen. I brought paperwork with me and was only trying to keep organized. That's when he asked me if I was OCD. I told him no, but that I just did not like being surrounded by clutter. Because I had come with my notes, and that he knew I had gone to so many doctor appointments for my current injuries (31 in January, and 27 scheduled for this month February), not to mention previous several months, he called me a "professional patient" and that I could end up spiraling downward like most of them do and that he did not want to see me ending up the same way as they did. I was really upset about that. I felt as if he was mocking me.

Each time I would bring up my psych issues, whether it was the urine in the face, the homicide of the inmate and its aftermath, and the current ordeal I was having now with the workplace violence, he seemed to shrug it off saying we will get back to that later. Well, before I knew it, two hours had passed and he said we were done. I paused for what seemed like a complete minute, motionless trying to think of what was missing. Finally, it came back to me that we never went over any of my psychological emotions other than a couple of questions on some score sheets. I wanted to be heard about how much this had been bothering me, so he gave me a few minutes to discuss this. While he might have agreed of how I was feeling, he offered no outlet other than asking me if I am currently still suicidal or had any other feelings of depression. I told him since my incident on 10/24/17, I had learned to cope somewhat with rejection and to walk away without making an immediate determination and acting out. However, my depression was up and down like a roller coaster, causing me sleepless nights even under meds, and days filled with four-hour naps.

On the instructions attached to the notice from the NYSIF, it stated: "This claim is established for a left shoulder injury and adjustment disorder with mixed anxiety and depression only." Although he conducted no physical exam on me, most of our interview surrounded my medical injuries and history. And since this was my first time going to a Psychological IME, I felt as if not enough observation, attention, or questions were made in reference to my psych claim from 5/9/17 workplace violence incident among the other incidents from the past at the prison as well. There was so much more to be told, but the opportunity to explain my thoughts was not given. I wanted to make this clear for the record so I sent a copy of this review over to my attorney's office, along with one to Dr. Ogulnick, who was very upset at how the exam was handled by the psychologist, and another copy to Nurse Jody. Now it was a wait-and-see approach to see what the exam report coming out in the next week or so will say. Then we will decide on where to proceed with the outcome.

The next independent medical exam coming up was scheduled for February 27th in Poughkeepsie with an orthopedic specialist who was going to check my left shoulder, as well as my neck. The State Insurance Fund had sent notice via First Choice Evaluations, which completes the scheduling, and on this notice it stated in the instructions to the orthopedic doctor, "Please examine areas of the neck, parts unknown." How in the world can an accurate complete medical summary be given on the injuries in the neck when the State Insurance Fund does not even know what parts? They have the same copies of the MRI exam reports that I do. There is no excuse for this. A doctor who has never seen or treated me before will be giving me a 15-minute exam and base his findings on what the paperwork says and what he had observed. Nurse Jody had accompanied me again to this exam. I know these are the injuries from Thompson's assault on me that day 5/9/17 that they are looking at, but my law firm is more concerned with the inmate-related injuries and the exams from those, rightfully so, when it comes down to the benefits. Afterall, a previous conversation and a pint of advice about the small claims court for the personal injury claim that I had filed on Thompson had been scheduled for February 21, 2018. However, we had to take care of some other issues first so this small claims matter was put on hold for the time being. I contacted the City of Newburgh Court Clerk's Office by phone and mailed them a written request to withdraw my application to pursue this matter at this time. I would consider dealing with this later.

I arrived home shortly after my appointment on the morning of February 23rd to find a UPS packet at my front door. At first glance I took a look at the address and thought it might have been more paperwork from First Choice Evaluations for me to fill out on the upcoming orthopedic examination this week. Once I got inside and settled down at the table, I opened it up to find a relatively large amount of documents that were from the Psychological IME done by Dr. Claus. There were many formalities inside the details of the paperwork, so I fast forwarded to the first page of the exam. It was almost word for word of how the exam was conducted. Much to my surprise, it came out much differently than what I originally thought in the beginning. I mean after all, having such prior bad experiences with these IMEs did not exactly lead me to having confidence with this one. It had started out with the usual summary and injury history, followed by the actual incident on 5/9/17 with Officer Thompson, and then onto a complete medical history. Sounds like a lot of medical for a psych exam but that's how the system works. Following that we discussed in great detail about my psychiatric history, which had noted, when I took this job back in 1994 and had taken the additional psychological exam and interview with a psychologist, I had passed it with no issues which indicated that there was no prior history with me.

We started talking about my educational background and all that I had accomplished in life thus far. As quick as that went, Dr. Claus then started a mental exam asking me assorted questions. Part of his statements on the reports were that his observations of me during the session included depression, extreme anxiety, trauma related symptoms, disturbed sleep patterns, irritable mood, and related marital discord. The State Insurance Fund, who arranged for this examination, had sought a conclusion of medical findings by Dr. Claus. In these findings, he found partial relationship between claimant's injury of 5/9/17 and his psychiatric conditions. Diagnoses included generalized anxiety disorder, major depressive disorder, single episode and post-traumatic stress disorder. The claimant, being myself, is partially and temporarily disabled at this time in terms of his work-related conditions. Dr. Claus states in his report, "He is not yet ready to explore other work options but he will NOT be able to return to his job in the Corrections Department.

"The claimant is not able to return to duty in Corrections, and by doing so, this would develop problematic symptoms upon his return. This is a job where one would have to make a split-second decision in times of extreme stress and crisis. If one cannot make these decisions, lives can be in the balance. As such, this claimant cannot be expected to return to work in a Corrections environment. It seems apparent that this claimant is not yet ready to return to an alternative work environment. But this should continue to be a goal for him."

Yesterday I had attended my second Independent Medical Examination with a Dr. Schoolman up in one of his offices he rents in Poughkeepsie. He is an orthopedic doctor. He spoke swiftly and stuck to the facts; apparently, he had a full schedule as I was his first patient of the day. Nurse Jody had attended this exam with me again, she was familiar with this office. Having been there before, she seemed relaxed about this routine exam. Nurse Jody knows of Dr. Schoolman, as was apparent when they greeted each other upon entry into the exam room. This exam was quick and to the point, almost everything he asked me were things that I had already filled out on my worksheet, so I had him refer to it when I could not recall details. Besides the neck and shoulder exam from the injury assault of 5/9/17, he began to ask me questions about my physical health history, past surgeries, medications, and other details. At that point, unlike others who would type this into a computer at the exam, he used a blank sheet of paper to scribble down short abbreviated versions of my replies to him. He then asked me to take off my jacket, and to stand up and turn sideways. He completed a rather fast range of motion exam on me, but did no measurements as I have had done in the past with certain medical instruments by other doctors. Within a minute of that visual exam, he told us we were done and he sat down to make some more notes. We left the room. Nurse Jody and I briefly spoke outside about how things looked and went on our way. It would be about 10-12 days before I would be hearing anything on the outcome from this exam. As it is right now, I am out on my own sick time and vacation, having exhausted my six months of benefits from the workers' compensation program. I was in touch with the girls in the Time office at Fishkill to keep tabs on my balances and to work up an estimated date of when those accruals would be exhausted. With this being the last day of February, I was now looking onto March's calendar, with 32 doctor appointments already scheduled for the month, if not more as the days continue. But I have not missed one appointment yet, and I will keep going and following the orders of my medical and legal staff as this case continues, all in an order to see fit that I will not fall into the cracks of this system and get the deserving medical treatments that is needed. This week I am getting called up to Albany for my third Independent Medical Exam with an ENT specialist, Dr. Service, whose office is right next to the Crossgates Mall in Albany. This issue also was found to have relation to the 5/9/17 case with Officer Thompson. The sudden deceleration from his impact upon my left shoulder caused multiple trauma that the major diagnostic exams, doctors' reports, and other tests had shown leading the State's Workers' Compensation Board judge to find prima facie medical evidence on for my case. This would be my third IME this month. I would be bringing another nurse with me up to Albany as well. I just want this process to finally get going. Coincidentally, within a week from now, I will again be back in Albany for my preliminary hearing on the charges I brought against our union and employer through the Public Employee Relations Board.

Here it is, March 8th, the day after a major snowstorm impacted our region. It even shut down the donut shops. Now you know if they close, it's a bad one out there. I had tried the day before to call around with First Choice Evaluations and with the State Insurance Fund to see if everything was on schedule. The weather map had included the Albany area, and in my neighborhood alone, we got about 18 inches of snow. Trees down, car wrecks, no power – pandemonium all around. No one was at their offices that day to answer phones so I could not even find out if my IME exam was going to be rescheduled the following day. Once I got up the next morning, all was clear. School was a two-hour delay, I dropped off the kids at a friend's house and met up with Certified Nursing Assistant Heather. She helped me out with this IME due to the numerous out-of-pocket expenses I had been incurring. I could not get through to their office so we took the ride up nonetheless. Roads were clear the entire way up, save for the tractor trailer off the road whose trailer was completely bent in half. It must have just occurred and we just beat the traffic nightmares that come associated with these incidents. The Thruway Authority and Troopers had just arrived on the scene. We ended up arriving early, by 30 minutes at Dr. Service's ENT office. The staff took a copy of my ID and had me fill out a three-page questionnaire pertaining to all of the details of my injuries as well as medical history, medications, and contact information. Within minutes, we were called into an exam room. Dr. Service told me he had already looked over my very thick folder of documents and knew the details of what happened. They knew at this point most of the information, other than a few questions with information that had been occluded in the prior documents. Before I knew it, he did a quick exam of my eyes, ears, and mouth, then had us move into another testing room where I was put into a sound proof booth. Anyone who had had a hearing test before knows exactly what these are. There were a series of tests done which took about 15 minutes. The technician handed over my folder to Dr. Service and had Heather and I come out to the hallway. I asked him about the outcome and he told me everything was exactly the same as the last test, I had hearing loss to my left ear. I asked him if he was going to do a balance test on me and he responded with a swift, "No, we are going to note in your file to the State Insurance Fund that you do have balance issues which we concur with and we will direct them to approve and set you up with physical therapy for your balance issues." Dr. Service was not very thorough with his examination, as witnessed by my attending nurse

Heather. "As for the TMJ problem, we do not specialize in that," he said, "you would need to see an orthodontist." At the time he told me that, I pointed out what the State Insurance Fund had instructed in the IME report. He made a note of that and told them that there would be nothing he could give opinion on with that issue. We wrapped up and were out the door, time for some lunch before the trip back down the thruway south. At that time, I had called Warren, one of my attorneys, left him a voicemail to update him on the IME exam findings so they had a heads-up before the report was sent in.

On March 13th, the UPS truck once again pulled up my driveway with a flat rate envelope. I figured it was from the orthopedic IME exam two weeks ago at the state doctor in Poughkeepsie, which my Nurse Consultant Jody had once again attended with me. After getting my hands on it, I took note that it was exactly that. Dr. Schoolman's report, albeit a lengthy 16 pages long, spoke in volumes about the outcome of the exam, everything from history to medications, test results, and his determinations based on his findings. "Based upon my medical evaluation, review of medical records, and the NY State Workers' Compensation Board's guidelines, the claimant has a moderate 50% disability secondary to the injuries sustained. His diagnosis was traumatic impingement syndrome, rotator cuff tear, and labral tear with arthroscopic surgery having been done in October of 2017. Additionally, he has traumatic cervical musculoskeletal disorder with mechanical cervical axial pain and strain, as well as anxiety and post-trauma depression. There is causal relationship between the injuries sustained and the incident of 5/9/17. He is not working and has not worked since the incident in question, and cannot function as a state corrections officer as he has restricted use of his left shoulder and cannot restrain inmates or do overhead activities." I called up my other attorney and spoke to Jason and spoke about the outcome of this exam. I was gearing up for my next surgery with my knees, which had been previously injured in a combative use of force involving an inmate back in the fall of 2016.

On March 23rd, another UPS overnight delivery, this time holding the 15-page report of the ear, nose and throat specialist independent medical exam that had been done on March 8th. It was quite the contrary to what Dr. Service explained to me in front of my escorting nurse, Heather. Although it is quite common for IME exams not to get into details of the outcome for the report during the appointment, Dr. Service was giving the impression to us that there was indeed some issues with causal relationship to my incident on 5/9/17. He did not have any prior audiograms to compare to pre-incident, so it was hard for him to make a case. This would be easy enough for me though, I have always had excellent hearing and I had planned on obtaining records from my prior physicals showing my hearing tests prior to this assault. It was just another road block, another hurdle, but we would get through this. I was determined to stand up for what was right in this case. Soon I was sending an email follow-up about this report to my law firm. Although Dr. Service does concur with the orthodontist report of TMJ, as well as the other reports reviewed from my specialists that I have been seeing for months and months, during his 15 minutes with me, he was able to magically conclude that none of the otologic injuries appeared to be related to the accident of May 9, 2017. I had found numerous errors throughout the report such as misquotes, diagnosis contradictions, among other things, so there would be a plan to appeal this under my rights within the Workers' Compensation Law. I located my most recent complete physical and sent copies of it to the State Insurance Fund, my law firm, the workers' compensation board advocates, as well as to First Choice Evaluations. Dr. Service indicated he had no prior incident audiogram to compare to, so I took these documents and made sure they were forwarded right away.

Chapter Twenty-Eight
Public Employee Relations Board Hearing

The time had now come for me to face the union, COPBA as well as the Governor's Office of Employee Relations which represented the Department of Corrections and Fishkill Correctional Facility. I reviewed the answers that both parties' attorneys gave to the charges, none of them making much sense at all, and according to those in the business, the usual typical response that these agencies would give to immediately deny anything hurtful. They basically admitted to the obvious, but since I was representing myself pro se in this matter, I gathered all of my statements, documentation, and prepared for the road trip to Albany tomorrow, to the Empire State Plaza, for a pre-trial hearing in front of the administrative law judge. I had checked into several previous labor lawyers and while I did pay for some consultations, it was not worth the thousands upon thousands of dollars to hire representation when in cases such as these, there are no punitive damages awarded, and rarely, if any at all, attorney's fees awarded. I had the proof in my hands and I was told by some of my own doctors well aware of this case and its corruption that no one else better than I could tell it like it was. The problem with telling lies is that after a period of time, things start to become inconsistent and contradicting. That was already starting to become transparent. The truth stays the same, always has, always will. I am looking forward to making some progress up there, I feel confident and ready to go. I think the only thing I am worried about is finding a parking spot when I get up there. And boy was I right; arriving early paid off. Everything was jam-packed, Albany Capitol Police had road blocks up on surrounding streets for what looked like some type of a union protest about to set in motion. A few rounds of the block and back into the tunnel area of the Empire State Plaza, pulled into the visitor parking area and quickly had a rare spot right next to the elevators to the concourse. It was quite a walk through there, felt as if I was in an airport with all the shops, etc. I still had time to spare so I made it to the elevators, arriving up to the 18th floor with a full suit and coat, briefcase in hand, ready to go. Apparently, with my appearance, I had been mistaken as an arriving attorney as I noted the schedule on the wall so I sat in the hall and waited for the other parties to arrive. I had heard a commotion around the corner of male voices who appeared lost, looking for the right room they were supposed to be in. As they rounded the corner, I noticed it was the Union President Peters and his lawyer. I was surprised thinking, he had to have been here before, so how could he be so confused. It was only moments later that the attorney from the Governor's Office of Employer Relations had arrived as well. Judge Rikers had come out of his office and introduced himself, and soon we were off to get started. We headed to Hearing Room "B" on the 18th floor of Building 2 in the Empire State Plaza. We all took our seats for this pre-trial conference and as the judge was explaining the process, we were signing in on a sheet being passed around the room. Not long after, Judge Rikers gave me the floor in which I had begun approximately 30 minutes' worth of opening statements, explaining the violations that they committed in their oaths as well as the constitution, and went into details about the State's Civil Service Law violations as well as Taylor Law. I had read off my complete list of charges and accusations against COPBA and its representatives who have been named. Judge Rikers had stopped me a few times asking me questions as to what I was referring to. After some explanation, I was able to carry on. I had done hours upon hours of research for this and it paid off. During this time, while I was reading off my list of charges against COPBA, President Peters, who was only sitting about ten feet away from me, appeared to be in anger as his entire head and face was boiling hot red in color. He had not said a word with the union's lawyer sitting at his side. We went into discussion about the directive that the Department of Corrections has called Directive 4960, Violence in the Workplace. The department claims it has zero tolerance against any infractions of this, but apparently this was not the case in my incident. I had further explained that due to the lack of the actions taken by my union to act and represent me after numerous emails, phone calls, and certified letters, I had suffered irreparable harm and pain from the controverted medical claim which arose from this case. It took nearly four months before I was able to get some approvals on my controverted claim. I had also noted for the record that I had never been contacted about the workers' compensation disability claim being controverted. This changes the whole game once they do that.

After some more questioning, the floor was turned over to the State Governor's Office representatives who had nothing to add at this point. The attention was then turned to the union's lawyer who had mentioned a few issues based on the answers to the charges. This was like playing patty cake. I had already given information verbally about the answers to the charges that they contested. One of them from the union was that my response was not "timely." How dumb can one be when I have been attempting for months at reaching out to them for assistance? Timely? Hardly not! Look in the mirror, guys! The union's lawyer did not have a lot to come back with, apparently underestimating what kind of individual they would be going up against. They had several charges being lodged against them from my written reports, and I was able to respond with more details and read off more about my statements, which included that they acted with depraved ignorance and chose to close their eyes to the obvious facts in the case. Soon after, the judge had excused all parties except myself; he came over from his area to sit next to me for about 20 minutes to go over my resolution in the case, what do I think could be done to be made whole again. One thing was for certain. I was not withdrawing my charges, nor was I going to settle. I wanted an outside agency, a federal agency, to come in and handle the workplace violence investigation based on all the evidence at hand. There was no way that a state agency could do this now, it would end up going into arbitration and being handled by the union. That would be a conflict of interest, like someone deliberately shining a flashlight on Punxsutawney Phil to get him to see his shadow, pushing for something in their favor.

Judge Rikers left me in the room alone and went outside to talk to the other parties. He came back within 20 minutes explaining to me what the union had offered and I rejected it. I firmly told the judge I wanted to proceed to trial with this, albeit the preponderance of evidence all weighed upon me. I had won this battle today, after doing so much research and fact finding, and by myself, without a lawyer, or as they call it in the legal world, a pro se case of representation. All parties were brought back into the room for a final briefing and notified of their expectations and what was going to be coming in the mail to us shortly, as the trial date is decided, witnesses are identified, and that we prepare for this. President Peters left the room without saying good bye, although upon entering he shook my hand saying hello. Looks like they had some work to do. I would be as prepared as they will be, this is not something I take lightly. I finished up writing down some notes in the room, being the last one to leave and Judge Rikers came up to me, shook my hand, told me thank you for coming today and that I did an absolute great job. I appreciated that wholesomely and finished up my notes. Soon, I was on the elevator to grab some lunch open the concourse level before making it out of the Albany area to get home to get the kids off the bus. I had multiple medical appointments the next two days to get my paperwork ready for as well. With my roller coaster rides of ups and downs during this entire case since May of last year, I was definitely up on the highest part of it, feeling exhilaration of some sorts, with quite a load taken off my mind, even if done so temporarily. For some reason when your mind becomes stress-free and you have a sense of joy about you, your body's immune system seems to get a boost in its powers during the healing process of one's injuries, and I had many of them. I felt good that day.

Eventually word had gotten out around family and friends of how the pre-trial hearing went for me and I had been congratulated by everyone all around. This was not something that was handed to me, I had worked long and hard to prepare for this, doing a lot of research, but I could not have done it all without the help of my wife, first and foremost, as well as my friends Dave, Mike, Al, and a few other unmentionables, who were all instrumental in assisting me in research and study. Of course, the support of my family and friends, neighbors, were always there as well. But this was just a starting point, we had more work to do, and it would be coming up sooner than later. After speaking to Judge Rikers, I was going to hold off on any extra leg work gathering the subpoenas and other evidential documentation until a complete review of the directives and the submitted documents in the Improper Practice Charge were completed. This was a slight indication that my burden of proof might not be as heavy for the upcoming trial since I had already done so much of the work already.

Chapter Twenty-Nine
A Patient's Patience

Well, not a weekday goes by these days that I do not have some sort of medical appointment scheduled. As I was saying before, my average count is around 30 appointments each month for the injuries that occurred from the incident on May 9, 2017. However, today was not just one of those routine days of office visits. It was March 20th, the first day of spring. One would love to see the signs of the change of season at this point, but according to every weather report, we were about to get hit with our fourth snowstorm this month. I started calling around to ensure my three medical appointments for the following day would still be on schedule. One of them in particular was for Dr. D's Office on Broadway in Newburgh. He was the orthopedic who did surgery on my shoulder and we were getting ready to work on my knees soon, those being from inmate-related assaults at Fishkill Correctional Facility. It was 3:15 p.m. when I called Dr. D's office and spoke to his receptionist staff. Looking at my calendar and appt. card, I wanted to be sure my appointment was confirmed for 12:30 p.m. the next day. After a minute of checking, the girl came back to the phone and said I was all set. If there would be issues with snow delays then to give the office a call the following day before going in.

I had just finished up my appointment with Dr. Newton in Goshen and he got me out of there in time at noon to get me back to Newburgh so I would make it on time to my 12:30-p.m. appointment. I arrived at the Broadway office of Dr. D's, signed in on the clipboard, and sat down. One of the girls, Noelette, walked over to me and asked me my name; I gave her the information stating I already confirmed it twice, plus I had the appointment card. She came back after making a phone call and apologized and said, "We do not have you in the computer for an appointment today, you would have to come back in April or go to Middletown today to see Dr. D's assistant."

I explained to Noelette, "Listen, my work note is due today, I have to have this done, this appointment was confirmed yesterday. I just drove here from Goshen, now you want me to go to Middletown?" She left me no good option so I said, "Ok, I will go to Middletown, but there must be a full waiting room there."

Noelette stated, "No, there won't be, I will call ahead. You will be seeing one of the assistants today, just ask for him and they will get you right in. So go now, run! Go, I will call for you."

I began my trip again down 84 going to Middletown. There still was no snow in the area yet – thank God – but once I got to Middletown, the school notified me that they were releasing students early. Great, I thought, what now?! We live in a great neighborhood, we all know each other and party together, we all do what we can to look out for each other. No other neighborhood in the area could compare to ours for that matter. I gave Eric a call who is retired, living across the street. He had an eagle eye for activities in our area so I knew I could rely on him to get our kids from the bus along with his grandson until I got home. I was just about to the office looking for its location off from Rt. 211. We had come upon a stoplight, as I glanced over thinking I saw the small sign and I ended up rear-ending an older car full of people in an accident. Good thing for my rubber mounts on the front bumper that cushioned the impact and caused slight cosmetic damage on the rear of the other car. Since we had a lane blocked and were all in a hurry, no one had any injuries so we moved on our way. This was caught on my dash cam as well so I would have it for future use if I needed it. I knew it was my fault but with the predicament I had been put in between what was required by my employer, the screw-up of the appointment system at the doctor's office, none of this should have happened if I did not have to be there. I pulled into the lot and entered the office of Dr. D. He has numerous locations all across the region from New York City and upward throughout the Hudson Valley. I checked into the office and the girls there had heard I was on my way, but the receptionist said that I would have to wait. It was now 1:30 pm, I had an appt for 12:30 pm, and she told me that Noelette should have known better than to tell me I would be "taken" right in to be seen upon arrival. She rushed me there for nothing. I had to wait for two additional hours just to be seen and have a work note signed. Following this, I went straight home and began to type up an email to send to Dr. D's office. The following day I got a call from one of his managers in

Poughkeepsie who said they were aware of the incident and that it would be looked into. She also offered an apology which I expected, but couldn't help feeling as if that was sufficient. This is what drives an injured patient into a corner.

And yet I am told by Dr. D's senior staff that he seems to go through office staff quite frequently. They find that they cannot keep up with the high demands of the caseloads of documents from the daily patients. Even if you have an appointment, there's no way you are getting in there on time, most likely up to an hour past your scheduled appointment. Yet they keep scheduling patient after patient to get the turnaround that Dr. D's firm is looking for. By doing so this creates so much potential for errors in the paperwork. Just with my case alone, this has happened several times. I've worked with some of the best medical specialists for my injuries but their bedside manners and factory assembly line of patients during your visits is what disrupts the doctor-patient relationship.

When it comes to ensuring that the Workers' Compensation documentation is filled out and sent in correctly, that's one thing, but then it's another to have them fill out your insurance papers such as AFLAC. Chasing them down after you mailed it in and it gets buried on their desk of folders, faxing follow-ups, phone calls, and even visits in person does not guarantee you certainty that this simple task will be done. Maybe if Dr. D's office hired more staff? Maybe slow down on the rate of daily patients who overflow into the hallways from the waiting areas? Something as simple as this could lead to better ratings, less stress on the injured patients, and to boot, happier people who would heal better. It's not my job to make sure someone else does their jobs, but like most of who have gone through the system or still are, we all said the same thing. Even with a lawyer, you have to advocate for yourself, each and every day. Maybe that's why my logbooks are getting so full of my documentation since day one. But with AFLAC, I have a secondary policy which supplements at about 30% of what I would be making if my photography business were up and running. But they have maximums on their policies so you have to take what you can get. Simple issues like not putting the diagnosis code onto the form can get a claim denied. This only creates more frustration and hardship on one's family. The entire system is a squash if you ask me. I am sure plenty of working people in this country have enough to say about the healthcare system let alone the Workers' Compensation Program. Between the bureaucracy, the State's Insurance Fund, lawyers, Workers' Comp, doctors, employers, etc., it's enough to weigh down the burden one has when he or she is injured and is only seeking the rightful deserved treatment that is necessary. I can bet that the Opiate Crisis was triggered by many of these patients who could not handle the system and tried to ease their mental anguish, pain and suffering, among other issues by abusing their prescribed medications. It's difficult enough to find a great orthopedic or a compassionate caring doctor who is able give you your treatment, but who also cares about dealing with your rights within the system and advocating on your behalf with the mountains of paperwork. Sometimes in order to find these specialists, you have to drive distances out of town. You are not going to find one right down the street from you, that's for sure. But in my case, I was lucky enough to find at least a couple of them in the area. But a patient is a human being too. We have the same feelings as everyone else. And everyone has a patience threshold. When it gets pushed over and over again, it's only a matter of time before the system no long works for this patient. He or she become a statistic. Then they end up becoming dependent on society as they get booted out for having shown their signs of weakness. Mental health is a huge issue with personal injuries today. Everyone has a different case, but mine are stacked up like Jenga blocks. I've been to the bottom, however, slowly but surely, I will climb up out of there and climb back to the top once again, taking the knowledge of these experiences I had endured and hopefully be able to help others with their situations. That's one of the main reasons I am writing this book, to bring public knowledge to what is really happening out there in the system, and inside of the system as well, right under our noses.

I came back to see my orthopedic surgeon Dr. D on March 27th who read over my MRI reports and although there were definitely injuries to my knees, he felt my best option for them was to keep doing physical therapy, medications, and pain management. I wear double knee braces that were measured and fit for me by his office. Since I had already had two knee surgeries before, he said that 3-4 months down the road if I had more surgery, I could be in the same boat again. Dr. D told me I was a good candidate for knee replacements but that I was too young for them so I would have to wait it out. The pain was too great for me during specific types of activities. And if it wasn't my knees, it was my lower back; if it wasn't those, then it was my left shoulder. I have permanent issues from my injuries. It was a constant battle.

A couple days later, I got another UPS overnight letter in the mail, containing an addendum to my orthopedic IME from Dr. Schoolman. In his original report he stated that I could not go back into this kind of work anymore, and that due to my injuries, it would be some time before I could do anything, but now he sends a report at the State Insurance Fund's request to fill out a Limited Physical Capabilities form which indicates light duty activities. I immediately contacted my law firm so that we could request a hearing with the State Workers' Compensation Board. I wanted to argue this and point out the discrepancies in the reports. As many exams as these doctors do, even they make clerical mistakes, which can make or break a judge's decision at a hearing. Once this was done, we could also start getting my approvals for my TMJ treatments, balance physical therapy, and cervical spine injections from the incident where I was assaulted back in May of 2017 by Officer Thompson. It has almost been a year and I am still waiting for treatments. This is unbelievable, unheard of, and unacceptable. They keep loading you up on medications, and right now I am on seven of them, using them to hold you down until the real work can be done on your injuries. The length of time, the psychological stress, and the pain and pressure while you are taking these meds are part of the reason that many patients end up abusing them. The state caused this broken system, it's all a game, a stupid game with a bunch of morons pushing pens onto the paperwork that they shuffle on their desk daily. It's only costing the state more money which in turn costs the taxpayers more money. It's there, you might not see it in your tax bills, but trust me, it's a line item in the state's budget, and the entire state of taxpayers, or at least those of us that are still here and have not moved out of New York yet, should be kicking down Albany's doors. Let me be the one who can show you the proof. They call this a game, but it's no game. Not when it involves one's own family, and let me say this. The other side of this matter may be laughing, sitting back worry free that yeah, we did our reports, we covered our asses, and pretending this never happened, well, here's a news flash, fellas, this is not going away. You are not going to hear or see the end of this for a very long time, if not ever. The old theme of delay, delay, go away is done, those days are over. People will be held responsible for their actions, and keep this in mind too. Nobody, and I say again, nobody put you in this position that you are in but yourselves. You made the wrong decision, and albeit being an uphill battle for me, I made the right one.

Chapter Thirty
Decisions, Decisions...

On April 11th, I was notified by phone from staff at the personnel office in Fishkill Correctional Facility that I was going to be taken off the Workers' Compensation injury case for my inmate related injuries of 9/11/16, of which I was getting treatments for through pain management, physical therapy, orthopedic, and cortisone injections. I had gone to two different professional specialists that deal with the knees. I am being told that Mark, who is the head of Personnel for State Corrections, had done a thorough review and decided to put me back on the 5/9/17 injuries from the Thompson incident. This meant I am now back out on my own sick time with no compensation benefits, getting treatments for inmate related injuries. Personnel also informed me they were going to request the State Insurance Fund to send me to another psychological independent medical examination to get clearance. I obtained the contact information for Mark and gave him a call at that time, but of course only to get his voicemail. I left a message explaining the situation and to give him my information to return my call. My next attempt was to contact my law firm in White Plains. I left them messages and then finally heard back from Nick within an hour or so of my initial call. "This is an employer issue, not a workers' compensation issue," he said. "You can't be out on two cases at once." While I was well aware of this, our conversation was pretty intense. There were certain contractual issues they were not aware of for my case as my firm represents many different law enforcement agencies. This created a dynamic sense of uncertainty in the matters of my case when many questions would arise. The conversation had gotten to me real fast, sounding as if he was coming from their side and not on mine, so I hung up and took some time to go clear my thoughts.

I got in touch with Dr. Ogulnick, my psychologist who I have been seeing since this all began back in May of 2017. We spoke at great length about what the state was now doing to my case. There were some ideas brought up and some suggestions made, which to me sounded good. He walked me through my anger and stress while on the phone and once I got home, I had sent an email to follow up with my lawyers group once again with Nick and sent him a lengthy message about that day's events and my dissatisfaction. It had been almost immediately that he responded to me and there was no discussion regarding my complaints I had made, only that he said there was no need to apologize. Nick went into numerous paragraphs about my complicated situation and how we are in a storm with this right now, but soon this would pass and there would be light at the end of the tunnel. His advice was just to keep going with my appointments and documentation until the next hearing. However, this did nothing to address my immediate need to plan for my reduction in pay and benefits in the certain and extremely near future. As I type this, I am looking at the clock and getting ready for three appointments today; I am on my way out the door now for the chiropractor, physical therapy, and the ENT specialists, all to be seen for my work-related injuries. This will make for seven appointments just this week alone. Out the door I go.

Back I come, nearly seven hours later after these appointments, having drove well over 100 miles and was able to obtain additional documentation from my ENT Physician Dr. Feldman over at ENT and allergy associates. I provided her with a copy of the ENT IME that was done in Albany. Although her name was listed on it to be served a copy of this document packet, she indeed had not received one. After further exam, assessment, and review of my worsening condition to my TMJ and left ear, she wrote up my report and I provided copies to my attorney law firm in White Plains. I also got some documentation from my lawyers in the mail requesting the hearing from the state's Workers' Compensation Board to address the independent medical exams I had mentioned earlier and to produce more documentation. I was hoping for something to be scheduled as soon as possible due to the amount of pain I was still in. Three weeks or so from now will make this the one-year anniversary since the Thompson Incident occurred. Can you believe how long it takes the system to get treatments necessary for an injured party which when the major diagnostic testing was done, had shown evidence of such injuries?! I thought we were in America, not some 3rd-world country. We deserve to be treated no matter who has to pay for it, the State's Insurance Fund or the Empire Plan. But in the end, I know it will be the State Insurance Fund's responsibility because that's where the truth leads back to. It's just unfortunate that one has to wait while caught up in the web as the wheels of justice slowly grind round and round. Now more delays have come as the Governor's Office of Employee Relations and COPBA's attorneys have discrepancies with PERB's new trial dates set for June. So looks like that's going to be set back another 60 days or better. They plan for a two-day trial, so this will give the state more time to prepare for their case, witnesses, as well as COPBA's sit-down with their testifying witnesses to go over the questions that will be asked of them during their testimony. In the meantime, I will be working on my cross examination.

While I was at physical therapy this morning, I got a call back from Mark, the head of Personnel up in Albany for Corrections. He explained to me the same thing that my local told me. But I was not hearing it. Not because of my left ear, but because it was unheard of to be released by my orthopedic doctor who did the left shoulder surgery. He was now going to start working on my injured knees, from a use of force altercation that had occurred on numerous dates while on duty. Why would it be fair for them to put me back out on my own sick time for the 5/9/17 case and get treatments and medical procedures for my inmate-related injuries? This was unheard of. But in the end, Mark had said that I needed to be cleared by the state's psych IME doctor in order for me to go out on another case. They had contacted Miss Jackie over at the State Insurance Fund to have another exam scheduled. Guess it's becomes a wait and see game now. It's a just a big game, that's what I keep being told. Well, this game is a big joke playing with the serious business of people's lives. Let them sort out the fraud through other means, but to put us all through the same path is just not fair, and it's discriminating to one's disability.

I had received a letter dated April 12, 2018 from Fishkill Correctional Facility's Deputy Superintendent of Administration's Office. His office oversees the duties of the human resources for all employees staffed at this prison. Since day one of this incident in May of last year, I have faxed and mailed in multiple doctors' notes and workers' compensation documentation as required by the department. But since Albany decided to move me back to the other case of 5/9/17 while I was now getting procedural treatments on my knees and back from inmate-related injuries during uses of force in combat, the Deputy Superintendent decided to send me out an official notice on state letterhead stating, "You are currently overdue for medical documentation. Failure to submit an updated, conforming medical document with seven days of the date of this letter, on April 19, 2018, will result you being placed on unauthorized leave retroactive back to last month." Doing such would cause severe harm to my case, salary, and benefits for my family. There was no need for this. They are the ones that put me out on the other case that I already provided the documentation for. This was pure harassment at this point, but I could see what they were up to, having after all being under the eye of numerous agencies investigating them for my case. I made a phone call to his secretary since today was now April 17th. I did not receive the letter in the mail until yesterday, and that would give me three days to get an appointment made and have this documentation made out retroactively. This would be impossible and was not fair. His secretary kept me on the line and said she was going to transfer me to Personnel, but I told her no, I had already dealt with them and I had the right to speak to him since it was his letter to me. After a quick placement on hold, he picked up the phone. We had a serious discussion about the matter regarding his letter to me. His voice was very broken, as if he was nervous after I had read off some narratives from the directives to him and notifying him that I was referring this matter to my law firm in White Plains. He kept pointing the finger at the Workers' Comp Board but this had nothing to do with them. This was both Fishkill and Albany's decision to keep me out on the same case longer and to request another independent medical exam to get me cleared. It made no sense and only wasted time, but that's what this system is good for, wasting time of injured workers in hopes that eventually they will just give up and walk away from the matter. I have lost all that I have ever cared for in that place, except for most of the people I still consider my friends. They all knew what I was going through and supported me when I needed it. They were also in agreement and loved the fact that I was fighting this corrupt system in hopes to make some changes for other officers' future careers in the prison system so they too would not have to endure the same type of treatment. I got off the phone with him with my mind rested assured that he knew I was serious about this and that action would be taken. No longer could they intimidate me. This fight would continue. I chose to do it for me and my family, but now it's also including all the rest of the Corrections officers who are working in New York's prison system.

I just did a count of the number of agencies involved with this assault and workplace violence incident of May 9, 2017. There are a total of 24. "That's insane," said another officer I work with who did not want to be identified. "You would think that just having a couple of them would get the job done to find an ending to this." Two of the most recent agencies to get involved are the State's Joint Commission of Public Ethics and the New York State Inspector General's Office. Following my receipt of my inquiry into the status of this incident, they both had me submit additional documentation, 47 pages in all. I sat here scanning them into the computer one by one and sent them off by email. That number is a single-digit percentage of the amount of paperwork I have on file regarding my case. It was about time to call it quits for the day to get ready for my three doctors' appointments tomorrow for physical therapy, pain management, and chiropractor care. I seem to be on this spinning wheel that doesn't have a brake to stop it or slow it down. Time and pressure have always been the test on whether or not one was able to get through a confined area. That's exactly what's going on here – time and pressure. Sooner or later, the truth will come forward as it has already been proven by other means in its existence. But the other side applies the opposite, waiting for the delays to drive this issue into the ground as if it never happened. The statistics show that most officers would not have gone this far and would have given up by now. They are not used to seeing this type of situation with the way my case is carrying on. The attention from all involved will soon get out to the public. Always has, always will, especially in this day and age.

It was April 19, 2018, just getting back home from a busy day of those medical appointments, and it was the pain management group, out of New York City, if you can imagine, that caused me the most grief. Although I thought it would be a typical day of going in for an exam as I had been doing for at least two of my cases for the last several months, this day would be the ending of myself being treated by this group. As usual the patients stacked up after signing in, awaiting to see the one specialist, actually a nurse practitioner, not an MD. The earlier you got there the better, but it seemed like an assembly line. It was like a factory production line. From past visits, she had always made me aware that she does not have that much time to spend with each patient. Now where are the bedside manners here? This just shows that they are rushing patients through the system in order to turn over profits from the insurance companies. I had not been called in yet, but while I was sitting in the waiting room, this nurse practitioner walked by me to her exam room to greet me with a hello by using her right hand to rub my upper right leg above my knee brace as I was sitting down. I thought of that as quite odd. Soon I was called in and as prepared as I usually am with documentation for my appointments, I had handed her a copy of the orthopedic IME report from Dr. Schoolman along with his amendment made out three weeks later which directly contradicted his original report of the IME three weeks earlier. I also gave her my typed-out medication list and she said to me, "Did you give this to the girl who interviewed you?"

I said, "No, she did not ask for it, just a few questions and then she handed me a urine cup for a urinalysis test." My nurse practitioner seemed very bothered by the fact that she was given extra paperwork to review. She began asking questions only to cut me in mid-sentence and talked over the top of me, not allowing me to finish. She further elaborated, "Paul, listen, we don't have time for this, I have several patients waiting." I looked at my watch, I had only been in there four minutes at that point. She went into a fit of rage and said she was calling her boss who headed this pain management group out of New York and would request to discontinue me as a patient. She then walked out of the exam room like a 10-year-old, and in front of about a dozen patients and staff, she loudly alerted her assistant to remove me from the charts and that she would not be seeing me anymore. There was no discretion on her part. I stayed in her room as she pouted outside. I was the one needing the treatment for the pain. I have already been wronged by this horrible system we have for injured workers. She came back in and got her cell phone and laptop, and then I left the room to meet with Dr. Habif, my chiropractor that originally referred them. We had a brief meeting and he asked me to please not report her for official misconduct. I left there going back to the exam room to notify the pain management staff that I would be reporting this conduct and contacting some lawyers. I went to their website and posted a review about the event that occurred. I spoke to my wife about the situation and we were on the same page about this ordeal and what to do about it. First thing I did was to make a call for another pain management specialist in the local vicinity who came recommended and accepted workers' compensation. After securing that, I would be preparing for my medical appointments tomorrow to discuss this situation with my other doctors for further guidance. Well, this has been a busy week. Nine medical appointments, some good and bad news as expected, some not so expected. These injuries from the assault case of 5/9/17 have a long way to go yet in the investigations, but right now I am also focusing on the other medical injuries from inmate-related combative uses of force. I am seeing about 14 doctors right now, ranging from orthopedics to pain management, two different physical therapists, psychologists, spinal and knee surgeons, ENT specialists, chiropractor, and an orthodontist for the TMJ, among others. I did get some good news; while waiting for the State Workers' Compensation Board to schedule a date for our hearing to go over the three independent medical exams with the judge and all involved parties, they finally approved my vestibular therapy for my balance issues due to the injuries from Thompson's assault nearly a year ago. I have been waiting and fighting forever to get this and today I went for the first time to Prime Care Physical Therapy in Goshen, New York, where Dr. Feldman had referred me to. I had received a C-4 authorization form in the mail from the State Insurance Fund that said approved vestibular therapy without prejudice, and my lawyer Nick also sent me an email to alert me of the approval. My first visit and a barrage of testing that lasted over an hour showed I had serious balance issues and left ear damage due to the incident from May 9, 2017. I was told that I would have to come in weekly for sessions and then also do home therapy as well. A day or so later, I get a phone call from Prime Care Physical Therapy. They had spoken to the case handler, Miss Jackie. According to her, she stated to my new physical therapy provider that "They could treat me but they would not get paid." I replied, "She has no authority over saying you are not getting paid, that's up to the Workers' Compensation Board judge to decide at the upcoming hearing. Furthermore, why would you stop treatment on a patient who is so much in need of this care?" Prime Care PT's reps replied back that they could not go forward and would have to cancel the remaining appointments. I was pretty upset about that, typical of this game that the insurance company plays, but soon our day for the hearing was coming and was certain to be ironed out. I also got a call from Dr. Ogulnick from Orange Counseling Associates in Newburgh the following morning. I thought for a second he was calling to reschedule but quickly he had told me with permission from another patient of his, that he had almost the same exact situation going on that Dr. Ogulnick was seeing him for. His name was Gregg, about 40 years old, an otherwise healthy individual save for the fact that he had a few injuries from an assault by a co-worker. He too was a state worker, in the Mid-Hudson Psych Center, and was also a union steward. His situation had mirrored mine so much, I was surprised, but not in disbelief. Even his case, with him being an official with COPBA, he too is facing the same mirror as I am. This is not an uncommon issue. He too was having issues with returning to work under the scrutiny of his case, the peer pressure, the harassment while in the workplace, the ability to feel safe in his work environment without reprisals, and get this, our union also was not giving him a fair shake on representation. This was causing the usual stress and PTSD, and the management at this work location was running away from the facts to avoid being held responsible for their failures to uphold the state's rules and regulations, laws and guidelines regarding workplace violence. Dr. Ogulnick had asked me if we could have a group session this week at my usual appointment time and I agreed. With 24 state and federal agencies already currently or passively having been involved in my case alone, I was surely able to point him in the right direction down the long road he was about to take. But that's what the employer wants you to see, that long road with no help in sight, all in an effort to get you to lay down on the issue and make it go away in hopes that everyone can go back to work unharmed who had fouled up in the first place. With the way this department is changing these days, there's far less protection as there used to be but in some circles. There are some surviving good 'ole boys' clubs still in service. Probably for the time being, but not for long. We were able to meet in session, the three of us there got to sit down and talk over the issues, surely not enough time to get into it all, but we hit some good ground on where things were headed. I had previously prepared a checklist to help him reach out to contact the right agencies that would assist him in his matter as well. In this case with him, it involved him being struck by an African American female. Everything was being done to protect the class status of the aggressor, but nothing for Gregg, also a white male. Now, I have never been one to make anything into a race issue, as many of my friends come from multiple backgrounds. On the other hand, though, when it comes to the State's Department of Corrections, the white male is the bottom of the totem pole, unless of course you had the executive connections to cover up the incident overnight.

Some more news came in the mail from the Industrial Board of Appeals' attorneys. Two envelopes, in fact. The first one I opened up stated that the Department of Labor's senior attorney had motioned for dismissal of my petition in my appeal of the DOL's investigation into Fishkill Correctional

Facility's handling of the workplace violence incident. The hearing officer and senior counsel for the Board of Appeals denied their motion and directed me to resubmit an amended petition within 30 days. Heck, I redid that in 30 minutes with much more narrated evidence, then made copies, typed up the proof of service affidavit, and got it notarized by Mike who's always been there for me; with it, off in the mail it went. I am not the kind of guy that knowing when something has to get done, I wait until the day of to complete it. I like to get things done proficiently.

I coincidently got a telephone call from the Governor's Office of Employee Relations and spoke to one of their representative attorneys. The dates for the upcoming two-day trial regarding my case of charges against my union COPBA were being pushed farther into summer, further away than I appreciated. I did not want this to drag out any longer, but as Judge Rikers said, they would be willing to work with all parties involved in order to get a schedule that worked for everyone. If I were them and needed to prepare for such a case like this, I would push for more time as well – like I said: delay, delay, go away. We came to a possible conclusion on some dates and I was waiting to hear back from the State's Public Employees Relations Board for further details. I had also been in touch with the State's Joint Commission on Public Ethics and the Inspector General's Office investigators, who confirmed that they all had received the 47 pages of documents along with their submission forms and were looking into the matter. I had informed them that there were well over 150 documents following this should they be needed to be reviewed, not including my 260+ pages of logbook legal material. The ball is in their court, now it was time to sit back and see. Tomorrow was another full day of doctors' appointments, routine as usual, only this time one of them was a new provider for pain management of the shoulder/neck/ear injuries caused by Officer Thompson. Everything was pointing back to him, even the state's independent medical exams and the Workers' Compensation Board's hearing where the State Judge found his testimony not credible and had awarded me my medical benefits to start the surgery I needed.

Chapter Thirty-One
Missing Out on Life's Pleasures

I look at the end of April's calendar, full of appointments, the new calendar for May being displayed as it appears, and that too will fill up with medical appointments. I just finished up making out my sixth mileage reimbursement request forms and emailed them to the State Insurance Fund with copies sent to my law firm in White Plains and the Workers' Compensation Board. To date, according to my mileage log, I have traveled a distance of 8,429 miles to medical appointments just for the May 9, 2017 incident where I was assaulted by Officer Thompson. The miles will keep adding up, my injuries are far from done being treated. So much time, so much travel. But I really wanted to talk about life's pleasures that most of us can say we enjoy in today's society. There are several occasions in which as I type this, my children are out playing and doing things that most dads would be out doing with them. I am very limited on what I can do. I mean if I were to try, I certainly would feel double the pain the next day, and with pain comes misery. You can only chew on so many medications and who knows really what that's all doing to my insides in the long run. With so many doctors giving me treatments, it's not unusual for many of them to be asking me why am I taking this, why am I taking that? Since I have been out, there has been attempts for me to remain an active part of our family. But of course, my wife, with so much more on her plate, often turns her anger toward me in this whole ordeal that I am in which is impeding on our household economically, physically, emotionally, and psychologically. I admit, we had a great life going, things were good. Everyone has their ups and downs, but this surely was a downer. This issue, with it being so long term and all, was a daily reminder of what we take for granted in life. I really wanted to see the light at the end of the tunnel. I have been reminded by many that there is one, this was a time where most of us in this position begin to fall into the hands of the system and give up on their fight for what they're entitled to from the job. After all, like I said before, I did not put myself in this position, the corruption of the system did. How do I go 23 years of service with so many great years and all of the sudden this happens? I am nearing the finish line for retirement.

I just want to move on and try to focus on what's important – my family. I was told this the night of the incident leaving the emergency room and I continue to be reminded about it every day. I hope in the end I will be able to make some changes in the system. I seem to be doing the impossible, taking on the state in so many ways with these agencies by myself, acting pro se. Sure, I have a group of lawyers for my workers' compensation and retirement disability, but so many other legal issues remain in the line of sight. I want this to be a win for all of us. This is something that goes on daily in New York's prison system. You don't always hear about it because the old saying goes: "What happens behind the walls, stays behind the walls." Come on already, that was so yesteryear.

My children are only in 3rd grade as of this year. I have been reminded how time flies and you need to really stay on top of their activities. As much as I am at home from not working, I am not home due to the daily runaround with all of these appointments. I have been doing lots of research and learning more about the rights an individual has according to the laws that were set about to protect us. The one thing I want is to have stability and to be made whole again, to replace the losses I have suffered, and to secure our future, with my decreased ability to perform in today's workplace market. Just because when they say this is a wrap, does not mean it will be a wrap for our family. This is permanent, life-altering injury after injury. And part of that research has shown that one's mind may be at ease with the PTSD issues from those traumatic events he or she once experienced, but it only takes one thing, a glance, a sound, a reminder of this, and you have triggered the mindset back to square one. I miss those good days, but I need to move onto the next phase of life. I know one day when I sit down to read over this book again, I will remember the hours upon hours of writing I did to put together such a memoir like this. The time to do the research, the interviews I have done with others, and taking my photojournalism experience, and finally putting it into a book for my first time rather than other periodicals.

My kids are active these days, the wife working her full-time job and taking on her role as a homemaker in addition to running around with the children. My son is doing well with Lacrosse after a couple years of playing little league baseball, and of course my daughter, who has been ever-so-busy with her cheerleading squad at school. There's a lot to keep up with especially during the season of play. Who knows maybe there will be a little bit of good in this after all, my ability to make it out to their events as I once could not when I was working all of my jobs. But, without all of this being into play as it once was, it is wreaking havoc on the home front with just about every level you could imagine. This kind of situation puts an unnecessary strain on anyone's relationships. It's the strength from the last couple of decades being together that will test the endurance of our bond to the commitment we made to each other.

I got a call from my mother and my brother this week, who separately both live out in the western part of the country, checking in on how I was doing, looking to see how my case was progressing and what was going on with the family. I had brought them up to speed and I could tell that they too, along with my other immediate family members, had me in their thoughts constantly. I was the only one in my family to enter this type of career, save for the fact that my stepbrother from my father's remarriage of over 30 years to Paul's mother. He worked upstate, pretty much back home where we grew up. Since I was out on my own sick time still and using up my accruals, time was chipping away and I began seeking out donations of time accruals from friends on the job that would buy me some extra time on the books before losing pay and benefits. As I was looking at the calendar, I had noticed that I had not yet heard back from the Corrections Head Clerk of Personnel in Albany. I had called his office on a Friday afternoon and was forwarded through two secretaries to his extension. I finally was able to catch up to him and inform him that Miss Jackie from the NY State's Insurance Fund had informed me that they were not going to be scheduling me for the additional second psych medical exam as requested by the Department of Corrections. This kept me out longer to prevent me from transferring my workers' comp case over to the injuries sustained from the inmate related use of force combat incident on 9/11/2016. At this point, medical professionals out of Manhattan were reviewing my multiple MRI films and suggesting an immediate lumbar fusion due to the severity of my low back injuries, as well as from having two prior surgeries to my lower back that did not remediate the problem as well as I thought it had. "Why is it fair that I would be out on my own time or no time or benefits getting procedures done from an inmate?" I quipped to the Head Clerk. He stated that "I cannot be out on two cases at once." I replied back to him that I had already submitted the medically conforming documentation to my facility's administration officials who approved it and moved me to the 9/11/16 case several weeks ago. Upon review by Albany's Office of Personnel, however, this did not work out to be the case. It was a matter of three weeks before they changed it back and never notified me in writing. I further told the clerk that when they send in an additional request for the second psych medical exam to get me cleared from that case, I would need something in writing from his office.

Later the following day, I had another appointment to go meet with Dr. Ogulnick. We sat down in his office, sometimes we switched where I would be in the opposite seat as opposed to my prior session. He had asked me one time if I ever saw the movie *Serpico*, starring Al Pacino. I had in bits and pieces but he referred to it as almost an exact replication of what I was going through in many ways with the department, trying to expose the cover-up and corruption. Coincidentally, two days later, that movie was on and I watched it in its entirety. I don't think the ending, albeit making its point, was satisfactory; it should have been a more drawn-out process, after all, the ordeal he went through was quite the drawn-out process as well. I was also seeing Dr. Ogulnick for the inmate-related use of force which was deemed a homicide by the Orange County Medical Examiner's Office. As I mentioned earlier in this story, a lot had happened that night and in weeks and months following it. It was exactly one month after the incident in April of 2015 that those officers involved received notification in the mail from the union's law firm that we were not to speak to anyone other than the lawyers or union officials representing us. While so much was going on in the media, out in the streets with this event, we had a gag order and could not say or respond to anything at all, and for that matter, the Department of Corrections did not have much response at that time either. As it has been researched, documented, and statistically shown, Corrections officers are often forced to bottle up the event and not show signs of weakness. It was not until that time period in August when we got cleared where many of us could actually open up about it freely and speak to medical mental health professionals about the incident. As of right now, I have a copy of the approximately 37-page report lawsuit naming multiple individuals in a civil case from that incident. Last I knew after speaking with the Assistant Attorney General from the State Attorney General's Office, they were eyeing Medical and the Office of Mental Health in this for their failures to act accordingly when dealing with this inmate who had died as a result.

Many of those who were involved have either transferred out, went to other state jobs, or resigned, retired, or otherwise quit altogether. I am told by every single officer from Fishkill that I have worked with, who I see almost daily when I go to my appointments, that it is getting really rough inside the prison. There were several issues being caused by Facility Superintendent Shields, Deputy Oblinski, and Captain Dryer. Each and every officer had the psychological fear in their minds that this was not the same environment anymore, where many of their authoritative rights were being diminished by Albany's new program of puppeteering. No longer did the administration control its own facility. Since the Great Clinton Escape of June 2015, Albany is now heavily overseeing the facilities and making the decisions. It is only each facility's administration now acting in the direction given to them in what was referred to as puppets on strings acting however Albany wanted them to. These officers were looking at ways to get out into an early retirement however they could. Even the good guys who always did the right thing had a new administration looking down upon them. But I would not trust those officials any farther than I could throw them. Funny how they turn a blind eye to politics of a serious situation such as mine but not to the minor petty issues like one of the supervisors parked in a handicapped spot and being suspended for it.

Chapter Thirty-Two
The Long-Awaited Workers'
Comp Board Hearing

My law firm and I had begun preparing for the upcoming hearing to ensure that we had all of our documents covered. I had a growing file of paperwork, as if it had been fertilized and watered. It just added up. Just like my appointments, 33 to be exact for this month alone, it was non-stop. Today's mail came with some good news; my low back injury that occurred in the inmate-related combat use of force on 9/11/16 was approved by the State's Insurance Fund so that I could go down to Manhattan and have lumbar fusion with a couple months of follow-up physical therapy. It was a step closer and some days I felt like I was eventually getting closer to more answers. It had been over a year since the incident with Thompson since I had worked. Sadly though, I still had weddings booked for this coming fall that I had not yet canceled. I was not sure of the timeline of these cases, if I was going back to work, or what. But I knew I had to act in good faith and start writing refunds and cancellation letters to my would-be clients in order for them to have enough time to locate and reserve the services of someone else reputable in this area that would be able to hopefully do the job I could have done, if not better.

My sixth workers' compensation board hearing for the 5/9/17 case was all set for Monday, May 21st. This past week has been hell in our community. On May 15, 2018, at about 4:30 p.m., a tornado and severe storms touched down in the Newburgh area, physical injuries to numerous civilians, toppling trees onto houses, cars, knocking over telephone poles, power lines trapping people in their homes, on their streets, and a few times in their cars, making roads impassable, widespread power outages, and pure chaos throughout the area after the storm passed. Not a cop to be found, they were so busy, as well as other emergency services' crews from the fire department and EMS. States of emergency were declared and the National Guard Troops were deployed to our region along with hundreds of utility crews from around the state. It is day 3 without power as I write this, running off our house generator to try to keep our home somewhat habitable. Without it, we would not have water service either, let alone phone, cable, internet, etc. I have had people come over for gas that I had on hand, to use our garden hose, ask for assistance in locating their loved ones during the storm aftermath by using our 4-wheel drive truck. Lots of neighbors and their children came over to our home last night so we could provide running water for their containers, places to charge their phones, a grilled hot meal and some cold refreshing adult beverages. They filled their buckets with our water just so they could flush their toilets. Even while going through everything I am, especially with my physical limitations, I still feel the need to want to help out where we can. My family is still in the hole and needs lots of help to get back to where we once were before these incidents with work, but somehow we still find room to offer a helping hand to our neighbors in the community during their times of need. We even offered our 33-foot RV camper to the neighborhood to use as a place to shower, prep meals, or get fresh water. I stopped down to my firehouse and they had been to over 80 fire calls since the storm came in, just in our district alone. These guys and girls were tired. But after a quick check in and a bite to eat there, I headed out to my medical appointments only to race back home and get some more writing done while the generator was still going.

May 21st arrived, and what a beautiful day outside. I arrived early to my hearing to check in at the window and to review my documentation and to make some logbook entries. After a short briefing with one of my lawyers Jason, we discussed what the plan of action would be once we went in there. The cases were running behind schedule; my 10:00 a.m. appearance was not called until nearly 30 minutes later. After our names were announced on the loudspeakers to enter into Hearing Room #1, I sat down with the other parties and the judge had asked me on record, "How are you doing today, Mr. Harrington?"

I replied, "I am stressed out and in constant pain."

His reply back, "Well, hopefully we can take care of that for you and get you better soon."

As the State Insurance Fund's representative and my lawyer identified themselves for the record into the microphones, the judge began asking questions and went into details. Documents were reviewed from the state's independent medical examination, as well as from my treating physicians. Arguments went back and forth as the judge made some determination that the state's IME documents were not fully consistent and had some contradictory details. One issue that came up was my hearing loss from my left ear. The judge wanted to hold off and have my ENT and the state's ENT both examined and interviewed for the record. This would be done eventually to show that there was evidence of left ear hearing loss consistent to the assault from the 5/9/17 incident. The hearing wrapped up quicker than usual after the determination was made that the State Workers' Compensation Board was accepting the TMJ, bi-lateral hearing tinnitus, and my cervical spine injuries as all part of the 5/9/17 case. We were only one step away from fully getting all of the injured body parts covered so that I may proceed with the treatments and procedures that were so badly needed after waiting over a year. This was not over for Thompson; once we established all of these injuries, our next step was for the upcoming hearings and trial this summer. It was almost a matter of time. All of the evidence was stacking up in my favor. This is what happens when you stick to your decision to do the right thing. There is a hefty price to pay for it, but as they say, you have to spend money to make money. Now I am on my way out to two more medical appointments today and will be scheduling my third back surgery from work-related injuries in the prison. It was already approved. This is something I really needed, I have exhausted all of my other attempts at remedies. So now I wait for the next Workers' Compensation board hearing to bring up all dates that I am being treated under so that the state can establish the awards. My lawyers told me once I go out for my back surgery, I should be back on that inmate-related injury case again and covered with full pay and benefits, but that would have to be brought up before the Workers' Compensation Board Judge. At this time, the Department of Corrections has not cleared me to go back to work from the Thompson assault case yet, and you can't be out on two cases at once.

I am officially scheduled for a two-level lumbar fusion on July 17th, to be done by Dr. Paul and his staff at Columbia Presbyterian Hospital in Manhattan. This was going to be my biggest surgery yet. I had done lots of research on it and was confident that after all I have exhausted in my attempts in the two prior back surgeries, therapy, pain management, medications, and exercises, this was going to have to be the right thing to do. I met up with Dr. D's office who referred me to Dr. Paul and his staff. Today they gave me cortisone steroid injections into my knee as soon as I finished my physical therapy for my knees down in Spring Valley. When I got home, I saw a message from Lieutenant Richards from Fishkill. If you remember, he was one of the first to respond to my critical stress incident on October 24, 2017, which involved my 12-gauge shotgun on the back deck of my house and a major police response that evening. In his message, he stated that on June 7th coming up, he has to report to Albany for an awards ceremony where he will be presented the Medal of Merit for his actions in preventing further crisis and saving my life on that day. I spoke to him on the phone briefly and of course I already knew, being on the job for so long already, when someone gets this kind of attention from the top, they tend to get their chops busted a lot by the rank and file. There were also some comments made by others, which I expected, that were intended to mean that this should have not been prevented so that this fight I am going through with the state and some of its representatives would go away. An easy win for them, right? They think so, but many people I have spoken to and kept in touch with from Fishkill do not concur with those statements made by those individuals. I am glad for Richards though, and while his family will be at his side during the event, I will coincidentally be at my attorney's firm in White Plains filing new documentation for my case. He will deservedly receive this distinction that will reflect on his record for as long as it will reflect on mine.

May 29th has arrived and off I went to another state independent medical exam ordered by the State Insurance Fund, who was seeking an opinion from a medical doctor that they hired regarding my lower back and bi-lateral knee injuries from another case. Coincidentally, and very unusual, they sent me to see Dr. Schoolman again up in Poughkeepsie. The exam took place in a chiropractor's office in a room that Dr. Schoolman rented out to do these exams. It's what we call "doc in a box." There had been a roomful of patients in the waiting area when I arrived to sign in and turn over the documents I had already filled out and given to the receptionist to make copies of for my file. I was waiting for about 30 minutes to be seen. Prior to that I had noticed an older gentleman with a walker wearing a badge around his neck. I looked up and it was a lieutenant who retired from Fishkill over 15 years ago, maybe more. He had lost his left leg and was wearing an orthopedic device. It took him a minute to remember me but we shared some memories before he was on his way as he was being assisted by his family. It had been good to see him, but what a wake up to reality to see how things in life can end up for us. We take so many things for granted and are given only one life to live. That's why it's very important to take care of yourself and each other because nothing is guaranteed. Finally, I was called into the exam room and sat down next to Dr. Schoolman. I had last seen him on February 27th for another exam regarding my orthopedic shoulder and neck injuries. We went over a stack of documents, he reviewed three MRIs, numerous doctors' notes, many, many questions about my current treatments, pain management, physical therapy, medications and the doctors I had visited. For each question Dr. Schoolman asked, he gave you about three seconds, and it had to be just that, any longer than that and then he would be onto the next question talking over the top of you as if he did not care about the necessary facts that were being relayed to him while he wrote down his notes on a scrap piece of paper. It was not very professional and his bedside manners had been checked outside at the parking lot. I know dozens of other officers who have gone through these exams and all say the same thing. Anyhow, after about 15-20 minutes, he had me stand up and remove my orthopedic knee braces to have me walk and then do some range of motion and pain range testing. The only tool he used in his exam was a measuring tape to measure the circumference of each leg above my knees. I had explained to him that I had numerous treatments and sessions with medical specialists regarding me knees and back, two knee surgeries and two back surgeries already. The next thing they can do for me is total knee replacement, but I am too young and will have to wait, but as I said earlier, I will be going for the lumbar fusion surgery in only a matter of weeks. Dr. Schoolman had me laying down on a chiropractor table that was higher at the feet. When he was done, he told me to sit up and he turned away as if he was doing something else so he could avoid helping me get up from the position I was in. I had a difficult time getting up without actually sliding off. Again with his bedside manners. Dr. Schoolman has no care in the world for any patients coming in there. As long as he gets the favorable results back to the State Insurance Fund and gets his paychecks, he is happy. It's Corruption in a broken system and it needs to change now. I put the capital "C" in it for a reason. He finished up with me and told me I was all done, not looking at me, not saying good bye, no hand shake, not a word. I was out the door past the receptionist to hobble down the flights of stairs using the wall to guide me due to my balance issues until I got back outside and into a waiting vehicle.

Chapter Thirty-Three
Fishkill Prison Is off the Hook

I had a chance to catch up with a couple officers I had not seen in a while and grabbed some lunch. We ended up going out to a new place in town called 125Fifty Food & Drink, it's owned by a friend of mine, located in the town of Newburgh, not too far away from any of us so it was a quick ride to meet up. We had placed our orders quickly and even though we tried to steer away from what we on the job called "shop talk," somehow we still ended up on the topic of the prison issues. "They're telling us at pre-shift briefings they do not want to see anymore search forms from each shift say "NCF," or "No Contraband Found." They don't care how small the item may be, they want it listed now. Either extra state property or even the minor cigarette butts."

I said to them, "What if you don't find anything at all?" in which they replied, "Does not matter anymore, they want to see the job being done on paper." Even if that meant lying about what you did or did not find. "Now the bosses are coming after our air conditioners." After hearing that, I could not believe it; as hot as it can get in those areas, one of the only refuges they have are the cooler areas. After all, I worked the tunnel areas underground for 14 years, and it got stinking hot down there, even with a fan. The boss would even complain on their rounds signing logbooks, and believe me, they did not hang out long making conversation. It's only a matter of time now more officers will succumb to the heat exhaustion factors we face on this job. More and more officers we knew were getting injured inside while on duty, there were more drug and gang problems ever than before, and even with the attempts to divert packages being delivered to prisoners by their families, or by using other tools and methods to fight the crime inside those tall fences, Governor Cuomo shut it down and had the department change its policy back in order to accommodate the inmates. Additionally, in recent headlines, Cuomo has restored voting rights to convicted felons who were in prison and now were out on Parole. Here you have murderers, rapists, robbers, drug dealers, cop killers, burglars, you name it, now getting out of prison not only with benefits of public assistance, but now they have the rights to vote. This is taking away everything that hard-working, decent, law-abiding citizens had a right to do. Apparently now though, with inmates getting brand new tablets to download music, books, send emails, etc., as well as free college, New York has become the place in which they reward the criminals and punish those who do the right thing in life, those raising families, paying their taxes, obeying laws. This is a slap in the face to every New Yorker out there. It's time for a change we said, and it starts from the top.

Inside the prison each day, there is some type of incident occurring. Every single move inside there is scrutinized now. An officer can't do his job without the fear of some consequence. It is each person for themselves now. So many of those good officers are being mistreated and disciplined for the tiniest infraction. Yet, those same infractions, when committed by a supervisor who is high up in the chain of command, that's a different situation. Case in point. Everyone coming inside the front gate now carries a clear bag that can be seen through. This is for their lunch items, dinner, etc., as it is not possible to leave to go out for a meal, we do not get a "lunch hour" during your tour. You must eat on the go, and when you can find a quick quiet minute or two to do so. But when a boss comes through, often times they pass right through without inspection, or even if so, a brief vague one at that. So if the top is watching over the lower ranks, who is there at Fishkill watching over them?

The newly-minted officers coming fresh from the academy in Albany arrive eager, yet nervous as we once were as well, to start their new jobs inside the prison. They have not seen how it used to be inside the fences, when staff morale would be at an all-time high and despite the dangers in place, we did not have the same amount or the same type of incidents occurring as they do today. Most of the men and women in there that have any time on the job are looking for ways to get out of there, transferring to other state agencies, retiring, resigning, among various other methods. You are entitled to a full retirement at 25 years, there are officers that stayed working there well past that, for as much as up to 35-40 years in some cases that I have saw. You will not see that anymore. If so, extremely rarely. As it is now, between the department's new policies, the lack of the state, or even the County District

274

Attorney's willingness to hold the prisoners accountable for their crimes inside the prison, it shows the convicts that where there's a will, there's a way. And they have 24 hours a day to figure out a way. It puts the ball in their hands, it creates the potentially explosive environment in some of the buildings where many of the gangs and drug dealers are housed. Cutting back on solitary confinement and restrictions only gives the prisoners more power. The state is scared to death of these guys, either all tying them up in courts suing them, or by taking over a facility in a riot situation. So what do they do? They feed them more crumbs. You give them an inch, they'll take a foot. In the meantime, the rank and file have to go into these trenches with a baton and some pepper spray to defend themselves and others with. And so help you god if you have to use that stuff. The microscope will be in the hands of the Monday morning quarterbacks to decide if the right split-second decisions were made or not. While I cannot get into other specific situations, it has not always been a typical outcome following an incident. And unless more cameras are installed which will be there to protect us all, everyone can then avoid any extra hostile or violent conditions.

Tomorrow is the day up in Albany when the Department of Corrections and Community Supervision holds its annual awards reception, done so in front of large crowds of dignitaries, politicians, family members, officials from the department and representatives from each facility. Often times as well the media will be there to cover the event. Following the awards, a reception is held for all to attend. As I mentioned before, Lieutenant Richards and his family will be making their trek up to Albany in the morning, wearing his freshly-pressed Class-A uniform and service hat where he will join other recipients getting various awards for their achievements throughout the year while sitting in front of hundreds of people outside the front entrance to the State Corrections Academy. Escorting him to represent Fishkill was the current Superintendent (Warden) Mr. Shields. Richards got the Medal of Merit for his actions in preventing a tragedy during a crisis that occurred at my residence on October 24th. The union was also there representing and he received multiple certificates, among just the medal itself.

Here it is, Monday June 11th, and with a quick phone call to the Payroll Office at Fishkill, I was informed that I am officially now out on 1/2 pay of my regular base salary. As if it was not bad enough to lose the photography business income, now my family has to survive on 1/2 of my salary. I have checked around to seek additional benefits but as it stands, we do not qualify for public assistance and certainly I do not have any more benefits from my AFLAC Policy. We had to break into the savings for now to keep things afloat and get us through these summer months upon us. We are getting daily calls from family checking in on us, from both sides. We certainly have a lot of people thinking of us during this long difficult period of time. Friends have also come out of the woodwork as well. Since I have not been working for so long, I was qualified to submit an application for social security benefits. I spent five hours going over tons of documents with both Nancy and Phontayne who had to fill out the application and input the numerous doctors, surgeries, hospitals, medications, and other pertinent information regarding the details of my injuries preventing me from working. Nancy had teased me about having so much paperwork, she called me a walking filing cabinet, but I mentioned to her that a few other doctors had referred to me as the Library of Congress. She got a chuckle out of that and liked that reference better. I had been told by one of my lawyers Nick that I was their firm's best client when it came to keeping documentation, having forms on file, organized and sent to them on a same day basis. If I did not do this, then who would? You have to advocate for yourself or you will soon find out you could be on the losing end of the stick. Certainly the other parties of my case, especially the employer, could not be solely relied upon in producing records, some of them from 15 years ago. I had to go out of the office twice to fill the meter up at the parking garage in White Plains, where their main office is at. I thought at first this would be a quick two-hour session, but it turned into three, then four, then five hours, finally, and we had to wrap it up for the day. I signed and initialed at least a dozen pages of papers for the law firm. I was then out the door on my way to physical therapy and the chiropractor. Since then, we have kept in touch as I have had to inquire about certain instances and documents. It was not long before I had already received a letter from the Social Security Administration's Office in Poughkeepsie notifying me they were in receipt of the application and had asked for additional documents for their review. I had noticed that the envelope they sent me contained additional pages. As I went onto the next few pages, I soon became confused because none of the paperwork pertained to me. Those documents have another man's name on it with his social security number, contact information, and other data which I should not have had sent to me. I separated the files and mailed them back to Poughkeepsie's office where they originated. Here we see on the news everyday how there is personal information that gets leaked from consumer transactions and other types of files, and no one knows nothing about how it leaked. Yet I get all of this information sent to me that had it fallen into the wrong person's hands, it might have been used for other misdeeds, thus creating the problem of this victim dealing with stolen identity issues which could take years to resolve. Albeit a blunder or some type of mistake on the Social Security Office's behalf bearing the fact that they handle hundreds of pages of sensitive information on a daily basis, it still leads one to wonder what kind of prevention they have in place to keep this from happening. After all, we are all human, and to err is to be human.

On June 12th, a pre-arranged telephone conference call had been scheduled by the State's Public Employee Relations Board Judge Rikers. I got home as soon as I could from two medical appointments and the moment I sat down, the phone rang and I had made it just in time. Representatives from the union's law firm, the Governor's Office of Employee Relations, and Judge Rikers, along with myself, acting as pro se in my case, all spoke in conference for 28 minutes in which we discussed the PERB Rules Section 211 about subpoenas, how the process works, and their approvals thereof. Then we went over what the order of the trial would be for Evidence Exhibits, Original and Amendment answers to the charges against the union and agency, and about the burden of proof being on me to produce the evidence and how they should be brought into evidence for the other parties in order for it to be included. Judge Rikers stated that I would be giving a narrative testimony without the addition of questions seeing how I am acting in my own legal capacity and how I will be subject to objections by the other parties. This is supposed to be a two-day trial, with each day inside the hearing running for several hours, starting at 10:00 a.m. and running until about 5:00 p.m. A few questions ensued during this telephone conversation and I brought up the fact that I am scheduled for major back surgery in Manhattan and will be hospitalized for numerous days. I informed the parties I had hoped and planned to be ambulatory by the time the dates arrive for court. I mentioned I may be bringing along others who will assist me where needed. After a few comments, we ended the discussion and at that moment, I spent hours and hours preparing my exhibits, in addition, making four copies of each page for the other parties. I had to gather my phone records, emails, US Mail certified receipts, logbook pages, as well as other legal and medical documentation that would be entered into evidence.

It was not long later that evening I got some of my usual phone calls from friends. Some text messages came through as well. One of them in particular was from Father K. He mentioned to me his interest from day one of this incident case and has been ever so supportive of it. Another friend Ed, who lives upstate not far from Albany, is an assistant fire chief I met at the State's Fire Academy several years ago. He also has been on top of this case with me. They both stated that they would be available to be there to help me carry the evidence, provide transportation, and anything else that was needed. That certainly was some great news to hear and these days it was surely needed.

I am awaiting word back from a few others who may be coming only as support. Somehow, I wonder how I will be able to take on the state's union, their law firm, and the State's Governor's Office and their attorneys all by myself without legal representation. While I do have great writing and organization skills, I also have some paralegal background. I have done plenty of research on this matter and have prepared myself well in advance. I am certain that the truth will finally come out, not for nothing, but I had proven my cases and the state's back was in the corner. If one thing is for certain, it's my daily logbook of activities, dates and times, names and subject matter that I have kept on file, with well over 300 pages so far, all starting with the assault incident that occurred on May 9, 2017. Those of course will be turned over as evidence as legal documents, along with all of my case files. We shall see when the time comes, until then its onward and forward with my 30+ average medical appointments each month.

I had a return call from Maria, an assistant attorney general with the NY State's Attorney General's Office. With the state's top lawman Attorney General Eric Schneiderman now being forced to resign over his scandals, that office is in the public eye. The corruption, scandals, cover-ups all seem to be seeping out of every crack of those concrete buildings up in Albany. With time and pressure, anything would soon break free. Maria had spoken to me about the homicide case at Fishkill that occurred on April 21, 2015. We had not spoken in several months but she said that even though we were criminally cleared by the Feds in August of 2017, the plaintiff's law firm was able to identify more officers who were directly involved. Prior to this, I was being named as a "John Doe," but now that my documentation was produced, she indicated to me that I am on the list and would soon be served to testify for the Civil Trial down in Manhattan at the Federal Court. We spoke over numerous details that have occurred since we had last touched base with each other. She asked me questions and seemed very concerned that after all I had been through with this incident, amongst the other issues to include the Thompson assault, the October 24th crisis incident at my house, and my current legal battles with the department as well as the union. It seemed as if my medical evidence and testimony would hurt the state's case more than help it, and she told me that we would all have to be on the same page under one lawyer representing us. Marie told me she had to make a lot of phone calls to get more details on my case and would get back to me. I am awaiting on her reply back, and to see when I will be served those documents to appear at trial. I already called her back a few days later and left her a message. She soon returned my call and stated I would be hearing from a man named Bruce who would go over all the details with me and hear me out on all of my pending matters with the department and the Officers' Union.

Chapter Thirty-Four
The Saga Continues

My other case following the Department of Labor's investigation's findings and the appeal that followed it with the State's Industrial Board of appeals has gone back and forth. Upon my original petition to appeal after the Department of Labor closed its case on Fishkill Correctional Facility's Workplace Violence Investigation, the DOL's Senior Attorney had requested motion to dismiss the petition but the IBA's Counsel had denied it, asking me to resubmit an amended petition. I had done so right away, the same day I rec'd the notice in the mail. I also had to do an affidavit of service and provide copies to the DOL's lawyers as well. As I lay in wait for that to happen, I was contacted by the COPBA Union's law firm who was looking for me to send them my documentation and evidence exhibits prior to trial. According the Judge Reich of the State's Public Relations Board, this could be done voluntarily amongst the parties, including the Governor's Office. I had strong feeling against doing this. Although they stated they had mostly witnesses, they did not have much for documentation to produce on their defense. I thought to myself, why would I proceed to helping them to benefit their defense and to prepare and "coach" the witnesses on how to respond to the evidence once they are on the stand? After all, it had been many months, many occasions where I needed help from the union and never got the response and assistance. What comes around goes around, so may it be as it is.

I saw a posting on the Mid-Hudson C.O.'s Facebook group page where another officer had committed suicide, all within a short period of time from one prior to that. In his post, he explained how important it was for him as a union steward at that facility at Green Haven, in Stormville, NY. He had stated in that online post, "Down back, we have to be vigilant 24/7. Our lives, our families' lives and the lives of our coworkers depend on it. So naturally, when someone in our line of work is having issues with depression, anxiety, substance abuse, family trouble, financial problems etc., you can imagine why they might feel the need to keep that to themselves. They don't want the people that rely on them knowing that there are some proverbial 'cracks in the foundation,' so they keep it to themselves, carry the burden on their own. More often than not after tragedies such as the several we have experienced at Green Haven over the last year, you'll see an outpouring of sympathy and support. Officers pronouncing their willingness to lend an ear and help anyone who may be experiencing hardships behind the scenes. However, we need to take into consideration the fact that many experiencing these issues simply don't feel comfortable sharing their problems with people they work with every single day.

"Because of this, I'd like to take a second to highlight the importance of programs that provide our troubled brothers and sisters the anonymity and confidentiality many need to help them feel more comfortable about reaching out for help. Specifically, COPBA's "Members Assistance Program", which has been created with the idea of empowering members to ask for help, all the while assuring them that they can receive quality assistance without having to tell a coworker. I will be posting several flyers detailing the program including contact info for anyone interested. So if you or someone you suspect might be going through hard times, I sincerely think looking into the Members Assistance Program is worth your while."

I have been there and done that and while his words are bringing light to the never-ending list of officers who have taken their own lives, I explained to him that the Members Assistance Program called "Catch a Falling Star" was put into place to provide Band-aids. I for one can bear witness to the fact that after several times that I contacted Cindy, the program's coordinator's office, just after the incident back in May of 2017, she listened but told me, "I really can't do anything to help you out, I am only a volunteer here, I do not work for the department." This statement truly would add to anyone's demise as they look to reach out to someone that is supposed to be there. I wrote back to him on his Facebook email about my situation with my own crisis and how I had reached out for help numerous times prior to the incident in October 2017. I also mentioned to him, why is it that police and other law enforcement agencies, even fire departments, have psychologists that are there on duty specifically for their needs following a critical stress incident? They are always mandated to get cleared from the psychologist prior to returning to duty. Those agencies are responsible for their personnel when they go back to duty. However, in the Department of Corrections and Community Supervision within New York's jurisdiction, no such program exists. In my 23 years of service, I have been involved in numerous incidents. The department never sent you off to get cleared. The stigma was amongst your co-workers and peers that you had to "Suck it up, Sally" and deal with it. Wake up the next morning like nothing ever happened and go back to work ready to deal with the next incident. We were essentially expected to bottle it up. If you showed any signs of weakness, you would then become the runt of the litter with little chance of survival when it came to working as an officer. Word would get around and soon you would be ousted, not trusted to back up others' reports of what happened, or be able to react and make a split-second decision that could come back to haunt you. The department really needs to get off their ass and stop worrying about the inmates so much, even though we are only considered a number to the state, it is with that which comes the responsibility to put well-qualified individuals in place within these dangerous facilities. It is a much different beat than that of a police officer. In the general public, not everyone is a dangerous criminal or felon. In our prison system, each and every inmate is, at varying degrees. You're always surrounded by them and far outnumbered, and at any given moment by letting your guard down, the violence can and will erupt, and it's up to you and others responding to the incident to handle the situation. The idea is to leave there the same way you came in.

Last week I had already been notified by Social Security Disability that I had been scheduled for two exams, only with three days' notice. Nick over at my law firm mentioned this was unusual that it would come so quickly and with such short notice. I had reported that day to fill out a dozen pages and since I had arrived early, I was seen by the psychologist first where we had the exam interview for nearly an hour. It was more of a formality, they already had reviewed my records and at the conclusion, the psychologist from Social Security's Disability IMA Office in Middletown had concurred that I did indeed have depression, anxiety, stress, and PTSD all related from the incidents at Fishkill. Going back out to the waiting room to compose myself, I was soon called in for the medical exam which I went through an extensive number of tests and review of my medical injuries. The staff there were so friendly and compassionate. I think I was there for about three hours in all. Once they forward the results to my Doctor's Office, I will be able to get them off to my law firm down in White Plains. I did not expect that kind of treatment at all inside the exams, figuring in a place like that we were just another number.

Now I am only two days away from getting my lower back fusion surgery with Dr. Paul at New York's Presbyterian Hospital in lower Manhattan. He is considered and documented to be New York's best spinal surgeon. This will be my third back surgery due to all of the violence at Fishkill Correctional Facility. I am told by staff that I will be admitted and should expect to be there for about four days. I feel anxious about it but at the same time, I have done so much research about this and this is a much-needed procedure since the first two operations did not last well for me. It will only be a matter of 10 days after discharge that I will have to make my way to Albany for my trial hearing against the Union and Governor's Office of Employee Relations on July 30-31. I will be representing myself pro se in the case and I have prepared for it as best as I could have. It's only a matter of time at this point.

In the meantime, my lawyer Jason wanted me to locate all of my prior audiograms that I had done before the assault incident on May 9, 2017. We needed to produce those as evidence along with the deposition from ENT Dr. Feldman at the next Workers' Comp board hearing to show medical evidence of my left ear hearing loss. I had to make a dozen calls, some to my fire district officials, some to the employer's personnel office, and others through my own family doctor. I was able to locate three prior audiograms all done recently that showed my hearing levels were normal and that I had no prior issues. I got those forms, as many as 30 of them, scanned and emailed down to Jason at the law firm so we would be ready to go for the next hearing.

Surgery day had arrived. I was brought to the Beacon Train Station by my wife who was on her way to work. A one-way peak trip to Grand Central Terminal plus a subway ticket with a five-minute walk to NY Presbyterian Hospital cost me only $25. I arrived down there early to ensure I would not be late due to transit issues, etc. I checked in and filled out my documents. Since I was early, I had hoped they would take me in earlier. Turns out, it was the other way around. Dr. Paul and his team had a difficult case in front my appointment. Turns out it would run them longer by several hours. At this point, I had not eaten since the previous evening, nor drank anything, and it was a hot day. I wanted to say forget it and go home, but part of me stayed there. I had been approached by the hospital administrator who urged me to stay and they even got Dr. Paul to come out to talk to me for a moment. It really wasn't the inconvenience for me at that point, it was the uncertainty, the pain, the fact that this was about to be the most serious surgery I would ever be having. After years of assaults and reinjuring my lower back from inmate-related incidents at Fishkill, two other back surgeries and multiple courses of treatments to make my injury better rather than have to get the fusion I would be on this day, now was the time to put myself in the hands of one of the best spinal surgeons. The plan was to get me prepped and into O.R. Upon arrival, I would then be hooked up to all the equipment. Dr. Paul, Agatha, and his staff were ever so careful with me and very polite to talk to me like I was a real person, not just another number in line as you see and hear about in many cases these days. I was undergoing surgery for both anterior and posterior lumbar fusion of the L4-L5 and L5-S1 with SSEP. The surgeries had to be split apart by one day due to the length involved, total duration being about 11 hours. All said, I lost close to 500cc of blood during these procedures. They were able to implant the two remaining disks that were at extreme loss with medical implants. I had to be cut open about seven inches on my left side abdomen area and another six inches straight down my low back for them to get access during these procedures. During this time, they located a blood clot in my lung. I had to be implanted with a filtering device for this and put on blood thinners after my recovery started. Dr. Paul's expert opinion was that this blood clot was more likely caused from a prior surgery I had for another work-related injury. I am very fortunate that they found this when they did. As my wife says, after all she's seen me go through, it appears I have more lives than a cat.

With surgery over, my original expected stay was up to four days. That turned into nine days at the hospital. I was in such pain and could barely move. They would not feed me solid food for seven days. I could have Jell-O, and chicken broth, and some Italian ices, but besides that I was looking at water and ice chips. Once the order came in for solid food, I was very disappointed by the selection and quality for the patients' meals. With a name like NY Presbyterian, you would think they would have a top-notch food service program there like other smaller hospitals I have been a patient at. They had set alarms on my bed, for that matter they might as well of put mouse traps around the edges too. Every simple move I made to get comfortable in that bed that was not meant for someone my height and size, the slightest bounce around and turn over would cause a loud alarm bringing and a minimum of three nurses to check on me to ensure I was still in bed. I had requested to go to the men's room on the second/third night there and with two female nurses, one male and another one who come with a wheel chair, they wanted me to stand with their assistance and walk over as they guided me to the bathroom. The moment I stood up, I felt the nurses let their grip loosen up and down I went to the floor crashing like a box of rocks. On my way down, I remember hitting face first into the heavier set nurse, planting my face into her large chest and then hitting the floor in extreme pain. They said I was too heavy to pick up so they called for additional staff. As they argued amongst each other, I found a breath of wind during my pain to yell at them for someone to just get me off the floor. Once they got me on the bed, they tied my legs to the ends so I could not get off myself. It had already been a week since I had even brushed my teeth. I wanted to feel clean again, and to freshen up. After a few requests, one of the nurses took care of me. Not every nurse cared as much there at NYP. Most of them did their jobs, some of them hid from doing it. My much-awaited family visit took place on Sunday night when my wife and my daughter came to visit for a while. They told me all I was missing out on back at home. I could not wait to be out of there, just to be in my own bed again. A few days later, I found out I would be eligible to get discharged. My ride Fr. Kevin, who lived down the road from us, was very familiar with Manhattan as that was where his last parish was that he served at. He took time from his busy schedule to get me out of there and home by 3 p.m. that day. I had to carefully guard all of my wounds from surgery as excited as my dogs were to be jumping all over me. It was good to be home again. It was not long before I had been sent a survey from the hospital wanting input about my lengthy stay. There were numerous issues brought up and I formally had typed up a two-page notarized letter, sent certified to the hospital, as well as five other patient health organizations. The pain in my legs should have already vanished but it appears my hard fall to the cold tile floor was possibly a contributor. But it was not long before I would be catching up on my mail, email replies, phone call messages, etc. After all, I still had a trial in Albany to be preparing for. That Friday as the weekend approached, I spoke to both the Union Law Firm and the PERB judge, who were well aware of my situation. I just needed to be sure that I was ready to go physically for this as they thought the same. I tried to rest it up, doing all I could to relieve the pain this weekend but to no avail. Monday morning came and I called Judge Reich, told him of my situation, and he granted an adjournment on my part due to physical health and he would immediately advise the other parties, and with a week or so, he would call me back to discuss other days that may work out for all parties involved. Just about that time, my inquiries into my medication that I requested to help in my post-surgical recovery were like as act of congress. Numerous phone calls to the doctor's office, the pharmacy, the hospital as well as a call from my lawyer's office helped to get things straightened out. All I needed what was right for the pain I continued to endure. As it was, I will still be using a walker to help me get around. The way my lawyers explained it is that the state keeps a pretty tight database on each patient's record of pharmaceuticals prescribed. You wouldn't believe the stories they told me of what people do with their medications. All I know is that my list is once again growing again, but that's for a guy who has so many issues abound at this time. While it is known for sure that the State will get what it wants, "The Fund's mission is to guarantee the availability of workers' compensation insurance at the lowest possible cost to employers while maintaining a solvent fund, as well as provide timely and appropriate indemnity and medical payments to injured workers." I am not sure what they consider timely but to you and me as well as other consumers, timely usually commits to a time frame, which is a typical period; for those guys, we are talking about several months.

You know, the Workers' Compensation Board has patient advocates that assist you with your case even if you do have an attorney, they help you out with any matters that you may have pertaining to your case and can direct you. But then there are others, like the State's Insurance Fund, that have a mission. "Achieve the best health outcomes for injured workers by paying indemnity and medical benefits in a timely manner, and facilitate appropriate medical care. Ensure that all New York businesses have a market for workers' compensation and disability benefits insurance available to them at a fair price." This may be a goal of theirs but it certainly fell short for hundreds of cases over the last decade or better. The best possible outcomes? You mean being put through the wringer, being denied benefits and those long-awaited approvals for major diagnostic testing that shows time after time that the patients and their medical staff were right all along? All of that just to deny, delay to save a dime? If there's corruption in New York, and we all know there is, then it's in both politics and insurance.

With the weekend upon us, I had tried reaching out to Dr. Paul's office. His staff there kept informing me it was the landlord's fault that their phone system was faulty. Since they were leasing the property, there was only so much they could do. I had asked them to ensure he gets my message and calls me back prior to the weekend. You could be hold for a long time only to get disconnected, repeatedly, no matter what phone I called from. I had other numbers I could call as well, the nurses' desk at New York Presbyterian. I left messages with them as well but was not confident with that information getting to my surgeon at once. With it being Friday afternoon and all, with Dr. Paul being down in New York City and all, this made it rather difficult to just get to his office. He, like many other doctors, have an "on call" doctor or an answering service. I could not bear the pain anymore. I had spoken to several people I know in the medical field that said my symptoms were not adding up and that I needed to go get checked out. It was now Monday afternoon. Once I got to St. Luke's Hospital in Newburgh, I was placed in Bay 15 and was taken care of rather quickly. They did an EKG, took some vials of blood, started an IV on me, and brought me in a turkey sandwich. They gave me plenty of meds both orally and through my IV. I tell you, my arms had so many holes in them from my surgery, they could barely find a spot to get an IV into me at St. Luke's. After some testing, a different doctor from shift change approached and told me all was as good as can be. He wanted to me follow up with my surgeon as soon as I could, got my electrolytes up where they needed to be and prior to getting my IV removed, they gave me one more dose of morphine, along with a script for additional pain medication. This had my med bottle count up to 12 now. I was like a roving pharmacy. I was looking forward to my next appointment when my other doctors start asking me about why I was taking this medication, that one, and so on. This has happened before and it was only a matter of time again. I am now waiting to see my surgeon on August 20th, which should be right around the time I get my prescription to start my physical therapy. I have been to numerous sessions in the past. To me I did not like the schedule, the pain, or the growing task to achieve my goal. But in the end, it would work out well, trying to get my abdomen and low back built back up where the surgeon performed back surgery on me. The front incision is about five inches long and on the center of my lower back it was about the same size. The only thing good about the lower back incision was that it covered up the scars from the previous two low back surgeries. Once I got word from Dr. Paul that I could stop taking the blood thinners, I could finally go and get those long awaited epidural injections under Fluoroscopy for my neck. It has been well over a year since the cervical injuries sustained from the Thompson incident.

Chapter Thirty-Five
Hurry Up and Wait

Nowadays, it was a game of sit and wait. Wait for the workers' comp board notice of my next hearing, wait for word from the NYS Public Employee Relations Board on the available dates to conduct the trial against the State's Correction Officer Union, and for decisions on my retirement 3/4 disability and social security applications. It seemed like I was so close to the end. This year has been pure hell for me, my family, and most of all, my wife. In today's mail came a certified return receipt letter from the employer, New York State Department of Corrections and Community Supervision. It was a two-pager, filled top to bottom. According to my mail lady, she said this was their second request sending this to me to get signed, but her and I both agreed there was no way that could be true. I had been there each day that week when the mail came, and in fact, it was mostly a junk mail kind of week. In the letter, the first sentence started out as: "Pursuant to Section 71 of the Civil Service Law and Rule 5.9 of the rules for the classified service, this is to notify you that your workers' compensation leave will end, and your employment will terminate effective September 7, 2018, beginning of business, due to your absence having exceeded one cumulative year. This separation revokes your Peace Officer Status granted under Section 2.10 of the Criminal Procedure Law." The letter goes on into details about my rights to appeal, the responsibilities to appeal in a timely manner, etc. There goes 23 years of my honorable state service. Nothing I did, or nothing anyone else does inside those prisons will be recognized or rewarded enough for putting themselves in harm's way. After reading it through, I went to my computer, scanned and emailed the contents to my law firm and reached out to Warren who was overseeing my case with the team of lawyers and paralegals we had assembled for my variety of items being addressed. Warren called me back while driving his car and told me he understood my problem and knowing that it is a month away from the date of termination, he would get on this at once to make some calls and get the process expedited due to the hardships my family was having. My response to him was, "Warren, there's no way you can rush this system, it has to take its course."

"I know, I know," replied Warren, "but I will be there to make sure we will protect your rights." After all, with no job, it also meant no salary, no benefits, no health or dental insurance. What was I supposed to do for my family? I hated like hell to knock on doors and ask for handouts. Since my own union couldn't care less due to the nepotism issues that I am taking them to court for, I reached out to Sean who was President of the Police Emerald Society. He had been checking up on me from time to time to see if there was anything we needed. I have been a member there for about a year now and several other officers I have known personally for a long time are also members as well. They were well in the know about what was going on. The night I spoke to Sean, he had kept telling me anything I needed I was to let him know. I hate asking for things, I have never been one to take hand-outs, but I was in a real bind. With school coming up and my twins about to enter 4th grade, each of them had lengthy supply lists given to them by their teachers and I knew we were going to need help with that. This was priority. Once I even mentioned it, Sean said it was taken care of. I tell you, for the first time in my life, accepting something like this was very humbling, bringing brotherhood and family together. Once word got out amongst the ranks, Brian from Duchess 10-13 sent me an email asking if all was ok and wanted updates. He mentioned that this week he would be approaching the board to get a check from the organization to assist a fellow member whose family hardship was looked out for in our time of need, and I tell you it came at a great time. I'd already used up my savings stocks, took half of my retirement on loan. Our parish helped us out with travel expenses for my medical appointments, among other aid. My sister Kate and her family from Colorado was sending up some help with getting the kids set with some new school clothing. My wife's mother and father also sent us some very helpful monetary assistance. They helped my family out immensely, way beyond what we expected. Again, this was a humbling experience from all that contributed. I am sure I could be one of those guys who could have put a post on the GoFundMe page with the large network I have, but I was only looking for immediate need of essentials. My family only wanted what was needed us to carry us. My Wife had been elated but somewhat embarrassed with the responses we got and we wanted to recognize these organizations helping out that week. Even Fr. K., over at the parish down the road from us, pulled me aside from the exodus of parishioners departing from mass and once things cleared, he spoke to me about what the church could do in terms of sending us any type of assistance we may need as well. He gave me further advice on staying away from credit card spending and informed me that if I needed food, gas cards, whatever the case, it would all be just a phone call away. The organizations I spoke to said there's nothing to be ashamed about in my situation. You would not imagine what people go through these days. One would think that after going through all of this, being medically released from 23 years of state service, that all of the various incidents that I had responded to and became injured due to the combative situations, that my facility would be making phone calls to say the least. Ironically, I am banged up from head to toe. Everything on my left shoulder, jaw, ear, bicep tendon, rotator cuff, as well as the labrum tears, multiple herniated discs in my neck, not to mention the psychological issues from the further trauma of dealing with the state agencies. This was no coincidence. The State Department of Corrections, Fishkill Correctional Facility, the State Insurance Fund, not to mention the numerous others, all had their hands in the filing cabinets to delay, deny, and continuously refuse that I had been assaulted by Officer Thompson. In our system we are only allotted a certain period of time to be out on comp. Personnel of the Albany office for Corrections joined in the defense to protect the department and the staff at Fishkill. Knowing I had only so much time left of full pay, they put me on half pay once that ran out. They locked me into the case date of 5/9/17 (The Thompson assault case) and would not clear me to transfer over to one of my other cases for use of available time. It would be the end for me. Did I lose the battle I was fighting so hard for and this was my punishment? If I had played the hand they dealt me and I did not fight this, would I be back to work on light duty? I think only two people know the answer to that question. Them and myself. I have plenty of compensation time months, several of them, over a year in fact, to use for my time while I was in recovery for my recent major back surgery and yet to come, more for the knees and neck. But they refused to let me use it, so here I am sitting out since June on what appears to be 1/3rd pay and only three weeks from now, a permanent separation of no pay, no benefits, no health insurance for my family, no peace of mind, all the while I take nearly a year to recover (this is from my professionals and doctors) from my abdomen and low back incisions each one being several inches, and then the low back physical therapy and then onto my neck surgery.

I used to run out the front of the house, out the door at all days and times for 30 years straight to help my community in need, or give to the local food pantry, make donations to charitable organizations, and even did a fundraiser with my World Trade Center photos that in less than two weeks raised several thousands of dollars which after expenses were donated to the FDNY's Widow and Children Fund and presented to the FDNY Union President Steven Cassidy, back in 2001. This effort had even warranted me an entire page in the *Times Herald Record* newspaper. It'd gotten so out of control for one person to handle, I had to enlist over a dozen volunteers to assist with this as it continued on. Having done this and more, now I am at the point where I need the help asking for simple things like school supplies. They say what comes around goes around and perhaps this was our turn.

So with all of this currently going on, I am hearing from many current officers still working at Fishkill about how the administration has been treating the "troops." It has gotten to the point that they are making your shift as difficult as they can for you. Many areas have lost their much-needed air conditioning units, there are even some areas where officers had a back room to throw their food in the fridge, warm it up in the microwave, lay down their bag and hang up their coats to keep secure while working their posts. Many of these areas in the summer months have air quality issues, it becomes hotter than hell in the tunnel areas, and most of the time if you're lucky you will have a wall-mounted fan which turns it into a giant hairdryer. That only compounds the problems. It's only a matter of time now before OSHA gets called to go in there, or other officers leave in ambulances for heat stress among other things. And this is happening statewide, not just Fishkill. Ever since the Clinton Escape in June 2015 in upstate New York for three weeks where over 1,200 law enforcement officers were called in from agencies all across the east coast; this could not have given a bigger black eye to the department than ever. Nowadays, they have each facility under close scrutiny, using the management as puppets. All they are now are the middle men, observe and report, the rest will come back on decisions made by the three-piece suits who have been given political positions but have yet to ever have worked inside a prison. A report came in the other day that while on rounds, the Deputy Superintendent of Administration, himself a few years fresh from a recent sting at Greenhaven where he got caught up in a major contraband ring inside the prison and was transferred to Fishkill as part of his discipline, happen to find a personal lock hanging off of the personal locker without being secured. After speaking to the civilian who claimed ownership of said lock, he took it upon himself to launch the metal padlock across the table striking the civilian worker on his front side. A complaint was immediately made about the incident, but rather than discipline the boss, the administration covered it up and just sent him out on vacation.

Ever since I had my independent medical exams numerous months ago, my employer's headquarters in Albany decided to keep me out on the Thompson case dated 5/9/17, from the date of the incident. This froze me from being able to move onto another case from my other inmate-related injuries that I needed surgery on. Even though I had gone through procedures for numerous dates of injuries I had documented on file, the state would not let me use any of my other "comp" time I had on the books. Their plan was to freeze my case, make me move onto my own time accruals, and after I used those up numerous months later, they would put me on half pay. Once the one-year mark hit, they had the power to medically terminate me. Even while I am out getting major back surgery from an inmate-related incident, I am stuck out on another case. They were playing a game, they had a full house sitting in their hand that was dealt to them, and they saw a good way of getting rid of someone who was fighting the system in order to make things right for myself and my family. With the numerous amounts of documented injuries I had and an upcoming homicide trial that I was going to have to testify at, they had only just seen the beginning. There was still a lot more to do yet and I needed to get those wheels in motion.

In recent news, Governor Cuomo and his entourage, along with the "Acting" Commissioner of the Department of Correction, Annucio, made a visit to Great Meadow Correctional Facility, an all-male maximum security facility, only one of 17 in New York's prison system. The night before there had been a large-scale fight involving about 25 inmates. Cuomo states that they are there to support the department's efforts in doing these lockdowns and to take preventative measures, recognize a potential situation, and get ahead of it to take control before injuries or death could occur. What a crock of shit. In my 23 years of state service, not once has Cuomo and his staff made special visits to prisons regarding these situations. This department has NEVER, EVER, EVER been proactive. Always reactive, always. You know it, anything from a simple pothole in the ground to another hazard. "Ahhhh, we will wait to see if anyone gets injured before we can put in a work order and have maintenance fill it in with asphalt." Or it could be something worse like an issue where we had constant issues with the fire alarm systems getting tampered with. There would be several days at a time going by before a populated secure building housing inmates would actually have a working fire system in place for such cases as an emergency. There were so many false alarms set up by inmates cooking or illegally smoking that time after time that would become the answer as to why the alarms were going off. It got old inside real quick when the administration stopped caring about safety and security procedures by dumping it into the building staff's hands to handle. This would soon lead into incidents that could have otherwise been avoided. If the state or prison facilities had been proactive in prior years, then for certain we would not have had these incidents which occurred causing the lives of families to change, who had loved ones working inside those facilities. These inmates have 24-7-365 to think of ways to manipulate the system, figure out our routines, among other things. If this department had been as preventative and proactive as the Governor calls it, these inmates would be chirping like jail birds, not moaning like beasts. Case in point, once again, referencing the Clinton Escape, having prior knowledge, being proactive in all that the state claims to be doing, I can assure you would not have happened. In fact, Clinton's superintendent requested lockdowns days prior to the great escape but was denied by the Department of Corrections and Albany's Central Office. So stop filling the public with your corruption, your empty promises, and your fake news about what really goes on inside those prisons. But wait a second now…it's election year, and in a few months, New York will be heading to the polls. So of course Cuomo is making a visit to the particular facility having issues. Many, many officers had been hurt and injured brutally and had been hospitalized, not during this one-time occasion, but on many daily operations inside these walls and fences. None of them were ever visited by Governor Cuomo or given the same recognition that such law enforcement authoritative figures would be due. I can't think of many officers in the department's ranks of nearly over 21,000 officers who concur, coincide, or even care of what

Cuomo has to say. His work will not change our broken system, and they won't certainly bring back the dozens of officers and staff that have committed suicides due to the perils of this job. I for one can personally attest to this just dealing with everything I have in the past year or better. There was no way up until 2015 when the Governor's office's hands were forced to purchase additional weapons, contraband screening, and other tools of the trade in which was used to help us in our fight to do the right thing. They even invested in heat sensors and other scanners to use by night shift to be able to ensure an inmate was present in his cell, something the typical $10.99 flashlight was not capable of doing.

I got a phone call from Bruce today over at the NY State's Attorney General's Office. He told me there were over 70 people going to be called in to testify for this 2015 homicide case which is to be heard in NYC. I have already been in contact with them numerous times and there were issues from the last year or so that had occurred with me that he had not been aware of. While I can't get into too many details, his job was to separate the groups who would all be represented by one attorney in order to sort out the facts should, as Bruce said, "Officer's testimony that could contradict the next on, and so on, so forth." It would be so easily given after all this time for those involved and going what they had gone through, not to inject fact with opinion.

My follow-up with Dr. Paul had been completed on June 20th. Right away he gave me a script to get over to Orange Radiology for some x-rays of my lower back. It did not make sense that there were still issues going on with my legs from my lower back. Now that this was completed, I received a call and a letter in the mail from New York Presbyterian's Patient Administration Services, who informed me that staff interviews were conducted but of course there were no findings. Then surprisingly, in their letter, they did admit to a fall, albeit in their own version, about how "I was safely lowered to the ground." That afternoon I sat down with my newly-retained personal injury attorney Mike, we went over all of my documents and he had me go over some of his. I had signed onto a retainer agreement from their firm while they began the process filing requests for medical records from various facilities. I gave him some copies of my documents that would be needed in future reference.

After numerous delays, I was finally booked for my cervical epidural injections I so badly needed to relieve the nerve pain in my neck. They had me stop taking the blood thinners for a few days to get this done. I had chosen to stay awake for the procedure, which was being done under fluoroscopy at Cornwall Hospital. It went as planned and not as bad as I thought it would be, having had bad experiences with needles in the back and neck before. I was able to drive myself home. A day or so later, I found relief had started to take effect in my neck. These injections were actually working for me. I know that they don't last forever but at least for now it had done some good for me since it had been since May 2017 with the workplace violence incident that I had more progressive cervical treatments that were previously controverted by the State Insurance Fund. While I was feeling pretty good about that, some good news and some not-so-good news came in the mail that day. The first one I opened was from the State's Industrial Board of Appeals. Their senior attorney had found that my amended petition for my appeal against the Department of Labor was found to be in my favor and that the second motion in an attempt to dismiss my petition by the DOL's attorneys was denied. It was now in their hands to get an answer to my charges that the DOL had failed to conduct a fair and unbiased investigation of the workplace violence incident at Fishkill Correctional Facility. While I was happy with that update, I then went to open the next envelope which was from the Social Security Disability. Reading the first line, I immediately could tell it was denied. As I had been told and having been forewarned by others about first-time decisions by the SSD, my hopes had fallen through. But this was just another long road ahead as I contacted my law firm's office to notify them of the findings. Something else to add to my plate. This could take up to two years to get a hearing for my SSD decision based on the submitted medical documentation and exams that were given to me. I would be expecting a call next week to get the appeal papers started and to submit our request for a hearing.

September 7th had arrived and after my morning appointment with Dr. Ogulnick, I was all packed up and ready to head over to Fishkill and turn in my badge and ID, among other things such as my manual book, keys, parking permit, and a whole bag of uniforms. I had not been there in a long time and as I pulled into the facility, it looked so much more open aired as it used to be. Turns out, the state finally had a contractor take down all of the trees surrounding the perimeter fence lines and parking areas. Those trees had quite the life span and one good storm could topple them, knocking down anything in the way. It was nerve-racking for me at first to walk in there knowing the past year's fight for justice and what havoc I had caused for the administration.

When I got to the gate, the female officer who I am not familiar with kept the gate locked and went to get the staffing lieutenant. He came back to the gate and asked me loudly through the plexiglass, "Are you here to turn in your stuff?"

I replied, "Yes."

"Wait here, I think the Dep needs to see you."

Moments later, Deputy of Security Oblinski came to the gate and told the female officer to open the gate to let me in. I followed him down the administration hallway, passing the watch commander's office. I glanced inside as I walked by noticing some familiar faces. Oblinski had me sit in the conference room as he got some forms. He sat down with me and he took my ID, badge, manual and parking permit. Writing out a receipt for that, I began filling out my "C" form, which is used to transfer weapons. It contains information about the weapon, both parties, and other details. It has to go through a background check ever since Cuomo overnight signed the SAFE Act into law. Prior to this, none of that had to happen. I could simply sell a weapon to another law enforcement officer and we had 10 days to file that "C" form, without approvals or background checks. Another officer, JR, who I have worked with for several years, agreed to purchase it from me so it could be released and taken out of the state's possession from when they confiscated it following the May 2017 incident. Within minutes, we were finished up and as I went down the hallway, I met up with another lieutenant who escorted me down into the basement locker rooms where I could empty out my locker, which only had a few uniform items in it, along with a 4x6 photo of my wife and myself that had been in there almost since I met her back in 2000. I closed up the locker, turned over the key, and walked down to check the mailboxes for anything I might have in there. Empty, no mail. Onward we went, up the stairs and out the gate. I headed down in my vehicle to another building in the lower part of the facility to go meet up with the quartermaster. I brought my bag of uniforms up to the second floor and spread them out on a table where inventory of them was done. As each item was checked off on the form, I signed off on it and then said bye to a few other officers there that I know. I had a feeling I would be back there soon, for one reason or another.

It was now Monday morning, and my scheduled Workers' Comp hearing was about to start. Representing me this time was Nick from my law firm. I arrived 30 minutes prior, just before Nick got there. The hearing was delayed almost an hour as we awaited hearings scheduled prior to mine. Once we were called, the judge asked the state and my lawyer to identify themselves for the recording into the microphone. He then asked me how I was doing and I replied, "Miserable."

"Sorry to hear that, Mr. Harrington, now let's move forward with your case due to the time constraints."

This hearing was to introduce medical documentation and evidence of my PTSD being a part of my injuries from the 4/21/15 incident involving the homicide that evening at Fishkill Correctional Facility. After some presentations, the judge had found sufficient causal relationship in my matter which the State Insurance Fund made exception to and requested an independent medical exam with a psychologist. The hearing was adjourned and I went outside to discuss matters with Nick. We had to wait for an exam to be scheduled by the state and then would be back in for another hearing at a later date.

Chapter Thirty-Six
My Legal Cases Continue

With matters as they are for my family, it seemed like pulling teeth to get decisions in a more timely manner and some help with our economic status. Of course, we appreciated all of the help we had received prior to this date but I had to start doing research and getting some benefits nailed down for my wife and children. After hours of researching, I came across NY State of Health. I called them up and they kindly walked me through step by step, on starting my account on their website. There were ways to electronically upload documents onto the account. It did not seem as bad, I figured something like this would have miles of red tape. After a few weeks of sending in documents, I found out we were qualified under Medicaid for medical, dental, vision, prescription, and anything else medically necessary for the entire family. They even gave us our choice of about six health plans, which we went with WellCare New York. It was a widely accepted insurance company so it did little to disrupt our current providers. This was just what we needed. Not even a deductible or co-pay. With that in place we now set our focus on my Social Security Appeal and the expedited Retirement Disability 3/4 Plan for disabled employees. Surprisingly, with having no pay coming in for the past 5 weeks, I received a check in the mail from the State Insurance Fund which was now paying about 90% of my salary. This, along with some disbursements from my Deferred Compensation Stock I had been saving the last two decades, had put us back on track and allowed me now to put my goals back to my recovery. I am still going to 29-30 medical appointments on average each month. It was like a full-time job along with handling all of my legal cases.

On October 3rd, there had been a scheduled conference call between the Governor's office, the Public Employee Relations Board, COPBA's law firm and myself to settle on two dates for the trial which had been previously delayed due to my complications of having the lumbar fusion surgery. We were all set for trial in Albany to start on November 7th and conclude on November 28th. I had been prepared since the prior scheduled date with my evidence and exhibits. I had no plan to call witnesses but many of my other friends who are still working as officers talked about getting together to come to the hearing. They also had opposition with the union. As I mentioned before, the prior elections only yielded about 7,000 votes out of over 20,000. The union was starting to see a pattern of no confidence from its membership. It often did nothing to see into the cases of those needing representation. Sure, they came along and entertained some grievances, or other matters regarding the numerous suspensions that were occurring across New York's prison system. With myself being the one dealing with their failure to have the Duty of Fair Representation, I wanted to take a stand against them. Many other union members who supported me, did so in confidence but did not want to be put on paper for fear of retaliation.

Also on October 3rd, I finally got another follow-up in the mail from the State Department of Labor. They had previously been given 30 days to answer to the denial of their motion to dismiss my appeal. The original went to the State's Industrial Board of Appeals' counsel office and a copy was sent to me. When I opened up the manila envelope, I began to review their response. This was becoming a game. It was a paperwork shuffle. All they did was change up some of the vocabulary and kept blowing smoke patterns stating board rules and sections of the labor law. My prior evidence submitted, along with my amended petition, and the acknowledgment of the Industrial Board of Appeals to find my response to be proper, just, and well-presented, was making them nervous. I have it on paper, in black and white, they can't continue to run from the truth. If I have to, this will not be let go as long as I can keep going at it. This is something that I know, standing up for what's right and what the truth is, will one day come out, it always has, and always will. One just has to be patient and willing to push for it, do not become one of their statistics, and most of all, know that cover-up and corruption needs to be dealt with. Even Governor Cuomo's office can't escape it.

In the past several weeks, I had been in contact with JR, who had been interested in purchasing my 9mm off-duty hand gun which was still in custody and secured at Fishkill Correctional Facility. Deputy Oblinski had accepted the "C" form documents completed by myself and JR, but we had run into some red tape. In order for JR to get the transaction completed, he would need to have the weapon in order to have a firearms dealer complete the forms with the state. Without this, there was nothing that could be done to process this transaction. JR had been in touch with Deputy Oblinksi and was told he was calling the Office of Special Investigations to get further direction on the matter. Well, it has been about five weeks already and I felt bad for JR having to go through so much unnecessary crap. It was clear inconvenience, *was* the operative word here, since I had reached out to outside agencies to stand up for my rights due to the Thompson investigation. So I reached out to OSI's central office in Albany while sitting in the doctor's office awaiting my appointment, I had a few transfers until I reached the right individual. I spoke to Sergeant Larry from the OSI's Special Operations Unit that deals with firearms. I gave him the complete layout of my situation and all of my information. He was in agreement with me that it should not take this long and was very cooperative. Sgt. Larry was going to give Deputy Oblinski a call and follow up on this. He told me he would be calling me soon once he was able to get further details and direction to the facility about my weapon. I sent JR a text message to inform him that I was already making the calls to take care of this process the best I could to expedite it for ourselves, and to get it out of Fishkill's arsenal.

I was on my way to a second psychological independent exam at the request of the State's Insurance Fund. The Workers' Compensation Board Judge had found prima facie medical evidence that my PTSD was also related to the 4/21/15 incident involving the homicide. The Insurance Fund had the opportunity to send me to one of their specialists to get a second opinion on the matter. On October 11th, as my wife and I went to the appointment all the way out in Bloomingburg, we showed up at 10 a.m. in the downpour of rain. I brought along my documentation and a copy of the lawsuit from this incident to show as exhibits during my examination to support my answers to all of the questioning for their psychologist. She and I had got to the office first, and like last time, Dr. Claus came driving quickly into the parking lot while we waited outside. It was minutes later when he came to the waiting room for me to fill out the paperwork for the exam.

We started around 10:15 a.m. and I had introduced my wife who had sat in the corner of the room, and using her cell phone, she began to record the examination in its entirety. I had last saw Dr. Claus in February of this year. He went to my file on his computer and pulled up my notes. He started typing

301

away, erasing lines and filling in the blanks. I made a gesture about him doing that and he laughed it off as if it was the normal thing to do. As we continued talking about my PTSD from the homicide case, he kept repeating questions that I had answered, but that did not fit the blanks he needed to fill in.

"Look, Paul, I don't even know exactly what the insurance company is looking for. I am just trying to make the connection of your symptoms to this case and the other ones as well," as Dr. Claus grieved to me. "I can't make it happen if you don't answer my questions directly!"

I looked straight at Dr. Claus and said, "Look, Doc, this session is over. I have shown you documents, I have given you my symptoms and answers as best as I can. You should be able to handle each of your client's needs that walk through this door!"

The Doc looked over at my wife and asked her a few questions about what she has observed in the changes of what I have been through. She began answering them and as she finished, Dr. Claus looked at her saying, "By the way, are you recording this?"

"No, just Paul," she stated.

He chimed back, "Well, technically you are, and that's actually a no-no."

I explained to him that it was likely that she only got the audio portion of him and he agreed. He then asked her to send him a copy of the video which she voluntarily did while we were still there. Per Workers' Compensation rules and regulations on independent medical exams, each party has the right to videotape or record the session, but must be notified in advance of the session. We went beyond the one-hour limit, and I had told Dr. Claus that it was our wedding anniversary that day. After some cordial greetings, we wrapped up the session and made our way out in the pouring rain to go out for lunch in Middletown. Normally within ten business days, the evaluation findings are mailed out to each party so I will be expecting it by next week.

I looked up Sgt. Larry at the OSI's Special Operations Unit in Albany again since I had not heard back from him yet about my personally owned handgun which I was trying to sell to another officer at Fishkill. We spoke briefly and he hadn't yet had the chance to call Deputy Oblinski at Fishkill about the matter. He told me he would follow up and I stated, "If this does not go through as it was originally supposed to, I plan on filing a claim with the facility to pay me the net value of that 9mm firearm." After an agreed time to call back, my phone rang from my pain management office at Cornwall Hospital. Staff there had informed me that the State Insurance Fund had notified them that my pain medications cannot be billed under the 9/11/16 case when I had the group altercation with an inmate that led to serious back surgery and knee injuries. They told me it would have to be billed under the 5/9/17 Thompson case which made no sense at all. I am being treated for the most recent surgery right now and the State Insurance Fund wants to bill this under a non-inmate related incident. This does make a difference when it comes down to the bottom line. But my pain management doctor had been treating me under the 9/11/16 case and this was his third time prescribing my pain medications under that date of injury and billing it on that case. Something was going on up in Albany with this prescription mess and I am awaiting a follow-up from my lawyers regarding it.

One of my biggest hurdles to overcome was the filing for my Retirement System Disability Pension which would be 3/4 of my salary, tax free. With the number of injuries I had sustained over the years, many of which became permanent, I had hired my law firm down in White Plains to also represent me in this case application as well. Normally, as one of my lawyers Nick had told me, I would have to most likely go to two-three of their doctors for medical exams. You also would usually have to wait one year from the date of your last surgery before being approved. But to my surprise and relief, on October 24, 2018, I received an email from the State's Disability Retirement system. In it stated, "Hi Paul, I did get your paper work you sent in last week. However, your case has been approved and the letter telling you that will go out in the mail today or tomorrow. You won't have to go to the IME exam since the doctors here looked at your records and all agreed you were disabled. Your case now moves to the Calculations Dept., where they will figure out how much money you're owed and what your monthly payments will be. You should see your first check at the end of December. There's a small chance you'll get it at the end of November, but plan for December." I was sent information to fill out and told that my first deposit was coming on December 14th, but even after submitting all of the required documents, another state worker in the retirement system's office appeared to be in a rush and typed in the wrong account information thus delaying my payment. I was told by case handlers that it would take some time to get the information input back into the system and I hope to get my first payments from disability retirement by January. Now that we were in the hole again and it being this time of the year, once again we got help from other charitable organizations such as Duchess County 10-13 of the Hudson Valley and through our Church Parish. The state's retirement system stated: "You will get a couple of letters in the mail explaining what I just tried to say to you but in the meantime, if you have any questions, feel free to contact me. It was nice working with you and good luck in your future." It turns out I did not have to go see any of their doctors or wait the full year following the lower back surgery, all due to the efforts of my law firm with Warren and Nick. My cooperation in providing documents on a moment's notice per the retirement system's requests also helped expedite the process as well, albeit for the calculations department mishaps.

Some of the best news I had heard in a long time. My stack of documents from nearly 18 doctors was enough for them to see that I was incapacitated. It was certainly welcoming to hear this after all of my fighting efforts in this case. Now that this obstacle is clear, it's time to get ready for the first date of the Public Employee Relations board hearing against the Governor's Office of Employee Relations, my former union, COPBA, and their law firm. The case will be heard in front of Judge Rikers in Albany. The date of the hearing is supposed to end on November 28th. I have prepared all of my exhibits and will be ready to go present my case at the first day of the hearing, the day after election day.

November 7th has arrived and with that, an earlier than usual wakeup to get ready, put on my business suit, gather my documents already set aside and off to pick up my friend, Fr. K., who was coming along as an observer of the trial and an advisor during our breaks. Upon arrival to the Empire State Plaza Building 2, it was through the long concourse and onto the elevator all the way to the 20th floor, but we think it was actually the 19th floor because there was no 15th floor listed on the elevator. Fr. K had helped me carry several pounds of documents for the case. A lot of it was reference material, while about 200 documents were exhibits of evidence each copied four times. The parties present for the trial were the law firm for COPBA, of which the President or any of his executive staff did not show up for this scheduled hearing, however two attorneys from the Governor's Office of Employee Relations and one individual representative from the State's Bureau of Labor Relations were there, along with Judge Rikers and other court staff. Each party was directed by the judge to go into the conference room and to identify the documents which would be presented as evidence. Having mine stacked in order, as I explained it in brief, I noticed glances between the union's law firm and the GOER attorneys, who 90% of the time had some questions and comments about my documents, while myself, acting pro se and not having the official law degree, sat there as they informed me that they would object to most of my documents. About 30 minutes later, we went back into the hearing room. Judge Rikers began to formally go on record about the details of this trial, and while being extremely thorough, walked to each party to ensure they recognized my prior filings with PERB regarding the union's violations of their duty to fairly represent me, as well as improper practice charges. I was then given the floor by Judge Rikers to give my formal opening statement, followed by the union's lawyer to give his. They did not have much to offer other than a blank copy of a grievance form and a new copy of the palm-sized handbook for the state's contract with COPBA and its members.

I was soon called by the judge to the stand, where I was sworn in and then sat down. For approximately five hours, I had been seated at the stand as I presented my case of the workplace violence incident, and a timeline of what my actions were following such. There were brief moments of silence as the judge reviewed each document and identified it to the court room that it would be entered into evidence. Over and over again, I had a total of 23 exhibits, with nearly 50 pages involved. After repeated objections by the GOER and COPBA's lawyer, the judge ruled in my favor all but one time when he sustained an objection over relevance of one of my documents. Additionally, he was going to disallow one document after both opposing parties had objected, but after allowing me to briefly explain the importance of its contents and having him look closely at pages 4-5, Judge Rikers reversed his decision, overruled their objections, and allowed for my document to be brought into evidence. I had everything on paper, from the first report of the incident, to copies of my private doctors, state doctors, the Workers' Comp Board and the NY State Insurance Fund. That one document attached to the union President's email reply to me which he assumed was Directive 4960 turned out to be correspondence between the Union's Office Manager, President and Vice President Mallory, wherein he stated, "This guy is going to sue us for DFR" in a simple one-lined reply to the Union President in Albany. GOER's attorneys were in question of this document and by observing the reaction of their faces after reading it, they were doing all they could to throw it out, but Judge Rikers allowed this to be submitted into evidence. It was a long day on the stand, some of it repetitive, yet necessary. Plans were made on what would happen at that point at the next hearing in three weeks whereas the union's law firm would be calling several union officials as witnesses. After a brief discussion, the hearing was adjourned and we hit the highway to get home.

I looked forward to doing my cross examinations. I already had them all typed up and ready to go. Prior to the hearing that morning, they asked what I wanted out of this since there is no monetary award, I looked the lawyers right in their eyes and said, "It's a matter of principle. I need to do this to hold those union officials accountable who did not perform the duties of which they took oaths for, and additionally, I want to set the standard that change should be considered in future cases so other officers facing similar sanctions, injuries, workplace violence, etc., should not be afraid of the system and should stand up for their rights." What I wanted would help those currently just joining on the job as well as those who have been there for many years. It's a broken system and the lack of nepotism directive within the department singlehandedly allows such protections afforded to those who have the higher powers connected in their family bloodline or otherwise, versus those who do not. If you have ever watched the show *Blue Bloods* on TV, starring T. Selleck, he was the NYPD Police Commissioner that held his family to the book, the ones who were also on the force as an officer and a detective, to the highest expectations. They did not get special treatment and if one of them got jammed up, they would have to go through the system just like the next person would have to. He would have it no other way and that's the integrity that I am referring to in the state's prison system. Favoritism has to go, it damages officers beyond repair, and often time follows them home affecting family members as well. That is not the job that most of us signed up for.

As the second day of the union hearing came upon us, the morning of November 28th was no different than most mornings. The house was busy as the wife and kids were getting ready for their day at school and work. Once I finished up with getting my tie on, I gathered my documents and loaded into the vehicle. I took a moment to kiss everyone good bye and I drove up the road to pick up Fr. K, who was once again assisting me with helping me get my materials up to the 20th floor. I am still unable to carry that much weight. It was a clear ride up to Albany, traffic lighter than usual, and the weather clear and dry. We arrived up there and found my usual spot in the parking garage right near the elevator. Once we took the elevator up to the 20th floor, I began to settle my materials and organize myself. Moments later upon the arrival of the other parties from the State's Bureau of Labor Relations as well as the GOER's office and the union's law firm, we began with Judge Rikers calling me to the stand. It had been three weeks since the last day we had been there so I had to collect my memory of where we left off. More documents from my medical providers were reviewed but allowed to be placed into evidence. As I sat on the left side of Judge Rikers, my head shifted between him and the row of attorneys sitting in the front of the hearing room. I was advised to speak loudly so that the stenographer could have a better time hearing what I was saying. The union's law firm began with their questioning of me. After some basic questions, he also brought up four pages of documents, the first page with a couple of short phrases while I was at the E.R. I had sent these to a number of co-workers in text messages to let them know I was ok, that I had hit my head causing a small laceration on the top part of my head. This had occurred about a month prior to the incident at work when I had been assaulted by Officer Thompson. The union's lawyer had questioned me on the matter and made references to it being related to my injuries from Thompson. So in a way, the lawyer had been admitting that Thompson had assaulted me, as was previously denied, but he was trying to get me to say that this was related to my case. My response back was that I had no head injury claimed with Officer Thompson in my medical report nor the workers' compensation claim form. Suddenly, all of the other parties started shuffling their documents to see what injuries were involved in the Thompson incident. Those were the left shoulder which I had surgery on following the incident, and my neck. I had also noted anxiety which might be referred to the head, but not actually a physical injury. At that point, the union's lawyer started asking if it could be the cause of my neck injuries, ear, or TMJ of the jaw. None of it was relative, but it was allowed to be admitted into evidence. I made notes to myself to obtain those medical documents from the hospital as soon as possible after this date.

Now it was time for the witnesses to be called in. Officer Nomore was the first to be called; his stay on the stand was brief, about 10 minutes long. After he was questioned by the state, I began my previously prepared cross examination of him. He seemed careless, lacking of memory from most of the incident. He recalled certain key facts but could not recall others. He was being somewhat cooperative in answering the questions but had a laid-back attitude, as if not taking this seriously. My questions of him were short in nature as he had been the first union representative I had contacted after the incident. Next up they had called was another union representative, Officer Smurf. He is typically a well-carried, intelligent person who knows his stuff when it comes to dealing with anything regarding the union, when representing other staff during any type of situations regarding another officer. He himself had been suspended from Corrections for several months when he was involved in a situation regarding an inmate who was on special watch confined in a cell. There was another partner of his that went down as well but eventually after obtaining the assistance of a law firm and that from the union, they had gained their jobs back. I am also familiar with Officer Smurf; he has been to my photo studio before to do headshots wearing multiple outfits to get a small portfolio for him to use for his side business outside of Corrections. Again, similar questioning under testimony had begun and he too was also up there for a short period. I had asked him numerous questions during the cross examination, taking notes of his responses. He surprised me as he appeared to not have any memory at all of this date in question, that he had no idea of what was going on regarding the workplace violence incident. He either denied or did not recall anything asked of him. Judge Rikers and I had made eye contact with each other from time to time as if to say that Officer Smurf wasn't being such a good witness and not as cooperative. As I said before, he is intelligent and knows the system. He was working on my shift in the same area of the building on the day this occurred yet he could not recall working that day either. We all carry calendar books given to us by the union each year. Everyone can easily refer to it to see what days they were off, had overtime, or worked regular shifts. On top of this all, Officer Smurf and I had some of the same days off each week, so this led to us seeing a lot of each other at work.

The state had called up their third witness, The Union's Vice President of the Mid-Hudson region, Mr. Mallory. He was being asked how he knew me and he stated that we had a good rapport and knew each other on the outside. He repeatedly said I had opportunities to reach out to him via social media, call him, or even stop by the office. He went into the history of his state employment, with the numerous positions he held and what his responsibilities were. After his questioning was done, it was now my opportunity to cross examine him as I had done with the others. Keeping in mind that I am not an attorney, I do have some paralegal experience. I had also prepared my questioning ahead of time as I took notes of what he was saying. Most of the time on the stand he was smiling. I had caught him a few times with some misinformation, perhaps perjuring himself. He had just testified to the state that he had not been contacted by me ever. But I informed Judge Rikers to refer to one of my exhibits and to show it to My Mallory. It was a typed-up letter cc'd to him; attached to it was a signed signature card signed by him. He then admitted he received it, read it quickly, and put it on the desk. Judge Rikers questioned him, "Did you respond back to Mr. Harrington? Did you try to contact him at all?"

Mr. Mallory stated, "No, sir. No, I didn't." I also referred to Mallory when he had stated that Officer Nelson was his brother-in-law and that he had represented him for Thompson's prior harassment incidents, and out of a 30-day no-pay suspension, he was able to get it down to three days' loss of vacation time only, no suspension, no loss of pay. He stated to the court that it was only two days, but I had corrected him that it was three days. Mallory responded carelessly as if there was no difference between two days and three days. The facts are the facts. I got into further testimony with him about his duties and what prior history did I have with him as being an active member of the union. Within 20 minutes or so, Mr. Mallory had been excused and smiled as he walked by me departing the court room. The state's last witness, an unnamed officer who worked for the union as their Head of the Grievance department, was called into the front of the court room, was sworn in and took his seat on the stand. The union's law firm submitted evidence in the case of a few blank grievance forms and the contact book, which was still being practiced although it was expired three years. Officers continue to work without any wage advancements, not even able to meet the cost of living. As the grievance official began his testimony, neither he or I had any knowledge of each other. He seemed like a well-educated individual. He had run off his list of experience within the Department of Corrections. His expertise in the grievance field seemed as if he was fit for the job and one of the reasons he was selected to fill that position. Part of his testimony was to just explain what the process was and some definitions of the contract language. Soon after, I had a brief few moments to cross examine. To my left, I had seen the GOER's attorney and the union's lawyer snickering and laughing quietly. I stopped during my questioning and looked at them saying, "Could we please keep the tone down and act professional here?" A gasp could be heard by numerous people and Judge Rikers immediately called the room to order and put us all on a five-minute recess. After we came back into the room, he put us all back on the record and proceeded with my cross examinations. The grievance representative almost appeared as if he had been testifying for the good of my case. Upon his questioning, he agreed that filing a grievance on a directive cannot be done, and one for a workplace violence incident would be handled differently. Those were relative to my case and gave false hope to the union's lawyer that he had selected a witness who was more for both sides rather than just the state's. We concluded and wrapped up the hearing as both sides rested their cases. Judge Rikers gave direction on how the proceedings would occur in the next 30 days and when we would have to file our final briefs and arguments. It had been a long strenuous day on me with my physical pain and mental anguish. I had taken on the role of a pro se attorney representing myself voluntarily, however at the time it was the only choice I had. Besides, no one can advocate and speak for you better than yourself. It was about December 3rd when I made a trip to the hospital to get copies of those medical records regarding my minor injury on Easter Sunday in 2017. Nothing in those 16 pages of documents indicated or projected the same type of injury as Thompson had done to me the following month. In fact, the CAT scan even showed my neck to be perfectly fine, having no disc stenosis as well as other things. I spoke to Judge Rikers about submitting these documents and I had to run them by the other lawyers first and of course both of them representing the Governor's Office and the union had defiantly stated their objections to the submission of these medical records. It would state the facts of my case and I found it unfair, so I had to write a complete motion up in legal terms and send off copies via certified mail to all parties including Judge Rikers. The day he asked me to do it on a conference call with everyone on the phone together, I immediately got to work on it and had it all done including the affidavits of service by mail. I have the burden of proof in this case to accompany those photos. These documents ultimately will prove the other party's theory wrong.

Chapter Thirty-Seven
The Finale of My Energy and Triumph

I am working on my next submission of Form C-257 which is a Workers' Comp Board Claimant's Record of Medical and Travel Expenses. As of this date, November 1st, 2018, I have documented well over 400 medical appointments just for treatments, surgeries, testing, physical therapy and many more from the assault that took place upon me on May 9, 2017. I average about 28 medical appointments a month right now, with many more in the future and currently being scheduled for me. With all of that travel, my mileage has added up enough that I could drive from my house to San Francisco, California on two different trips. Looking back at the Notice of Hearing under the case of Harrington v. NYSDOCCS Fishkill Correctional Facility, a highlighted area from the hearing officer ordered the respondent, Department of Labor, to provide a copy of its investigation report no later than seven days prior to the pre-trial conference on November 26th. Once I called in for the conference that morning, it was noted that such files had not been submitted. Without penalty, the State's Industrial Board of Appeals gave the Department of Labor a second chance to submit those files by November 30th. As agreed upon, I awaited the whole week for those files so I could begin putting my case together. As of December 1st, I still have not received those files. Someone is covering up something and delaying the process. If there were no issues with their files, why would they continue to delay sending them? I called and left a message for the Industrial Board of Appeals' hearing officer asking him to call me back on Monday regarding this urgent matter. On or about December 14th, we had a 45-minute phone call, with the Department of Labor's counselor being nearly 15 minutes late, once again not complying with instructions given by the hearing officer, yet their misdeeds went without scrutiny or penalty. This was to update what records were missing from my personnel file and also what the new dates of the adjournment be for at this hearing. Over the holidays, I was asking for the extra time due to the Department of Labor's delays to allow me ample time to research more items and to print up my case materials to be brought into evidence. What I am really trying to do with these two state cases is to change the system, hold those responsible, possibly set up a different procedure on how to handle these types of cases in the future. It was a lot of work and many have told me they would have quit a long time ago. That's what the state wants too, but they picked on the wrong guy to do that. I am working on behalf of the officers and staff members working in NY's prison system to be free of what I went through, and to enable them to stand up for their rights. This is for those current and anyone new coming into the system.

I finally got word back from the State's Office of Special Investigation Special Operations Unit Sgt. Larry. He made contacts with the State Police and with Fishkill that I could have the weapon transferred to a gun dealer for the background check before it is released for sale. I spoke to an owner at a local gun shop in Wallkill who was going to make arrangements as a federally licensed dealer to transport weapons. This came with a small fee but was well worth it to get it into the hands of another officer rather than having the state seize it. Now that I was gaining ground with that matter, more bad news came in. I found out at Dr. Habif's office during my appointment that one of my other lawyers had quit the firm as well. That makes two in less than 40 days or so. First Jason and now Nick. From what I understand, there were some transitions going on at the firm and the workload was just too much for them to handle. Now I was left with Warren, the "of counsel" of the firm. Ever since they started representing me, that large firm had downsized and there were several changes. I was uncertain about how this would be for me in the future of my cases but Warren assured me he was on it and going to see through the rest of my representation. I mean after all, I did have about 7-8 injury cases there, a retirement disability case, and a social security case with that firm, which means that me being one single client, I was a big client for them and in the end, they would certainly see their end of the settlements. I also had two separate law firms, one in Kingston, New York and the other in New York City, all representing me in medical malpractice cases overseeing the processing of the lawsuits regarding my treatments at New York Presbyterian Hospital in Manhattan. Even though myself and other officers I have spoken to prior to that, had done much of our own legwork finding paperwork, scanning documents, calling in for this and that, we saved the lawyers a lot by advocating on our own behalf when it came to our cases. You would think we should be allowed to invoice the lawyers as well after receiving their billing, but that would be in one's dream. I just found out from a colleague today that Sgt. Oswald transferred to Otisville Correctional Facility in Orange County, N.Y., about a 40-minute ride from Fishkill. Not sure why he changed assignments, but like they say, it's like kicking the same old can down the same road.

Things are on the move for me right now, with the holidays past us, I am gathering my documents that will be used in evidence of the Department of Labor hearing this coming January 23, 2019. I will be working hard to go over the stacks of paperwork I have to ensure what my plan is for the hearing. Acting pro se in your own cases is a lot of work, but work that I would be getting charged thousands and thousands of dollars for. I am taking this fight on by myself along with my evidence. In the end, I hope that I am proved right as I have been up until this day. This will help the future of other officers in similar incidents to have a case to reference back on.

Later that day, I sent a notarized, certified letter to Superintendent Shields at Fishkill, asking him the status of my retirement badge and ID. It had been over 10 weeks already since the State's retirement system approved my disability pension retirement. I had made previous calls to personnel at Fishkill, as well as to Albany regarding this issue but it was getting nowhere. I even spoke to the Deputy Superintendent for Administration's Secretary who told me that she would pass along the message but he never returned my calls. Normally once you retire, staff in personnel would order your retirement badge and an ID would be issued by your facility. It was a game of wait and see what happens next, if anything at all. A few days following that, I received via email, the closing brief and affidavit of service from the Respondent Lawyers representing COPBA in my improper charge case. It contained numerous pages citing their belief that this situation never occurred and was all due to an off-duty injury at home. Despite my possession of a 16-page set of documented medical records from my treatment of minor injuries from the E.R. at St Luke's Hospital, the respondents pulled all they could out of their hats to ensure that these medical documents were not able to be submitted of evidence. After all, as compelling as they were to show absolutely no connection to the injuries caused by Thompson, this was in their best interest to persuade the Board to look the other way. The respondent's lawyer claimed numerous objections to my submission of additional medical documentation after I had rested my case. I did not have access to those records as they were still at the hospital. This was not planned for because it was not part of this incident in any way, shape or form.

As for the evidence I had gathered for the Department of Labor's investigation of the workplace violence incident and their final conclusion of it being "unfounded," I had numerous documents showing contradictions in the witnesses, reports, lack of documentation submitted, and a less-than-professional presentation of what would be an official investigation of one state agency from another. After a good three-hour stint at Office Depot making well over 1,200 copies of my documents (which totals up to be five copies of each page for the hearing, one of which is sent to the Department of Labor prior to the hearing on January 23, 2019), I had a total of 84 exhibits, all starting from the beginning and running through to present day. Of those documents of evidence were almost 22 copies of my annual employee performance evaluations, all marked "Excellent" and one being "Outstanding" by my supervisors, along with nearly 8-9 commendations for my service and being referred to as an asset to facility operations under previous administrations. These were important to show when establishing my character and performance of duty during my 23 years of service. In addition to that were several medical documents from my doctors and state doctors' exams/treatments showing that my injuries were consistent with the incident of 5/9/17 with Thompson. I was also able to submit some of Thompson's disciplinary records that showed a pattern of abuse prior to the physical assault. I was getting everything all set up with that, despite having ten doctor appointments this week and a workers' comp board hearing. I was now aiming my focus in the direction of the transcripts of the union trial which were priced at about $1,300. This extraordinary amount was something to be considered but I ended up making an appointment to go to Albany to review them prior to writing up my closing brief on this case. I had some homework to do but since I had come this far, I kept pushing forward to get closure on the matters at hand.

So as I tirelessly make calls after calls to the law firm, State Insurance Fund, doctor's office and Walgreen's Pharmacy, I begin to feel like I am caught in the web of this broken system, trying to get medication refilled with no problem, only to find that the State Insurance Fund is not approving the payments thereof. The red tape has led to further exacerbation of my symptoms. I thought we were supposed to be taken care of to ensure the best possible recovery. In the meantime, as I await medications, I have just looked at the calendar for this month of January, and I counted 34 medical appointments this month. That's a bit above the average. But even still, the injured worker loses all rights in his or her case and it's left up to the suits and lab coats on what happens next. In the meantime, while I go through this process, many of the illegal, undocumented immigrants in New York City, only an hour's drive away from me, are now receiving free 100% healthcare all on the taxpayer's dime. Speaking of the taxpayers, tens of thousands of dollars so far, and probably several thousands more after this, not to include the settlements, will all be going into my treatments, surgeries, medications and testing for the permanent injuries I sustained from Thompson on that warm and sunny afternoon in May of 2017. Yet, with the fights I have put forth, the agencies I have involved, the cover-up continues and the money keeps adding up, all in an order to protect this individual and numerous other superiors inside the facility itself, and all the way up to Albany. There's a lot at stake here and these guys are in it for the long run, willing to take the denying and delaying as long as they can run with it. I am not the only one having issues either, almost weekly I am getting back word from good sources about the workplace violence that continues to plague Fishkill Correctional Facility. So many of the senior officers and supervisors have already transferred or retired to get out of the system, before the system gets them, or for whatever reason they had chosen to do so.

For the past few months, I had been inquiring with my former employer about the status of my retirement credentials. Having made several calls in a three-month period to their Personnel office, as well as to the Administration Deputy Superintendent, I was getting nowhere. Finally, I had written a certified notarized letter to Superintendent Shields. Within two weeks, I received a letter from the Department's Head of Personnel up in Albany. This letter was asking for proof of my retirement. I thought to myself, interesting, here I had letters from the Comptroller's Office and Retirement System from back in October of 2018 that they had notified Fishkill that I was now retired based on a 3/4 medical chapter 722 disability. So I called the office up in Albany and got some questions answered. I ended up mailing out three documents to them that day showing proof of my retirement. It would be some time before I heard back and once it is approved, I most likely would have to go to Albany to get my retirement badge and identification card. In the meantime, I had a scheduled date for my IVC filter removal at New York Presbyterian Hospital in Manhattan. With some preparation instructions to follow, I attempted to arrange for medical transportation but that was not possible. Neither the State Insurance Fund nor my doctor's office made those type of arrangements, so I was able to take the train down to the city and a cab from Grand Central Terminal. It was a brutally cold day out on January 30th, 2019, when I went down to finally get this device removed. It was a same-day procedure so I was not admitted. Since I had gone alone unescorted to the hospital, the staff decided it was best for me to proceed with the operation under a local anesthetic and an IV with pain meds being fed through it. It was an hour past my scheduled procedure before they took me into the operating room. As they rolled me in, they put warm blankets over me, raised my legs higher up and began to hook me up to several machines. The initial pain began when they put needles into my neck to provide me with the local anesthetic. That was fist-gripping, as I tried to remain still. The hardest part was yet to come. They placed a tent style tarp over my head so I could not see the procedure. My head was turned to my side as they made access to my jugular on the right side of my neck. My doctor who originally did the implant of this IVC filter back in July of 2018 during my back surgery was there for the removal. I heard instructions being given as multiple staff were in the room. I felt a sudden jolt of pressure into my neck as they placed a tube the size of a soda straw into my neck. I yelled, "Meds, meds, meds!" as the anesthesiologist ran back over to continue another dose of Versed and Fentanyl into my IV line for the pain. That helped somewhat and I felt a cooling sensation all through my body. Suddenly they injected dye into me and quickly my insides turned into a fire as a blast of heat from the dye injected through my veins and made its way from my head to my toes. It only lasted for a minute before it wore off. I kept hearing the staff of doctors guiding the device of wires with a clamp on it inserted through my neck, make its way down into my inner right thigh. A few attempts were unsuccessful. As time passed, they finally got a hold of the filter and were able to fish it out of there through the tubes. Finally, they took the tent tarp off me and showed me the filter device which had some blood stuck on it. It was put into a container and bagged as evidence for my law firm in

New York City. The pain I had experienced from this device in my inner thigh through my abdomen and crotch area suddenly felt relief after six months of having it in me. The only pain I was experiencing at that point was the right side of my neck which I could barely turn side to side. They brought me into recovery and fed me. I was released to go home and as I walked outside, news had reported that a polar vortex was about to hit the city with severe snow squalls. It was mass hysteria, people running up the streets, traffic blocking the boxes, horns blaring even more so than usual. I flagged down three different cabs, all of them telling me no they were going home. I saw another cab stop to let out a passenger and I jumped in and was able to catch a ride from there up to Grand Central. Finally making it home by that evening, a few days had passed of wearing a soft neck brace and I began to experience more relief from the pain on the right side of my neck.

The night after I got home from the hospital in Manhattan, in the US Mail I had noticed a reply letter from the Director of Personnel in Albany for my former State Corrections employer. In it came some more bad news. The adverse actions I had faced since day one still continued from the department even after I had retired. It read: "This is in response to your letter dated January 14, 2019, responding to my letter dated January 10, 2019, regarding your request to obtain a retirement badge issued by New York State Corrections. After a review of the documentation you provided (from the State's retirement system and Comptroller's office), we are unable to approve your request for a retirement badge. Therefore, you are denied at this time." Coincidentally as I type this, my phone rang with a call from the NY State Retirement System. Mike called me back saying everything was done with my case, even the calculations, and had been closed since I was now retired. After I explained to him what was happening and my reasons to believe this was an adverse action due to the ongoing hearings against my former employer at Fishkill Correctional Facility, he was very helpful and said that he was going to take care of this and get back to me. I had also notified Warren at my attorney's office who represented me on my retirement disability. Prior to this, back on January 23, 2019, the first day of the Department of Labor's hearing on my appeal with the State's Industrial Board of Appeals began at the State Office Campus Building 12 in Albany. I went up there that day with Al who carried my two heavy cases of documents for me and served as my resource person during the hearing. I had over 80 exhibits of documents to submit as evidence.

Having sent copies to the Senior Counselor Attorney for the Department of Labor prior to the day of the hearing, gave him an opportunity to review each document. He showed the hearing officer and myself a list of about 20 exhibits he would allow for me to submit with an objection. It took nearly four hours plus to identify with many objections by the State's Senior Labor Attorney, however, after my rebuttals to those, I was found in favor and they were overruled many times, allowing a total of about 62 of the 80 to be submitted into evidence. Those remaining were marked for identification purposes only. I then began my testimony while the court reporter was recording transcripts of the given dialogue. I had come prepared in my mind of what to say without having any written statements to read from which the State's attorney had done the opposite. It was a victory for me that day, but due to inclement weather that afternoon, it was decided to adjourn the hearing for another day which was scheduled for Friday, February 8, 2019, same location. I had more evidence come to light after the adjournment and prepared to submit those on day two as we commence the hearing on my case involving the Department of Labor's investigation into the assault and workplace violence incident at Fishkill on May 9, 2017.

I had taken a separate trip up to Albany to the Empire State Plaza once again to the Public Employee Relations Board for an appointment I had to review the two days of transcripts regarding the hearing held for my improper practice charges brought upon my former Union, COPBA, for the absence of their Duty of Fair Representation, which was also in accordance to the workplace violence incident. I sat in an empty conference room for about two hours or more reviewing the typed transcripts, finding mistakes throughout it which I made notes of. I had to go over this material since I was still representing myself pro se in the matter and had to prepare for my written final brief to be submitted before February 8, 2019. This whole ordeal has been physically, emotionally, and mentally exhausting but somehow, I had to keep moving with this, to bring out the truth and expose the wrong-doings which left me with a vast change in my lifestyle and careers I once had. Once I got home, I began compiling my research and documents to compose my packet containing over a dozen pages for my final closing statement for the union trial, and with that copies were sent to all parties involved along with affidavit proof of service upon them. I mailed all of them out certified mail after getting it notarized by my friend Mike who had helped me out anytime I asked for it.

Now it was time to focus back on day two of the Department of Labor hearing at the State Office Campus in Albany with the State's Industrial Board of Relations. This time around, my good friend Ed, who lives up north of Albany, came down on the morning of February 8, 2019 to be my resource person at the hearing and to carry my bin of documents into the building for me. The hearing started off right on time at about 9:30 a.m., and I had surprised the hearing officer with five more exhibits showing more adverse actions from my former employer. After a review of those, one of the packets was entered into evidence prior to the beginning of the Labor attorney's questioning of me. He had prepared a list of his questions for me as he did for his witness. Mine seemed to be the usual, nothing I did not already expect. Pretty simple stuff, I thought. Moments later, his witness, Jeff, who is one of the Department of Labor's Safety and Health Inspectors, as well as a Labor Investigator, had taken the stand and was sworn in by the hearing officer. The Labor attorney, who shall remain unnamed, began his list of questions for Jeff. These questions were pretty standard, most likely much of it he was most likely "coached" for prior to the hearing. During this time, I took several notes, trying to write as fast as I could, and I noticed the hearing officer peering over to what I was doing. He stopped the proceedings, went off the record, and said, "Mr. Harrington, I noticed you're writing on the back of some sheets of paper. Would you like a note pad?"

"Yes, that would be helpful," I replied. With Ed sitting on my right side behind me, he was able to take in the whole room of events and make mental notes of which he informed me about during breaks. Once the questioning for Jeff finished up, the hearing officer made a note of the time and motioned that we would all go on lunch for one hour and then return for my cross examination. Ed and I had gone downstairs to the basement of the building where a cafeteria was located along with a large dining room with tables that were spaced out pretty far apart. It took us about 20 minutes, then we went up to the lobby where I made some phone calls and returned some messages. I was starting to get my head into the game. We proceeded back to the hearing room where I had been seated and left all of my documents and evidence. I started to review the notes I had scribbled during Jeff's testimony so that I could formulate how I would proceed with my questioning of the state's witness. I did not prepare any questioning prior to the hearing, I am pretty good at bringing up points straight from memory. I gained that from my numerous years of doing public speaking. Once everyone returned to the room, the hearing was brought to order on the record and we had now resumed where we had left off at prior to lunch break. Much of my questioning began with what experience he had with the position he is working in now. I dug deeper into the prior years where he stated he had worked in security and for the sheriff's office. I continued further by asking the parties to refer to petitioner's exhibits as well as the state's. There were numerous contradictions in the Department of Labor's investigation which was appealed and why we were at this hearing to begin with. I was able to bring up facts regarding the validity of their findings. Surprisingly, when I had showed them logbook pages that Fishkill Correctional Facility had provided, Jeff did not really have a clear answer as to why illegal changes were made and why some portions had been blacked out. He stated they had the right to do such when it is not relevant material, however, there were blacked-out lines in my own incident that had been entered by the watch commander's office at Fishkill. I kept referring back to my notes as I paused between questions to gather my thoughts. A few times I had been objected to for compound questions and asked to simplify. With the fact that I am doing all of this work pro se by myself, it was severely mentally exhausting to go through all of this questioning I had for Jeff. In all, it took over 90 minutes in time for me to question him about numerous issues. The biggest of all was that he stated that their investigation was solely based off from the documents I submitted and that from the state. This was not an investigation. It was a review of documents, hearsay items, and yet nothing had been done to question its validity. It was easy to sit at the desk and shuffle this paperwork. Not one interview in person had been conducted, not one site visit to Fishkill Correctional Facility, and not one look at any of the other logbooks from my tour of duty. Additionally, I had requested phone records from the area in which the workplace violence incident occurred. They had failed in obtaining those as well. Their findings, as Jeff stated, were simply done by reviewing the employer's response. I was tearing the defense apart, limb by limb. For the record, Jeff's statements were barely audible for he had been told about 3-4 times to speak up louder, even the microphone in front of him could not pick up his sound. After I got done with my questioning, I had rested my case. The hearing officer stated that he had a few questions to ask of the witness. They had to do with my questioning and one in particular he had asked Jeff, "If Harrington's case says the color blue and the state's says red, what leads you to conclusion of the correct color?"

Jeff basically replied, "We base the findings on what material was provided by both parties and then make our decision from there." During questioning, Jeff stated the word "opinion" numerous times. The last time I checked, an opinion had no basis or finding in an official investigation. It is only that of the facts and when you have one state agency investigating another, a serious conflict of interest occurs.

One of the questions asked of me by the state's senior labor attorney was, "Mr. Harrington, what do you want to see in the end result of this case, what do you want to happen?"

I simply replied, "I do not know what the results of this hearing will bring, and for that matter to the individuals involved in this case who have violated several departmental regulations and state laws. That would be up to the entity handling this matter in the findings." We wrapped up the hearing with a 30-day time frame being set for me to submit a final closing statement. I told the hearing officer for the Industrial Board of Appeals I only needed two weeks and he smiled saying, "I will still give you 30 days regardless. Make sure you include a copy to the Department of Labor, there is no need for an affidavit of service." We shook hands and departed the building. Ed carried my documents for me to my vehicle and from there we went to grab a drink at a local establishment in Albany. My phone began to ring off the hook as numerous friends and supporters were seeking the big news of what happened at the hearing. It made for a quick ride home and once I arrived, I shed my three-piece suit and laid down giving my kids a big hug. My wife and I spoke about it in some detail but she herself was getting exhausted of how long this whole ordeal had carried on for. I definitely owe her a nice vacation away once we get through with this. It was now time to await decisions from both the Public Employee Relations Board and the Public Employee Safety and Health agencies for these cases. It would be then that press releases would be in the works to get the public aware of what has been occurring in this system-wide cover-up.

With February 8, 2019 now come and gone, I had finally received via USPS a large yellow manila envelope with no return address. I figured it to be something from Albany. As sure as it seemed, it turned out to be the final statement/argument from the Governor's Office of Employee Relations, written by the Acting General Counsel. Not only did it not contain a required hand signature, as any legal document of this type, but upon review of this 11-page document, I had found numerous spelling errors, inconsistencies, and other false statements claimed by GOER's office as it was addressed to the Assistant Director of the State's Public Employee Relations Board. As I mentioned previously, she had now been assigned to take over my case and Judge Rikers who oversaw all three days of this procedure, suddenly disappeared, not even working there anymore or listed on the website. I had showed this document to other officers familiar with labor law and civil service laws. What I could not believe, but I was not surprised about, was the fact that this document was composed on the deadline date and obviously with the deficiencies noted; it had been a rush job. This is something I had planned on keeping handy should there be an appeal on the findings. I have always said to myself that this should be handled at a federal level due to the state agencies involved having conflicts of interest. That's where the cover-ups and back-door deals happen. Albany is the biggest one of them all and when they tolerate it, this effect trickles down the pipe all the way to the smallest entity within the state's government.

Looking back on some emails that were sent to me, a colleague of mine, Dave, had sent me some information about a recent bulletin dated December 3, 2018 from the Governor's Office of Employee Relations in Albany. It appeared as if some changes had already started to take place due to the lower level cover-up of many discrimination cases that would often end up in court. The state only reacts to situations.

They do not issue such memos just for the sake of it, something, like my own case, had to have happened in order for such order to be handed down to each state agency. As I said before, for every action there is a reaction. The memorandum was short and read:

"Effective December 1, 2018, all complaints of protected class employment discrimination will be investigated by the Governor's Office of Employee Relations (GOER) Anti-Discrimination Investigations Division. If you have any questions about what constitutes protected class employment discrimination, please refer to the Equal Employment Opportunity Rights and Responsibilities Handbook for New York State Employees (*Handbook*) located at https://goer.ny.gov/equal-employment-opportunity-rights-and-responsibilities-handbook-employees-new-york-state-agencies, and at www.doccs.ny.gov. The handbook is the state's anti-discrimination policy."

It had been almost two weeks from my prior contact to both the Retirement System and Albany Personnel and still no response from DOCCS personnel in Albany regarding the issuance of my retirement credentials. Prior to this date, numerous phone conversations had taken place and that led to certified mail being sent out to both Fishkill Correctional Facility and to the Director of Personnel in Albany. I was awarded disability retirement on October 15, 2018 and even with confirmation from the Comptroller's Office, and with help from Mike in the State's Retirement System, the DOCCS Personnel Director, Kelly, had continued with deliberate ignorance to avoid that I had legitimately retired and DOCCS refused to issue such credentials that I was entitled to for my 23 years of state service. Speaking to others who went on retirement due to disability, they did not face similar circumstances. Their credentials had come available to them in a rather expedient manner. It was obvious that due to my actions against my employer and other state agencies for numerous discrimination and adverse actions, this was their last attempt to play hard ball with me. Coincidentally, this also remained the fact with my off-duty weapon that was still being held by Fishkill.

Just a few days later, I received a call from a representative at the Department of Corrections and Community Supervision's Personnel Office in Albany. The woman calling sounded cheerful, so I unexpectedly did not know what the call was immediately in reference to. After some short conversation, she notified me that after review of my request for my retirement credentials, it had finally been approved that they would be mailing me my retirement certificate and badge. After the past four months since retirement, numerous phone calls, emails, and letters had been completed with the assistance of Mike at the State's Disability Retirement System in coordination with the Comptroller's Office in Albany. It had come as good news to me, finally one step closer to getting much of this behind me. As a friend and past colleague mentioned, "Great job! Persistence pays off, my friend!" to which I replied in my message, "So far it does, thanks, Commish." I had inquired at the time about my photo ID that accompanies the badge and she had no knowledge of it even though they previously directed me to go to Albany to get it, they would look into the matter and get back to me by phone.

It was now March 6, 2019 and I had to run to the post office to sign for a certified package sent to me by the Department of Corrections. I had a positive inclination as to its contents, but I reserved those thoughts since up until this point, they have not done anything beneficial in my favor. Once I opened up the packet, I found a brand-new shiny gold retirement badge and a photo ID card with a leather wallet and what was a diploma style hard-cover binder with the Corrections logo on it, and inside was both a certificate of appreciation and a letter from the Acting Commissioner, who also signed both of these items. The first part of the letter opened up by stating: "This is to acknowledge your decision to retire from the position of Correction Officer with the Department of Corrections and Community Supervision on October 15, 2018, after 23 years of state service." It read on like the usual form letter ending with "Best wishes for a happy and healthy retirement." Hardly the case, I thought, here it is five months later and I now just received my credentials. Technically with 23 years of service, you don't automatically get to make the decision to retire unless certain conditions are met. I did not exactly choose to retire, I was forced to due to my numerous injuries. As for being happy and healthy, this is hardly the case, but I can only hope for the best. Nobody, not even the Acting Commissioner, has a glass crystal ball and can see into one's future. After what I have been through, it will take a vast amount of time to get over it. Every day I see the scars endured from the surgeries due to my work-related orthopedic injuries, I am reminded of those haunting memories. While I was thankful that I finally received and was acknowledged for my retirement as I was entitled to just as any other person on the job, this certificate and letter would be put into storage. I am not exactly in a rush to go frame these and hang them up with my other awards.

A copy of my Retirement Certificate that finally came over five months later of fighting for what was rightfully mine. This came in the mail with the badge and ID as well. Photo by P. Harrington.

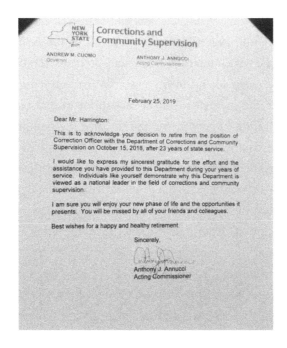

A final official acknowledgment that I was indeed retired. This was in a binder similar to a graduation diploma. I will not be framing this as a reminder of all I had to do for it, but certainly will remain in my office to reflect upon. Photo by P. Harrington.

Recently, I had been directed to go to another state independent medical exam in Albany to see Dr. Copps, who was a psychiatrist. I had done a review of him online, looking at his poor ratings given by his regular patients, and I was skeptical of attending a session exam with him. I had asked my insurance case handler if she could reschedule me with someone else but her reply was, "No, you are not allowed to choose who you see for these exams. You are being directed to report on time for your appointment." The State's Insurance Fund had sent me there for him to review the medications I was taking for my symptoms which included pain management. I had walked into the office area and was greeted by a receptionist, after she checked for my name in the computer, she took my driver's license and made a copy of it for their file. I had got there early since it was about an 80-mile trip one way. Within 15 minutes of my arrival, Dr. Copps had taken me into the office where I sat down adjacent to him, face to face. I had gone to this exam by myself this time. He had his computer on and I observed on the screen some of my case files. Dr. Copps reported that he had spent six hours reviewing the paperwork on my case. He began to ask me some questions and before I knew it, we were into the incidents which were rehashed and had triggered some of my ongoing issues. I had gone into specific details about all of the turmoil which I had faced. He had reviewed numerous notes and progress reports from multiple doctors who I had been seeing in my case. We had gotten into the depths of the timeline since the incident of 2017, and prior to that dating back to my childhood days. Before I knew it, we had finished up the interview and I was on my way out. I decided to grab lunch at the nearby mall before the drive home. It had been about two weeks, maybe give or take a few days, and in the mail I received a copy of the 19-page report from Dr. Copps. I reviewed it twice in its entirety, along with my wife, and I had found well over a dozen discrepancies within it. How could such details become disorienting for a professional doctor who does these exams on a regular basis for the State Insurance Fund? I am told by other doctors I see for treatments that most of the time before the appointment, they already have their reports filled out based on the case files they review. It's a basic quick fill-in-the-blanks type of exam. This reminded me of other exams I had been sent to in which the same had been occurring during the interviewing. The whole system is a sham. It's all about the money, about getting paid. No one cares really in the end, they only care for themselves. They might give the appearance of caring in the performance of their duties, but it is for certain that this reality exists. I highlighted the areas of sections contained in the exam report and typed up an email to notate in detail the conflicting facts that were placed in the report by Dr. Copps. It was sent off to my law firm and the State Insurance Fund for review. Almost immediately I got a call back from Warren at my law firm telling me how brilliantly it was written and that it appeared to be the work of an attorney. I guess with all of my past paralegal experience and representing myself pro se in my cases, has given me the ability to express the language and legalities of local and state laws. But for now, I will await my next scheduled Workers' Compensation Board hearing, and the decisions to come from both the Public Employee Relations Board hearing as well as the Industrial Board of Appeals with the case against the Department of Labor and Public Employee Safety and Health. For sure I will be kept busy with my weekly average of 6-8 medical appointments until then.

I received an email today that was sent to me from Dave stating: "You must have shook the bush somewhere, we just got reissued the harassment in the workplace order." Attached to it was a file from the State's Governor's Office of Employee Relations, titled "Executive Order 187," Ensuring Diversity and Inclusion and Combating Harassment and Discrimination in the Workplace. To further promote the effective, complete and timely investigation of complaints of employment discrimination harassment and to ensure that such investigations are not subject to any potential conflicts of interest, the Governor today signed an Executive Order directing the Governor's Office of Employee Relations (GOER) to be the primary entity responsible for conducting all investigations into such complaints filed by employees, contractors, interns or other persons engaged in employment for state agencies. Any person engaged in employment for state agencies will continue to have the right to additionally file complaints with the Inspector General's office who may conduct investigations into conduct that may amount to fraud, abuse, criminal activity, conflicts of interest, abuses of office, or waste. The change will be effective December 1, 2018, and will involve staffing adjustment to ensure that GOER has the full staff it needs to accomplish its investigatory goals. The change will also include updated training on the process for all investigative staff, as well as all agency staff that are involved in address claims of discrimination and harassment. This tasks the Chief Diversity Officer and the Commissioner of Civil Service with responsibility for statewide workforce diversity and inclusion. Today's executive order directs the establishment of the Office of Diversity Management within the Department of Civil Service. The Office of Diversity Management shall be responsible for assisting the Commissioner of Civil Service and the State's Chief Diversity Officer in the effective development and implementation of statewide diversity and inclusion plans, policies and programs. Building on Governor Cuomo's legacy of expanding opportunities for New Yorkers and the recommendations of the Governor's Advisory Council on Diversity and Inclusion, the Executive Order tasks the Chief Diversity Officer and the Commissioner of Civil Service with the creation of statewide Diversity and Inclusion guidelines by December 31, 2018, and with overseeing effective implementation of agency-specific plans. The executive order also creates an Executive Committee for Diversity and Inclusion to advise the Governor, the Chief Diversity Officer, and the Commissioner of Civil Service in the formulation and coordination of plans, policies and programs relating to diversity and inclusion in all state departments and agencies, and in ensuring the effective implementation of such initiatives. In my case, I would call this a day late and a dollar short, but this is the #1 reason I fought this through anyhow. I wanted change in the system. For too many years I have both witnessed and been a victim of the abuse that is widespread throughout DOCCS' prison system. This seems to only be the beginning of changes being made and with that the new coming of measures to be put in place to deal with these problems. No more of the "good 'ole boys club" will be found if and when the state finally puts the hammer down on this old culture and way of going about routine business inside the prison system. The bullying does not stop at the school level, unfortunately it is carried past it and into the prison system and has so for decades.

Today, I got a call back from the State's Attorney General's Office and spoke to one of Assistant Attorney General lawyers who would be representing me in the 2015 homicide case from the incident at Fishkill Correctional Facility. I had asked her for a follow-up since I had not heard anything as to what was going on. She informed me that the case was still ongoing, but that they were in discovery and that the law firm representing the plaintiff's estate had been dragging their heels and the state had made some motions for dismissals. Soon the time would come when we would be called in for depositions prior to the trial which was planned to be heard by the Southern

District of New York in Manhattan. She also told me we would be notified in advance and called in to meet with them so we could prepare for the next step and to familiarize ourselves with the details of this incident which happened four years ago. In the meantime, this continued to become harder on my family situation. Because of my depression, PTSD, stress and anxiety issues, not to mention my nine injury cases in which I had so many medical appointments for, I had been falling short on my ability to keep up with my marriage. I will admit, it was beyond my ability to absorb anyone else's issues, including that of my wife. I had a hard time listening and trying to resolve her feelings and frustrations when I could barely deal with my own. It was not looking good for us on the home front. Anyone being in my shoes who had my personality would equally find it extremely challenging to add this to your plate. I thought I was doing the right thing, just to lose it all, everything I had worked for. My home, my successful business venture, my community leadership, my family, it had all begun to dissipate from the day of May 9, 2017 when this incident took place. These incidents continue to be covered up. But now I am told that soon Fishkill officers will be wearing body cameras. That's laughable. They can't even keep a unit radio working for one shift without the battery dying waiting for a replacement that could take an hour or better in some cases. Albany was of no help either. Cuomo was busy giving himself a pay raise and deciding which prisons to close next. They had enough of their own worries and I was just one person.

I also recently received the CD of the transcripts of my appeal against the State's Department of Labor. I had issues trying to open the files so I contacted the Industrial Board of Appeals and asked for them to possibly send me a hard copy, but that could not be done without cost. Literally hundreds of pages at 25 cents per page would add up pretty fast. I suggested that they could be put on a USB, but the office manager told me that they did not have them and said, "Would you like me to go out and buy one so I can do that for you?" My reply was simply that I could not believe a government agency's office did not have any USBs on inventory. In this day and age, there are rarely any computers that come with drives on them anymore for DVD or CDs. So my last request would be to simply email me and within an hour I had the files sent to me via email and readily available to read over without any issues.

Later that day after an appointment, I was waiting for my vehicle to get worked on and a friend of mine had approached me. Surprised, I turned around without expecting him. We had a little conversation about how my incident with Thompson continues to come up in the gossip columns within the prison system. Recently, a walking tour of a local prison facility in Ulster County was done and Thompson's brother-in-law, Mallory, who is still the Union's Vice President, was part of that visit to the facility to look at some issues that had been reported. There had been an entourage and the subject of an incident regarding one similar to mine had become the topic amongst the group. Mallory had stated that it is not a good idea for one officer to approach another officer about how clean they keep their areas and work stations. "How would that be an issue?" another had asked of Mallory.

"Well, you see, there's this guy Harrington who had an incident with another officer over an incident like this. The officer had left a threatening note in his logbook and it became a bigger issue and that there had been an allegation of being pushed or something like that. Now he's retired out on 3/4 disability." After hearing that, it started to pique my interest. I was hardly infuriated by this matter, it is so typical in Corrections for rumors to get around and get mixed up quicker than your frozen beverage in a blender. In fact, the issue is so bad that during the academy they gave us training about how to handle it and deal with those issues. But one thing I did comment to my friend was that Mallory should know better, nobody can go out on 3/4 disability injury and retire unless it was inmate related, of which I had several cases involving surgery and hospital admissions for that led to the state's decision to retire me on disability. Not for anything, but at the time I worked that post, there was no such logbook in my office as one was not required at the time. I had recently spoken to some colleagues who indicated that Fishkill's correction officers will be required to start wearing body cameras. This comes under regulation per the New York State Senate's Bill Number S4437. This would affect many prisons in New York. Body cameras worn by law enforcement officers have been shown to improve safety, provide meaningful oversight of officer interactions with civilians, and reduce the number of use of force incidents in nearly every criminal justice organization that has tried them. From large police departments to small local jails, body cameras have produced measurable results and have saved money, lives, and heartache. In order to employ body cameras successfully, there must be sound policies behind their usage, ensuring that the cameras are on during critical encounters and that the footage is accessible when needed. This bill would require DOCCS to initiate a body camera pilot program in a NYS correctional facility to help evaluate such cameras as tools to increase facility safety. DOCCS could work out the protocols necessary to implement the program on a larger scale should the cameras prove to be effective. Ironically, the problem with the handheld radios has existed for numerous years. There was always an issue with batteries being worn out and become inoperable sometimes even an hour after going on duty. Fishkill's response to the problem would be to add to the job description of another officer who had a mobile post to make rounds in areas to replace these batteries as needed. Each and every time my radio went dead, I would make an entry in the logbook about the issue and the time I had notified the arsenal that I needed a replacement.

Depending on the ongoing routines of the shift, it could be less than 15 minutes until a replacement would arrive, sometimes up to an hour or more. In some areas of the prison where there is no phone close by, that radio is your lifeline. It also serves as an information source for inmate movement. When you do not have this information, sometimes you must reply on a nearby post to advise you of such announcements over the radio. So now here comes another battery-operated device which is capable of recording up to four hours. It is intended only to be activated when you are dealing with an inmate. These cameras, when attached to the flimsy strength of the uniform shirt, can and will fall off easily when running to an incident or when there is an altercation. At this point, this is only a pilot program. According to the Senate's bill, no less than 50 officers per shift will wear and utilize these cameras. In Fishkill alone, there are over 60 housing units not counting the various areas such as yards, mess hall, gymnasium, medical, school, and religious areas among numerous other checkpoints and locations where inmates are. The general attitude toward this new change is being taken slightly given the fact that with the camera recording, everyone changes their demeanor knowing that they are being watched. Inmates may use it as a way knowing the camera is facing them only so psychologically they may intend to use it toward their advantage.

After numerous lawsuits against the state at Fishkill's Prison in the last decade by inmates who alleged that they had been physically assaulted, there were countless settlements done. The state intends to curb this trend by applying body cameras. It is now up to them to record and document such incidents at a significant cost. There appears to be issues with the body camera use since they were first implemented. It has been reported to me by a supervisor at Fishkill that only sergeants and officers will wear them. Recently, one officer inadvertently forgot to turn his camera on during an incident and he was under investigation for disciplinary action by the administration. These cameras that are used in an incident are turned in and as per the department's new directive on them, nobody below the rank of captain may review the footage. This is an effort to keep those involved from collaborating their reports along with what is shown in the footage. So if one's report does not match up to the details, it sets up entrapment should that individual not recall every single detail. They should be allowed to review their actions, after all, it is their assigned body camera, and regardless, you can always change a report, but you cannot change a video. What's done is done. This just puts into concrete that the administration is out to protect their asses and not that of the sergeants or officers involved and on video. Like I have said earlier, there needs to be permanent, hard-wired security cameras mounted inside the many blind spots and areas needed inside Fishkill's buildings. This could be the beginning of the end for many hard-working well-intended officers who may make a mistake in their written reports. When I was involved in many incidents, there were no body cameras then. I can recall numerous times that I needed to alter or amend my written reports so that it matched up to the watch commander's report to the command center in Albany following the "unusual incident." Not for nothing, but it is my name signed on the report, not theirs.

More updates came in for my repeated attempts to follow up with Fishkill's administration, to include Superintendent Shields. I had written him a letter to point out the fact that I had documented numerous days and times of which I had called the facility to speak to Deputy Superintendent Oblinski. Every single time I would end up getting his secretaries. At one point they even agreed with me that they could not believe how long this was taking and that it should have been done already. This was the same response I got from the gun dealer as well. Within 10 days or so, I got a reply from Superintendent Shields stating:

"This letter is in response to your April 9, 2019 letter to my office. Please understand that the storing of this weapon at the facility is an inconvenience. We would like nothing more than to resolve this matter. The weapon in question was not confiscated, you are no longer able to legally possess this weapon. Your efforts to transfer this weapon to C.O. JR in September of 2018 was not approved because Officer JR failed to provide the necessary background check required by law. The DSS has spoken to you regarding the disposition of this weapon. Clear direction has been given to you on how to resolve this issue. You must either obtain a NYS Pistol Permit or transfer the weapon to another individual that can legally possess it. This individual must have a Federal Firearm License or a Pistol Permit C4 with the necessary background check as required by law. The DSS has spoken to that firearms dealer and informed them that the facility would require their information. The representative was advised to contact the facility but has failed to do so. When you meet the above-mentioned requirements, please contact the DSS so arrangements can be made. Signed, Superintendent Shields."

Further information was sent to me by one of the department's technical specialists. Sgt. Larry in Special Ops was sent a copy of my letter to the facility. He forwarded it onto this specialist who emailed me back, telling me that I need to quit playing the "blame game" and to follow the instructions given to me in order to precipitate this process. After reading that, I sent him a reply in which he responded briefly with DSS Oblinski's official email address. None of the responses I received from Superintendent Shields or the Central Office in Albany were factual. It was a smoke screen to cover up their misdeeds. This for certain was deliberate ignorance on their part. Since September 2018, I have been following the instructions given to me and not once, not even on my phone records, does it show a call from Fishkill Correctional Facility as they claimed several times. This continues to be an adverse action which is typical and common when any staff report incidents to outside agencies. Until this current date now in May 2019, no action has yet to be taken to get this firearm released. It's as simple as the facility setting up an appointment for us to go there and sign out the weapon to be turned over to the gun dealer.

My 9 mm off-duty hand gun that I had carried for 90% of my 23-year career. It took over nine months to get Fishkill Correctional Facility to release it to Wallkill River Small Arms in Wallkill, New York, for sale now that I no longer had Peace Officer Status to carry off-duty. Photo by P. Harrington with cooperation of Wallkill River Small Arms.

Another Workers' Compensation Board hearing was held on May 8th. This time it was a "virtual hearing" done by video and/or telephone loud speaker. All parties including both of my law firms, the State Insurance Fund and the

Board's judge were present. The state has begun closing down the locations and offices that conduct these hearings. It saves on time, typical building costs, security, utilities as well as travel for them to do it this way. During this hearing I was on the phone loud speaker but I could not see anyone there. A few brief questions were asked of me but we did not get done what I had hoped to. The State Insurance Fund requested an extension to get the deposition done from another one of my orthopedic surgeons. The board concurred with their request and also gave them 60 days to send me in for another independent medical exam regarding my hearing loss that he found prima facie medical evidence on. I had already been to one IME exam for my hearing up in Albany. This makes no sense to send me again but a call to my lawyer Warren led to his direction for me to not dispute this and to go if directed to do so. This long process with Workers' Compensation usually concludes with a Section 32 Permanency Hearing. This is where all come to a final decision on the percentage of disability I have for my numerous injuries. I am told this should be occurring this summer. I just want to get this over with and behind me so that I can manage my own health care without the constant say of the insurance fund on authorizations for testing, treatment, and medications, etc.

It has been several months since I had taken the trip to work at Fishkill Prison on the routes through Beacon as I used to do. Some would call it a trip down memory lane but I felt quite the opposite. As much as those who worked there felt depressed about having to go to work at this facility, I had that plus the anxiety of having to deal with the unknown once I got there. I had Frank, the firearms dealer from Wallkill River Small Arms following behind me so he would know the direction on where to go and park, etc. Upon arrival at my scheduled appointment time with Deputy Superintendent Oblinski, I had called ahead of our arrival to advise him we were enroute. We walked up to the entrance of the administration building. We showed out ID cards and signed in to the visitors' log.

Where I once entered on a daily basis, surprisingly made me feel like I had never been there before. It was a different perspective, a different vibe. As we waited for the paperwork to be shuffled for me to fill out and sign, the firearms dealer and I made for some small talk as I explained why things worked the way they did in his observations at the facility. It was sort of an unofficial unguided tour. Soon we had been directed to wait outside by the arsenal window gun port. The window is tinted very dark, so dark, Cuomo wouldn't let that tint pass on a New York State Inspection. A sliding metal drawer, like the kind you see at a drive-through bank, was used to receive or turn in weapons. It seemed forever that we waited. As we were casually talking, I was leaning over the metal railing looking out toward the parking lot. Low and behold, talk about timing and coincidence.

Walking up to the parking lot carrying some bags was Thompson's wife who worked there as a secretary. She made eye contact from afar but as she got closer to the front entrance to go inside, she did not look at me or say anything. With over 30 minutes having passed, the dealer looked at me saying, "They knew we were coming, there is no way there is that much delay with getting the key to unlock this. I never have to go through this with others. Why are they doing this to you?" I responded back with a watered-down version of what had occurred and that they had been put through a few investigations due to my complaint of the workplace violence incident and that this whole ordeal is not over with yet. It was plain and simple we both thought, this was one of the ways to make life difficult for me as a payback. After all, it had been nine months and change that it took in all efforts to retrieve my 9-mm weapon with its two clips and about 18 rounds of ammunition with a leather belt holster. It was now in the hands of the firearms dealer where it will be displayed in his showcase for sale. I personally think it should be put up in a museum showcase as a big part of this story and how it all occurred.

The other day, I ran into two civilian employees that use to work at Fishkill. One was the facility locksmith, the other a head cook. We saw each other at different locations. The conversations were quite interesting. The locksmith no longer works at Fishkill, he transferred out. Nobody knew better about the facility's locking or security systems than he did. For a facility as large as Fishkill, they only had one locksmith whereas facilities in the region would have two/three working and available for full coverage. As usual, he too felt the same about how operations at Fishkill are sliding downhill quickly. He was overworked and could not get a raise. He had a family to support and thought best of their needs. It was not safe at Fishkill anymore so he transferred out to another state prison within an hour's drive. "My blood pressure and stress levels are down considerably, my attitude has improved and I actually love where I work. I have the full support from administration, and the staff there are decent people to work with," he stated. I agreed with him that he had made a good move. He told me he has been keeping up on my progress now that I am retired throughout social media. We both had our hands full of some items at the store so we checked out and parted ways with the promise to keep in touch. Later that day, I had to make a stop to pick up something at the mall and I had run into the civilian cook, who still works at Fishkill. He told me it was great to see me and glad that I was doing somewhat better. I had asked him about how things were going in Fishkill. While at the current time I try not to think of that dreaded environment, I am still concerned about some of my friends and fellow colleagues who still work there. "It is getting bad," he said, so many new faces and he made a slicing motion with his finger going across his neck to indicate that so many staff are going out of work because of the violence and cover-ups. He told me he had about two years left to finish up so he could retire. I told him it might not be worth it, perhaps a transfer, but one thing was for sure, he needed to get out of there like anyone else. I know of some bosses in there as well on other shifts who all hate it there. They tell me they are counting down their days until retirement and trying to burn as much vacation time they can to stay out of that environment at Fishkill. We were both soon on our way and said goodbye, wishing each other well. I only hope the best for those that deserve it inside that place. I hate to say it but something major could happen there soon, and this wouldn't be an "I told you so," just a prediction that contained all of the right issues that needed to be in place for such an incident to occur.

Speaking of running into former co-workers, I had recently attended a long-time friend who had reached his 25 years of service at another prison facility in New York State Corrections. We were at a popular establishment in New Paltz where many of his co-workers, family and friends had gathered. It was a good time catching up to some of the people I knew there. One person in particular, who I used to work with as an officer at Fishkill back in 2000, also attended the party. She had flown up the ranks and is now superintendent at a maximum security prison in this area. At first we did not recognize each other but she approached me asking me if I recalled who she was. It took me a second but it popped in my mind as soon as she mentioned the time that Cardinal Dolan had visited Fishkill and I was assigned to do all of the photography while he was there on his tour. She had been assigned there as a deputy superintendent. We got into conversation about the current environment within the department. I told her it was good that she was not assigned to Clinton Prison upstate where the infamous escape of David Sweat

337

and Richard Matt had taken place in June of 2015. Clinton is having huge problems right now with violence within its walls between rival prisoner gangs. One thing that stood out in our conversation was when she mentioned, "Paul, there is nothing we can do right now to make our own decisions in the prisons, we are like puppets. The Governor is still mad at us about the escape and has put Albany in charge of us." Without a doubt in my mind, I believed what she said. It was evident when I was working in the system until 2017 when I went out on disability from my work-related injuries. The superintendents can't make decisions without getting the ok from the upper ranks at the Corrections Command Center at Building 9 in Albany. Without being there to see the situation for themselves, they rely on a summarized listing of the incident to make their decision on authorizing the prison superintendents on what they can do. That's kind of like what happened with Clinton Prison just days before the escape when Albany refused to permit the superintendent to lock down the facility and to bring in extra staff to search the entire areas. This department has always been reactive, never proactive, and probably will always be. It's all about money, budgets, etc. Soon enough, it's going to be an officer's life. As if the amount of staff suicides is not enough to bring changes to the table.

Speaking of retirement, I had conversations with a number of officers who are retired and already received their retroactive back pay after the new contract had been ratified between the union and the state. Since I have been retired for numerous months now, I had wondered how come I did not get mine yet. I decided to make a call to the Payroll Office at Fishkill's Prison Administration. Our conversation was brief and after looking me up, she replied to me, "You're still listed as terminated, medically terminated, so you're not on the list to get the retro check. You might want to call the union in Albany so here is their number…get a pen, here it is…" After we hung up, I decided to get payroll in Albany on the line. Thinking perhaps maybe they had my status listed correctly, I thought wrong. Not only would the older lady I spoke to on the phone not give me her first name for the record, she would not give me the direct extension to their office so I would not have to go through the switchboard again. She was very rude and uncooperative. I now understand the frustrations of the general public who call to make inquiries with these agencies and have to deal with such nonsense. At that point I had followed those instructions from Fishkill's Payroll Office and ended up calling the guy who runs the retiree program for COPBA. Right away he was very blunt toward me, told me I had called "You might better call Vice President Mallory who is making a list of those still waiting on retro checks." One thing was for sure I thought, I am not going to call him, I am better off putting it in writing and sending him an email. After speaking to Al and some other colleagues, I sent Mallory an email requesting that I be placed on such list and gave him information about my retirement status. Not expecting much of a reply back that soon, he surprised me within a couple hours; he wrote back a simple phrase: "I'll add you to the list." I decided while I was at it to type up letters to both New York's PERB and PESH to inquire about the status of the hearings held earlier this year.

These decisions had yet to have been made and handed down, as well as to be posted to their individual website. I asked them about the process and informed them that these matters were of timeliness concerns due to further actions to be taken. At this point, it was a game of sitting back to wait and see. Nothing moves fast in New York's government agencies, except on a Friday when they are all hitting the thruway to get their weekends started. The Officer's Union's contract had expired in 2016, and staff had been working without a contact for two years. It had finally been ratified once they came up with the best possible deal they could get its membership. I had been on the payroll until September of 2018. In the contract those that had resigned and had been terminated, were not entitled to back wages which we refer to as "retro." I had heard that all those currently working had received their retro and many who had retired had done so as well. I decided to call Fishkill's Payroll Office up and spoke to them about the status of my back pay. After a few moments, the lady got back on the phone saying, "We still have you listed as terminated, medically terminated."

I said, "That can't be, I have a retirement number, certificates of retirement, my retirement badge and ID, and plus, I have been collecting retirement checks for the last 8 months."

I am not feeling confident about it but will give it some time to see how it works out. I am in no emergency to get it, but certainly I am entitled to it and deserve it when everyone else gets them.

Today I met with three officials of the State's Attorney General's Office out of New York City. Those that would be representing us at trial in the Federal Court, Southern District of New York, wanted to meet with each of the officers involved with the 2015 homicide at Fishkill. They had to travel the whole region, visiting numerous prisons and locations to catch up to us. I had brought a bounty of documentation, much of it not needed, however I had forgotten my folder with the documents for the homicide case. I called home and had my wife go into the files and pull out the folder to bring it down to our location where we met, not too far from my house. Within minutes, she arrived and I was able to pull out evidence needed to back up my statements. Much information discussed was what I had taken a part of that night, and the issues at the hospital with BCI Forensics, as well as the incident in its full detail upon my arrival to the unit in which the Code 10 emergency had been called over the radios. I had felt some stress and anxiety prior to our meeting, and this was not even the deposition. I had attended by myself with the three representatives sitting around me all asking questions and separately taking notes.

Basically, it was a review of the federal grand jury testimony from months ago with additional questions asked about my ongoing case regarding the department, the union, and the facility in reference to the workplace violence incident with Thompson. They looked over much of that documentation from other agencies. The #1 question that Marie, the Assistant Attorney General, had for me was whether or not I would have issues testifying regardless of my ongoing cases. The last thing they needed was someone turning state's evidence. I explained to her that these issues had nothing to do with the incident going to trial and that I would testify just as I did at the federal grand jury. We were there in this interview for nearly 150 minutes. It had to be cut short due to their train schedule back to New York City. I was told we would have to meet again.

They mentioned I had very organized files of records and to keep them handy for the next meeting. Prior to our departure, they had me sign two forms to release medical records regarding the incident. I was also told by one of the gentlemen not to delete anything off my social media pages regarding this subject matter. Our next meeting was going to be soon but no date was scheduled. There were still more questions they had for me that went into depth about the facility. They told me depositions were not expected to begin until at least the end of the year. I thought to myself this was going to take forever before the case was over and decided. Like others, we just all wanted this behind us. So many had hardships over the entire incident, and as I did in October of 2017, I had severe PTSD from this as well as other cases, and I nearly took my life with a Savage Arms 12-gauge shotgun. They all got to see the photos from the video cameras we have around our house with the gun barrel resting on my forehead.

To their shock and dismay, I explained to them that many officers had taken their lives by suicide during my two plus decades assigned at Fishkill. There was no assigned departmental psychologist at the facility to deal with staff trauma. Just an Employee Assistance Program Officer who handed you a list of telephone numbers to call. The psychologist on site at Fishkill was there strictly for the inmates, although I had tried to talk to them a few times as they strolled past my checkpoint. They did not deal with staff. I gathered my records and left to go home after our meeting ended. It was not a happy day for me, but nice at arrive home to my children and two dogs.

I had a busy week coming up. It seemed none of this was going to go away anytime soon. On the calendar I had seven medical appointments, a workers' compensation hearing, and another state independent medical exam for my knees and low back up in Poughkeepsie. A ruling had already been made in regards to my injuries and conditions of those orthopedic areas but they were sending me back again for another exam with the same state doctor I had seen previously for this issue. Now that the medical depositions had been done, I could only conclude that this was for a final opinion prior to the permanency judgment in which we would be closing out the nine injury cases and being awarded a settlement in the near future. I was also waiting on the upcoming board decisions from the administrative hearings held last season.

On July 30th, I was on my way home from seeing my ENT for the work-related Thompson case injury in Middletown at Crystal Run. I had given her an update from my last hearing and I was having incredible difficulties getting my prior audiograms submitted. I had delivered them via email numerous times in June 2018 over a year ago, to my lawyers. It has been a battle getting my treatments approved for what the Workers' Compensation Board judge found as prima facie medical evidence that this was related to the incident. I had called up Warren two days before the hearing to go over what I would need to be prepared for. He did not seem very concerned with this hearing telling me not to worry. Later, as the hearing began, Warren had sent one of his younger newer guys to represent my case. I ended up advocating on my behalf and kept interjecting when the state spoke about their case files, and what was given to the board.

There were so many errors in their statements and nothing was being said by my new lawyer. The judge allowed me to explain issues and I stressed to the board that these prior audiograms, which they have been asking for us to produce many times, still did not appear. My new guy was shuffling files and did not have them. So with that, I was told this issue would be held in abeyance until the next hearing. Dr. Feldman and I had finished up our discussion about the notice of decision issued from the hearing and had me scheduled for a follow-up. I got in my vehicle and headed home. As I got off Interstate 84 and headed north on Route 300 almost home, I was about two miles away when I noticed a commotion in traffic.

I pulled around because I noticed that there were a lot of people out of their vehicles. It did not take long for me to see what was going on. An older gentleman had been pulled out of his car by other motorists since he was unresponsive. Others called 911. No emergency services had arrived yet. My past training kicked in and I grabbed my first aid kit, and working alongside an off-duty West Point Firefighter, he did numerous compressions as I took out my CPR mask and checked the man's mouth for any obstructions and began mouth to mouth. Numerous police from Town of Newburgh and State Police arrived to control the crowds and traffic, allowing us to continue our efforts. It seemed forever but under five minutes, EMS arrived and took over. From what I hear, he had been worked on for a long time by medics. The ambulance pulled away to rush to the hospital where after about an hour at the emergency room, he passed away. We all tried.

I had been on my knees kneeling down and it was extremely painful but what had to be done was done. It soon became a crime scene, traffic was crazy as they closed down the road for the Police I.D. Unit to document the scene. Apparently, there had been some contraband found in the car that turned this into a police investigation. A lot of us there turned and shook hands as total strangers. We got to meet people in a way that we will remember for times to come. It took those of us involved over an hour to get out of there after speaking to police investigators. My wife had come to the scene with bottled water that was sorely needed. It had to be about 95 degrees outside and no shade where we were. Soon it was all wrapped up and I was finally on my way home.

Days later, I showed up to my monthly appointment with my pain management doctor at Cornwall Hospital. I had been seeing this staff for several months now where I had been prescribed pain medications, ordered a new medical back brace, and given epidural shots in my low back and my neck as well as my shoulders. It was an early morning appointment, straight from home after breakfast, arriving on time, had my vitals taken and then waited to be called in to see the doctor. We spoke briefly about my pain levels as I sat across his desk from him, with his nurse to the right of me by the door overlooking the exam. "I'm afraid we had a bit of bad news here, Paul, your urinalysis from May came back positive for THC marijuana." I looked at him with a brief pause, my jaw dropping as I said, "No way this can be right, I have never done any illegal drugs and have always been responsible with my medications. I swear that I have never done this, I want to challenge the legitimacy of this testing, done by Millennium Health in San Diego, California." I asked for an immediate copy of this to send to my law firms. It was referred to as a radar report. I was given another drug test right then on the spot, with the doctor telling me if this one comes out negative, we will go back and see where we can start back on your treatments. If not, this can be a violation of your narcotics contract, you would lose your pain prescriptions and further treatments. I could not have been more concerned and as soon as I left and got in the car, I contacted Dr. Habif where I had been getting the CBD oil 1000 mg from on numerous occasions. At that time, Dr. Habif got back to me and said yes, it does contain trace amounts of THC in it. "I never knew that, I was under the impression this was only hemp seed oil, this is not prescribed and you can buy it everywhere these days." Speaking later on that day with Dr. Ogulnick, he did some research and found out my numbers that showed up (between 15–21 nanograms) were bottom of the barrel low and had to been positive from the CBD oil. Anyone actually consuming THC marijuana would be much, much higher than that. "50 nanograms is the presumptive to trigger a positive result, therefore your numbers do not indicate actual use and could quite be a possible false positive result," mentioned Dr. Ogulnick. When I got home, I had taken a urine drug test my wife picked up for me at Walgreens, that too, being 99.9% accurate, came out negative. Additionally, my law firm in White Plains who is assisting Warren with my injury cases sent me several links of pages showing the medications I was prescribed could trigger a result as this. At this point I was pretty stressed out about the whole thing. I told all of my family, everyone who knows me are aware that I am not ever involved with illegal drugs. I was actually quite upset with pain management for pushing this test result without considering its low numbers as indicated above.

I stayed pretty busy this month, summer has flown by fast. Just finished up putting the kids' supplies in their book bags that came in the mail. Looking at my calendar, I still had the usual 18-20 appointments this month, a far cry from the 30-35 I used to do for several months straight.

Hard to believe all this time has passed already. I am trying to get through my cases. Right now, my workload involved four law firms and multiple state agencies, nine workers' compensation injury cases, three personal injury lawsuits, and two administrative pro se hearings against the state, not including the upcoming social security hearing and the homicide civil rights suit in Federal Court, Southern District of New York. Between this and all of my medical appointments, it's a full-time job. But speaking of jobs, my latest independent medical exam by Dr. Schoolman once again showed that I could not work and sedentary jobs for more than one hour per day. The Workers' Compensation Board found me to be at 80% disability. I decided that after speaking with two book publishers, it was time to do some research on finding a law firm to represent me upon its release. I had spoken with one in particular who was interested in joining my side as the book was in its last phase of wrapping up before going to edit. I wrote up a five-paragraph press release and it was sent out to a dozen news agencies around NY State to announce its forthcoming. I had been notified by Warren that soon the State Insurance Fund was preparing a settlement for my combined cases from work injuries and surgeries acquired from incidents at Fishkill. I believe this was future medical expenses and indemnity as well. One they contact me, if I decided that I agreed to that amount, then the guidelines indicate that they have a certain amount of time to make payment or they could be fined as much as 20% of the settlement, payable to me as well. I certainly had my plate full and was eager to get all of this put behind me. My goal for doing this book release was to put pressure on both PESH and PERB to release their final decisions on the hearings that took place last winter. Previous inquiries were made about the status of them but no future date had been indicated to release such decisions. I know that acting pro se in these cases, I was able to bring out the truth and present my cases in the best way that they could be told. So many lies and smoke screens were blown out by not only the union, but also from the State Department of Labor, all of whom were brought to these administrative hearings in regards to the cover-up and converting of my medical claims under workers' compensation following the Thompson case.

Chapter Thirty-Eight

Light at the end of the tunnel, I can recall that many supervising sergeants would have to hear the grumbling of how unfair it was that male officers were held to tighter standards than female officers, especially those of color. This was true as I observed daily many females coming into work with their hair down past their collar, extra makeup and in many cases, extra-long finger nails and uniform pants that were too tight. It brought attention to the male inmates in the housing units and made our job that much more worse by having to watch the inmates' movements and eyes when a female officer would be in the area. It was enough for us to handle many situations but this too as well? Much of the administration, with the exception of one or two female bosses, would turn their heads and look away for fear that any comment or suggestion on their appearance could lead to misconception and complaints lodged against the administration. It was not fair that if I were to go into work with any facial hair other than the authorized trimmed mustache, as soon as I would walk in the gate I would be ordered to remove the violation of the uniform Directive 3083. Most males in there wore goatees, even a lot of the new guys. The rest of the males would be ordered to get a doctor's note and then have to make a trip to Albany to get examined by a state doctor who would issue a permit for that particular male officer to wear his facial hair. Looking at today's *New York Post*, Fishkill was in the news again making headlines. The administration had suspended two male officers who were Muslim. For years and years that I worked there and knew these two officers, they had always worn a beard and were never in any type of trouble for it. The administration at Fishkill called it "an undue hardship and burden on facility operations." They had refused to shave their beards due to their religion yet other officers were allowed to keep theirs without incident. Not long before their return, they were reinstated and determination was made to grant their requests and given full back pay. Under

Cuomo's legislation, there are exemptions and prohibition by employers based on religious attire, clothing, or facial hair. With morale as low as it has been in some time, and with overtime at its highest, many staffers are out on compensation for work related injuries while others make use of their sick time. Years ago, with previous administrations who were allowed to run the prisons as they saw fit, things were much lighter, morale was always high, you had great turnouts at extracurricular activities for things like "Make a Difference Day," blood drives, and fundraisers that were done annually from what was called SEFA, the State Employee Federation Appeal. These have almost become a thing of the past. With Albany still pissed off about the Clinton escape, facility superintendents have become string puppets and take orders from the suits up in Building 9 in order to run their facilities. This has employees in an uproar and many have retired or resigned due to this, while a new generation of officers fresh from the academy walk in and take over, not knowing what was once there. With the systematic breakdown in each state prison having their own qualms with their union bosses or administration officials, this department is on the brink of a major incident occurring, quite possibly revisiting the Attica 1971 riots again where several died as a result. The worst part is that so many officers in the system now are newer and do not have that experience needed in such situations. As I mentioned, with the fear of something happening, it places unjust stressors on officers who want to make it home safely to their families. These administrations around the state need to wake up and when the public calls for prison reforms, they need to point their eyes at Albany and hold each deputy commissioner responsible for their actions, many of whom do not even have the experience of walking into a state prison.

I had a sit down at the State's Capitol with an investigative reporter named Brendan from the *Albany Times Union*. We spoke in whole about the entire Thompson investigation and the lack thereof, along with submitting my three logbooks and well over 110 documents and several emails of information. The story was being looked into by Brendan who has several years of experience of investigating state corruption which happens in several agencies. There was some homework to be done by him, reviewing all the documents, researching files, making contacts to do more interviews, etc. It was a story that Brendan told me he was going to use. It was a matter of time before it hit the fan at this point. The public needed to know what was going on. If it is so important for them to know about the good side of the department, it's also just as much for them to see the other side by having transparency. I had gotten some phone calls from Warren's office staff and we were in the process of dealing with the State's Insurance Fund to get my cases closed out and to settle for my numerous injuries. "Medically, you are a train wreck, Paul, nothing personal, but you are a disaster, and this is too much money for the insurance fund to want to settle this case at the amount of money it would take to cover your lifetime medical."

I said to Warren, "You promised me so much yet you do not have a crystal ball. How can you predict and tell me this is what's going to happen? You do not know any more than the next guy."

Man was I upset. This is something that would be affecting my family's future for years to come. It was time to go back to the drawing board and approach the State Insurance Fund again to come back with some other counter offers. If I keep my medical open, it means that I am stuck dealing with this insurance fund for decades to come. I am going to research my options at this point and see what else can be done. In the meantime, it is going to be a sit and wait approach, especially as we head toward the Social Security Hearing in November coming up.

It has been back and forth with me in the middle, which it should positively not be. The State Insurance Fund has ceased communications with all parties except the law firms. My case handler in particular, is almost 50 days past due with my mileage reimbursements alone on over 1,300 miles traveled to medical appointments over the last couple months. I have been trying to see a neurosurgeon about my neck pain, having been seen by pain management, a chiropractor, and a neurologist. It has been like pulling teeth trying to get approvals done for my treatments. It really adds to one's stress and where does that stress get dumped off at? The family. They are the ones around you who see the tension release. I know this is wrong, but those who have my specific diagnosis would feel the same way about how wrong it is for the insurance companies to pass the buck. It puts burden on my law firm, and with Warren at the helm, he often replies to my emails or messages pretty fast, but he does so while he is in the middle of multi-tasking and he takes his emotions out on me by yelling over the phone. He has not done so much as when I first signed over my eight medical cases to him in the summer of 2017. Since then, he is in a new law firm and has paralegals working my cases. Nothing that has been

348

promised has surfaced yet, and I keep getting told that I am going to get this and get that, etc. The system with work-related injuries in New York is just plain broken. I would not wish this turmoil on anyone. It wreaks havoc. It's like pulling a scab off a wound, not allowing it to heal. In order to heal, one has to be stress free. Stress is a killer. It adds onto the pile of PTSD victims in the system and causes them to diminish. The system is not there to help at all. It only adds to the problem. I called back the neurosurgeon's office in Tarrytown only to be told that my lawyer has to handle it. "We are familiar with Warren, not good," said the receptionist. "He won't pay the bills here, we need word from the case handler at the State Insurance Fund before we can see you as a patient."

I said, "What does this have to do with anything? I have been going to several doctors in the recent past who are all treating my neck injuries, and nobody else at these offices have had me go through any of this."

This week, I am waiting word back from Brendan at the *Albany Times Union*. I sent him more information to contact my lawyer regarding my neck and shoulder injury case.

I mentioned to Brendan that a TV news station had called me and wanted to interview on camera but after some email exchanges, it was decided I wait until his work is complete to release the story and let him have the lead on the case. Sometime by the end of the week I should be seeing something about this in print. I anticipate quite a bit of feedback once this gets out there. Many I am sure will have comments, others questions. But one should know I sure may have picked this job and steadily worked it for over two decades, but I certainly didn't pick this fight!

I want to skip back for a moment and talk about the people who run that department and those that work for it. Every person I see out in public, whether it be a gas station, store, or even the same medical appointment as me, they all say the same thing. It's time to get out of Corrections. Many of them are retirement eligible soon, and many are not.

But this job may include working in a prison, but that does not necessarily mean you are the prisoner. There are many other professions out there for one to choose from. Throughout the years, so many colleagues transferred into other state jobs. All of them that I keep in touch with are very happy they did what they did. And then there's the one that keeps going back into the prison, with the gate crashing behind him or her as they walk in with their child-sized plastic see-through lunch bag, moping about not getting the personal day they put in for off from work, or having to work with a partner who swapped the shift with the regular officer they worked with. Bottom line is, we all have a choice. But to go into a dangerous and unknown expectation of a daily job like this, it leads one to believe that they are brainwashed as a prisoner in itself to the job. Many will say, where will I go? What will I do? There is nothing else out there for me. Well, yes, there is. Look for it, it's there. The dangers of the job have changed drastically since the escape at Clinton Prison in Dannemora, New York back in June of 2015. Albany Building 2 houses the Department of Corrections' top ranks of numerous deputy commissioners and the acting commissioner. This is where the prisons are run from now. When the officers use to run the prisons, morale was good, and things were quieter at times. But those are days long gone. Nothing can be done without getting permission from the higher authority other than your usual daily routine assignments. Anything else goes to a sergeant, then he or she will call the lieutenant, who then calls the captain, and likewise will contact the Deputy Superintendent for Security, and then the Superintendent. He will then call Albany Building 2. That's for certain situations and during certain times of the day when administration is working. As for nights, weekends and holidays, that process is usually cut in half, otherwise those officials are called at home. So an officer's hands are tied behind his or her back in many situations. Daily, it only gets worse. Up top on the pile, they certainly do not want the embarrassment of another escape or an incident that will be costly as much as Dannemora was. Keeping a tight leash has changed the job for so many senior staff. Those fresh out of the academy already know what to expect as they are trained and readily except the department's new goals and mission.

It was Thanksgiving Eve 2019 when I was laying down almost ready for bed. I got a phone call from Warren. He surprised me by calling that late in the evening. When I saw his number on the caller ID, I figured something had to be going on. It had been good news. I had a notice of decision issued from my Social Security Administration hearing. This normally took a month or more but was done in about a week. The decision had been favorable for my case. Warren informed me that I was approved for my disability benefits, giving me an estimate of what those would be. I was owed back pay all the way since May of 2017, plus a monthly benefit, all tax free. The long road traveled had begun to show the fruits of my labor. Now things were really looking up for my family's future.

I had thanked Warren for his time and great news. I also sent an email to his office to thank the other lawyers and paralegals who all worked so hard on my case. Soon I had shared the news with my family. It had been well-received by all. Now that this load was off my shoulders, I focused on finding out more information about the status of my cases against COPBA and the DOCCS, as well as the Department of Labor. I had sent out requests on the status of the notice of decision, with affidavits being served upon all of the other parties involved. It has been a long year and with that, I had anticipated these decisions way before now. As complex as these cases were, it would be up to each of those hearing officers to respond in kind.

Eventually, I received a reply back in regards to the notice of decision status. It was nothing I had not heard already from my previous inquiry on the matter. It seemed to be delay after delay, however, I had done some research on this matter and found that other cases, not relevant to mine, had long delays, sometimes two years on average, to be issued a notice of decision. While that did provide some explanation to me, I had still wondered about this. After all, I had been through all the red tape of New York's governmental administration on many occasions.

The day finally came for my cervical fusion surgery down at Lennox Hill Hospital in Manhattan. That was a rough ride all the way around. When I was scheduled the day before, they put me in for like a 1:00 p.m. showtime, and that I had to be there two hours prior. I immediately asked for a change in time, hoping for something earlier that morning. Like most surgery, you are not supposed to eat after midnight before it, and taking the train and subway to get there the next morning was not going to be fun. I usually like to eat breakfast like most. They could not change my time because there were older people who had to go in first. I knew this would be an issue, we were not even allowed to drink water on surgery day, but I took a bottle with me on the train anyhow and sipped from it. Upon arrival off the subway to Lennox Hill, I was greeted by registration and processed shortly thereafter. I was then sent several flights up to sit in a waiting room to be called in. Things seemed to move quickly but once you got into pre-surgery, it was a long game of sit and wait. Literally, I was in there for about four hours. I was like the last one to be seen. I was rolled into the very cold operating suite where I briefly met the surgical team before being sent off into la-la land. I was scheduled for neck fusion where they placed metal hardware into my C-Spine and a cadaver bone to replace the herniated disc that was injured back in May 2017 by Thompson while at Fishkill Correctional Facility.

I woke up in recovery where I finally had a bite to eat before being moved into my room where I would stay for at least the next 36 hours. There was no rest during that time, albeit an hour or two here and there. Staff came in on a regular basis for some type of care, and between that and the older grumpy man on the other side of the room, it made for an eternity. This man always complained and berated the nurses and staff on a regular basis. He was due to be discharged but he kept going on and on about needing to stay there. When he wasn't ringing the call bell, he was snoring badly. If only my arm had been longer to reach over there. The following morning after breakfast was brought in, I was told that I would be going home that day, released with a neck brace and other medical items. I had not received my medications to take home since the hospital pharmacy did not accept workers' compensation insurance. As crazy as that seemed, it made for almost four days without meds before my surgeon's office called my order in and for it to get approved before I could pick it up. Finally at home, I was able to start my treatment with my cervical stimulation neck brace which sped up the bone growth process. Between that and rest, I was chewing on oxycodone tablets daily to help subside the pain. In time, months later, I had done two separate x-rays to confirm the healing process that showed good progress. Inside me though, I felt the pain to be the same. Especially when sitting at the computer, driving, and other daily activities. I was told it would be a lengthy healing process before I would notice total recovery. It took time before I could start physical therapy sessions for my neck. There had been some anxieties about getting into this activity again but it was pretty much par for the course.

Soon after my initial session, the country got hit with Covid-19 which literally shut down everything in New York State, save for the fact that we still needed our essential workers up on the frontlines. My appointments were all canceled and within weeks they became tele-med appointments, mostly over the phone, and others did them by Zoom video. It soon became a different time for all of us. I had heard from many corrections Officers at Fishkill's Prison that they had been hit very hard with the virus. After several weeks of pleas with Albany about getting Corrections in line with the current standards set by the Department of Health, officers would soon be able to wear face masks, giving them some form of protection against each other as well as from the vast inmate population within that prison. The conditions were reportedly deplorable at Fishkill.

Well over 200 sergeants and officers were out sick having tested positive with the virus. They also led the state's prisons in the ratio of inmates infected with Covid-19. Stories came out about many being stuck there after their shift was over which was not uncommon, but was surely more frequent. It was already hard for staff to be inside this facility with such a large amount of the virus coming out, but sincere hardships were endured by all of those affected by this policy. After all, they were down by over 1/4 of their manpower. Corrections officers soon became recognized more by their counterparts and the general public in communities all across New York as a broader light was cast upon them while working inside these prison institutions on the frontlines.

Many of the retired officers also shared their grief and sorrow for those that were still inside working in those environments. Also felt by them was that ever so humble feeling of relief that they no longer had to be a part of that system. Recently, my wife had taken the state's civil service exam in hopes to broaden her career path. Anyone who takes this exam knows all too well that it could take a long period of time before you get your exam results, however she got hers back in a timely fashion. She scored a high grade, well in the 90s, and some of her friends had taken the same test as well. By now they had told my wife that they had received calls about job interviews in our region. More specifically, Fishkill Correctional facility's Administration was hiring from the test list. Wondering why she had not heard anything yet, she called the Department of Civil Service and spoke to a nice woman who offered her an update. We had been confirmed on her original suspicions. She was being passed by the list due to my departure from Fishkill. When she advised me of this, I was both angry and also laughing at the same time. They are continuing their games as usual. Like I said earlier in the book, the hiring practices at Fishkill are not exactly textbook. It's really more about politics then it is a grade on your exam. I was not surprised so much with this information from Civil Service. I had seen many times in the past that there had been hiring from the inside, and those civilians coming in for their interviews all dressed up really had no idea of the program there. It looked legitimate, but so many pockets had been fleeced there from the insider favors to hire from their own households.

It was such a shame, but again, everything had its touch of the corruption that was common inside Fishkill's Prison.

Chapter Thirty-Nine
The Long-Awaited Decision

A quick trip to the mailbox while expecting the usual junk mail surprised me when I saw a large manila envelope addressed to me from the State's Industrial Board of Appeals. It had been what I had highly anticipated, my notice of decision regarding my discrimination case against DOCCS and the State Department of Labor. It took 15 months, with two written inquiries submitted to Albany requesting the status of the decision. In all. it was 13 pages long, and throughout it there had been multiple other OSHA, PESH, and labor law cases cited. I was named the petitioner during this case with the State Department of Labor being the respondent. An excerpt from the judge's decision on the case was not surprising to me. As stated, "The petition alleges that the determination was unreasonable because respondent's investigation documents contained numerous discrepancies. The amended petition further alleges that:

1) There were discrepancies in certain witness statements collected by Harrington's employer;
2) Respondent performed an inadequate investigation by failing to obtain telephone records from the date of the workplace violence incident;
3) Petitioner's employer failed to notify Harrington that they were controverting his workers' compensation claim;
4) Harrington was required to pay out-of-pocket costs due to his injuries sustained from the workplace violence incident;
5) that Harrington filed a timely complaint with Respondent, and;
6) Harrington's post was moved by his employer in response to his workplace violence complaint.

"Upon notice to the parties, a hearing was held before Honorable Matt D. Robinson-Loffler, Associate Counsel to the Board, and designated hearing officer on this matter, on January 23 and February 8, 2019, in Albany, New York. Each party was afforded a full opportunity to present documentary evidence, to examine and cross-examine witnesses and to make statements relevant to the issues. We find on record evidence that Harrington met his burden and proved that the Respondent's determination that his employer did not discriminate against him in violation of Labor Law 27-a(10) was unreasonable. Respondent failed to rebut Harrington's proof with credible and reliable evidence, and we find its determination dismissing Harrington's complaint and declining to take further action was therefore unreasonable.

"We remand this matter to the Commissioner for further proceedings in accordance with this decision and to request the New York State Attorney General to bring action in the Supreme Court against the person or persons alleged to have violated the provisions of this subdivision as required by Labor Law 27-2(10)."

The documents in this decision went on into such great details. At that moment, after I initially read this packet, I became so exuberant that I had to read it over and over again. After a while I thought to myself, not bad for a layperson to be able to accomplish all of this. It had taken numerous days of long exhausting research, copying, filing, mailing, getting notary stamp and signatures, all in an order to prepare myself accordingly. I had a number of guys that helped me out on this case either through peer support, assisting me with administrative research, or even attending the hearings with me in Albany. Thank you to Mike, David, Al, Kevin, Ed, and many other family and friends who saw the truth as I did and went after it in an attempt to extinguish the corruption within New York State's government agencies and beyond. Although we won this fight, it was onto the Supreme Court now and I decided I will not represent myself in this matter any further, so I contacted one of my many attorneys, Warren, and filled him on this update. It was decided that his firm would take over on this case as we proceed. I can't wait to hit Albany and Fishkill where it hurts for all that I had endured and gone through.

A long-awaited Worker's Compensation Board hearing was held on August 20, 2020, albeit virtual by teleconference still due to Covid-19. As usual, the hearing was in front of Judge Alade. My attorney representing me on this case was Victor, also from Warren's Office in White Plains. We had spent hours going over the deposition from Dr. Feldman, and to prepare for my testimony to be given. Alade was one of the better judges that the Worker's Compensation Board has, but he is very hard to understand, especially over the phone, due to his strong accent. About thirty minutes into the hearing, Alade found in favor of the State Insurance Fund, stating that Dr. Feldman was found to be not credible and that Dr. Service in Albany, who did one exam on me, was indeed credible. It was extremely surprising to hear him give this decision, as to this date I had won everything else presented to him at hearings. Furthermore, my thoughts were, how can he find her not credible? I had been seeing her for treatment every six weeks or so for three years! I saw Dr. Service for 30 minutes on one day for an insurance exam, regarding my bilateral hearing loss. A decision based on that was very surprising.

Fortunately for me, my hearing has gotten better, save for the tinnitus. Victor was thanked by myself for his hard work, but he was really let down about the decision. He did say that he respected Judge Alade's efforts in preparing for this hearing by reviewing the transcripts from both Service and Feldman's depositions. But this is not over yet. I am keeping steady on course to move forward with this appeal.

Lately I have been still pretty busy with all of my doctor appointments, about 20-25 that I go to per month. It's been unsettling to say the least, but well worth the relief I get from treatments. One of the best reliefs I ever got was from doing acupuncture. Up until now I had never tried it before, due to restrictions from the State Insurance Fund. We are approved for 10 sessions per body part injury. Following those sessions, my provider also does suction cups and hot stone therapy. Apart from a few red circles imprinted on my back, it made me for a new man. How ironic is it that one can get better relief from this as compared to surgery? I plan on repeating these treatments as much as I can, and I have even referred others who have not done it before. Some of those others I have been in frequent contact with and we are trying to align our schedules and be able to have a group luncheon. Today I met up with my friend Kris, who worked with me at Fishkill. He is out on injury, having had several surgeries, and we were talking a lot about his cases as well as numerous other officers and sergeants who are out on work-related injuries. Kris brought up a great idea, one that had been mentioned before amongst other professionals in my circle.

"Hey, how about you do a conference or something, maybe have some special guests who can come give some advice to others," Kris said as he grinned. I stood straight upward in response thinking how perfect it would be. So with that I made a few phone calls. Warren liked the idea as well, saying that he would be more than happy to be a guest speaker there covering the legal side of these issues. Definitely worth looking into doing something local in our area since there are so many prisons in the Hudson Valley region.

About a month ago, I sent a letter to the State's Attorney General, the Honorable Letitia James, to advise them that I am still acting pro se on the matter and that I requested further action from her office regarding the pursuance of this case that had been referred to them. With the amount of blood, sweat, and tears that has gone into this case, I certainly was not planning to sit on it anytime soon. I know how things can be pushed aside by the state if it was not a part of their agendas. Now that I have accomplished everything I had so far, I intend to be heard all the way until the end. As it is, I am still dealing with these injuries by getting treatment from several medical providers upward of 22 appointments per month. According to the statements I get on occasion from the state, they depict all of their costs including medicine, treatments, surgeries, mileage and other factors. My cases to date have more than hit near the one million mark, and they still have yet to be settled on indemnity and medical proportions. As of this point, my outlook on these cases could carry on for a few more years.

Currently, my discrimination case against State Corrections is sitting idle awaiting to be heard in New York's Supreme Court. DOCCS has been given an opportunity to respond back to the DOL's case prior to moving forward. This case has no monetary award or request for settlement. The Department of Labor's suit against Corrections is to address their violation of State Labor Law. I was asked by the Criminal Division Chief of the State Attorney General's Office on what I would be seeking for injunctive relief. I want there to be more changes in the system with respect to workplace violence statewide. There needs to be new training and awareness, along with holding a higher accountability and to see a revised directive with this issue, and to add on a new directive for nepotism. For far too long there has been major cover-up in most of the incidents I have experienced. I only seek this relief in order to prevent this happening again to the next officer. This vicious cycle needs to stop now, starting at the very bottom and working its way right up to the

Corrections Commissioner and the State Governor's Office of Employee Relations.

As for my case pending against my former union with the State's Public Employee Relations Board, a notice of decision was handed down to dismiss the case in its entirety. I was given a chance to offer an appeal but I rejected it on the grounds that any injunctive relief offered to me at this point is moot. A lot of money was spent by the state on this case. Hitting the union in their wallets was satisfaction for me.

For where there is injustice anywhere, there is a threat to justice everywhere. As of lately, Warren and Victor over at my law firm are working on settling all of my on-the-job injury cases for indemnity only. This means that I would get all future earnings in a lump sum but medical treatment options of these injuries from work would still be left open and available to me for life. Sometimes this works out well for some, others not so much. Each case is different, and the figures would have to add up in order for it to be worth it. You're probably thinking, wow, sounds great, what a deal. It's actually not though. It's like giving yourself a loan and then paying yourself back.

Anything from a settlement would be offset from my disability retirement and other benefits. It is designed so that you can't get ahead of the system. Basically, I would be stuck in this system for life and have to live within my means without the ability to broaden my horizon financially. Some people looking from the outside say those of us who are in this system have it made. That could not be farther from the truth. At my age, I would love to continue onward with my future endeavors but in the meantime, I will look upon ways of keeping myself healthy for myself and my family. I also plan on continuing my involvement with the community and the many law enforcement organizations that I hold memberships in. I am also going to be advocating for law enforcement officers facing injustice and starting a fight to change New York's broken Workers' Compensation System. If it takes lobbying in Albany, then so be it. I am also making plans to open up an advocacy office with a fellow co-worker who herself has experienced severe hardships within her law enforcement career. Together we will help those whose trying times have fallen on deaf ears by having a network of medical and legal professionals, and other organizations who reach out to those law enforcement officers needing assistance. When their union officials only care about themselves or play politics on who they choose to help, we will be there. When their lawyers do not return their phone calls, we will be there. When their agency is discriminating against them, we will be there. I will take a stand against those government officials at both local and state levels who turn a blind eye to injustice, and to hold them accountable and making them do their jobs or face the consequences. If these are my new goals, then let the ball roll, this is just the beginning.

In the meantime, I will focus more on my family, community, and to become a productive member of society once again. Looking back on all of this, I probably would have not gone into the career of law enforcement that I did, but rather perhaps staying with my business management goals. I do hope for the best for the many wonderful officers and supervisors I had to work with during my career. It was them who made things on the inside a little easier to deal with. Many of them are retired now, or have departed from their positions in pursuits of other dreams. After all, there is more to life than staring at the inside of a wall and razor-wired perimeters multiple hours a day.

Fade to black...

CPSIA information can be obtained
at www.ICGtesting.com
Printed in the USA
BVHW010811300622
641015BV00003B/9

9 781649 797018